Beyond MORALITY

In the series

ETHICS AND ACTION,

edited by Tom Regan

Beyond MORALITY

Richard Garner

TEMPLE UNIVERSITY PRESS
PHILADELPHIA

Publication of this book
has been supported by a grant from
the National Endowment for the Humanities,
an independent federal agency

Temple University Press, Philadelphia 19122

Published 1994
Printed in the United States of America

The paper used in this publication meets the minimum requirements of
American National Standard for Information Sciences—Permanence of Paper
for Printed Library Materials, ANSI Z39.48-1984 ♾

Library of Congress Cataloging-in-Publication Data

Garner, Richard, 1936–
Beyond morality / Richard Garner.
p. cm. — (Ethics and action)
Includes bibliographical references and index.
ISBN 1-56639-076-1 (alk. paper). — ISBN 1-56639-108-3 (pbk. : alk. paper)
1. Ethics. 2. Religion and ethics. I. Title. II. Title: Morality. III. Series.
BJ1031.G376 1993
170—dc20 93-7399

To the memory of Leslie D. Krebs

A Good Father

Unthinking people have a tendency to assume that some things are just naturally good and others bad, and some actions right and some wrong, and that we need only to discover which is which.

—*Richard Taylor*

CONTENTS

PREFACE xi

INTRODUCTION 1

1. *Moral Arguments and Morality* 4
   - Conversations and Conventions 4
   - Moral Discussions 7
   - Moral Philosophy 11
   - The Burden of Proof 14
   - Moral, Amoral, and Immoral 16

2. *Doubts about Morality* 20
   - Dogmatism 21
   - Universalism 21
   - Relativism 22
   - Skepticism 29
   - Non-Cognitivism 30
   - The Function-of-Language Argument 36
   - Anti-Realism 37
   - First Conclusion 41

3. *Morality and Its Denial* 43
   - A Literary Example and a Warning 43
   - Moralism versus Amoralism 46
   - What Is the Difference between Moralism and Amoralism? 48

4. *History, Hallucinations, and Human Nature* 70
   - Original Humans 70
   - Hobbes 71
   - Rousseau 73
   - Human Nature 76
   - Human History 80
   - Agriculture, Cities, and the Goddess 82
   - Murder in Mesopotamia 83
   - Law: Marduk and Hammurabi 85

Divine Messages 87
Explaining the Messages 89
Early Morality 94

5. *Moralism and Amoralism in India* 98
The Āryans 99
The *Vedas* 100
The *Upaniṣads* 101
Karma and Reincarnation 105
Heterodoxies 106
Cārvāka 106
Jainism 107
Buddhism 108
Persuasive Definitions 122
Moralism and Indian Thought 126

6. *Moralism and Amoralism in China* 130
Confucianism 132
Moism 140
Daoism 141
Mencius 147
The School of Names 149
The Yin-Yang School 150
Legalism 151
Buddhism in China 154
Moralism and Chinese Thought 157

7. *Moralism and Amoralism in Greece* 161
Minoans and Mycenaeans 161
The Āryan Harvest 162
'*Agathos*' and Its Persuasive Definition 163
Hesiod 164
Government and War 166
The Philosophers 168
Socrates and Plato 171
Justice and the *Republic* 175
The Theory of Forms 182
Aristotle 186
Moralism and Greek Thought 188

8. *Gods and Religious Morality* 191
The Enforcers 192
Some Unfamiliar Deities 196

Revelation and Divination 200
What to Believe? 202
The Genetic Fallacy Fallacy 207
God-based Moralism 210

9. *Experience and Reason: Secular Morality* 220
Rationalist Attempts to Make a Secular Morality 221
Empiricist Attempts to Make a Secular Morality 223
David Hume 225
Richard Price and Thomas Reid 230
Immanuel Kant 232
Intuitionism 234
Making Moralism True by Definition 243
Conclusion 247

10. *A Survey of Moral Theories* 248
Metaethics 249
Normative Ethics 253
Value 255
Obligation 258
Rights 268
Virtue 272
Conclusion 274

11. *Amoralists, Critics, Pseudo-Amoralists, and Backsliders* 276
The Amoralist Need Not Be an Immoral, Heartless, Selfish Jerk Who Denies the Obvious 279
Some Responses to the Amoralist 280
Pseudo-Amoralists and Backsliders 284
The Amoralist 292
What Is Wrong with Morality? 294

12. *Desires and Emotions* 297
What to Do about Desires and Emotions 298
One Extreme: Eliminate Desires and Emotions 298
The Other Extreme: Indulge Desires and Emotions 299
A Middle Way 300
Another Middle Way 307
Conclusion 312

13. *Decisions, Control, and Harmony* 313
Making Decisions 313
The Bicameral Brain Again 315

Socialization 317
Force and Control 326
The Way of Harmony 329

14. *Language, Truth, and Non-Duplicity* 341
Language 341
Truth 352
Non-Duplicity 355

15. *Applied Amoralism* 362
Applied Ethics 362
The Alternative—Applied Amoralism 366
The Questions 367
Last Conclusion 382

WORKS CITED 385

INDEX 397

PREFACE

SOON IT WILL be determined whether earth's experiment with humans was a success or a lethal mistake. If we were just another biological organism, we would be considered out of control—extinguishing species after species, devastating the environment with war and disregard, and magnifying our limited ability to do harm with diabolical inventions capable of poisoning all life and destroying the planet. But we are also capable of love and language, creation and understanding, and it is within our power to solve our problems, save the planet, and make happiness the rule rather than the exception. The problem is, and always has been, how to plant ourselves firmly on the path of creation, cooperation, and healthy competition, rather than the path of destruction, unhealthy cooperation, and lethal competition.

Some of those who have noticed that we remain the greatest threat to our own survival have sought ways to stop the destruction and mutual slaughter that have been with us for so long. But it is one thing to see a path, something else to take it, and something else again to persuade or convince others to take it. Morality, often supported by religion, points to virtues, values, duties, and demands. We are told that God commands us, or the Universe requires us, to act one way rather than another, to eat only certain things, to be unselfish, honest, courageous, or celibate. We are also told that these are not just requirements we have placed on ourselves. But what if they are?

Morality and religion have always tried to guide us to a "better" world, but the actual effect of moral and religious commandments is debatable. We learn that God commands us not to steal or kill, and that everyone has a right to life; but we also learn that God has ordered massacres, that every rule has exceptions, and that there are rights capable of overriding even a person's right to life. Because of their flexibility, neither morality nor religion is good at dealing with people who reject their requirements, and, to be honest, both are easy to doubt and dismiss.

Anyone who looks closely at what is happening in the world will be saddened by our treatment of each other, by the pain and misery we inflict on other sensitive creatures, by the damage we are doing to the environment, and by the legacy of debt and decay we are about to leave for our children and grandchildren. But none of this has to happen. We can change most of the things we want to change, fix most of the things that are broken, achieve most of the goals we are capable of setting for ourselves—if we are willing to make the appropriate choices.

What we have tried so far has not worked, or it has only worked well enough to get us into our present trouble. Morality and religion have failed because they are based on duplicity and fantasy. We need something new, and I believe that if we can get beyond the fictions and deception inherent in religion and morality, the traps set for us by our language and those who use it for manipulation, we can find what we need. Only then, I argue, will we be able to develop the beliefs, attitudes, and habits that will result in the kind of world we want. Paternalistic lies and convenient fictions give us a warped picture of reality and necessarily result in inappropriate behavior. What will actually heal us is a radical diet of true beliefs, as fully understood and as deeply realized as possible. The choices we make will not be appropriate if we do not understand the context in which they take place, and as long as people are not telling us relevant details, and we are not capable of listening when they are, we will not understand what is really going on.

I hope I have not offended anyone by my attitude toward religion and morality, but I truly believe that many of the goals cherished by religious thinkers and moralists will never be sufficiently realized till religion and morality are left behind. But even if I am mistaken about this, the position I present is shared by more people than you are likely to think. Some of the kindest, most gentle, most helpful people I know are motivated neither by religion nor by morality, and this leads me to hope that my suggestion that we leave those illusions behind us, restrain our habits of moralizing, and learn to listen to others and to ourselves may be exactly what we need to lead us out of the darkness.

Throughout this book you will find boxes containing quotations. They illuminate and illustrate things being said in the text, but I do not discuss them explicitly. I trust my readers to make appropriate connections. In the text, double quotation marks are used around quoted phrases or sentences, or as "scare quotes" to draw attention to some peculiarity warranting note but not mention. Single quotation marks signal that the item inside is being exhibited or mentioned—there is a 'cat' but no cat in 'catalog'.

Indian words are written with the standard marks scholars use to guide pronunciation. An *ṛ* is pronounced with a light trill, and both *ś* and *ṣ* are pronounced *sh,* as in 'ship'. An *ā* is prolonged, as in 'father'. For more help with pronunciation, see the appendix on pronunciation and accents in Radhakrishnan and Moore.

I have adopted the pinyin spelling of Chinese words favored by the Chinese government, but in Chapter 6, on the first occurrence of a Chinese term, I provide the once-standard Wade-Giles romanization if it differs from the pinyin. 'Daoism' is a good example. The Wade-Giles spelling of the word is 'Taoism', but the pinyin romanization makes it 'Daoism'. This makes sense because the Chinese way of *saying* the word is with an initial *d* sound. I shall spell it with the *D,* but in translations and quotations from other sources it will often turn up as 'Taoism'. The *Dao De Jing* and its legendary author Lao Zi turn up as the *Tao Te Ching* and as Lao Tzu in quotations or bibliographic references, where proper names are written as they appear in the original. Throughout, I remain faithful to Chinese authors' spellings of their own names.

I owe a debt of gratitude to many people who have encouraged and criticized me through the years. Richard Taylor, Tom Regan, Ray Martin, Andy Oldenquist, Kathy Bohstedt, Wayne Alt, and Justin Schwartz read all or part of the manuscript and made many helpful suggestions, only a few of which I ignored. My students and colleagues encouraged me to persevere, showed me things I needed to see, and taught me things I needed to know. Scott Lloyd helped in countless ways with the preparation of the manuscript. Everyone at Temple University Press has been reasonable, helpful, and cooperative. We should all be grateful to Jane Cullen, whose advice helped me to write a shorter and a better book, and to Lesley Beneke, the best copy editor on the planet. I am particularly grateful to The Ohio State University for my Faculty Professional Leave during the academic year 1990–1991. Without that, this book would still be on my hard disk.

Beyond
MORALITY

Introduction

WE HAVE convinced ourselves, and taught our young, that our conventions, laws, practices, and principles are subject to "higher" standards. We subscribe to natural laws, acknowledge eternal values, respect inalienable rights, and agree that we ought to avoid evil. We fear that if morality were "merely" conventional, "merely" a product of evolution and intelligence, it would lose its authority and become, in Immanuel Kant's words, "a mere phantom of the brain" (Kant [3], 48).

We learn our lessons and our language so well that the lines we are taught to draw appear as inherent features of an independently organized reality. We qualify as "moralists" if we believe the world contains values to discover, rules to follow, or rights to recognize. Moralists take morality seriously, believe in its authority, and consider themselves and others bound by its requirements. Amoralists, on the other hand, believe morality *is* a phantom of the brain, a projection, an invention, a convenient fiction, a subterfuge that works only when we mistake it for something it is not.

Moral emotions, moral judgments, and moral arguments permeate our social life and our private thoughts. Someone who does not know "the difference between right and wrong" cannot even be tried in court and held responsible. As we live our lives, we assimilate moral concepts, distinctions, slogans, assumptions, argument-fragments, principles, dogmas, and guilt. In this way our lives, our behavior, and even our desires are regulated.

Familiar traditions and practices have a built-in moral weight, a presumption of correctness, a moral inertia. Any attempt to alter them is resisted on moral grounds, and unless reformers meet this resistance with moral arguments of their own, they can forget about trying to change things. As new issues are propelled into the public consciousness by this or that disaster, network special, protest, or scandal, the one thing that remains constant is the moral tone of the discussion. Whatever the topic, we find people occupying both extremes of the spectrum of possible positions and all the points in between. Everyone claims to have correct answers, and everyone has plenty of reasons and arguments to defend their preferred options.

I call this book *Beyond Morality* because I believe that this moralist approach to questions about how to live and act is inherently flawed. It is too easy to find moral arguments to support both sides of any dispute, too hard to explain the claim that we are bound or required by morality, and too unsettling to see such widespread and apparently irreconcilable moral divergence among even well-meaning humans. It is time to face these facts and to explore other alternatives, such as the informed, compassionate amoralism I recommend.

Moralists assume more than they can prove and promise more than they can give. They say we are "subject to" objectively binding moral requirements but never explain what this means or why it is so. For example, strong moralist pronouncements appear in a recent book by Jeffrey Stout, who writes that it is a knowable truth, independent of human contrivance or agreement, that "slavery is evil" and that "knowingly and willingly torturing innocents is wrong, impermissible, unjust" (Stout, 245). He says he is more certain of these things than he is of anything he might use to support them—so he does not support them. The skeptical amoralist reminds us that neither Stout's strong belief nor his inability to support his moral intuitions is evidence for the truth of what he claims.

The amoralist rejects Stout's dogmatic intuitionism, and all the other forms of moralism, whether offered by Hindus, Platonists, Buddhists, Christians, or atheistic proponents of natural laws and rights. What is required from the amoralist is not a collection of refutations of an endless column of moralists so much as a responsible and critical survey of the case for and against moralism, followed by an attempt to explain why people hold the moral beliefs, and beliefs about morality, they do. In the first eleven chapters I treat the origin, history, and nature of morality, and I explain and defend the amoralist alternative. In the final four chapters, I explore a variety of ways to achieve the very goals some moralists set for themselves, and for others: a reduction in suffering and an increase in the happiness and contentment of those capable of happiness and contentment.

Amoralism, the rejection of the characteristic claims of moralists, is neither a philosophy of life nor a guide to conduct. But neither is moralism, as such. Everything depends on which moral principles one holds, and then on how closely one follows them. I argue that we can easily do without morality if we can supplement our amoralism with *compassion*, a desire to know what is going on, and a disposition to be non-duplicitous. By 'doing without morality' I do not mean doing without kindness, or turning ourselves into sociopathic predators. I simply mean rejecting the idea that there are intrinsic values, non-conventional obligations, objective duties, natural rights, or any of the other peremptory items moralists cherish. To reject morality is to reject these beliefs, something very few people have ever been willing to do.

In the final chapters of the book, I explain why informed and compassionate amoralism offers a better chance to create the kind of world we want to inhabit than does any moral system ever invented. Before we are through, I hope to have explained what morality is; what is wrong with it and right with amoralism; and what we can do to construct, without self-deception, superstition, or duplicity, a satisfying personal and social strategy for living.

1

Moral Arguments and Morality

> I like parties. I don't think there's anything wrong with that at all. And if people think that's glamorous, fine. But if people think that's something bad, I'd like some reasons for it.
>
> —*Simon Le Bon of Duran Duran*

Conversations and Conventions

WE SPEAK so effortlessly that we rarely notice how remarkable the use of language is. Our ability to communicate links us with others as nothing else could. Language is a group creation, nourishing and nourished by shared beliefs and conventions. Conventions, which are like unspoken agreements to conform to certain ways of doing things, can be found at every level of interaction. Shaking hands is a conventional act used to say hello or goodbye, to seal an agreement, to congratulate, to end an argument, and even to make fun of people who shake hands. The act "means" what it does, when and where it does, because of the beliefs, thoughts, and intentions of the shakers, and the conventions in force among them. Flapping your hand, firing your pistol, and hitting your forehead with the side of your hand only amount to saying goodbye, starting a race, and saluting because of conventions in force among people who do those things in those ways.

Words are conventional instruments for modifying the world, including the minds of others. The thoughts, intentions, expectations, and behavior of those who use the word 'dog' generate the conventions that give that word the power it has to play a role in episodes of communication. When we combine words into sentences we exploit further conventions—the conventions of grammar. Although these conventions are so complicated that philosophers of language and linguists are only beginning to understand them, *we* follow them without any conscious awareness.

By using words, sentences, and other signs, we get into and out of contracts, we transfer ownership, we notify and announce, we warn, blame, promise, bet, encourage, argue, and assert. We perform these "speech acts" by exploiting conventional rules, but only when the surrounding circumstances and accompanying intentions are in order. If I *warn* you, I am supposed to be trying to alert you to some danger—real, possible, or imagined. If you are already taking the danger into consideration or if there is no danger, the warning is compromised, inappropriate, unnecessary, or pointless. We might say that it was not a warning at all. What we finally say will depend on how we understand the circumstances and the conventions about warning.

Our words, with their conventional meanings, are combined according to the conventions of grammar to make sentences. Thanks to further conventions, we use these sentences to perform speech acts. Other conventions determine who gets to talk and when, tell us how to interrupt or change the subject, and even regulate the way we talk over the phone. There are conventional rituals of greeting, parting, bargaining, and rebuking, and there are conventional and comfortable patterns of small talk. Finally, there are conventional ways to discuss subjects such as sex, politics, religion, and morality.

Unless alerted by some peculiarity of expression or context, we habitually (and usually correctly) assume that people who are talking to us intend to be heard and understood in a straightforward way. But when messages are vague or ambiguous, directions unclear, words mumbled, mispronounced, or unfamiliar, we resort to familiar ways to ask for help. It is nearly always appropriate to ask a speaker to repeat something we have simply not heard. When we have heard what was said but failed to understand it fully or sufficiently, we may ask for a clarification; though there are times when "What did you say?" is appropriate and "What did you mean (by ———)?" is not. Both questions are normally in order because of the natural, but perhaps optimistic and certainly too simple, assumption that the point of talking is to be heard and understood.

One other question permitted by the conventions of conversation, though in fewer situations than the two just mentioned, is a request for support for some claim or judgment. If I tell you one thing and you believe another, you are likely to ask me to supply reasons for my belief. There are many ways I can meet this request, but if I do not want you to discount what I have said, I must do something—I cannot just stand there. No one who is habituated to the eating of meat is going to be moved to vegetables by the unsupported remark that "it is morally wrong to eat meat." If we say that to a "meat-and-potatoes" person, we can count on being ignored, assaulted, or asked to support our judgment with reasons. In fact, anyone who makes a moral judgment (or even a suggestion) to a skeptical audience should expect to be asked for grounds, reasons, support, or justification. This is not a feature of the conventions of modern Western society, or an artifact of individualism. It turns up wherever there are clashes and conversations. The demand is such a standard reaction to an unwelcome moral judgment that we have all learned how to satisfy it. In the case in question I might reply that life is sacred and that by eating meat you are killing yourself and encouraging others to kill the animals you eat. Or I might claim that animals have a right to live and not be molested by humans.

> The notion of living according to ethical standards is tied up with the notion of defending the way one is living, of giving a reason for it, of justifying it. Thus people may do all kinds of things we regard as wrong, yet still be living according to ethical standards, if they are prepared to defend and justify what they do. We may find the justification inadequate, and may hold that the actions are wrong, but the attempt at justification, whether successful or not, is sufficient to bring the person's conduct within the domain of the ethical as opposed to the non-ethical. (Singer [2], 9–10)
>
> When people say that something is morally right or wrong, it is always appropriate to ask them to give reasons to justify their judgment, reasons for accepting their judgment as *correct.* (Regan [2], 8)
>
> Philosophers are not concerned merely with finding answers to their questions; they are concerned with finding answers that can be defended by rational argumentation. This means that philosophers need to think up reasons to support their answers. (Brody [2], 3)

Moral Discussions

One feature we cite to distinguish ourselves from other animals is our rationality. Though the word 'rational' can be interpreted in a number of ways, rational creatures are often described as ones who act on the basis of reasons. The idea that rational beings have reasons for their actions and beliefs influences many of the conventions that govern our interactions. It opens the way for discussion, persuasion, debate, criticism, and compromise. Also, the idea that rational beings will or should have reasons for their moral judgments makes it easy to support a convention that allows us to ask our fellow rational beings for their reasons.

One surprising thing about the demand for reasons is the ease with which it can be satisfied. When we make a moral judgment in public we are usually ready with argument-fragments, slogans, and information to offer in defense of our claim. You can see this is so if you participate in this little experiment. Think of something you believe to be definitely morally wrong (littering or treason, for example). Write it in Box A below and then fill in Box B with a reason why that thing or kind of thing is wrong.

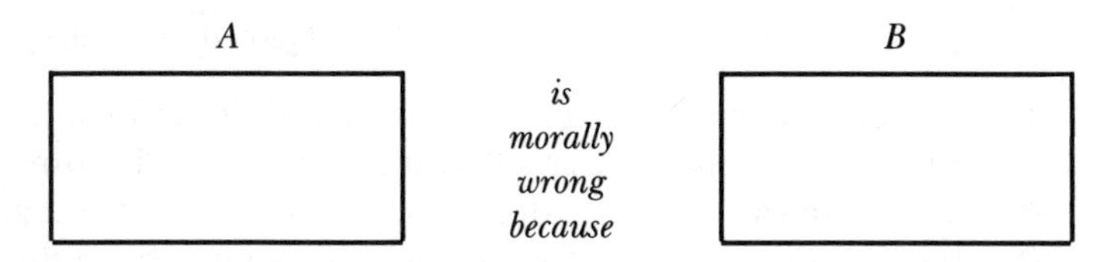

Probably by the time you finished writing in the first box you thought of several ways to fill the second: Littering is morally wrong because it is inconsiderate; treason is morally wrong because it hurts your fellow citizens. We can all fill Box B with reasons no matter what we think of the moral belief inscribed in A. If we take the trouble, we can even come up with a moral defense for actions we think are morally wrong.

Why are we so good at this? Why are we so rarely at a loss for words when it is time to defend moral judgments? Perhaps it is because we have learned to expect those who do not agree with us to ask us for our reasons. Knowing this, we are prepared. Fortunately for us, the reason we produce does not have to be a super-reason, powerful enough to convince any rational being. Almost anything not obviously false or irrelevant will do for a start. If we associate with people who share our moral beliefs and pay attention to what they say, we will develop an arsenal of reasons that will see us through most challenges. For example, trappers and people who wear furs can find writers who say things they can use to defend their habits. They might subscribe to "Trapline Ramblings," by trapper-reverend Roy Johnson of Hammond, New York. Johnson argues that there is no question of a trapped animal's feeling pain and says: "If a man beats his wife every day, she suffers because she has an immortal soul. But if he beats his hound-dog, it may yelp some but it won't suffer because it has no soul and no consciousness" (Amory, 219). From this we are apparently supposed to conclude that since dogs and trapped animals have no soul and no consciousness, we can beat and molest them as often as we please—they will not suffer. *Animals and Men: Past, Present, and Future,* a book sponsored by the fur industry, is designed to justify or rationalize the ends and methods of trappers and hunters.

> I have the impression, based on field observation, that many shot animals do not especially show feelings or pain.
>
> There are no 'rights' in the natural world—to the victor belongs the spoils.
>
> It is hard to know what people mean by 'cruel' or 'inhumane'.
>
> (Quoted in Amory, 244)

Each of these remarks can be exploited in some defense of hunting and killing animals. If someone says that it is "cruel" or "inhumane" to use steel traps, we can ask for a definition of 'cruel' or 'inhumane', and then attack the definition. If someone talks about the rights of animals, we can insist that only humans have rights and that in the "natural world" it is every beast for itself.

Our example has to do with the treatment of animals, but we can use any past or current practical moral issue: abortion, capital punishment, sexual morality, the treatment of the environment, or any of the moral problems connected with attempts to distribute the benefits and burdens of society. Around each of these issues there has developed a pattern of disputation involving everything from one-line slogans to complex and subtle arguments. Many of these slogans are insulting in their simplicity (abortion is murder, an eye for an eye), and many of the arguments play fast and loose with language and involve hidden assumptions. But the one-liners sink in, and the arguments will be similar enough to standard patterns of rational debate to satisfy the minimal demands made on those who wish to hold a moral position.

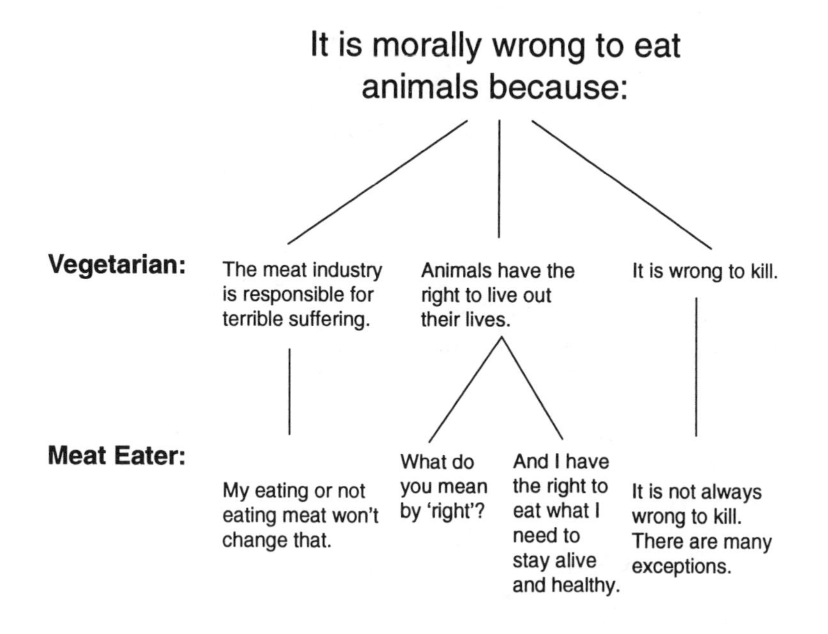

Figure 1-1

We can see how this works by returning to the debate between the vegetarian and the meat eater. The vegetarian says it is wrong to eat animals and then supports this claim with a reason. There are many reasons available, but in every case a dedicated meat eater will be able to find some reply (see Fig. 1-1). If, on the other hand, the omnivore supplies the arguments, the vegetarian can, with little trouble, find a first-line response (see Fig. 1-2). These arguments can be continued, but not indefinitely. When each side has made its point, the argument can be allowed to dissipate and antagonists can turn their minds elsewhere with no fear of being thought irrational, arbitrary, or dogmatic.

Arguments about moral issues can unfold in many ways. Some degenerate into theological disputes and others come to an impasse over some difficult or abstract philosophical problem (What is the nature of goodness? What is a person?). Sometimes moral arguments evolve into disputes about meaning (the meaning of 'life', or 'rights', or 'humane'), and often they come to a standstill over some factual claim that neither side can prove or disprove (Does capital punish-

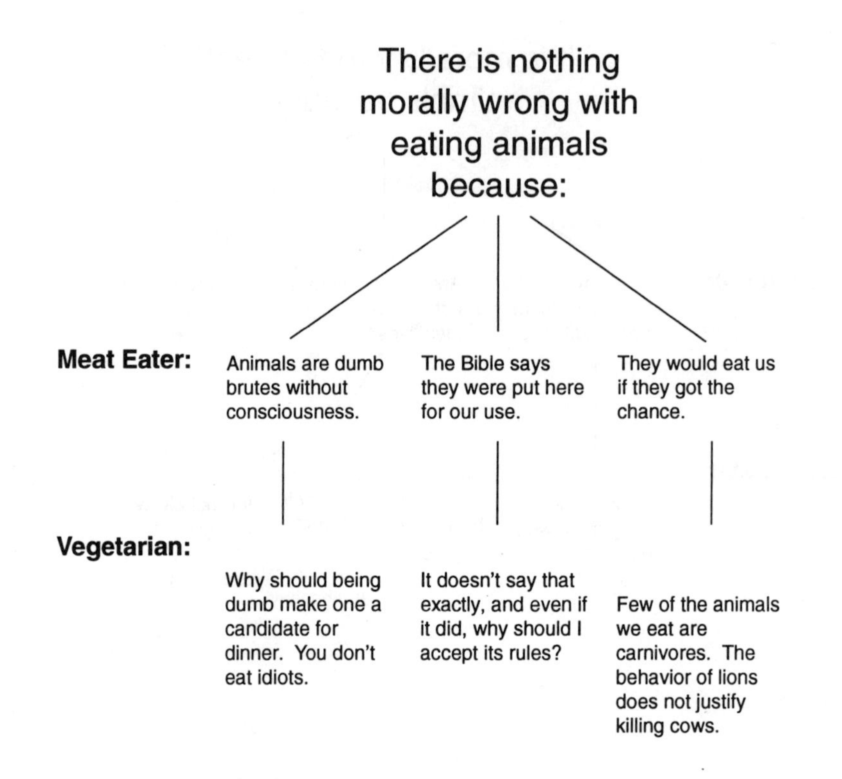

Figure 1-2

ment decrease the number of offenses or only the number of offenders?).

When we move from the question of whether it is wrong to eat animals to the question of what a person is, or from the question of whether abortion is wrong to the question of when human life begins, we have replaced a difficult question about morality with a certifiably unanswerable philosophical question. This does not bring the argument any closer to a resolution. Usually it turns out that our theory of human life or of personhood takes the shape it must to bolster our more personal and practical beliefs about diet and abortion. This shift to a more "basic" question will usually guarantee that the protagonists will arrive at an impasse—the natural end-state of a philosophical dispute.

Of course those involved in disputes about values and related philosophical questions are not trying to arrive at an impasse: They are trying to convince someone whose beliefs and attitudes differ from theirs. Since value disputes concern our behavior or character, when a cool and objective approach does not move our opponent we may resort to other methods, such as trying to gain an advantage by giving new meanings to words, by claiming that our moral principles need no defense or that they are true by definition, or by presupposing principles or facts we need to help prove our conclusion. In our eagerness to be declared blameless, or even justified, we imply that someone would have to be stupid or evil to disagree with us. When our initial efforts fail, we may become insulting, domineering, rude, or even obscene. When those who are arguing are unevenly matched in skill, experience, energy, information, or eloquence, it is usual for the apparent loser to feel that the apparent winner has capitalized on an unfair advantage, not that his position has been shown to be wrong. The ritualistic, hypocritical, and rhetorical nature of our arguments about morality helps explain the fact that after discussing an issue like abortion for hours, the only change in the minds of the antagonists may be in their estimation of the intelligence or the sincerity of the opposition.

> Suppose you and I argue. If you beat me instead of my beating you, are you really right and am I really wrong? If I beat you instead of your beating me, am I really right and are you really wrong? Or are we both partly right and partly wrong? Or are we both wholly right and wholly wrong? Since between us neither you nor I know which is right, others are naturally in the dark. Whom shall we ask to arbitrate? If we ask someone who agrees with you, since he has already agreed with you, how can he arbitrate? If we ask someone who agrees with me, since he has already agreed with me, how can he arbitrate? If we ask someone who disagrees with both you and me to arbitrate, since he has already disagreed with you and me, how can he arbitrate? If we ask someone who agrees with both you and me to arbitrate, since he has already agreed with you and me, how can he arbitrate? Thus among you, me, and others, none knows which is right. Shall we wait for still others? (Chuang Tzu, in Chan [1], 189–90)

Moral Philosophy

Here the philosopher steps in and says: "Now wait a minute—of course people cheat when they argue, *if they can get away with it.* But we are here to see that they don't get away with it. We can sort out the good arguments from the bad ones, the legitimate moves from the fallacies, we can classify the fallacies and clarify the reasoning." It is impossible to ignore the fact that philosophers have worked long and hard to help us see how to make the distinction between good arguments and bad ones. Now, thanks to that work, fewer people are likely to be convinced by bad arguments and fallacies. But this has not improved our ability to resolve moral disputes. With or without the hard work of the philosophers, if two people who disagree about some moral question can stay cool, avoid gross errors, and keep talking, both can be declared rational and unrefuted. Philosophers have no argument or device powerful enough to compel rational beings to accept their evaluations and principles. The most they can do is to show some people that, given their own assumptions, consistency requires them to accept this or that moral belief.

Suppose you argue that *A* is true and offer as your reason, *a*:

$$a \rightarrow A.$$

If I do not want to accept *A*, I can deny that *a* is true, deny that *a* implies *A*, or claim that you have not given an argument for *a*. If I ask you for your argument for *a* and you give it, then I can start all over again. If I deny that *a* is true, then you can then ask me for *my* argument. I may give as my reason *b*:

$$b \rightarrow \text{not-}a.$$

Now *you* can deny that *b* is true, deny that *b* implies not-*a*, or argue that *I* have not given an argument for *b*. This explosive set of options alone is enough to guarantee that *if we want to*, we can argue till the cows come home, and then some. Add to this the fact that either of us can question the meaning of the other's basic terms, or the truth of some subsidiary assumptions, and we can see that unless some parameters are taken for granted, nobody can be forced (rationally) to accept *any* conclusion. Those who feel strongly about some difficult moral issue like abortion or the death penalty will almost certainly be unwilling to accept any parameter that undermines their sincerely held moral beliefs; so the outlook for cool, rational debate about moral issues is not promising.

Some philosophers, sensitive to the potentially interminable nature of moral arguments, contend that since the concepts of morality are so confused and confusing our time is better spent clarifying moral notions than attempting to resolve moral issues. They say that if we are not clear about what 'good' and 'right' mean, or how they are used, we will never discover what things are good and what actions right. Or again, they say that we must investigate the nature of moral argumentation, so that when the time comes to support our own moral judgments (or to attack those of our opponents) we will be ready. In these ways, even the clarifiers lead us to believe that their clarifications will eventually help us find correct answers to the moral questions that confront us.

In the 1950s and 1960s, moral philosophers devoted themselves to this "disengaged" critical approach to morality. They were disinclined to moralize and so they concentrated on questions about the meaning and the use of moral language, and about the nature of moral disagreement and moral arguments. Some may have hoped that this digression would be of use when they returned to actual moral issues, but eventually it became clear that there is no limit to the available digressions. Can we study the meaning of 'good' without studying the meaning of 'meaning', and can we study *that* without studying the relation between language, thought, and reality? By the end of the 1960s everyone, even moral philosophers, had become impatient with analysis, clarification, and questions about meaning. In the 1970s and the 1980s, "practical" or "applied" ethics replaced "theoretical" ethics; and "the analysis of moral concepts" (if that is what really went on) has given way to discussions of concrete moral questions about abortion, capital punishment, genetic research, nuclear war, and the environment.

Challenges to morality itself and questions about its ultimate foundations are less welcome now that moralists have turned their attention to applied ethics. Moralists who are dealing with specific moral problems typically acknowledge the existence and the concern of skeptics, subjectivists, nihilists, relativists, and amoralists and then insist that it is not their business to answer these characters. Baruch Brody, in his textbook *Ethics and Its Applications*, admits that "the moral dimension of human life" presupposes that there is an objectively knowable and important difference between what is right and what is wrong. He identifies challenges to this presupposition by the nihilist, the subjectivist, the skeptic, and the determinist, and then he declares his intention to ignore all of these challenges.

> *Theoretical ethics* is concerned with critically evaluating the foregoing presuppositions of the moral dimension of human existence in light of

> these theories which challenge those presuppositions. This book, however, is not about theoretical ethics. Therefore, we will accept the presuppositions of the moral sphere of life and go on to deal with the ethical problems described in the next section. (Brody [2], 6)

It is hard to deny that moralists are in a peculiar situation. The conventions at work in our society allow us to ask each other to support the moral judgments we make. We can begin to meet this demand, but given what usually happens when people disagree about morality, few if any moral controversies are going to be resolved by argument. Any actual moral judgment will rest on some unjustified starting points and assumptions. The viability of applied ethics depends on a conspiracy to keep the lid on theoretical ethics by assuming that the challenges and objections of the skeptics, amoralists, and nihilists are not lethal. But if the critics of modern moralism are correct, this assumption is fatally mistaken. One may think that the ability to raise these unanswerable challenges is merely an artifact of modern Western civilization, but it is probably more universal than that. When circumstances allow us the freedom to reflect about our lives and about the requirements placed upon us by our social group, forms of moral skepticism, relativism, and amoralism are inevitable.

The Burden of Proof

Sometimes moral philosophers try to keep people from traveling down paths that lead to skepticism, relativism, or amoralism. But since they are philosophers, not behavioral engineers, physicians, or parents, they are not allowed to use persuasive and effective techniques such as drugs, electric shock, or appeals to emotion, fear, and guilt. What remains is talk, and the best way to block the path to amoralism is with a clear description of the foundation or ground of morality. If moralists believe that morality is objective and not subjective; that moral principles are binding on those who understand them; that moral judgments, principles, or ways of life can be justified, let them come forth with the explanation of what they mean and with convincing reasons why we should believe them. For reasons that have already begun to emerge, this is not likely to happen.

Fortunately for the moralist, there is a less strenuous method available. The moralist can try to convince budding amoralists that they cannot get to amoralism without arguments that clearly refute those who believe that there are moral facts, or that morality has a foundation. If anyone can be talked into serving up an argument to prove *that,* the moralist is in business. Any fairly skilled student of philosophy can find a flaw or uncover an unproved assumption in any argument aimed at proving anything the least controversial. Someone who is able to get an opponent to provide the first argument, or at least to admit that it is incumbent upon him to provide the first argument, is likely to do well in philosophy. He has the knack of "placing the burden of proof on his opponent."

For example, in *After Virtue* Alasdair MacIntyre says that emotivism "rests upon a claim that every attempt, whether past or present, to provide a rational justification for an objective morality has in fact failed" (MacIntyre [2], 19). The emotivist who allows himself to be talked into making that particular claim will find himself or herself burdened with a Herculean task. Only God knows how many attempts to provide a rational foundation for morality there have been, and not even God would be capable of making sense of most of them. So how can it be fair to ask the poor emotivist to identify, interpret, and then refute each and every one of them?

The burden of proof is an interesting bit of philosophical foreplay. It is always more difficult to prove something than it is to criticize someone else who has tried to prove the opposite. So it is very unlucky to have the burden of proof placed on you. But how is it done, and how does one avoid it? In the simple cases, it is not difficult to see how it works. We put the burden of proof on the party with the *positive* claim. Suppose a Christian missionary goes to a remote country where nobody has even heard of Jesus. He cannot start off by demanding that the natives prove to him that Jesus was not the son of God or did not rise from the dead. What could anyone do who wanted to prove that two thousand years ago something he does not understand did not happen to someone he never heard of?

Of course there can be arguments over what should be called positive and what negative. The moralist might argue that it is the amoralist who must prove the "positive" claim that most people are deluded about morality. But then the amoralist can ask for the moralist's proof that the claim that people are deluded is indeed the positive claim. You see how it goes.

Clearly it would be foolish for the amoralist to begin by asserting that no moral judgment that has ever been made can be proved, justified, or defended. Anyone starting in that way would be stuck not only with the job of proving that negative generalization, but also with the task of defining more clearly the nature of the thing that allegedly can never be done. It is not the amoralist's job to construct all possible forms of morality and then show that each is baseless, or to consider all the ways morality might be given a foundation and then show that and why every one of them must fail. The amoralist's strongest and most honest position will be one of aloof innocence. Since moralists suppose some moral judgments are preferable to others (or to none), why not let them explain and then defend the objectivist assumptions embedded in the moral language they are pleased to use?

Moralists will say that this attempt to shift the burden of proof is unreasonable. They do not want to admit that until their basic assumptions are established, every belief and claim that presupposes those assumptions can be held in doubt. But why should they be given this kind of a break? If the moralist can ask the amoralist to prove that *every* actual and possible attempt to establish morality fails and that every principle that has ever been held or crudely defended is mistaken, why can the amoralist not make the superficially more reasonable request that moralists defend the moral principle or principles they wish to impose on themselves and others?

Moralists are not silenced here. They may try to offer, not a proof of one type of morality, but of the objectivity (in general) of morality. The argument, which involves another attempt to place the burden of proof on the amoralist, runs like this: The very fact that morality is so widespread is evidence that at least some moral judgments are correct. How could so many people be completely wrong about something so central to life? You can guess how amoralists will respond to this. They will insist that the fact that people believe something is never by itself evidence for the truth of that belief. One might as well argue that the fact that most people believe in a god shows that one or several gods exist.

Much more can be said on each side of this dispute. Moralists who own up to the burden of proof *have* attempted to explain and justify their forms of moralism. They have been criticized both by other moralists and by moral skeptics and amoralists, who have, in turn, tried to justify their own beliefs. In the pages that follow, we will have ample opportunity to pursue some of these disputes.

Moral, Amoral, and Immoral

Before continuing, we need to attend to two crucial terms—'morality' and 'ethics'. Philosophers and non-philosophers sometimes use these words interchangeably. They speak of an ethical (or moral) code, and of ethical (or moral) principles. We make moral (or ethical) judgments and criticize people and actions for being immoral (or unethical), but here a difference begins to insinuate itself. *Immoral* actions seem worse than *unethical* ones. A merchant who overcharges or a used car salesman who turns back the odometer is unethical, but that criticism is too mild for a mass murderer, a rapist, or a sadistic torturer. If I hear you have been charged with unethical conduct I will think of your profession, but if I hear you have been charged with immoral conduct I will expect some more serious breach.

'Ethics' comes from a Greek word, and 'morals' from a Latin one, but both words make reference to what is customary. The *Oxford English Dictionary* identifies ethics as "the science of morals," and "the department of study concerned with the principles of human duty," a definition that gives the right flavor but is a bit too close to what was once taught in British universities.

Moral (ethical?) philosophers speak of applied ethics and of nursing, medical, and engineering ethics but not of applied morality, or of nursing, medical, and engineering morality. This may be because 'morality' suggests non-conventionality or universality. 'Ethics', on the other hand, implies a kind of relativity—as in medical or Hopi ethics. Perhaps when we study *ethics* we abstract from actual moralizing and retreat to a non-judgmental, conventional standpoint. This difference carries over into the distinction between a *moralist*, one who believes in and promotes morality, and an *ethicist*, one who studies it.

If we feel comfortable with this distinction, we might be able to say that the amoralist does not reject *ethics*, because ethics is no more than a set of conventions, practices, and habits that people promote and follow (or the *study* of those conventions, practices, and habits). What the amoralist denies is *morality*, which is to say that the amoralist denies moralists' distinctive (but yet to be examined) beliefs about the objectivity and prescriptivity of rules, prohibitions, virtues, vices, rights, and duties.

In *Ethics and the Limits of Philosophy*, Bernard Williams invokes a distinction between ethics and morality. He identifies the "ethical" as a vague area that includes ideals, virtues, obligations that arise from agreements and from one's position, and all kinds of rules that guide and shape us. To say that every society has an ethical code is only to say that every society has a set of recommended and inculcated ways of acting and being. This means that amoralists, nihilists, and utter monsters have their own ethical codes, their own ways of doing things.

Morality, by contrast, is only "a particular development of the ethical, one that has a special significance in modern Western culture" (Williams [2], 6). Morality emphasizes the idea of "moral obligation" (6) and a universal concern (14).

The members of any society understand the basic rules and values of that society—rules that require and recommend certain patterns of behavior, and values that rank things as more or less desirable. It is impossible to grow up without having a clear impression of what is wanted, and impossible to function in a group without a set of guidelines. In this sense we all have an *ethical* code, one that comes initially from those around us. Only after some code of ethics has been formulated can it be questioned, and only after it is questioned do we hear appeals to objective duties, divine commands, natural laws, moral rights, and intrinsic values. Only after our simple, unquestioned, ethical rules and policies have been questioned are they likely to transform into moral requirements.

The difference between ethics and morality lies in the moralist's claim that there is some objective and binding reason for being or behaving in a certain way, that when we are morally required we are *really* required. If we merely rank things, if we merely recommend, discourage, and require behavior, we are not yet acting as moralists. But when we support our rules, rankings, and recommendations with "objective" reasons, when we suggest that we have measured some actions or individuals by an objective criterion, or assessed something by standards that are more than mere conventions, we have moved in the direction of moralism. Moralists have beliefs about what people ought to do and about how they ought to be, beliefs about what is "intrinsically valuable" or "objectively right," beliefs about virtue, vice, wickedness, and worth. Even if we have not formulated these beliefs, we qualify as moralists if our (sincerely expressed) words make sense only on the assumption that we accept them.

The amoralist wants to criticize the fundamental beliefs that constitute moralism, but there are other similarly expressed beliefs no amoralist needs to reject. The language of better and worse, and the language of obligation and duty are available in technical and conventional contexts. Any amoralist can say that some people play the piano *better* than others, or that some people, because of their roles or past actions, *ought* to do this or that. An amoralist can admit that some traits are *good* for society, or *good* from the point of view of the rich. But for the amoralist, all goodness and all obligation is of this relative and dependent kind. Nothing is "good in itself." The amoralist believes that everyone is strictly equal in value in the sense that the "intrinsic worth" of each person is the same: zero. That some people have *more* "intrinsic worth" than others—the "philosophical" basis for racism, sexism, and aristocracy—is, to the amoralist, a joke.

The amoralist has developed an understanding of ethics (in Williams's sense of that word) that results in a rejection of some claims made about it by moralists. People who do not *follow* the ethical and moral requirements of the society to which they belong can be called *immoral* (at least by the moralists in their society), but a person who is *amoral*, an amoralist, does not believe certain claims made about those requirements, however he or she behaves. The moral standards we accept (if any) determine who (if anyone) we call immoral, but everyone should call an amoralist an amoralist.

William Frankena quotes Jim Casey from Steinbeck's *Grapes of Wrath*, who says, "There ain't no sin and there ain't no virtue, there is just stuff people do." (Frankena [3], 75–76)

In the play *Caligula*, by Albert Camus, we find the following dialogue:

> *Caligula:* So, I take it, you believe in some higher principle.
> *Cherea:* Certainly I believe that some actions are—shall I say?—more praiseworthy than others.
> *Caligula:* And *I* believe that all are on an equal footing.
> (Camus [2], 52)

One who has yoked his intelligence [with the Divine] (or is established in his intelligence) casts away even here both good and evil. (*Bhagavad Gītā*, 2: 50, in Radhakrishnan and Moore, 110)

Subhuti, though we speak of 'goodness' the Tathagata [Buddha] declares that there is no goodness; such is merely a name. (*The Diamond Sūtra*, Section 23, in Price and Wong, 62)

2

Doubts about Morality

> Tao is hidden by partial understanding. The meaning of words is hidden by flowery rhetoric. This is what causes the dissention between the Confucians and the Mohists. What one says is wrong, the other says is right; and what one says is right, the other says is wrong. If the one is right while the other is wrong, and the other is right while the one is wrong, then the best thing to do is to look beyond right and wrong.
>
> —*Chuang Tzu,* Inner Chapters

THE SUSPICIOUSLY unresolvable nature of moral disputes, their ritualistic character, and the impressive variety of potentially incompatible moral stances, have raised some disturbing questions about morality. If countless opposing moral theories can be defended by those who know how to argue, and if evenly matched opponents need never concede defeat, then is not moral argumentation merely one more strategy for altering the attitudes and behavior of others? Those who think so are fortified by the fact that centuries of debate have left us with a variety of theories so complex and vague that we cannot even agree about how to interpret them.

These are disturbing facts about morality—and they call forth a variety of responses. Some moralists harden their positions and sharpen their skills in order to defend their theories against all who hold opposing positions. Others look for ways to deny, or to minimize, the impact of the data. Perhaps, they suggest, widespread moral disagreement is more apparent than real. Still others move in a relativistic or skeptical direction. And finally, there are those who do their best to "look beyond right and wrong." In the next few sections we will sort out some of these reactions.

Dogmatism

One way to respond to widespread variation in moral beliefs and principles is to hold fast to your own beliefs. The *dogmatists* say that no matter what others believe, and apart from any objections they may raise, their own views are the truth. There are times when all of us are more or less dogmatic about something, and there is room for mild dogmatists who believe that their views are correct but who are willing to listen to alternatives and to criticism. But when the issues are moral, the stakes are high. Since the considerations that support one or the other side are never conclusive, dogmatism easily becomes extreme, and dogmatists tend to lose the ability to listen sympathetically to alternatives. At the most extreme point, the "mad dogmatists" stand by their own moral principles in the face of *all* criticism, manage to see all objections as irrelevant, and suppose that deviations from their views are at best mistakes and at worst willful and deliberate acts of immorality.

Universalism

Another way to respond to the widespread disagreement about moral beliefs is to say that the disagreement is not so widespread and that it is superficial. The *universalist* holds that however much disagreement there may be about specific moral questions, there remain some moral principles that everyone believes. These may be general principles like "Everyone ought to honor commitments," but they cannot be empty ones like "We all ought to do what is right."

The term 'universalism' might be used to refer to the claim that everyone accepts one or more moral judgments (universalism in a *descriptive* sense), or to the claim that one or more moral judgments applies to everyone (universalism in a *normative* sense). The present discussion concerns universalism only in the descriptive sense—the claim that there is some moral judgment that everyone accepts.

We might wonder why anyone would be attracted to universalism. A universalist will find it almost impossible to explain what is meant by 'everyone' and what is to count as "accepting a moral judgment." Some may support universalism because they believe universal acceptance of a moral principle would show that the principle is correct. But that would be a mistake—the truth of a moral principle no more follows from universal acceptance than its falsity follows from universal rejection. At best, universal agreement creates a presumption in favor of what is universally accepted. But remember, we do not *find* universal agreement, what we find is a changing pattern of agreement, disagreement, and misunderstanding,

The universalist is different from the dogmatist. If the dogmatist is right, some moral belief is true; if the universalist is right, some moral belief is *held true* by everyone. The belief that everyone holds some particular moral belief is not itself a moral belief, but a belief about moral belief. Nevertheless, the universalist who believes that everyone holds some particular moral belief probably holds that belief as well. So, serious and consistent universalists will also be moralists.

Universalism may be reassuring to moralists, but it is hard to defend and easy to attack. If just one person manages to believe *no* moral principle is correct, then universalism is false. It is also false if just one person rejects the moral principle the universalist claims everyone holds.

Relativism

The dogmatist admits that widespread moral disagreement exists and then says that everyone *else* is wrong. The universalist acknowledges the disagreement, and then denies that it is deep, basic, or ultimate. Neither "challenges" morality. The relativist offers a third reaction to the disagreement and the inconclusive and ritualistic character of moral debates, a reaction that moralists *have* seen as a challenge to be met. In one of Plato's dialogues, as Socrates and Protagoras are arguing over what virtue is and who teaches it, Protagoras says to Socrates: "And you say: Where are the teachers? You might as well ask, Who teaches Greek? For of that, too, there will not be any teachers found" (Plato [3], 26). His point is that each member of society helps pass along the conventions, rules, and practices that make both language and society possible, and that apart from these conventions, there is no true description of any item, and no true prescription about how to act. It is as wrong to ask what true virtue is as it is to ask what is the true word for a dog.

This relativism is not alarming when we are talking about language, but when we turn to morality, to virtue, rights, and obligations, it is a different story. The idea that the way we must treat dogs (or people) is as conventional as our way of referring to them can cause widespread concern.

Relativism about morality will not be found among members of isolated and self-contained societies. But when people learn of alternative social and political forms of life, they are forced to confront the *possibility* that at least some of the other sets of values and requirements are reasonable alternatives to their own. At this point moral relativism becomes an option.

We all recognize and work with some kinds of relativity. The look of a thing is relative to the conditions of observation; our willingness to act is relative to the circumstances; and what we believe about the world is (or had better be) relative to how things are. But these are forms of "relativism" that offer no threat to morality or the moralist. The "moral relativist," who *is* considered a threat to morality, tells us that "morality is relative." That is ominous in its vagueness, and we hear it often, but it needs to be made more explicit. To what, for example, is morality relative—custom, choice, circumstances?

Descriptive Relativism

Universalism probably cannot be defended. Even if we find some non-trivial candidate for a universal moral principle, we would have to overcome countless difficulties (of language, finitude, and human contrariness) before we could claim that *everyone* accepts it. There may be moral principles we think it would be nice for everyone to believe, and follow, but it will always be possible to find someone who disagrees with any moral principle we choose to mention.

Descriptive relativists begin and end with actual moral disagreement. Their modest assertion is that it exists. Descriptive relativists who remain content with the modest assertion have no quarrel even with the universalist, who acknowledges moral disagreement but not *ultimate* moral disagreement. If there *is* ultimate moral disagreement, then *no* moral belief, principle, or set of principles is accepted by everyone, universalism is factually mistaken, and what can be called *extreme descriptive relativism* is true.

The question whether ultimate moral disagreement exists is probably one of those that will never be given a conclusive answer. But let us note two things. First, even if, as the universalist claims, there is some universally accepted moral principle, it does not follow that this principle is true, correct, rational, or justifiable. Second, even if the extreme descriptive relativist is correct and there is no universally accepted moral principle, it does not follow that no moral principle is true, correct, rational, or justifiable. Neither the universalist nor the descriptive relativist can say that—or which—moral judgments or principles are true. They are talking about what people believe, not about which beliefs are correct.

Naive Moral Relativism

The descriptive relativist says that different people, societies, and groups have different and incompatible values and moral principles; the extreme descriptive relativist applies this to their most basic values and principles. But it is only when we take another step and claim that two conflicting moral judgments or principles may both be true that we advance to what I call *naive moral relativism*. The descriptive relativist notes that while it was considered morally acceptable in ancient Greece to leave unwanted children on the hillside to starve, the same action is held to be morally unacceptable in modern Greece. The naive moral relativist goes further and concludes that both the ancient and the modern Greeks were correct in their judgments and that what was once morally permissible is now morally wrong. Nor is it simply a matter of time. Even now, differing moral judgments may be made of the same action: "What is right for you may be wrong for me."

Naive moral relativism may appeal to moralists who have given up defending their own versions of morality and hope to buy tolerance with tolerance. And it will appeal to those whose values are at odds with the prevailing morality. It is also possible that many moral absolutists are too polite to tell others what they really think about their morality, and cover disapprobation with insincere expressions of tolerant relativism.

We can understand why someone may be inclined to *want* naive moral relativism to be true, but it is hard to think how such a view could be supported. It does not follow from descriptive relativism; the undeniable fact that different societies or groups have different views about what is right and wrong does nothing to show that each or even any of them is correct. Normally one would think that such widespread disagreement would be a reason for mistrusting a subject, not a reason for supposing that all the participants in the debate are in the right.

Naive moral relativists get into trouble because they uncritically adopt, and then violate, the language we use to describe reality, a language that does not permit literal contradictions. It is natural to assume that an action is morally required or morally forbidden because of some feature it has, and that if two actions share this feature, then both must be judged in the same way. Yet the naive moral relativist appears to be saying that of two killings of innocent people, one may be wrong and the other not wrong. If these different evaluations are backed by different principles (one permitting and the other forbidding the killing of innocents), our naive relativist will be content to say that both principles are correct. But how, if we take morality seriously, can some action or principle be right in one place (or at one time) and wrong in another? Naive moral relativists are called "naive" because they do not even get to this question.

Subjective Moral Relativism

The truth of individual moral judgments may be relative to general principles and to circumstances, but this is not the sort of relativism that alarms the moralist. Relativism only becomes a threat to morality when it demands that we abandon the belief that there are basic values or basic moral principles that apply to everyone.

If we say that some action is wrong for a person if and only if it is forbidden by the rules of his or her society, then head-hunting will be wrong for a person from a society that forbids it, and not wrong for someone who belongs to a society of headhunters. This, however, is not true relativism, because it presupposes a universal moral principle that says that what society forbids is wrong.

The subjective relativist may try to avoid this deeper commitment to a non-relative moral rule by adopting a "subjective" definition of some important moral word. Such a definition will make it possible to equate moral claims with statements about the beliefs, principles, needs, interests, or desires of one or several "subjects." Not all such definitions yield relativism, but many of them do.

The following definitions of 'right' and 'wrong' are subjective definitions that seem to result in a form of relativism. '*D*' stands for an action.

D is right $=_{df}$ *D* is permitted by the rules of *some* society.
D is wrong $=_{df}$ *D* is forbidden by the rules of *some* society.

Given these definitions, the very same thing (for example, head-hunting) may, without contradiction, be said to be both right and wrong. But the definition has done its job too well, because it has purged all the moralism from the claim that something is right or wrong. Anyone who says that head-hunting is both right and wrong, for example, would be saying no more and no less than that it is permitted in one society and forbidden in another. The same thing might then be both right and wrong even in the *same* society, if that society has inconsistent rules—some that permit the action and others that forbid it.

Now consider some other candidates for a definition of 'good' (or 'bad').

(*a*) *X* is good $=_{df}$ God likes *X*.
(*b*) *X* is good $=_{df}$ The majority of people like *X*.
(*c*) *X* is good $=_{df}$ I like *X*.
(*d*) *X* is bad $=_{df}$ I dislike *X*.
(*e*) X is good $=_{df}$ *X* is desired by someone.
(*f*) *X* is bad $=_{df}$ *X* is detested by someone.

The first definition results in a non-relativistic account of good if we assume God is consistent, and so does (*b*) if there is an answer to the question of what the majority likes. Definitions (*c*) and (*d*) are different. They allow one person to say that *X* is good, another to say that *X* is bad, and both to be right. The sting is removed from this apparent contradiction because, given the definitions, the speakers are not talking about *X*, but about themselves. Unlike (*c*) and (*d*), (*e*) and (*f*) allow the *same* person to say, without inconsistency, that something is both good and bad. They are only saying that someone desires *X* and someone *else* is averse to it.

Gilbert Harman defends a form of subjective moral relativism that he applies to what he calls "inner judgments." The judgment that someone "ought not to have acted in a certain way," and the judgment that "it was right or wrong of him to have done so," are inner judgments. These judgments are "relational," in the sense that if: "*S* says that *A* (morally) ought to do *D*, *S* implies that *A* has reasons to do *D* and *S* endorses those reasons" (Harman [1], 193). If Harman is right about this, we cannot morally criticize a cannibal or a Nazi who does not share "our" moral principles. To say that such a person *ought not* to have acted as he did is to say, or to imply, that he had reasons not to act in that way, and he may have had no such reasons. Harman says it is "a misuse of language" to say it is morally wrong for hardened criminals to steal and kill. "Since they do not share our conventions, they have no moral reasons to refrain from stealing from us or killing us" (Harman [2], 113).

Harman admits that those who go along with his way of thinking will have to "think again" about morality. It has traditionally been assumed that "basic moral demands are demands on everyone," but if relativism is true, this assumption is false. In that case:

> The ordinary notion of morality is based on a false presupposition and we find ourselves in the position of those who thought morality was the law of God and then began to suspect there was no God. Relativism implies that morality as we ordinarily understand it is a delusion, a vain and chimerical notion. (Harman [3], 113)

This threatens morality if the notion of morality essentially involves the idea that basic moral demands are demands on everyone. Harman thinks we can abandon this idea and still have "a reasonable substitute for" and "a good approximation to" morality. He suggests that we use moral language with an explicit awareness of its relativist implications and acknowledge that there are "various moralities, each involving different basic moral demands . . . which certain people accept or have reasons to accept" (Harman [3], 113). Moral principles are "binding only on those who share them or whose principles give them reasons to accept them" (Harman [2], 90). This "local bondage" gives us some of what morality is supposed to provide. The bondage is real, in a sense, but it is also "internal" to some system one can reject without being irrational or factually mistaken.

Situational Moral Relativism

As morality is commonly understood, if it is right for me to do something and wrong for you to do that same thing, then there is something about me, you, or the situation that accounts for that moral difference. We get *subjective* forms of moral relativism when obligation is relativized to principles we hold, or to other subjective features. The subjective definitions result in relativism when different people hold different principles, or disagree in their attitudes and desires. But if our definitions depend on non-subjective factors, it is not so easy to make them produce forms of relativism. Hence, when we say that what is right and wrong is relative to non-subjective circumstances, moral relativism is not so readily forthcoming.

The subjective relativist *speaks* as a moralist, but the subjectivist analysis of moral language shifts the subject from obligation or value to whatever subjective thing the definitions introduce. The situational moral relativist, on the other hand, really *is* a moralist, but one who believes that what is right and wrong varies with the circumstances.

Situational moral relativism is not a serious threat to morality because it contradicts only those few moralists who believe some things are right or wrong *no matter what the circumstances*. When situational relativists say what morality is relative to, they speak as moralists—otherwise they are merely claiming that the correctness of some (unspecified) moral judgment depends on the circumstances in some (unspecified) way. This is not a specific form of moralism, but the abstract form of all moralist positions. Subjective moral relativism, by contrast, can be seen either as supporting or as threatening morality. It threatens morality by offering to replace it with something different, but it also appears to support it by retaining moral language and a limited and local form of bondage, thus providing a relative kind of objectivity.

The dogmatist says "I am right and everyone else is wrong." The naive moral relativist says everyone is right. The subjective moral relativist says we are right when our judgments are consistent with our principles, and the situational moral relativist says that the circumstances determine when we are right. Not only are these views no threat to moralism, each can be seen as a form of moralism. Universalism and descriptive relativism are not forms of moralism, but neither are they hostile to it.

If a man sleeps in a damp place, he will have a pain in his loins and will dry up and die. Is that true of eels? If a man lives up in a tree, he will be frightened and tremble. Is that true of monkeys? Which of the three knows the right place to live? Men eat vegetables and flesh, and deer eat tender grass. Centipedes enjoy snakes, and owls and crows like mice. Which of the four knows the right taste? . . . Mao Ch'iang and Li Chi were considered by men to be beauties, but at the sight of them fish plunged deep down in the water, birds soared high up in the air, and deer dashed away. Which of the four knows the right kind of beauty? From my point of view, the principle of humanity and righteousness and the doctrines of right and wrong are mixed and confused. How do I know the difference among them? (Chuang Tzu, in Chan [1], 187–88)

Skepticism

Another reaction to the variety of moral beliefs and the inconclusiveness of discussions about them is *moral skepticism*—the belief that there is no way to know which of the many moral theories and judgments that can be heard are true and which are false. Skeptics in ancient Greece fall into two categories: Academic Skeptics (so called because they taught in the school begun by Plato, the Academy) and Pyrrhonists (named after Pyrrho of Elis). The Academics claimed not to know anything, while the more radical (and perhaps more consistent) Pyrrhonists tried not to commit themselves even to that negative claim. Sextus Empiricus, the most famous Pyrrhonist of the ancient world, amassed a collection of skeptical formulas and arguments that he used to counterbalance any argument for any dogmatic claim about how things "really are." These arguments could not be used to prove anything positive, but Sextus was able to deploy them against his opponents and thereby to remain in a state of suspension of belief. He claimed that this suspension of belief led him to tranquillity.

How shall we understand "moral skepticism?" In his book *Ethics*, John Mackie calls his belief that there are no objective values "moral skepticism," but he is not *skeptical* about objective values; he is sure there are none. A moral skeptic will not be so certain. One who resembles the Academic skeptic will claim not to know whether there are objective values; but Pyrrhonist moral skeptics will not even make that claim. They will try to refrain from making moral judgments and, since they do not claim to know that they cannot know, they will leave open the possibility that a right answer exists. A skeptic, say the Pyrrhonists, is a seeker.

So now it seems that both forms of moral skepticism, like moral relativism, are compatible with the existence of objective values and obligations. Skeptical beliefs flourish in an environment filled with inconclusive moral disputation, but neither the relativist nor the skeptic comes out directly and denies morality—one says that the truth is relative; the other claims not to know, or says nothing.

> Our assertion up to now is that the Sceptic's end, where matters of opinion are concerned, is mental tranquility; in the realm of things unavoidable, moderation of feeling is the end. His initial purpose in philosophizing was to pronounce judgment on appearances. He wished to find out which are true and which are false, so as to attain mental tranquility. In doing so, he met

> with contradicting alternatives of equal force. Since he could not decide between them, he withheld judgment. Upon his suspension of judgment there followed, by chance, mental tranquility in matters of opinion. For the person who entertains the opinion that anything is by nature good or bad is continually disturbed. When he lacks those things which seem to him to be good, he believes he is being pursued, as if by the Furies, by those things which are by nature bad, and pursues what he believes to be the good things. But when he has acquired them, he encounters further perturbations. This is because his elation at the acquisition is unreasonable and immoderate, and also because in his fear of a reversal all his exertions go to prevent the loss of the things which to him seem good. On the other side there is the man who leaves undetermined the question what things are good and bad by nature. He does not exert himself to avoid anything or to seek after anything, and hence he is in a tranquil state. (Sextus Empiricus, 41)

Non-Cognitivism

A more serious challenge to morality arose from the Logical Positivists. This group of logicians, scientists, and mathematicians took a no-nonsense, anti-metaphysical approach to philosophy. The task of the philosopher, they thought, is to analyze language and thereby uncover disguised nonsense. They said that any non-trivial utterance is meaningless if analysis reveals that no observation can establish its truth or falsity—if there is no way to verify or falsify it. They argued that if ethical utterances can be reduced to factual ones, then they are meaningful but completely descriptive, the business of scientists rather than philosophers. If these utterances cannot be reduced to factual ones, then they cannot be verified or falsified, and we can classify them, with religious and metaphysical utterances, as "nonsense."

In *Language, Truth, and Logic*, Alfred Jules Ayer announced that our "exhortations to moral virtue are not propositions at all, but ejaculations or commands which are designed to provoke the reader to action of a certain sort" (Ayer, 103). He denied that statements about what is right, wrong, good, and bad are ever statements describing the world. They are all disguised expressions of emotion and covert attempts to influence our attitudes and behavior. Since we never evaluate expressions of emotion, exclamations, or imperatives in terms of truth or falsity, Ayer concluded that moral judgments have no truth value. He was careful to distinguish the belief that moral judgments have no truth value from subjectivism, the view that their truth depends on subjective factors.

In the 1950s and 1960s, moral philosophers pursued this positivist-inspired challenge to morality, and the debate was between the cognitivists and the non-cognitivists. Cognitivists tended to assert, and non-cognitivists to deny, the following sentences and their implications:

(1) There are moral facts.
(2) Moral judgments are either true or false.
(3) We can have moral knowledge.

These three formulations are not equivalent, but their rejection is supported by Ayer's analysis of moral language and his assumption that all meaningful utterances are capable of empirical verification. *If* moral judgments are nothing but shouts and disguised commands, then they are not statements about facts, which means that they are no more subject to evaluation in terms of truth and falsity than are actual shouts and undisguised commands.

There are, of course, impressive differences between moral judgments and shouts and commands. Moral judgments look like statements, and people react to them as if they are statements—they attack and defend them by giving reasons, and they see themselves as seeking the truth about what is good and right. These differences lead some non-cognitivists to abandon the claim that moral judgments *are* expressions or commands for the more moderate claim that they function as expressions and commands, or that they have features in common with expressions and commands. This weakens an already weak case against (1)–(3).

Since the "Verification Principle" raises more questions than it answers, philosophers have backed away from the confident anti-metaphysical nihilism of the early positivists, and even non-cognitivists have found it harder to reject (1)–(3). When the connections linking facts, truth, knowledge, meaning, and verifiability dissolve, new possibilities appear to moralists. We can interpret 'fact', 'true', 'false', and 'know' in ways that make it correct to say that moral judgments can be true or known, or that moral facts exist. For example, if *truth* is understood as a matter of agreement, then moral truth exists where moral agreement does. If *moral facts* are social phenomena, then it is hard to deny that there are moral facts. But it is also hard to believe that they have any more force than a request or a command from a group of strangers.

Before we become enmeshed in epistemology and metaphysics, let us note that the denial of (1)–(3) was originally thought to be a *result* of the non-cognitivist analysis. What *makes* someone a non-cognitivist is not some opinion about (1)–(3), but a special understanding of moral language and its meaning or use. The non-cognitivists say that, like commands or cries of joy or pain, moral utterances have no "factual" meaning, and that when we express them we are not stating facts or describing reality. These non-cognitivists base their denials of (1)–(3) on their understanding of moral language and on an argument we can call the "function-of-language argument." After taking an initial look at (1)–(3), we examine the use of this argument. It emerges that a clear and unequivocal rejection of (1)–(3) does *not* follow from the non-cognitivists' claims about the use of moral language, which, in any case, are complex, confused, and, in important ways, false.

Moral Facts

Friedrich Nietzsche demands that the moral philosophers "place themselves *beyond* good and evil." He says that this demand "follows from an insight first formulated by me: *that there are no moral facts whatever*" (Nietzsche [3], 65). We can thank Nietzsche for giving us an explicit formulation of (1), but not for helping us understand what the non-existence of moral facts amounts to. What is the difference between a world with moral facts and a world without them? What are moral facts supposed to be, and where?

The British philosopher G. E. Moore appears to have believed in moral facts. In *Principia Ethica*, he says that the word 'good', like the word 'yellow', is the name of a simple and indefinable property. It is a simple fact that some object is yellow, and Moore holds it to be an equally simple fact that some things are good. The difference between the two cases is only that yellow (yellowness) is a "natural" property while good (goodness) is a "non-natural" one. We get a moral fact when something has a moral property (goodness or badness) just as we get a natural fact when something has a physical property (yellowness or roundness). We see the natural property with our eyes but we "intuit" the non-natural one.

Many moral philosophers cannot bring themselves to agree with either Nietzsche or Moore, and settle for a compromise called *ethical naturalism*. Ethical naturalists reject Nietzsche's claim that there are no moral facts. But the ethical naturalist parts company with Moore and the intuitionists by claiming that these moral facts *are* natural facts. The naturalist believes that when we say that something is good or right, we are simply reporting the presence of one or another completely natural (scientifically respectable) property—like the property of promoting survival, or of being pleasant, desired, commanded, or customary. Traditional ethical naturalists try to establish this conclusion by claiming that 'good' means the same thing as 'desired', or that 'right' means the same thing as 'leads to the greatest pleasure for the greatest number of humans'. As reports of actual usage, these definitions oversimplify and distort, and as recommendations about how to talk, they may be accepted or not, as one chooses. But even if one accepts such a definition, resolving henceforth to use 'right', for example, to mean 'productive of the greatest human happiness', nothing is accomplished by this lexical resolution. One has certainly not thereby established, grounded, proved, or justified the claim that we ought to try to make everyone as happy as possible.

Gilbert Harman's explanation of 'ought' in terms of reasons is an example of ethical naturalism. Harman says that there are no "absolute facts of right or wrong, apart from one or another set of conventions," but he adds that there are "relative facts about what is right or wrong with respect to one or another set of conventions." Moral facts exist, then, as "relational facts about reasons" (Harman [2], 132). The fact that *A* morally ought to do something is both a moral fact and a fact about *A*'s having certain kinds of reasons to do it.

Naturalism is designed to make it possible to speak of moral facts even while one believes that there are no "independent" moral facts existing in the "fabric of reality." Moore's motto for *Principia Ethica* was: "Everything is what it is, and not another thing." By this he meant to indicate that goodness is goodness, and not pleasure, or flourishing, or being desired, or anything other than goodness itself. Naturalists, of course, can agree that two things or properties that are really different cannot be identified, but they refuse to see that goodness and their favored property are really different.

Nietzsche's "original" insight about moral facts will never be allowed to stand unchallenged for long. People, wanting to believe in moral facts, have devised subtle ways to support this practice. One alternative is to lower the requirement for facthood, thereby flooding the world with new and exotic facts. Another is to raise the requirement for facthood so drastically that even science and daily experience yield no real facts. As a result, moral facts will be at least no worse off than facts of any other sort. Eventually we shall explore these strategies, but here we need only observe that, like the practical question of vegetarianism, the theoretical question of moral facts offers willing philosophers an unlimited field for combat and a smorgasbord of options.

Moral Truths

The second sentence cognitivists usually affirmed and non-cognitivists denied is:

(2) Moral judgments are either true or false.

If there are moral facts in any sense, then of course there are truths about them in some parallel sense. But is there a way to support (2) without directly appealing to (1)? One argument used in support of (2) starts with the fact (if it is a fact) that people, if asked, would agree that moral judgments are true or false. But answers people give depend not only on what they are asked but on how the question is framed. People who are asked if it is true that genocide is morally wrong will usually reply that it is. If, on the other hand, we ask the same people whether they believe that moral judgments are "objectively true or false," their answers are likely to be more pleasing to the non-cognitivist.

Still, non-cognitivists, who would not have answered even the question about genocide in the affirmative without reservations, appear to be in conflict with common sense here, and sometimes this is held against them. Harman, for example, says that the view that moral judgments are never true or false runs "afoul of a maxim or rule of thumb for philosophers, namely that, if a philosophical theory conflicts with ordinary ways of thinking and speaking, examine the argument for that theory very closely, since something has probably gone wrong" (Harman [2], 34).

This is a very useful rule of thumb because philosophers often tell us things that go against ordinary beliefs. They say that we cannot know anything, that matter does not exist, that time is unreal, that there is no God, that morality is an illusion, and that we all have a moral obligation to improve ourselves and promote the happiness of others—to mention just a few examples. When there is a conflict between what is ordinarily believed and what philosophers say, then it is a good idea to examine the philosophers' arguments, but it is also a good idea to find out why ordinary people hold their beliefs. The things that lead ordinary people to believe in God, morality, and astrology need to be looked into no less than the reasons of the philosophers who reject those beliefs.

Cognitivists say that there are moral truths and non-cognitivists deny it. Ordinary people who have not been exposed to philosophy may take the side of the cognitivist, but what are we to make of this? It is not obvious what philosophers *or* ordinary people mean when they say, or deny, that there are moral truths. Both use the expression 'moral truth', but that does not guarantee that they are using it in the same way, or with the same meaning. Given their different approaches, interests, and activities, they probably do *not* mean the same thing when they assert (2). In that case, the ordinary person's agreement with the cognitivist about moral truth does not really support the cognitivist belief in moral truths.

There is another way to arrive at the conclusion that there are moral truths. One can introduce a theory of truth that is loose enough to allow moral statements to count as true. We could do this by making truth a matter of consensus rather than correspondence. If judgments of moral obligation and value are true only if they correspond to some moral fact, then moral truths will rise and fall with moral facts. If, on the other hand, we call a statement true when it meets our community standards for being called "true," then many statements that were once questionable will now be capable of being true—including statements about our rights and duties, aesthetic statements, and (unless we can figure out how to stop it) statements about gods, ghosts, and goodness.

Moral Knowledge

Moral truths and facts are of little use if they cannot be known, so cognitivists who are moralists also support:

(3) We can have moral knowledge.

Moore, for example, believes that our knowledge that a thing is good is like our knowledge that something is yellow. But of course the difference between moral knowledge, as Moore understands it, and knowledge about physical features of the world is enormous. We understand how our senses give us knowledge about how things look, sound, and smell; we know the physical structure of these organs and we even know how to influence their operations in precise ways. There may be unsolved problems and unanswered questions about perceptual knowledge, but there are no *mysteries*—other than the ultimate mystery of consciousness itself. On the other hand, we can say nothing about any physiological mechanism underlying Moore's intuition of goodness. We smell with our nose, but with what, other than "our intuition," do we intuit?

Intuitionists argue, with some plausibility, that knowledge is not limited to what we can perceive with the senses. But how is it limited? It appears that anyone able to gain control of the standards for knowledge will be able to claim "knowledge" at will. If we say that to *know* something is merely to be warranted by the norms of one's society to believe it, then much may be known that a stricter account of knowledge would exclude.

The Function-of-Language Argument

In *Ethics and Language*, C. L. Stevenson draws a distinction between "descriptive meaning" and "emotive meaning." He defines the descriptive meaning of a sign as its "disposition to affect cognition," and its emotive meaning in terms of speakers' use of that sign to influence the attitudes and emotions of their audiences. *Purely* descriptive language is used to describe (state facts), and is subject to evaluation in terms of truth and falsity. *Purely* evaluative language is expressive or imperative, and has no fact-stating or truth dimension. As soon as this clarification is made, it becomes obvious that many if not most evaluative and factual judgments have both sorts of "meaning." Thus, arguments based on the non-descriptive function of evaluative language lose much of their weight. If moral judgments are mere expressions of feeling (like "Ouch!") or commands (like "Do it!"), then they probably do not state facts or have a truth value. But if they are like expressions and commands in some ways, and like assertions in others, then they might well be used both to command and to state. This is the way "You will take out the garbage" and "Trespassing is forbidden" seem to work.

The non-cognitivists' use of the argument from the function of language to show that moral judgments are not fact-stating was based on an important insight—namely, that evaluative language is different from language that is not evaluative. But no conclusion about the existence or non-existence of moral facts, truth, or knowledge follows from the fact that moral language has an expressive or an imperative function. Cognitivists agree that moral language is used in all these expressive ways and then point out that it may still be used to describe the world.

The argument now threatens to boil down to the question of which use is *primary*, and whether anything at all about moral facts, truth, and knowledge follows from any answer to that question. In "The Emotive Meaning of Ethical Terms," Stevenson claims that the *major* use of ethical judgments "is not to indicate facts but to *create an influence*" (Stevenson [1], 16). Instead of merely describing people's interests, they change or intensify them. Ethical terms, he says, are "*instruments* used in the complicated interplay and readjustment of human interests" (17). But what is supposed to follow from the claim that the "major" use of ethical language is to influence? One thing that does not follow is that ethical language is not used to state moral facts.

Anti-Realism

John Mackie describes a "second order moral view" as a "view about the status of moral values and the nature of moral valuing, about where and how they fit into the world" (Mackie [1], 16). He calls his own second order moral view by two different names, "moral subjectivism" and "moral skepticism," but a less misleading designation might be "anti-realism." In contrast to non-cognitivists, Mackie claims that moral judgments have a truth-value, and in contrast to moral realists and ethical naturalists, he holds that they are all false. Moral judgments are false because they all involve the mistaken claim, or assumption, or presupposition that there are "objectively prescriptive" moral properties or facts, intrinsic values, or binding categorical imperatives.

According to Mackie, objective prescriptivity is embedded in our everyday moral language, and it is an explicit feature of moral theories that depend on intrinsic value and binding moral duties. Morality is seen as having a kind of authority over us, its commands and prescriptions are thought to be objective requirements, not ones we invent or imagine, and not ones we can avoid. Mackie is not alone in identifying this cluster of puzzling beliefs as central to morality. Kant said that reason "commands what ought to happen" (Kant [3], 20), and the contemporary British moral philosopher Philippa Foot, commenting on Kant's idea, identifies inescapability as the mark of the commands of morality. "People talk," she says, "about the 'binding force' of morality, but it is not clear what this means if not that we *feel* ourselves unable to escape" (Foot [2], 162). Another contemporary moral philosopher, Bernard Williams, rejects what he calls the "morality system" and, like Foot, sees inescapability as a fundamental feature of moral obligation. He says that this inescapability means that there is no opting out of morality, and he identifies this idea with Kant's claim that morality is "categorical" (Williams [2], 177–78).

Foot points out one way morality and etiquette are both inescapable: In societies where rules of morality and etiquette are in force, "behavior does not cease to offend against either morality or etiquette because the agent is indifferent to their purposes and to the disapproval he will incur by flouting them" (Foot [2], 162). That is, our indifference to the imperatives of etiquette (Don't eat peas with a knife.) and to the imperatives of morality (Don't use people for selfish ends.) does not mean that our actions will not "offend" against the respective systems. But it is one thing for my behavior to violate a conventional code, another thing for me to *feel* bound by that code, and yet a third thing for me to *be* bound by that code. We can escape the imperatives of etiquette by moving in different circles, but no move will free us from moral imperatives. Moral bondage, unlike the bondage morality and etiquette share, is non-relative, non-derivative, and inescapable.

It is clear why moralists claim that the judgments of morality are inescapable, but it is not so clear what that claim means. Foot explores several ways of expressing the "fugitive thought" that morality binds us, that there are things we *must do*, or *have to do*. But she finds nothing standing behind the words and concludes that there may not be such a form of bondage, and that our belief and our feeling that there is results from education and training. "Perhaps," she suggests, "it makes no sense to say that we 'have to' submit to the moral law, or that morality is 'inescapable' in some special way" (Foot [2], 163).

Even though the meaning of 'moral bondage' remains unclear, and we have no clue as to the nature or source of an "objective demand," the thought that we are inescapably bound is an indispensable part of the institution of morality, as it is understood by those who participate in it. According to Mackie, herein lies the failure of naturalist and non-cognitivist analyses of moral language: Both fail to capture or explain the "apparent authority" of ethics—naturalists by excluding "the categorically imperative aspect" (the prescriptivity), and non-cognitivists by excluding "the claim to objective validity or truth" (Mackie [1], 33). Whether it is possible to combine these elements or not, our use of moral concepts requires both. Moral judgments that are *objective without being prescriptive* make no demands and require nothing from us. They merely inform us that our action has a property of "wrongness" or merits the term 'wrong', in which case learning that something is wrong is like learning what time it is—its relevance depends on other commitments. Moral judgments that are *prescriptive without being objective* are "mere" commands or demands. In their overt form ("Leave the room!"), they make no claim to objectivity; and when they are presented as statements, it is not the fact apparently being stated that is supposed to be objective ("You will leave the room.") but the demand. To be objective, a demand would have to result from something more than any subjective item like a desire or a need of some person or persons.

Despite its obscurity, moral realism is a pervasive feature of our lives and is embedded in our language. "Ordinary moral judgments," says Mackie, "include a claim to objectivity, an assumption that there are objective values in just the sense in which I am concerned to deny this" (Mackie [1], 35). Those who use evaluative language may not comprehend all this assumption involves, or how peculiar it is, but this does not prevent them from making it, and from being wrong every time they do. Obligations exist, but they are hypothetical and institutional. We value things, but not because we have discovered that they have intrinsic value. No matter how bound we feel, or how bound others want us to be, it is we who project objective prescriptivity and intrinsic value onto perfectly natural and intrinsically neutral items.

The idea that users of moral language are uniformly mistaken about the objectivity of morality does go against deeply held beliefs and common sense. Mackie acknowledges this and concedes that it means that his theory needs "very solid support." He finds this support in the argument from relativity and the argument from queerness.

Mackie offers the argument from relativity as an argument from moral diversity to the best explanation of that diversity. "The actual variations in the moral codes," he says, "are more readily explained by the hypothesis that they reflect ways of life than by the hypothesis that they express perceptions, most of them seriously inadequate and badly distorted, of objective values" (Mackie [1], 37). Recent moral thinkers have not been kind to this argument. Thomas Nagel expresses surprise at the popularity of what he calls the "argument from disagreement." He says that radical disagreement "is a poor reason to conclude that values have no objective reality," but then he turns around and uses an "argument from agreement" to support the objectivity of morality (Nagel, 147–48). The arguments, of course, neutralize each other, since there is both agreement and disagreement everywhere—in morality, in science, and in daily life. Mackie's anti-realism could be true even if everyone agreed about what is right and wrong; and moral realism could be true even if no one realized it. As things stand, there is disagreement *and* agreement, both within and among cultures, and Mackie's argument says that the best explanation of both the agreement and the disagreement need not go beyond human feelings, needs, interests, and traditions. We agree about morality and have strong moral "intuitions" because we have learned our lessons; and we disagree because we have not all learned the same lessons, and because our interests often conflict.

If we want to support anti-realism in morality and realism regarding the objects of everyday life, we dare not argue from bare disagreement, which occurs everywhere. We must argue that the best overall explanation of the actual patterns of agreement and disagreement leads to anti-realism about goodness and to realism about tables. When we try to say more about this difference, however, we are forced to confront the claim that moral facts and properties are unique, and this leads directly to the argument from queerness.

Mackie offers both a metaphysical and an epistemological version of the argument from queerness. The metaphysical version says that objective values would have to be "entities or qualities or relations of a very strange sort, utterly different from anything else in the universe," and the epistemological version says that our awareness of these strange qualities "would have to be by some special faculty of moral perception or intuition, utterly different from our ordinary ways of knowing everything else" (Mackie [1], 38). Nothing so different, so unrelated to everything we know and understand, so "queer," should be said to exist, so there are no values, obligations, or rights—morality is an invention.

If judgments of value and obligation concern actual rather than fictional moral properties, we ought to be able to say something about them and about our apprehension of them. Color has a scientific explanation, and color blindness a physical basis. We learned color words in front of observable objects, and properties like yellow "exist" in a network of beliefs about the relation of color to light, prisms, paint, physiology, and photography. Intrinsic values and objective obligations do not fit into any such system. We have no duty receptors or instruments to detect the presence of value. We do not know where moral properties reside, how they relate to other properties, and how we come to know of them. No one has ever explained how some feature of an object could impose an "inescapable" duty on a person. It is not just that moral properties fail to help us explain our moral experience, their "queerness" undercuts any explanation that involves them.

Not everyone accepts this point. Some have argued that moral properties and qualities are not really queer, and others that since non-moral properties are also queer, queerness does not count against the moral ones. Some give Mackie everything he wants and then deny that they ever held anything like the theory he criticizes. Others simply attack his two arguments and then say that the burden is on him to offer further reasons for rejecting what so many people believe. Even Mackie backs away from the most extreme consequences of his anti-realism. As the subtitle of his book, *Inventing Morality,* indicates, he does not want to do without morality, but to create it, or at least creatively to modify the purely conventional one we find already in operation. But this business of exploiting a system you know to contain a fundamental error is problematic in its own way, since it requires deception by "wise philosophers" who alone understand what is really going on. We return to this topic later, but here we can at least say that the strongest challenge to morality will resemble Mackie's anti-realism more closely than it resembles any of the forms of skepticism or relativism we have been discussing.

First Conclusion

The failure of the non-cognitivist to make a good case for denying (1)–(3), the weakness uncovered in the function-of-language argument, an unwillingness to believe that everyone who seriously makes a moral judgment is making a mistake about what exists, and a pervasive unwillingness, even by someone like Mackie, to throw morality out the window, have led many moral philosophers to swing back to the traditional beliefs that the non-cognitivist was trying to undermine. But before we swing with them, let us consider more carefully this matter of a challenge to morality. In Chapter 3 we consider ways to give voice to the doubts that spring up in the face of serious moral disagreement and depressingly predictable moral arguments. We characterize more clearly than we so far have the concept of morality, so that we can be clear about what someone who wishes to challenge it must do. Finally, we identify the strongest form of challenge to moralism and call this challenger the *amoralist.*

If the moralist claims that there are moral facts, the amoralist denies this. If the moralist claims that goodness is the name of a non-natural property open to intuition but not to empirical testing, the amoralist refuses to allow that such properties exist. If the moralist says that preferences create value, the amoralist insists that preferences are simply preferences, and that there is a difference between something being valuable (in some objective sense that would satisfy a moralist's needs) and the fact that someone values a thing. In her book *Wickedness,* Mary Midgley clearly identifies the critical and variable nature of amoralism, though she speaks of it as "immoralism."

> Serious, sophisticated immoralism . . . is not a single position at all, much less a solid creed, a negative counterpart to morality, which can be preached and make converts. It is a range of critical enquiry, and one which continually changes. It consists of a set of widely varied criticisms of existing moralities, which are themselves various and changing. (Midgley, 24)

3

Morality and Its Denial

> The difficulty of seeing how values could be objective is a fairly strong reason for thinking that they are not so.
>
> —*John Mackie*, Ethics

WHETHER WE MEET them in literature, in philosophy, or in life, amoralists will be in some way "against" morality. Formally, amoralists are like atheists—that which they refuse to believe in (morality in the one case and God in the other) is many things to many people, but nothing to them. Yet it is possible to "reject morality" without rejecting the language of morality, and possible for those who "abandon" morality to act in ways people would describe as morally admirable. One's amoralism does not reside in what one says, or even in how one acts. It is a matter of *what one believes* about morality. The conflict between the moralist and the amoralist occurs on many fronts, but its initial character is determined by the moralist who is willing to affirm and defend one or more moral judgments.

A Literary Example and a Warning

Literature provides us with a plentiful supply of amoralists. In the following passage, one of Fyodor Dostoyevsky's characters, Stavrogen, describes his realization of the truth of amoralism:

> On that occasion, sitting at tea and chatting with the crew, for the first time in my life I clearly formulated the following for myself: I have

> neither the feeling nor the knowledge of good and evil, and not only have I lost the sense of good and evil, but good and evil really do not exist (and this pleased me) and are but a prejudice; I can be free of all prejudices, but at the very moment when I achieve that freedom I shall perish. (Dostoyevsky, 604)

Like Friedrich Nietzsche's claim that there are no moral facts, Stavrogen's claim that "good and evil do not exist" is simple and dramatic. But it is not immediately clear what the claim is supposed to amount to. What does it mean to say that good and evil do not exist? The answer to this question depends on what someone who says that good and evil do not exist intends to be denying. If Stavrogen wants to reject commonly held beliefs, he will have to use the relevant words as they are commonly used. He cannot introduce a special sense of 'good', 'evil', or 'exist' that makes what he wants to say true by (re)definition.

Existence

A consideration of the following sentences reveals some of the difficulties we face when we talk about what exists, or about what does not.

(*a*) Kangaroos exist.
(*b*) Unicorns exist.
(*c*) God exists.
(*d*) Hell exists.

Many who believe that only (*a*) is true could be convinced that, given certain ways of understanding 'God', (*c*) is true as well. If 'God' is used to mean 'the universe', (*c*) says that God (that is, the universe) exists. That is true if anything is. We are allowed some latitude in our language when God is the topic, but when we are talking about unicorns and kangaroos we must stay closer to common meanings. We do not neutralize a debate about the existence of kangaroos by saying "Well, it depends on what you mean by 'kangaroo'."

All of this relates to the subject terms of the above four claims, but we can also mean different things by the predicate 'exists'. Philosophers regularly take up questions about existence, and some of them have even argued that it is impossible to deny that anything exists.

Philosopher: Now my friend, what is it you are saying doesn't exist?
Other Person: Unicorns.

Philosopher: Aha! So a unicorn is *something* that doesn't exist. But if it is something, then it does exist after all, for a something isn't a nothing.

We were saved from the conclusion that everything mentionable exists by the decision that "things" like unicorns do not really exist, they *subsist*. Things that subsist are just real enough to be said not to exist. Whatever kind of "reality" that may be, like fictional and mythological existence, it is not going to help settle any theological or ethical disputes. Nobody denies that unicorns exist in legends, and they may well "subsist," but for all that, there are no unicorns.

And so with God and Hell. No believer will be satisfied that we belong to the faith if we allow God no more than subsistence or mythical existence. If two sects of Christians disagree about whether Hell exists, nothing will be resolved by agreeing on what they mean by 'Hell' and then allowing that in one sense of 'exist' Hell does exist (people take it seriously and worry about it), and in another sense of 'exist' it does not (nobody dies and then goes somewhere to be burned forever and poked by devils). That compromise would be a real defeat for the believer, for it would amount to the view that while Hell does not really exist, people think it does.

Whether out of kindness, confusion, or a lack of courage, we occasionally try to impart a non-standard meaning to some word or phrase so that we can "truthfully" assent to sentences we no longer believe. By fooling around with words like 'God' or 'exists' we pretend we are not misrepresenting ourselves when we say we believe that "God exists." But this violates our usual linguistic policy, which is to use words with their normal meanings, and it sows confusion and mistrust.

Where questions of religion are concerned, people are guilty of every sort of dishonesty and intellectual misdemeanor. Philosophers stretch the meaning of words until they retain scarcely anything of their original sense. They give the name of 'God' to some vague abstraction which they have created for themselves; having done so they can pose before all the world as deists, as believers in God, and they can even boast that they have recognized a higher, purer concept of God, notwithstanding that their God is now nothing more than an insubstantial shadow and no longer the mighty personality of religious doctrines. (Freud [2], 32)

Good and Evil

When we turn from easy questions about unicorns and difficult ones about God, to the question "Do good and evil exist?" we must feel an initial sense of bewilderment not felt in the other cases. As we learn about unicorns and kangaroos we soon realize that the unicorns belong with Donald Duck and the kangaroos with Uncle William. God is a problem because it is not easy to discover whether he is, like the unicorn and Donald Duck, a mythical beast, or, like the kangaroo and Uncle William, a real one.

What about good and evil? 'Kangaroo', 'unicorn', and 'God' are nouns used to talk about definite things (whether they exist or not). But 'good' and 'evil' are more often used as adjectives. We don't say "I saw a good," we say "That was good." "It is good" is straightforward, but "It is a good" sounds esoteric and philosophical, or else invites the question "A good what?" When we use 'good' as a noun ("Good exists."), we are using it as some people use 'goodness'. Now goodness, like beauty, is not a concrete thing but an "abstract entity." Plato is given credit for believing that goodness (or Goodness) is an abstract entity, and that the things we experience are as good as they are because of their relation to Goodness, which we do not experience unless we study philosophy, or lose our senses, or both. Amoralists would be first in line to deny that, but they would be followed by a horde of moralists unwilling to base their evaluations on anything so esoteric as an abstract entity. Plato's views are discussed in Chapter 7, so we can turn our attention now to the more natural use of 'good' and 'bad' as adjectives and say that the moralist believes that some things are good and others evil, while the amoralist believes that everything is neutral and without value.

Moralism versus Amoralism

By denying that anything is good or bad, amoralists put moralists in a position to go on the offensive. "How," the moralist will ask, "can anyone deny that slavery, misery, and malice are bad, or that friendship, pleasure, and freedom are good?" According to these moralists, amoralism can be rejected because it is so out of line with what is ordinarily believed. We encounter a version of this in Chapter 2, where we see how Gilbert Harman criticizes the non-cognitivists for saying that moral judgments are neither true nor false. His advice is that when a philosophical theory conflicts with ordinary ways of thinking and speaking, we "examine the argument for that theory very closely, since something has probably gone wrong" (Harman [2], 34). We see that something does go wrong when the non-cognitivist uses the function-of-language argument to cast doubt on moral facts. Now we find Harman applying the same test (Does the theory conflict with ordinary ways of thinking and speaking?) to the position of the amoralist (or, in his terminology, the "extreme nihilist"), who believes that "nothing is ever right or wrong, just or unjust, good or bad" (11). This position, Harman says, is hard to accept because "it implies that there are no moral constraints—that everything is permitted. As Dostoevsky observes, it implies that there is nothing wrong with murdering your father. It also implies that slavery is not unjust and that Hitler's extermination camps were not immoral. These are not easy conclusions to accept" (11).

One way to respond to this charge is to point out that Harman, whose relativism is discussed in Chapter 2, must also say that it is not wrong for some people to kill their fathers, or even to operate extermination camps. He says that those "who do not share our convictions" may not have moral reasons to refrain from stealing from us or killing us, and that if a person has no reason to adhere to some moral demand it is not true that he *ought* to adhere to that demand. But then only those who accept moral principles that forbid slavery will find it hard to accept the conclusion that slavery is not unjust. If your moral principles permit slavery, you will find it hard to accept the conclusion that slavery *is* unjust.

The amoralist's first line of defense, then, is to note that a relativist like Harman will also be forced to say things that go against what "we" ordinarily believe. Both the relativist and the amoralist are in the same boat—both oppose ordinary beliefs about morality. But the fact that Harman's objection can be turned upon him does not help the amoralist. If it is a good objection, then amoralists and relativists, who both deny there is a single true morality, have strikes against them. Fortunately for the amoralists, the criticism is a weak one, and there are other things that can be said in response to the claim that their deviation from what is ordinarily thought counts against them.

There is a sense in which the amoralist will agree with Harman's "extreme nihilist," who claims that nothing is right or wrong, just or unjust, good or bad, and who is described as believing that everything is permitted. But while amoralists do not believe in binding moral obligations, intrinsic value, or natural rights, they are fully aware of conventional rules and obligations. One does not have to believe in intrinsic value to believe that some things are good or bad (by this or that standard), and everyone knows that much is forbidden and required. So, amoralists who say that everything is permitted should not be taken to be rejecting all conventional and practical assessments. They are more likely to be emphasizing the conventional nature of conventional morality.

The amoralist is not denying that we have a conventional morality, and the moralist is not merely claiming that we have constructed a set of conventional rules or rights. The moralist wants to say that the immorality of death camps and slavery does not depend on what people happen to think, want, accept, believe, buy into, or choose. The amoralist can join with the moralist in this rejection of subjectivism, but must demur when the moralist continues by saying that death camps and slavery are, nevertheless, immoral—suggesting thereby that their immorality depends on something objective rather than something subjective, or, more strangely, that it depends on nothing at all. According to the moralist, some things are *really* wrong—forbidden, as it were, by Reality itself. Moralists have both moral beliefs and beliefs about the authority and objectivity of morality. Amoralists are aware of conventional morality, and of conventional moral language, but they have no moral beliefs, and their beliefs about the authority and objectivity of morality contradict the most fundamental beliefs of the moralists.

Amoralism is a set of beliefs about the claims and presuppositions of moralists, and has no necessary relation to the way amoralists feel about genocide, parricide, or slavery—or to what they do about them. The amoralist who says "Hitler's extermination camps were not immoral" is probably trying to illustrate the claim that no moral judgment, not even one about Hitler's extermination camps, can be given the sort of objective status most moralists want it to have. Sensible amoralists will refrain from saying that Hitler's extermination camps were "not immoral," because those who hear them may take them to accept the institution of morality and to be giving not unfavorable marks to extermination camps. If we do not want to be mistaken for moralists, we must avoid moralist ways of expressing our beliefs and attitudes and making requests and demands.

What Is the Difference between Moralism and Amoralism?

Before we consider any further moralist attacks on amoralism, let us pursue the quest for a true challenge to moralism by sharpening the distinction between the moralist and the amoralist. What is involved in being a moralist? Or, as some moral philosophers put it, what it is to adopt "the moral point of view"? One way to explain the "moral point of view" is to contrast it with other points of view: the aesthetic, economic, political, religious, or ecological, point of view, or even with the point of view of self-interest. To take any one or any combination of these or other points of view is to be prepared to think and talk in characteristic ways, to hold certain beliefs, to count some things important and others irrelevant. The concept of a 'point-of-view' shifts slightly as we move from one to another of them, but the idea, though flexible, is not empty.

We can distinguish between *taking* a point of view and *looking at something* from a point of view. One cannot *take* the religious point of view without believing in God (or some god, or at least Something), but even atheists can *look at* things from the religious point of view. They can do this by imagining (or remembering) themselves as believers, and then asking how they would (or did) understand events.

We may likewise distinguish between taking the moral point of view or the point of view of self-interest and looking at things from those points of view. Looking at things from the point of view of self-interest or of morality only involves determining what the self-interested or the moral solution to a problem is. To *look at* things from the moral point of view is to consider the advice of morality, but to *take* the moral point of view is both to consider the advice of morality and to acknowledge its "authority." In the next few sections we explore what is involved in taking the moral point of view. Only if we know this will we know what it is to be a moralist—or an amoralist.

Making Moral Judgments

William Frankena says that taking the moral point of view "involves the making and/or using, and perhaps on occasion, uttering, of evaluative or normative judgments about rational beings, their actions, traits, intentions, motives, etc." (Frankena [2], 111). This seems right. If we do not formulate (at least to ourselves) some such judgment, we use no moral concept and establish no connection with morality. If our response to some event is merely one of anger or delight, we are still outside the system of morality and none of the further elements we are about to discuss has any application.

The moralist will make moral judgments, but will the amoralist refrain? Not necessarily. Frankena notes that someone moved only by a love of others and a desire for their well-being might still make moral judgments, intending *others* to treat them as objective, categorical, and binding. He would say that this friendly being makes moral judgments, but has no morality. Such a person knows that others have a morality, and exploits this information to influence them. This person is not a moralist, but an amoralist posing as one.

Both the amoralist who hopes to promote some end like human happiness and the amoralist who hopes to rule the world must face the practical question of whether or not to exploit the language of morals. An amoralist who decides not to pose as a moralist can still accomplish much with words. If you always place your interests ahead of those of your spouse, your children, and your parents, even amoralists can accuse you of being selfish. If you ask "What's wrong with being selfish?" the amoralist is not required to supply you with a proof that selfishness is objectively wrong, forbidden by nature, or irrational, though he might try to explain why he does not like it and wishes to see it diminished. By using the word with its conventional negative force, an amoralist can, without inconsistency, exploit that aspect of its use and join with others to put down selfishness. What the amoralist cannot do, without deception or error, is to use this charged language in a way that implies, and will be understood to imply, that moral judgments are objectively binding.

Amoralists are free to use words like 'good', 'best', 'bad', and 'worst' when they are willing to accept certain non-moral standards. There is no reason why amoralists cannot speak of good students, bad apples, good knives, bad plans, good movies, and bad restaurants. These evaluations are what John Mackie calls "objective evaluations relative to standards" (Mackie [1], 26–27). Given the standards, the evaluations are "relatively objective." Nor are the standards arbitrary, since they are based on human desires and projects. Amoralists may also use 'right' and 'wrong' if they relate their evaluation to some purpose (the right weapon, wrench, or word) or to some role-generated duty (the right thing for a brother, a promiser, a senator to do).

When we use moral language, or the language of any other institution, we represent ourselves as believing what the use of that language implies. But we do not become moralists by merely using moral language. Genuine moralists (as opposed to amoralists faking moralism) actually accept, or unthinkingly operate as if they accept, the traditional implications of their use of moral language.

What are these implications, and what is it to accept them? Most of them have already been mentioned. Moralists see moral principles and duties as binding and values as intrinsic. They are the philosophers who, like Samuel Clarke, believe that some things "are in their own nature Good and Reasonable and Fit to be done" and other things "are in their own nature absolutely Evil" (Clarke, 9). They are the contemporary moral realists who believe that "there are objective moral facts and . . . true moral propositions" (Brink, 111), or that "moral reflection and moral judgment are a matter of discovery, rather than of invention, projection, expression, or even self-discovery, because the good and the right are 'in the world' " (Zimmerman, 80).

In the following sections we consider some of the features that have been attributed to morality. The moralist and the amoralist need not disagree about how morality is seen by those who indulge in it. Indeed, if they cannot agree about this, their disagreement is an illusion.

Universalizability

Although there is controversy about the formulation of the principle of universalizability, the basic idea is that we can make no distinction without a difference. If it is wrong for me to eat animals, then it is wrong for you to eat animals unless there is some relevant difference in our situations. I might, for example, be a Buddhist, and you an Eskimo. Universalizability in this sense must be acknowledged as a feature of the moral point of view, if only because consistency is required from every point of view. Someone who claims that some course of action is morally right in situation *A* and morally wrong in situation *B* owes us an explanation of the difference. Spock once blew the circuits of identical robots by telling one that he loved her and the other that he hated her *because they were identical.*

This "logical" interpretation of universalizability leaves it open which differences count, insisting only that if you are going to discriminate, it cannot be based on numerical difference alone. It is called "logical" because to abuse it is, or is close to, a contradiction. It is also called "logical" because it is a feature of the *form* of morality, or of any other type of discourse that requires consistency, and because, like logic, it has no specific content.

Universalizability, so understood, allows us to put the burden of proof on moralists who withhold moral consideration from some groups, or who support systems that feature some form of inequality. Moralists who acknowledge a duty to help one neighbor, can be asked why it is not also a duty to help the rest of them, when their need is as great. Anyone willing to say that human suffering is intrinsically bad may be asked why non-human suffering of equal magnitude is not equally bad. By asking these questions, moralists can use the requirement of universalizability against those with limited sympathies or biased evaluations, a group that includes almost everyone.

Sometimes universalizability has seemed to offer moralists more. If actual moral judgments could be derived from universalizability, and if universalizability could still be taken as a logical (and not as a disguised moral) principle, then the moral rabbit would at last emerge from the philosopher's hat. Universalizability might then be used to establish the moral unacceptability of racism, sexism, and other forms of feature-based discrimination.

Unfortunately for aspiring moral magicians, while universalizability can rule out different evaluations of *identical* items, it cannot be used to show that racism or sexism is morally wrong. To defeat racism or sexism we need to show that it is wrong to use features like race and sex as if they were morally relevant, and it is beyond the power of universalizability to show this. The only strategy available to the moralist hoping to employ universalizability against some kind of discrimination is to wait like a spider for some other moralist with a limited sphere of concern to become tangled in the web of trying to justify discriminating on the basis of some arbitrary feature like race, sex, or species.

The one person who will not get tangled in this web is the amoralist, who does not believe, and who would be ill-advised to claim, that any feature morally justifies discrimination. Nevertheless, amoralists have likes and dislikes, and sometimes express these feelings with charged language. Universalizability does not prevent this. If you call someone lazy, you are not required to prove that laziness is wicked, bad, evil, or immoral. It is enough to say "Well, I don't like it." If someone asks you *why* you don't like it, you can *explain*, but you are not committed to the claim that being frugal with your energy is bad or wrong, or to the belief that everyone else ought to feel as you do. Universalizability only forbids you to deny that similar cases are also cases of laziness, or to evaluate your own laziness differently from that of those who are like you. Both the moralist and the amoralist can say that moral judgments are universalizable—that *if* something is morally wrong, anything relevantly like it is also morally wrong. But this means that we cannot use a belief in universalizability to distinguish between moralists and amoralists, so we need to move on to another feature.

Non-Egoism

Morality is sometimes said to be incompatible with egoism. Frankena says that "prudentialism or living wholly by the principle of enlightened self-love just is not a kind of *morality*" (Frankena [1], 19). Indeed, no one who makes decisions consistently on the basis of self-interest will be described as a "moral" person, or as living a "moral" life. As Harman says, "We ordinarily suppose that someone who acts solely out of self-interest does not act from a moral reason" (Harman [2], 151).

The *psychological* egoist claims that we always do (or must) choose the course of action that promises to lead to the best outcome for ourselves. But what concerns us here is *ethical* egoism, an account of what we ought to do, or of what we have a right to do. In a word, the ethical egoist believes that we all have an obligation or a right to act as the psychological egoists say we all do act. The amoralist will join with the majority of moralists in rejecting this belief, but even if ethical egoism is dead wrong and there is no such obligation or right, it can at least be *offered* as a true and complete statement of our moral rights or duties, an answer to one fundamental question of morality—"How should we act?"

So is it or is it not a form of morality? The truth is that while ethical egoism can be treated as one moral theory among others, most people are unwilling to use the honorific word 'morality' to characterize anything they want so strongly to discourage. Ethical egoism conflicts with a widespread conception of morality as something that requires us to take others into consideration. To the extent that proponents of this conception of morality are allowed to define moral reasons as reasons that refer to the welfare of others, ethical egoism will not be seen as a moral theory. On the other hand, if one is looking at things from the point of view of taxonomy, it is convenient to have ethical egoism as the extreme limit of confined generosity. For *our* purposes, the alleged incompatibility of egoism with the moral point of view is of no help in distinguishing between moralists and amoralists. No amoralist and few (if any) moralists will be ethical egoists, and moralists and amoralists differ among themselves about whether ethical egoism is conceptually excluded from the realm of morality.

A Special Point or Object

As we have just seen, some think that ethical egoism is not a form of morality on the grounds that morality is defined by its purpose, point, or object, which, they say, is to promote the good, happiness, well-being, desires, needs, or interests of humans. G. J. Warnock, for example, says that "the *relevance* of considerations as to the welfare of human beings *cannot*, in the context of moral debate, be denied," and that if we consider a question from the moral point of view, we *must* take these features into consideration (Warnock, 67–68). Philippa Foot makes the same point when she says that "a moral system seems necessarily to be aimed at removing particular dangers and securing certain benefits" (Foot [1], 4).

Frankena considers the question of the "object of morality" in his 1980 Carus Lectures and disagrees with Warnock's and Foot's claim that morality is defined by reference to some purpose, point, or object (O). A "genuine" morality, he says, must point out a direction that is "categorically right or good" and not just aim at some desired end, even if that end is the happiness of all. "The direction must be seen, more or less consciously, as right, good, or oughty," and the belief that actions and traits get their value from their tendency to bring about some O promotes the mistaken belief that "right doing and being virtuous (in short, being moral) have no intrinsic value" (Frankena [2], 121).

The amoralist and the moralist can agree that unless we make moral judgments we are not participating in the institution of morality, and that being willing to universalize and to treat equals as equal are necessary conditions for being taken seriously, whatever point of view one takes. Few moralists and no amoralists take ethical egoism seriously, and both are free to believe or to reject the claim that ethical egoism is a moral position. Finally, moralists and amoralists differ among themselves about whether morality necessarily has some object and about what that object is, with the result that these beliefs cannot be used to distinguish between them. Even someone who chooses to be guided by an ideal such as increasing the happiness of sentient beings will only be a moralist if this ideal is seen as "right, good, or oughty." What *this* means will become clear as we turn to those beliefs that *are* useful in distinguishing between the moralist and the amoralist. The first of these involves the notion of "moral bondage."

Bondage

The claim that we are *bound* by the rules and principles of morality is important, metaphorical, and misleading. It means that moral principles *apply to* us, that we cannot escape their authority, that they are directives that require us to act in certain ways. It is said that morality has both authority and power over us. The authority legitimizes the demands, and the power motivates us to comply. Our present concern is not with the power, but with the alleged authority. It was not for nothing that non-cognitivists identified moral judgments with imperatives. Imperatives do the work morality wants done—they are stronger than requests and suggestions, and they are often (at least conventionally) authoritative.

At the end of Chapter 2 we note Philippa Foot's remark that it is not clear what people mean by the "binding force" of morality if it is not that they feel themselves unable to escape. I suggest that there had better be more to it than that, or the bondage is an illusion. Foot, at least, is unable to find any other way to explain this "fugitive thought" and finally suggests that the belief that morality binds us might be "only the reflection of our *feelings* about morality" (Foot [2], 163).

We also note the connection between bondage and authority. Binding commands do not emerge from thin air, but from some authoritative source. A command not backed by the proper authority, we think, may be ignored, or even disqualified as a command. An imperative may *move* anyone, but it only binds those who are "subject" to its "authority." If I say to you, a total stranger, "Close the window," my imperative is categorical, but it has no intrinsic authority, nor do I. You are not required, and certainly not *morally* required, to obey. Given the way we think about these things, a polite request is more likely to be seen as placing a moral obligation on us than any (purported) order out of the blue.

When people associate in cooperative organizations, an order from an authority creates a conventional obligation, one called into being by the formulated or unformulated rules of the organization. Those rules say who can give and who must take orders, what may and what may not be ordered, and they set, and set limits to, the penalties for disobedience. If you are a servant, an employee, a child, or, in some places, a woman, you may have a conventional obligation to obey someone. A letter carrier, for example, has a postal obligation to deliver the mail. Amoralists can understand and either reject or participate in this form of bondage. They can recognize and observe conventional obligations to keep promises, tell the truth, and keep their genitals covered. But when they do these things, they do them for their own reasons, which can even include the fact that the things are required by conventional morality. Just as an atheist can choose to follow the Ten Commandments, amoralists can choose to follow moral and other conventions. But amoralists will never have, in the set of causes of their actions, the belief that they are inescapably bound, or in any way objectively required, by reality itself or by the wishes or directives of its inhabitants, to act or to be this way rather than that.

Since morality needs to be able to speak of an obligation that goes beyond the conventional one, which is local and mutable, it is natural to seek for a non-local, immutable, and "moral" source for the authority of morality. The natural move at this point is to turn to religion. Who but a god is awesome enough to bind everyone with commands and to give humans inalienable rights? In a well-known paper, Elizabeth Anscombe attributes the contemporary concept of moral bondage to the "law conception of ethics" promoted by Christianity and found in the Hebrew idea of divine law. "In consequence of the dominance of Christianity for many centuries, the concepts of being bound, permitted, or excused became deeply embedded in our language and thought" (Anscombe, 30). When people began to abandon the theistic assumptions that make sense of divine law morality, the concept of moral obligation lost its moorings. Today it survives "outside the framework of thought that made it a really intelligible one" (31). Modern ethicists would be wise, she says, to drop it.

Anscombe's rejection of the concept of moral obligation will be music to most amoralists' ears. That concept makes more sense in a slave society, which is what the Hebrew, Mesopotamian, Greek, and Roman societies in which it thrived were. Now the thought that anyone is absolutely bound by the will of another strikes few of us who are not "masters" as inevitable or natural. Today it is even possible to doubt that the command of a transcendent, all-powerful, omniscient creator can generate the thing we call moral obligation (see Chapter 8).

Fortunately or unfortunately, even if we do manage to put the notion of obligation as bondage out of business, moralism will not be stopped in its tracks. Instead of moral obligation, we can speak of moral rights, justice, or virtue. In each case the operative concept will come with its own form of bondage, and with its own way of requiring something from us. The rights of others "hold us back" from some actions; justice makes demands; and virtues are "good" traits, traits we ought to have, traits we would have if we were functioning properly.

Even the intrinsically good emerges as that which is desirable, that is, that which ought to be desired.

Whatever words are used, the effect of morality (and so, of utterances ascribing value, obligation, rights, and virtues) is to demand and forbid, to require and constrain. Tossing away the idea of moral obligation as bondage will not eliminate the very thing moralists respect and amoralists reject—the external and authoritative demand. As far as this demand is concerned, intrinsic value, moral obligation, moral rights, and moral virtues are all in the same business.

It does not really help to move from a theistic to a secular form of moralism, according to which the commands of morality do not come from an authoritative commander, but are nevertheless real and binding. The idea that there are intrinsic values and demands built into "the fabric of the universe" is easy to attack and hard to defend. Yet it is an assumption on which much of our thought and practice appears to be built, whether people explicitly entertain anything so patently implausible. When Mackie presents his "error theory," the error he thinks the moralist makes is that of believing (or at least of "implicitly claiming") that moral judgments are "objectively prescriptive" in that they announce, sometimes truly, that a situation has "a demand for such-and-such an action somehow built into it" (Mackie [1], 40). When we make a moral judgment we want to say something about what we are evaluating, something that, he says, "involves a call for action or for the refraining from action, and one that is absolute, not contingent upon any desire or preference or policy or choice" (33).

If the values and commands do not come from a divine being, and are not "out there" in the world, but arise from some other source, that source will either be ourselves, other people, or some abstraction such as reason. We have "moral autonomy" when we choose or ratify our own values and command ourselves, but moralists are likely to be nervous about this because it makes it too easy to dismiss values and duties, or to choose different ones. If you have deliberately and knowingly adopted your rules (autonomy), and if you arrive at a situation where it seems silly to follow them, then you will not find it easy or even reasonable to ignore your own good sense and follow the rules. But if you believe the rules come from outside (heteronomy), and if you respect (or stand in awe of) the source, you will be more likely to ignore your good sense and follow the rules. Hence, we need more than autonomy in morality. Even so, it is possible to wonder if we can get more, and possible also to wonder if we need morality. Do we really want people to ignore their own good sense, and to believe that they are bound from outside if they are not?

If it is hard to see how self-legislation can be morally binding, it is even harder to see how the preferences and values of others can result in inescapable moral demands on us. What could make the demands of others authoritative and objectively binding? To this question, many self-serving answers have been provided, each one as arbitrary and fanciful as the next: the best people, those with the right to command, have pure gold in their systems, or are stronger, or smarter, or lighter, or taller, or related to the king or to someone else with power, or were appointed by the gods.

It should now be clear that moral requirements are in trouble. If they are neither imposed by a god nor built into the world, if we cannot place them upon ourselves (or if we can replace them with others, or with none at all), and if other people have no non-conventional authority to impose them on us, then it is hard to avoid the conclusion that the binding authority of morality is an illusion or an invention.

The only way to escape from that conclusion may be to show that we impose them on ourselves, but with a kind of necessity. Perhaps what is needed, if such a thing is not a contradiction, is a kind of heteronomous rational autonomy, according to which our better half (the rational part) prescribes moral behavior. Some moral rationalists believe that something like this is going on. Immanuel Kant claims that "reason of itself and independently of all experience commands what ought to happen" (Kant [3], 20). He says that reason commands "pure sincerity in friendship" (20), and he attempts to generate (by arguments that are widely acknowledged to be less than cogent) prohibitions against suicide and lying promises, and injunctions to develop our talents and give aid to others (30–39). There are countless difficulties with Kant's view, but the idea that reason generates moral demands remains to this day a popular alternative. We discuss it below.

The moralist and the amoralist can agree that morality is supposed to bind us, and that moral beliefs play a role in the causal story of many actions. What separates them is their beliefs about the inescapability of duty and the objectivity of value. It is not always a theory about moral properties, facts, or language that makes someone a moralist; it may be the belief, or even the unreflective assumption, that we are bound by objective and inescapable demands, requirements, and standards. To the amoralist, on the other hand, a demand from a person, or from any source, is just that—a demand from that source; and no demand is ever intrinsically authoritative.

> For certainly the consciousness of a principle of action as freely decided upon is very unlike the consciousness of a moral principle, which is rather of something that has to be *acknowledged*. If it is then said that there is just a psychological explanation of that—then moral thought seems a cheat, presenting itself to us as too like something which it is not. (Williams [1], 38)
>
> Obligation needs to be 'peremptory and absolute', as George Eliot famously said; it often needs to be perceived as something sufficiently external to us to act as a *constraint* or bound on our other sentiments and desires. The chains and shackles of obligation must come from outside us. Can anything both be felt to have this power, and yet be explained as a projection of our own sentiments? (Blackburn, 6–7)

Objectivity

We now shift our attention from the claim that we are bound by morality to the claim that morality is objective. Mackie included both ideas in one phrase when he said that philosophers and non-philosophers alike attribute a kind of "objective prescriptivity" to moral judgments. If morality is objective, then our bondage is not invented or imagined, but real and imposed on us by an independent world. Anything less than objective bondage leaves too many loopholes—some of which open up because of the absence of objectivity, and others because of the absence of bondage.

The *objective* is contrasted with the *subjective*, and morality (or anything else) is subjective when it depends on subjects—on their feelings, desires, purposes, or points of view. A subjective point of view is a point of view of an individual with beliefs and biases. One family of uses of 'subjective' is already familiar from Chapter 2. A "subjective definition" of some moral notion equates moral judgments with statements about the beliefs, principles, needs, interests, desires, or attitudes of one or several subjects—as when '*A* is right' is said to mean 'I approve of *A*', or '*X* is bad' is said to mean 'Most people don't like *X*'. Another way to develop a subjectivist account of moral language is to explain moral language in terms of what those who use it mean, as David Hume does when he says that "when you pronounce any action or character to be vicious, you mean nothing, but that from the constitution of your nature you have a feeling or sentiment of blame from the contemplation of it" (Hume [1], 469).

These forms of "meaning-subjectivism" are rarely embraced today—by moralists or amoralists. People who actually express moral judgments and make attributions of intrinsic value almost never take themselves to be expressing or describing their own states of mind. In fact, if we allow ourselves to be influenced by what users of moral language take and intend themselves to be doing, we end up thinking, with Mackie, that moral judgments express a *claim to objectivity*.

Not only is "meaning-subjectivism" implausible, it undermines the bondage just identified as a basic element of morality. If my saying that *A* is wrong is saying no more than that I (or we) do not want you to do *A*, then the objective prescriptivity has disappeared, and you have a reason to refrain from doing *A* only if you want to satisfy that desire of mine (or ours).

Crazy Objectivity. As we have just seen, and as Mackie and others often insist, those who make moral judgments rarely consider themselves to be stating or expressing personal preferences or desires. On the contrary, they typically take themselves to be advancing claims about a world not of their making. People say that justice is good; they do not say, "I like justice," or "Hurrah for justice," because that is not what they mean.

If the objective is contrasted with the subjective, then objective moral judgments, properties, or facts will be ones that are independent of our thoughts, beliefs, attitudes, and desires, and it will be something about the non-human ("objective") world that makes good things good and bad things bad. We can identify the *crazy objectivist* as someone who subscribes to this belief in a naive and literal form. Crazy objectivity is a *fundamentalist* account of value or obligation, according to which values are real, eternal, self-subsistent, and independent of the desires, and even the existence, of humans. The crazy objectivist claims that there really exist, in the "fabric of reality," moral properties and facts, properties and facts that involve a call for action, a call "that is absolute, not contingent upon any desire or preference or policy or choice" (Mackie [1], 33).

Mackie, who sees his dispute with the moral objectivist as a dispute about what exists, takes his opponent to be the crazy objectivist, and he is at his best when arguing that there are no such entities as moral properties, and no special form of knowledge to detect them. But moral realists and supporters of moral objectivity often remain undaunted by Mackie's attack on crazy objectivity. They simply deny that objectivity, as they understand it, involves any peculiar properties or queer entities.

If the distinction between the moralist and the amoralist is drawn in terms of the moralist's belief in crazy objectivity, moralism will become a form of superstition, and an easy target. But, if the abovementioned moral objectivists are to be believed, there are various non-crazy forms of objectivity that have nothing to do with suspicious items. In the sections that follow, we search for some not-so-crazy form of objectivity that is still strong enough to do the work of a moral system. But as we move on to these sophisticated ways of understanding objectivity, let us not think that no one has ever held crazy objectivity, or spoken or written as if there were objectively real moral properties "out there" in the world. Assumptions close to those of the crazy objectivist underlie many moral beliefs and patterns of moral language use. Few people may actually believe that the world is furnished with Platonic Forms, "queer" properties, or demands as real as trees and as authoritative as orders from headquarters, but it is possible (even likely) that in making the claims they do, and in defending those claims, moralists are committed to some such beliefs.

Objectivity as Impartiality. Crazy objectivity is a metaphysical view, but we can approach objectivity epistemologically by turning our attention from objective moral facts and properties to objective moral beliefs. Objectivity may be gained by adopting an impartial way of looking at things—the more impartial, the more objective. Moral beliefs (and believers) are objective to the extent that they depart from limited and incomplete (subjective) viewpoints. Hume rejected all forms of crazy objectivity, but he said that to look at things morally is to look at things from an impartial point of view. It is "only when a character is considered in general, without reference to our particular interest, that it causes such a feeling or sentiment, as denominates it morally good or evil" (Hume [1], 472).

"Ideal observer" theories, which are also called "impartial spectator theories," have always insisted on the impartiality of their observers. These theories promise objectivity without abandoning the Humean insight that morality depends on subjective factors. Some say that value or obligation is a function of the feelings and reactions of an impartial and well-informed, but otherwise normal observer, while others identify moral truth with what such an observer would *believe*.

But the strength of these theories is also their weakness. We cannot convict them of crazy objectivity, but they fail even to try to answer the question the crazy objectivist answers so badly. They make no effort to say what makes valuable things valuable and wrong things wrong. Ideal observers approve of some things and not of others, but unless they operate on ideal whims, there will be some basis for their approval. The groundless approval of a wise, impartial, well-informed, and relatively sane, spectator cannot *make* a thing valuable. But if something "objective," some feature of the thing judged, is responsible for the correctness of the observer's reaction or belief, then that is the objective source of the moral truth, and that is what we need to identify.

There are other problems with ideal observer theories. We, who are considerably less than ideal, and who rarely come near impartiality, have no way to determine what one of these imaginary observers is likely to think or feel, and that means that we have no genuine way to know what is right or wrong. Even more troubling is the possibility that someone who attains a serious measure of impartiality will no longer have moral feelings or make moral judgments. In any case, even if we could know that there is something any impartial spectator would favor, we would still want to know what feature of that thing elicits and merits that approval.

Objectivity as Intersubjectivity. In the writings of Sabina Lovibond we find another attempt to give us moral realism without crazy objectivity. Her aim is to defend "a form of moral realism derived from the later philosophy of Wittgenstein" (Lovibond, 25). According to what Lovibond identifies as Wittgenstein's "homogeneous" conception of language, it is impossible to distinguish between those "parts of assertoric discourse which do, and those which do not, genuinely *describe* reality" (36). Since there is no clean way to distinguish between facts and values, or between factual language and evaluative language, we have no business saying that moral utterances do not state facts. We are confronted with a plurality of language games, and if the rules of one of them (the "moral language game") permit us to talk about moral facts or intrinsic value, we are free to be realists and to claim objectivity for those rule-spawned facts and values.

One might think that it is one thing for there to be objective values and quite a different thing for people to talk as if there are. As Mackie said, subjective agreement (agreement in valuing) "would give intersubjective values, but intersubjectivity is not objectivity" (Mackie

[1], 22). Lovibond disagrees. When intersubjective agreement exists, she says, "the particular discourse grounded in it can properly be called 'objective', regardless of its subject-matter" (Lovibond, 42). According to this rather lax interpretation of objectivity, our discourse about values, gods, souls, and beauty is "objective" because (apart from occasional heretics) we believe in these things, agree about them, and match our words to our beliefs.

Lovibond calls her position "moral realism" and "moral intuitionism," but she differs from traditional moral realists by making her realism a matter of what people agree to call real, and she differs from the intuitionists because she does not claim to intuit actually existing characteristics (as a genuine crazy objectivist might) but treats her intuition as skill in knowing what to say.

Because of our training in our language and traditions, certain things are *seen as* good or bad, and certain actions are *seen as* right or wrong. Our evaluations are not perceptions of unique properties, but spontaneous "observations" that present themselves with force and authority. The world of moral facts, says Lovibond, is "*compulsively* present to the will" (Lovibond, 13). This very phenomenon was probably one of the things that drove the intuitionists to their crazy objectivity. But Lovibond, and others who look to intersubjectivity for objectivity, are too sophisticated to think themselves directly aware of genuine mind-independent moral properties. Their form of moral objectivity replaces crazy objectivity with intersubjective consensus and then calls *that* objectivity.

We say more about Lovibond's moral realism in our discussion of justification. Not everything can be justified, but if we count intersubjective agreement as objectivity, we would have a way of getting moral arguments off the ground because we would have some "objective" starting points—namely, those beliefs (pain is bad, it is a duty to tell the truth, etc.) that most people accept.

Justification

When we make moral judgments we are open to requests for justification. The less welcome a moral demand, the more likely it is that justification will be required, and the more closely any purported justification will be inspected. Our beliefs about bondage and objectivity underwrite the conventions that permit us to ask for justification from those who make moral judgments. If we are indeed bound by morality, then there must be something that makes this so, and pointing out what that is will justify the bondage claim.

There is no doubt that we can justify some moral judgments if we are allowed to assume others. But since we obviously cannot justify everything, hard-pressed moralists often say that *basic* moral assumptions need no justification. Jeremy Bentham, the father of utilitarianism, admitted that the principle of utility cannot be proved, "for that which is used to prove every thing else, cannot itself be proved," and he added that "to give such proof is as impossible as it is needless" (Bentham, 4). Granted it is impossible, but why is it needless? If our conventions allow us to ask for support for moral judgments, why should there be an exception for first principles? Are we supposed to accept the principle of utility just because Bentham and his friends enunciated it?

As important as the ability to justify moral judgments is, it does not seem that justifiability is as close to the heart of morality as are objectivity and bondage. Moralists habitually embrace moral principles and values for which no justification is available. G. E. Moore believes that judgments about intrinsic value cannot be justified, but he also believes that when such judgments are true it is because of the presence of a "non-natural" property of goodness. And so, in a way, we can justify the judgment that something is good by claiming that this property is present. What we cannot justify is the claim that this property is present. That can only be determined by intuition. H. A. Prichard, another intuitionist, says that the judgment that something is our duty can never be supported by an argument. Lovibond, who also sees herself as an intuitionist, dismisses the demand for justification by arguing that since there will always be things we accept without justification, ethics is no worse off than any other field. Moral knowledge she insists, can stand without foundations (Lovibond, 38).

We have seen how it follows from Lovibond's permissive form of moral realism that our discourse about values, gods, souls, and beauty is "objective" because we agree about these things and match our words to our beliefs. But if intersubjectivity is objectivity, then objectivity is intersubjectivity, and that is a hard pill to swallow. Lovibond's good news for the moral realist is that ethics "is promoted to the metaphysical status enjoyed already by the sciences." The bad news, which is likely to go underreported, is that "natural science is demoted to the metaphysical status formerly allotted to ethics" (Lovibond, 42–43). And so, we might add, are statements about tables. Natural scientists can fend for themselves if this demotion makes them uncomfortable, but we should all be uncomfortable when the truth about rocks and tables is relativized to intersubjective agreement. The objectivity attributed to rocks and tables is more robust than anything we can gain from intersubjectivity, and considerably more fundamental than that attributed to quarks, rights, or intrinsic value.

Lovibond's mistake is to try to gain objectivity and justifiability by abandoning the very aspect of morality that makes it useful and powerful. If all we mean by 'objectivity' is 'widespread agreement within our group', then moral objectivity lacks both the authority and power to bind us that it has been supposed to have by moralists. The announcement that something is intrinsically valuable will not terminate the chain of requests for justification if it is just another way of reporting intersubjective agreement in valuing.

Whether or not final justification is to be hoped for, whether or not the idea even makes sense, most people do not question the conventional practice of asking "Why?" They just assume that lying, stealing, and other conventionally objectionable deeds are morally wrong, that they are wrong for some reason, and that anyone who took the trouble could discover that reason. Actual moral disputes are conducted on the assumption that it is fair to appeal to basic and undefended moral principles. If we insist that there is a moral obligation to feed the hungry, can we be required to defend every moral assumption we make, and to clarify the moral language we use? Before we can claim that you have a moral obligation to alleviate suffering, must we explain what we mean by 'obligation' and prove that suffering is bad?

These questions may sound rhetorical, but they have an answer, and the answer is: "Yes." By claiming that you *ought* to give to charity, we open ourselves to the question "Why?" If our initial answer appeals to some more basic moral principle, then, like it or not, we are liable to be asked to say something in its defense. Our whole procedure of asking for and giving reasons takes it for granted that our basic principles, our moral premises, are not arbitrary, not misguided, not mistaken, but are, in some way or another, superior to the alternatives. It is just that most people are more than willing to leave the *complete* justification of particular judgments, including the proof, derivation, and explanation of their basic moral principles, to the moral philosophers. By farming out these chores they are left with time and energy for more immediate and pressing matters.

Philosophers have long held out the hope that true and basic moral principles can be discovered and justified, and non-philosophers, unwilling to admit that their way of life is "irrational" or "groundless," have not been inclined to disagree with them. Hence everyone speaks of Morality or The Moral Law, and everyone supposes that there is more to this than they are themselves able to explain. This Moral Law is not arbitrary and not conventional—conventions are evaluated according to *it,* not vice versa. Gods are brought in to legislate it, and perhaps the very idea that conventional morality needs and can be given a non-conventional backing is a remnant of religion. But remnant of religion or not, the idea is no longer the sole property of religion. Moral philosophers show that they take it seriously when they describe themselves as attempting to "ground" morality, to establish its foundations, to *justify* it. That this aim, which Alasdair MacIntyre calls "the enlightenment project," is doomed to failure is the message common to MacIntyre's critique, non-cognitivism, Mackie's cognitivistic moral "skepticism," and what is here called amoralism.

Rationality

To justify something is to give reasons, and we tend to think that giving reasons is the essence of being reasonable and rational. We have seen that while anyone who is allowed to assume some basic moral principles can justify any number of particular moral judgments, there will come a point when one or several of these principles will have to be accepted without justification. This is an embarrassment to the moralist, who will inevitably be asked if anything can be said in favor of these most basic of all assumptions.

Moralists have answered this question in two ways. Some try to turn the tables on their critics by saying that since no justification advances without assumptions, we might as well say that justifiability just *is* intersubjective justification from accepted assumptions, that this is enough for rationality and objectivity.

Alternatively, a moralist can acknowledge that basic assumptions, just because they *are* basic, cannot be justified, if justifying them means deriving them from *more* basic assumptions. But, the moralist may then try to show that it is *rational* to accept them, or at least that it is more rational to accept them than it would be to accept alternative ones or none at all. Here, of course, everything depends on what is meant by 'rational'. There is something of a stigma attached to anything irrational, and for this reason most of us would describe ourselves as rational even before we were clear about what it means to be so.

In one sense of the word 'rational', to be rational is to be *logical*; a rational person is one who draws all (and only) the conclusions a reasonably alert human would draw from a set of premises. If we accept the moral principle that it is wrong to cause suffering, and believe that eating meat contributes to the total quantity of suffering in the world, then we are not rational (in this sense) unless we are willing to admit that it is wrong for us to eat meat. The ability to determine what follows from what is useful because things do follow from what we say, and because there are so many bad arguments; but this notion of what it is to be rational is too thin for the moralist because logic can only derive moral conclusions from moral premises.

Sometimes rationality is interpreted as calculating selfishness. One is rational when one's choices are directed to maximizing one's own interests, or the interests of some narrow circle of friends and relatives. It then becomes irrational to put the interests of others first, irrational to act in the way morality often directs us to act. One who is always trying to figure out how to make the largest profit and the smallest contribution will be "rational" according to this way of thinking, but few would be willing to apply the still honorific word 'rational' to such an egoistic sociopath.

A third way to think of rationality is to identify it with the ability to draw conclusions, accept new data, and figure out explanations. That would not give us basic moral principles to justify specific moral judgments either, but it would at least explain why someone might want to recommend rationality. It is an open question how sympathetic someone who is rational in this sense would be to moralism.

Many moral philosophers think morality needs a rational component because they underestimate non-rational information processing and decision making. Peter Singer, for example, contrasts the claim that ethics has a rational component with the view that it is "no more than an outpouring of our emotions," as if those were the only two options. This leads him to claim that even if we are finally forced to admit that we must choose our ultimate premises, we can "question the assumption that reason plays no role in ultimate ethical choices" (Singer [3], 85–86).

Singer tells us that sociobiologists have solved the "puzzle of altruism" toward kin and those who can reciprocate, but that they have not explained "genuine non-reciprocal altruism toward strangers" (Singer [3], 139). That is, while there are genetic causes of kindness to our kin, and to those in a position to be kind to us, sociobiologists find it hard to understand why we have any tendency or motivation to help unrelated people who can do nothing for us. Here is where Singer thinks reason comes in. His explanation for extended altruism is that an initially restricted application of altruism will be "extended to a wider circle by reasoning creatures who can see that they and their kin are one group among others, and from an impartial point of view no more important than others" (134)

We are able to draw this egalitarian conclusion, Singer says, thanks to our unique ability to reason. Reason gives us the power to see through our mistaken assumption that we and those dear to us are special and deserve more goods or more consideration than others who are essentially like us. This power, however, is no more than the power to see through a bad argument. We can use it to strip away popular but fallacious groundings for discrimination, but this will still not touch the selfish and partial motivations the argument was produced to support.

Any actual kindness to strangers, behavior Singer calls non-reciprocal altruism, seems to result not so much from reason as from compassion, or from some mistake like failing to distinguish between those who are kin and those who are not, believing that the stranger we help might turn up in our hour of need to help us, or supposing that by performing a good deed we earn merit, or good karma.

On the question of the objectivity of morality, Singer stands with Mackie and the amoralists. He quotes Mackie's argument from queerness with approval and embraces its conclusions (Singer [3], 107). He also claims that we can "debunk" ethical principles by giving biological and cultural explanations for them. But he is not willing to allow that we can debunk *all* our ethical principles. If we do, he thinks, we are stuck with a "deep ethical subjectivism" where being a Nazi is "in the end no less justifiable than" resistance to the Nazis (84). We can, he thinks, be rescued from this possibility only if there is "a rational component to ethics that we can use to defend at least one of our fundamental ethical principles" (85). And he wants to be rescued.

The trick he uses is one we have already seen. He waits until someone makes a moral judgment, and then resorts to universalizability in order to make them responsible for justifying any partiality. If we already agree that it is wrong to cause pain to humans, then he will ask us how we can justify causing pain to non-humans. Any attempt to ignore the suffering of anything short of oysters is deemed unjustifiable and arbitrary (as indeed it probably is). The minute we make a moral judgment to the effect that one person, being, or group deserves consideration, reason steps in to show that any limitation we make, any reluctance to extend consideration to similar beings, is unjustifiable. The only thing that reason cannot do here is show that the initial moral judgment was unavoidable.

This suggests that the way out of this trap is never to get into it. If the amoralist can refrain from making moral judgments in the first place, Singer will never be able to get the argument started. There would be a problem, of course, if the amoralist were not able to stop making moral judgments, but there seems to be no reason to assume that this is the case. As we learn in the next few chapters, moralism is an ancient and a widespread institution—but it is not an inevitable one.

4

History, Hallucinations, and Human Nature

> Hereby it is manifest that, during the time men live without a common power to keep them all in awe, they are in that condition which is called war, and such a war as is of every man against every man.
>
> —*Thomas Hobbes,* Leviathan

Original Humans

THE AMBIGUITY of the word 'original' allows us to deal here with two distinct but often confused topics. When we ask about "original" human nature, we may be asking what humans *were* like and how they behaved just after the emergence of *Homo sapiens*. But we may also be asking what humans *are now and always have been* like, abstracting from historical, environmental, and social influences. The first question is about what happened in the past—about human history. The second is a question about human nature, as it is now and as it has been since humans have been human.

Myths and legends offer answers to both questions. Other answers have been thought up by philosophers, historians, and anthropologists. Both Thomas Hobbes and Jean-Jacques Rousseau write as if they are describing actual developments in human history. But as they offer competing accounts of human nature and society they make it clear that they do not consider their arguments overturned if the history is not completely accurate. Rousseau goes so far as to say that his claims "must not be taken for historical truths, but only for hypothetical and conditional reasonings better suited to clarify the nature of things than to show their true origin" (Rousseau [1], 103). This means that he thinks we can tell a truth about human nature by making up a story about human history. Let that put us on our guard as we turn to the accounts of "original human nature" given by Hobbes and Rousseau. First, we discuss what they say about humans living in a "state of nature" (that is, without the benefit or curse of society) as if it were the historical account it often appears to be. Then, noting why neither would be right if they were offering historical accounts, we can ask what the real message is, if it is not historical. It is too simple to say that Hobbes's message is that humans are naturally evil and that Rousseau's is that they are good, and it is misleading, but it gives an important clue to the difference between them.

Hobbes

Thomas Hobbes was a "hard-headed" mechanist, a materialist who believed that all change follows fixed natural laws, and a psychological egoist who insisted that "of the voluntary acts of every man, the object is some *good to himself*" (Hobbes, 112). On the grounds that we want to attain and secure a contented life, Hobbes attributes to humans a "perpetual and restless desire of power after power that ceases only in death" (86). This universal quest for happiness, and for the power to preserve it, leads to conflict, and unless checked, to what Hobbes calls a condition of war.

> So that in the nature of man we find three principal causes of quarrel: first, competition; secondly, diffidence; thirdly, glory. The first makes men invade for gain, the second for safety, and the third for reputation. . . . Hereby it is manifest that, during the time men live without a common power to keep them all in awe, they are in that condition which is called war, and such a war as is of every man against every man. . . . In such condition there is no place for industry, because the fruit thereof is uncertain: and consequently no culture of the earth; no navigation nor use of the commodities that may be imported by sea; no commodious building; no instruments of moving and removing such things as require much force; no knowledge of the face of the earth; no account of time; no arts; no letters; no society; and, which is worst of all, continual fear and danger of violent death; and the life of man solitary, poor, nasty, brutish, and short. (Hobbes, 106–7)

Fortunately we all have "passions" that incline us to peace: the fear of death and the desire of "such things as are necessary to commodious living" (Hobbes, 109). Reason enables us to arrive at a number of "laws of nature," or rules "by which a man is forbidden to do that which is destructive of his life or takes away the means of preserving the same and to omit that by which he thinks it may be best preserved" (109). These are not *moral* principles but maxims of prudence. The first law of nature tells us to seek peace whenever we can, but adds that when it is impossible to attain peace, we may use all the "helps and advantages of war." The second says that each person should give up the "right to all things, and be contented with so much liberty against other men as he would allow other men against himself" (110). The third tells us to keep our agreements. More than a dozen other laws of nature advise gratitude, sociability, forgiveness, equality, arbitration, and other good ideas.

The problem is that if each of us is programmed to increase our power and satisfy our selfish desires, we will each realize that while we would all be better off if everyone followed these "laws," our own interests might be best served if others followed them and we broke them when we could get away with it. This "free rider" problem leads Hobbes to conclude that in spite of our ability to think them up,

> the laws of nature—as *justice*, *equity*, *modesty*, *mercy*, and, in sum, *doing to others as we would be done to*—of themselves, without the terror of some power to cause them to be observed, are contrary to our natural passions, that carry us to partiality, pride, revenge, and the like. And covenants without the sword are but words, and of no strength to secure a man at all. Therefore, notwithstanding the laws of nature . . . , if there be no power erected, or not great enough for our security, every man will—and may lawfully—rely on his own strength and art for caution against all other men. (Hobbes, 139)

It is easy to see why some believe Hobbes thought humans are basically, originally, and naturally evil; and it is easy to see why those who think we have natural passions "that carry us to partiality, pride, revenge, and the like," have concluded that humans are evil. But Hobbes does not put it that way, though Rousseau accuses him of it: "Above all, let us not conclude with Hobbes because man has no idea of goodness he is naturally evil" (Rousseau [1], 128). In fact, Hobbes says things that suggest classifying him as an amoralist, or as some kind of subjectivist. He says that people call things they want *good* and the "objects of their hate and aversion" *evil*, and that words like 'good' and 'evil' "are ever used with relation to the person that uses them, there being nothing simply and absolutely so, nor any common rule of good and evil to be taken from the nature of the objects themselves" (Hobbes, 53).

While Hobbes may not think our self-interested "passions" are evil in themselves, he sees how they can lead to trouble. Given his assumptions about human nature, no agreement is strong enough to restrain us when we anticipate an inalienable advantage from breaking the rules. Since most of us can see this for ourselves, Hobbes concludes that the only sure way to avoid "war" is to create a "sovereign" with enough power to guarantee that violations of laws of nature do not pay. This agent—be it a god, a king, or an assembly of people—must have the power to make uncivil behavior unprofitable, and a self-interested motive for doing so.

Rousseau

If Hobbes has been interpreted as believing that humans are evil, Rousseau has, with more accuracy, been accused of holding the opposite view. In fact, in a letter written in 1764 he says that *Émile*, his treatise on education, is "a philosophical work on the principle . . . that *man is naturally good*" (Rousseau [3], ix).

In his *Second Discourse* Rousseau produces a detailed (if hypothetical) reconstruction of the steps along the way to society and civilization. He characterizes the earliest humans as self-sufficient loners. Males and females only associated in response to their appetites to procreate, and "this blind inclination, devoid of any sentiment of the heart, produced only a purely animal act" (Rousseau [1], 142). After the act, the couple thought no more of each other, and the mother abandoned the child to its own devices at the earliest possible opportunity. As these creatures walked about alone in the woods, they had to figure out for themselves (anew each generation) how to use sticks and stones, how to defend themselves, and how to find shelter. On their own they discovered (again and again) fire, the fish hook, the bow and arrow, clothes, and concepts. They neither spoke nor reasoned, and they cared only for nourishment, sex, and rest. They had no thought of death and no idea of the future. Their projects were limited; and with few desires, no capacity for planning, no pride, greed, or ambition, they wandered about like lost but resourceful boy and girl scouts.

Sometimes one of these individuals would notice that the behavior of the others was like his own, and from this he would conclude that "their way of thinking and feeling conformed entirely to his own." This comparison and reflection launch an individual out of the blissful ignorance of the state of nature. "Taught by experience that love of well-being is the sole motive of human actions, he found himself able to distinguish the rare occasions when common interest should make him count on the assistance of his fellowmen" (Rousseau [1], 144–45). The result was a temporary free association that "obligated no one and lasted only as long as the passing need that had formed it" (145). But this stage did not last forever, and eventually men began to build huts. "This was the epoch of a first revolution, which produced the establishment and differentiation of families, and which introduced a sort of property—from which perhaps many quarrels and fights already arose" (146).

It was at this point that another instinct (in addition to self-interest) was activated. This (alleged) natural instinct is one Rousseau takes very seriously. He calls it *pity* or *commiseration*, and identifies it as "a natural repugnance to see any sensitive being perish or suffer, principally our fellowmen" (Rousseau [1], 95). Because he believes in this instinct and sees humans as naturally non-aggressive, Rousseau says that we are naturally good.

Rousseau does not forget the "quarrels and fights," and believes that as soon as people start building their huts in the same area, trouble is guaranteed. "Jealousy awakens with love; discord triumphs, and the gentlest of the passions receives sacrifices of human blood" (Rousseau [1], 148–49).

> As long as men . . . applied themselves only to tasks that a single person could do and to arts that did not require the cooperation of several hands, they lived free, healthy, good, and happy insofar as they could be according to their nature, and they continued to enjoy among themselves the sweetness of independent intercourse. But from the moment one man needed the help of another, as soon as they observed that it was useful for a single person to have provisions for two, equality disappeared, property was introduced, labor became necessary; and vast forests were changed into smiling fields which had to be watered with the sweat of men, and in which slavery and misery were soon seen to germinate and grow with the crops. (Rousseau [1], 151–52)

Hobbes and Rousseau assume that, "love of well-being" is the major, if not the sole, motive of human action, and that social groups are formed and preserved because they provide individuals with what they want—assistance and security. In reality, however, there was never a time when humans lived as solitary hermits, and society does not owe its existence to primitive private egoistic calculation. Higher primates are, with few exceptions, social. Anthropologists agree that the earliest *Homo sapiens* moved about in small bands of thirty to fifty individuals, living on what they could find and catch, and sharing what they had. In fact, our ancestors cooperated and lived in groups eons before they had the mental equipment essential for devising or following a policy of dedicated self-interest, or for conceiving a social contract.

Even if much of what Rousseau says about the origin of society is historically inaccurate, we must remember his claim that it did not matter if he had the history wrong because his aim was to tell us something about human nature, something that goes directly against the picture offered by Hobbes. Hobbes thinks that self-interest is the *only* motivating factor, but Rousseau believes that innate self-interest is accompanied and modified by innate pity or commiseration. This is a very important difference.

Our beliefs about how to deal with our own problems are influenced by how strongly we think humans are motivated by self-interest. The more we believe in the existence of cooperative, harmonious, and affectionate instincts, the less we will feel the need for strict laws and severe punishments. Hobbes wants a sovereign with the power to enforce agreements because, as he says, "covenants without the sword are but words, and of no strength to secure a man at all."

We have distinguished two different questions about "original" humans, one about human nature and one about human history, and we can be sure that those who follow Hobbes and those who follow Rousseau will have different answers to both questions. One set of answers emphasizes cooperation and harmony, the other features competition and struggle. One is optimistic about human nature, the other pessimistic. In the next two sections we explore these different accounts of human nature and human history.

Like Hobbes, Rousseau believes that in a state of nature certain moral distinctions are not yet made; since there is as yet no property, there is no use for the concepts of justice and injustice. But it does not follow from this for Rousseau that *no* moral predicates as yet have application. Natural man, following his impulses of need and occasional sympathy, is good and not evil.

> The Christian doctrine of original sin is as false as the Hobbesian doctrine of nature. (MacIntyre [1], 184)

> Man in the state of nature was not virtuous, since true virtue requires control over natural impulsions and therefore depends on thought and social experience. But by nature, man is *good*—self-sufficient, compassionate to others when they do not threaten him, and incapable of pride, hatred, falsehood, and vice. Society, precisely because it develops a man's faculties, corrupts him. (Masters, 20)

Human Nature

Plato was perplexed by a puzzle that has come to be called the "*Meno*-problem": Inquiry into the unknown is impossible, for if we do not know the answer to a question, we will not recognize it even if we stumble upon it. His solution was to say that when we seek knowledge we are looking for something we have forgotten. To learn is to recollect what we knew before our souls were imprisoned in our bodies at birth. Two thousand years after Plato, philosophers were still appealing to "innate ideas" to explain how we come to have concepts—like *God, infinity*, or *perfection*—that we could not have picked up from experience. These ideas, they insisted, are part of our original equipment.

Gottfried Wilhelm Leibniz goes beyond this, claiming that *everything* is innate. Each living thing, or "monad," is a separate and completely independent individual that "contains" its own future. No monad is influenced by, or directly aware of, any other monad. Each has a program that contains its future deeds and experiences, a virtual reality correlated by God with the virtual realities of all other living things. At the instant I have the experience of stepping on your toe, you reach the part of your program that gives you the relevant pain. Leibniz calls this view "pre-established harmony."

John Locke attacks the rationalist belief in innate ideas and says that all our *ideas* come from experience. But he grants that we have some innate *knowledge* and *dispositions*. Behaviorists deny everything internal and refuse to talk about human instincts, and Jean-Paul Sartre says that there is no such thing as human nature.

The truth, if there is one, must lie between the view that nothing is innate and the view that everything is. There must be some instincts, drives, tendencies, and aptitudes we get by being who and what we are. Other characteristics we pick up from those who socialize us. But how much of what we do is a result of our biological natures, and how much can those natures be modified by what happens to us? Geneticists, biologists, sociologists, sociobiologists, anthropologists, psychologists, ethologists, educators, philosophers, and politicians would love to know the answers to these questions. What we think about "nature and nurture" is bound up with dozens of other beliefs in a complex, open-ended understanding of the world, our plight, and the available remedies.

We can line up opinions about human nature on the basis of how powerfully and inexorably our natural endowments are thought to lead to anti-social, inharmonious, aggressive, or selfish behavior. Hobbes falls near one extreme, not because he thinks we are never nice to each other, but because he thinks we are only nice when we expect to get something out of it. If we have no such expectation, watch out! Rousseau is closer to the other extreme, not because he thinks we are always nice to each other, but because he insists that while we have much natural selfishness, many of our emotions and actions flow from "a natural repugnance to see any sensitive being perish or suffer, principally our fellowman." Those who, like Hobbes, stress the pursuit of self-interest in their accounts of human nature can be called *hard-liners*; while those who, like Rousseau, find a significant amount of natural kindness, sympathy, or benevolence can be called *soft-liners*.

Human Nature: Hard-Liners

Robert Ardrey is a hard-liner who stresses an instinct of territorial aggression, an innate disposition to seek and defend territory. "Man," he says, "is a predator whose natural instinct is to kill with a weapon" (Ardrey [1], 316). Sigmund Freud makes the same point (though without the incautious reference to weapons) when he says that the truth is that "men are not gentle, friendly creatures wishing for love, who simply defend themselves if they are attacked, but that a powerful measure of desire for aggression has to be reckoned as part of their instinctual endowment" (Freud [1], 85). A third hard-liner, Konrad Lorenz, claims that we are to a great extent motivated by the "big drives"—feeding, reproduction, flight, and aggression (Lorenz, 85). He says that aggression does not occur simply as a reaction to features of the environment, but regularly and inevitably as a result of stored up pressure that eventually must be released.

Hobbes, Freud, Ardrey, and Lorenz believe that anti-social activity flows from assorted inner drives. But admitting an innate disposition to promote one's interests does not make one a hard-liner. What makes one a hard-liner is a tendency to emphasize aggressive, selfish, anti-social tendencies. Hard-liners make these features central, or they make them the foundation of more gentle and generous tendencies, as Lorenz does when he traces the emotion of love to aggression.

We need not restrict our attention to modern or Western thinkers to find hard-line views about human nature. In ancient China, the Confucian Xun Zi is best know for his teaching that humans are basically evil.

> The nature of man is evil; his goodness is the result of his activity. Now, man's inborn nature is to seek for gain. If this tendency is followed, strife and rapacity result and deference and compliance disappear. By inborn nature one is envious and hates others. . . . Therefore the sages of antiquity, knowing that man's nature is evil, that it is unbalanced and incorrect, and that it is violent, disorderly, and undisciplined, established the authority of rulers to govern the people, set forth clearly propriety and righteousness to transform them, instituted laws and governmental measures to rule them, and made punishment severe to restrain them, so that all will result in good order and be in accord with goodness. (Xun Zi, in Chan [1], 128–31)

Human Nature: Soft-Liners

What are the options for someone who wants to take issue with the hard-line philosophy of human nature, or with the remedies derived from that philosophy? If we deny there are any instincts, we automatically deny the instinct to be selfish or aggressive. Ashley Montagu takes this line, and so does Morton Hunt, who says that "the whole concept of instinct is superfluous" (Hunt, 32). Given what we now know, this is unlikely, but in any case it would not help the soft-liner, who would also be forbidden the "commiserative instincts."

It may make more sense for the soft-liner to admit that there are hostile, selfish, and aggressive instincts, and then propose that they are balanced or even outweighed by instincts of kindness, compassion, or love. In the passages just quoted, Xun Zi is reacting to the views of Mencius, who says that "if you let people follow their feelings (original nature), they will be able to do what is good." This, Mencius says, "is what is meant by saying that human nature is good." Like Rousseau, he believes that "the feeling of commiseration is found in all men"

(Mencius, in Chan [1], 54). Hard-liners do not have to deny that humans feel pity or commiseration, but they are hard-liners because they minimize these feelings.

A third response to the hard-liner is to admit there are selfish or aggressive instincts, but then to deny that they inevitably manifest themselves in war or lethal competition. On this view it is within our power, individual or collective, to minimize our inherited aggressive tendencies. Some soft-liners argue that the absence of aggression on some islands in the South Pacific shows we are not condemned by our genes to continue to fight with each other.

The existence of saintly individuals and peaceful societies does count as evidence that aggression is not inevitable; but the hard-liner can still say it is built into our genes, and that individuals and societies are peaceful only when they have found ways to turn it into something less dangerous, like sports, hunting, lavish giving, or philosophy. There is certainly something to this, for one can find much aggression in these activities. However, the main thing we take away from these debates is the realization that we will never settle the question of whether we have many, some, or no aggressive instincts by appealing to the way people act. Those who believe we have an instinct for aggression are unimpressed by pockets of non-aggression, and those who reject that belief do so in full awareness of our violent history.

Finally, the soft-liner may criticize the hard-liner for suffering from a gender bias. Carol Gilligan argues that an adequate understanding of human development takes into account the fact that while males and females have many of the same lessons to learn, they learn them in a different order. Males first develop competitive abilities and the skills that set them apart as individuals. Females first develop cooperative skills and only later move on to problems of competition and individuation. She argues that this gender-differentiated development has been neglected by educators, who for years studied only males. Without understanding the full range of human development, hard-liners take the aggressive male pattern as standard, just as Lawrence Kohlberg took the morality of rights and duty of the males he studied to be definitive of the highest stage of moral development.

The Political Character of the Debate

Both hard-liners and their opponents operate as if they are divided by a question of fact; but by now the political character of their debate should be apparent. There is as much disagreement about human nature as there is about what is right and wrong—and the explanation is the same in both cases. We assimilate moral principles and the slogans and argument-fragments we use to defend them from our social environment, and the same is true of our ideas about human nature. Our understanding of the world comes in a semi-consistent and constantly evolving package, one that includes moral principles, political and religious views, ideas about human nature and human history, and remedies for the perceived ills of the day. When our moral principles are questioned, one way to support them is to appeal to a "theory" of human nature. It is no accident that the theory of human nature that seems most correct to each of us is the one that best underwrites our set of moral beliefs and attitudes. A belief about the morality of capital punishment or abortion comes linked with a compatible theory of human nature and a supporting world-story. Even our beliefs about history are shaped to support acquired prejudices and moral opinions.

Human History

Those who see selfishness and aggression as the dominant features of human nature are easily led to view history as a record of acts of violence. And those who find compassion, cooperation, and altruism in human beings characterize early hominids as living in harmony with their environment and each other until, as Rousseau says, agriculture and a more complex society brought on slavery, disharmony, and war.

Human History: Hard-Liners

The hard-liners claim that if life for primitive humans was not a war of all against all, it was at least a war of most against most. What made humans human, they say, was not cooperation but competition and the invention of weapons. This position is developed in a number of popular books by Ardrey, who argues that Rousseau was led into "towering hypocrisies" by "his unshakable belief in the original goodness of man" (Ardrey [2], 99).

Whatever Rousseau might have been doing, Ardrey is definitely trying to say what things were like for early *Homo sapiens*. Against Rousseau he (correctly) insists that humans were social from the very beginning. But since the other primates were also social, Ardrey is led to ask how we differed from them. His answer is that "*man is man, and not a chimpanzee, because for millions upon millions of evolving years we killed for a living.*" We were, throughout this long period, "*dependent on killing to survive*" (Ardrey [3], 9).

Human History: Soft-Liners

Lorenz makes claims about early humans that are consistent with his emphasis on aggression. "One shudders," he says, "at the thought of a creature as irascible as all pre-human primates are, swinging a well-sharpened hand-ax" (Lorenz, 233). What evidence could we ever find to support the claim that pre-human primates were naturally *irascible*? It is just as easy to hold the opposite belief, which is what Montagu does when he criticizes Lorenz. Montagu reminds us that almost *all* present primates are extremely peaceful and adds that "there is not the least reason to suppose that man's pre-human primate ancestors were in any way different" (Montagu, 12). Lorenz assumes that "neighboring hordes" were regularly at war, but this too is denied by Montagu, who says that " 'neighboring hordes' would have been few and far between, and when they met it is extremely unlikely that they would have been any less friendly than food-gathering hunting peoples are today" (Montagu, 13).

Richard Leakey and Roger Lewin argue that our discovery of the division of labor made a "mixed food-sharing economy" possible, and that we became human because we learned to share. The key was the "economic pact between suppliers of meat and suppliers of vegetables"—between the men and the women (Leakey and Lewin, [2], 131). Sharing, the division of labor, mutual trust and expectations, and conventions all required us to take each other seriously and to develop complex and interdependent patterns of expectations. We become more aware of others and of their awareness of us. As our relationships became more complicated, our brains became larger, and we developed language—and thus, by sharing, cooperating, and taking others into consideration, we became human.

Politics Again

Versions of the past are as varied as theories about human nature. Those who teach us about the past also give us our views about human nature and the arguments and slogans we use to support them. Did early humans kill and eat strangers? Was there a time when women held major positions of power? Did religious and moral beliefs flourish among early hominids? In a way these are simple questions of fact. But the facts are past facts, long gone and subject to the distortions of time. Our beliefs about such things must be even more tentative than our beliefs about recorded history or current events. If we want to get close to the truth, it is better to keep an open mind and consider a variety of alternative accounts than to adopt one position and then look for flaws in all the others. Keeping an open mind is the way to overcome the tendency to design history to fit our prejudices, but given our habit of rewriting even recent history to match our preconceptions and political requirements, an open mind is not an easy thing to keep.

Agriculture, Cities, and the Goddess

Around ten thousand years ago, in what is now Israel, Lebanon, Syria, and Iraq, nomads were abandoning their mobile way of life and settling in small agricultural communities. These settlements soon developed into villages with brick houses, storage facilities, carefully tended fields, and areas for domesticated animals. There is evidence that farmers there planted wheat and barley as early as 7000 B.C.

We do not know when the basic connection between copulation and procreation was discovered, but until it was, the mother was the only identifiable parent. This meant that when property or power was to be passed on, it was through her line—there being no other. In matrilineal agricultural societies, the analogy between birth and the growth of plants added a universal significance to the female as the source of life and nourishment. A combination of ancestor worship and matrilineality resulted in the worship of a powerful ancestress and in the goddess worship that flourished in the agricultural villages of Mesopotamia, Canaan, Anatolia, Egypt, Africa, Crete, and Greece. H.W.E. Saggs speaks of a Mother-goddess who, representing the female principle, "was probably the oldest divine power of all, probably already implicit in prehistoric fertility figurines" (Saggs, 277).

In *When God Was a Woman,* Merlin Stone argues that in the earliest agricultural settlements the high status of women was associated with matrilineality and veneration of a female deity, and she traces the process by which Goddess-worship was replaced by the God-worship of invading Indo-European nomads. This "herstory" is documented more fully in Elinor W. Gadon's book *The Once and Future Goddess.*

According to Gadon, "the death blow to Goddess culture was delivered by monotheism in which one male, all-powerful and absolute, ruled both the heavens and the earth. Monotheistic faiths were implacable foes of the Goddess. As we know, the Bible records the continuous battle waged by the ancient Hebrews against the worship of the Goddess" (Gadon, xiii–xiv).

> Then all the men who knew that their wives were burning sacrifices to other gods and the crowds of women standing by answered Jeremiah, "We will not listen to what you tell us in the name of the LORD. We intend to fulfill all the promises by which we have bound ourselves: we will burn sacrifices to the queen of heaven and pour drink-offerings to her as we used to do, we and our fathers, our kings and our princes, in the cities of Judah and in the streets of Jerusalem. We then had food in plenty and were content; no calamity touched us. But from the time we left off burning sacrifices to the queen of heaven and pouring drink-offerings to her, we have been in great want, and in the end we have fallen victims to sword and famine." (Jeremiah 44:15–19)

Murder in Mesopotamia

Between 5000 and 4000 B.C., the Ubaid people entered the area between the Tigris and Euphrates Rivers and established their temple at Eridu, near the Persian Gulf. They introduced irrigation, a male god named Enki, and kingship. Other invaders developed further centers of population and imported additional masculine gods—Enlil, a volcanic god from the mountainous home of the Āryan invaders; An, a sky god; and Marduk, the son of Enki.

These Sumerians used writing, engaged in trade, devised laws, and developed art and technology, but by 2300 B.C. they had disappeared and Sargon unified the land between Egypt and India in the world's first empire. He filled his new capital with spoils from all over the world, but by 2200 B.C. it had been destroyed by rampaging barbarians. Before long, Utuhegal threw the barbarians out, only to be deposed by his general. The general was then killed in battle, but his son ruled Ur until the capital was taken by the Elamites. The Elamites in turn were driven out by Semitic Amorites who made Babylon their capital. What fools humans turned out to be, building great cities and then destroying them, betraying and enslaving one another, and fighting one war after another as if there were no alternative. And it gets worse.

The Amorites who conquered Babylon started a dynasty in 1850 B.C. A hundred years later, their leader was Hammurabi, known for his code of laws. In another fifty years Hammurabi was dead and his empire in ruins. Around 1600 B.C., Hittites, speaking an Indo-European language and riding in light chariots drawn by swift horses, traveled five hundred miles down the Euphrates and made a raid on Babylon. They burnt it to the ground and then, unexplainably, turned around and went home. Order was restored and the Kassites, whom Stone identifies as a group "ruled by the northern invaders, the Indo-Europeans," controlled Babylon for the next four hundred years (Merlin Stone, 42).

As invaders from the north poured into Mesopotamia, Anatolia, and Canaan, a pattern was established: Warriors using horse-drawn chariots, and acknowledging male gods of conquest, enslaved the defeated inhabitants, replaced the female gods with their own sterner divinities, and instituted kingship, aristocracy, and conquest as a way of life. In the early stages of this invasion, a king could rule only with the "consent" of the goddess of the city, but this requirement became a formality, and eventually it disappeared. By the time of Hammurabi, the priest-king of a Mesopotamian city was seen as the god's official representative, his steward. The land, the crops, the animals, the slaves, and the city walls and buildings all belonged to the city god—but it was up to his representative to run things in a way consistent with the needs and whims of its true owner.

In 1350 B.C., the people of the city of Assur regained their independence after four hundred years of oppression. At first they were dominated by Babylon, but eventually they conquered all their neighbors, including the Babylonians, and gained a reputation for their cruelty. Tiglath-Pileser I was fond of "total war" and sought to wipe out every trace of his defeated enemies. The Hebrew prophet Isaiah grasps for an explanation and comes up with one when he delivers the following message from God:

> The Assyrian! He is the rod that I wield in my anger, and the staff of my wrath is in his hand. I send him against a godless nation, I bid him march against a people who rouse my wrath, to spoil and plunder at will and trample them down like mud in the streets. (Isaiah 10:5–6)

Listen to the Assyrian way, expressed in the demented boasts of a later king named Ashurnasirpal:

> I built a pillar over against his city gate, and I flayed all the chief men . . . and I covered the pillar with their skins; some I walled up within the pillar, some I impaled upon the pillar on stakes . . . and I cut off the limbs of the officers. (Kramer, 58)

It is a long way from a world full of nomadic gatherers to a society of peaceful farming villages, and even further to the vast and terrible empire of the Assyrians. Even if we are naturally selfish and aggressive, did we really have to spawn Assyrian monarchs? Apparently. A city is a storehouse, a bank, a source of slaves, and an annoyance to nomads and to other cities. Anything of value is a constant temptation to those who believe they have the power to appropriate it and are unconstrained by religion, morality, or compassion.

Law: Marduk and Hammurabi

Only careful planning and human drudgery stood between the Mesopotamian cities and the natural consequences of floods and droughts. As the cities grew, wars multiplied, which placed greater responsibility and power in the hands of the priest-kings. But it was also the job of the king to help settle personal disputes. When villages were small, elders resolved disputes as they arose, but in a city as large as Babylon this was no longer possible. According to the records, the gods and their stewards devoted major portions of their time trying to resolve squabbles about property and payments.

Since so many of their decisions were routine, the priest-kings simplified their work by developing precedents that crystallized into unwritten, and later into written, law. One treasure that has come down from this period is an eight-foot stone on which a god, possibly Marduk, is pictured consulting with Hammurabi. The text on the stone begins with an elaborate preface in which Hammurabi praises the gods, sets forth his divine connections, and announces his mission to "make justice appear in the land, to destroy evil and the wicked that the strong might not oppress the weak." Then we are given some down-to-earth decisions regarding problems endemic to the times:

> If a man has stolen property belonging to a god or a palace, that man shall be put to death, and he who has received the stolen property from his hand shall be put to death. (Nice, 24–25)

> If a man has broken into a house, they shall put him to death and hang him before the breach which he has made. (Nice, 27)

> If a man incurs a debt and Adad inundates his field or a flood has carried away (the soil) or else (if) corn is not raised on the field through lack of water, in that year he shall not render (any) corn to (his) creditor; he shall not pay interest for that year. (Nice, 31)

These laws were stricter than the Sumerian laws that preceded them and milder than the Assyrian ones that were to follow. They contained provisions for deferred payments and a form of insurance, but the penalty for most crimes was death.

Law is a fascinating, complex, and perhaps inevitable institution. Anarchists think it is neither necessary nor desirable, and Confucius did not approve of it, but a group of thinkers in China (called Legalists) believed that laws and severe penalties were enough by themselves to maintain perfect order. Our own society seems absolutely committed to laws, and we often refer to our government as a government of law.

Law is not morality, though they are sometimes confused. They overlap, as can be seen by the fact that killing is considered both legally and morally wrong; but each has its own special character and method of operation. Laws are established by those in power and are usually written down and accompanied by a list of penalties. Communities give some of their members the means and the authority to enforce the laws and to punish offenders. There is nothing metaphysical or otherworldly about laws or legal obligations or rights. In some societies, laws are clearly and openly stated, and officials who violate them are themselves subject to penalties. In other societies, what may legally be done to a person is limited only by the sadistic imaginations, or the compassionate impulses, of those in power.

Morality (like etiquette) covers many matters we consider beyond the scope of the law. Moral rules differ from laws in that there is no (agreed upon) schedule of penalties for moral offenses, and no official enforcing agency. One may defend a law on moral grounds, but it would be odd to argue in the other direction. To "legislate morality" is not to pass moral laws but to pass laws in an effort to enforce an already existing morality. Moral laws are neither passed nor decreed. According to the moralist they are discovered and according to the amoralist they are evolving constructions.

One reason laws work as well as they do is because society backs them up with as much force as it takes to ensure they are obeyed. A powerful king or emperor was not likely to be asked to defend either his laws or his authority to make and change them. But when some defense was required, people looked first to religion. Hence, Hammurabi clearly set out his relations to the gods, Western monarchs spoke of the "Divine Right of Kings," and Chinese emperors claimed "The Mandate of Heaven." When religion is taken seriously it not only bolsters the authority of the secular powers, it can work alongside them to help maintain order in the community.

Divine Messages

A. L. Oppenheim notes that we are justified in drawing few conclusions about Babylonian religion, but he adds that "the king could receive divine messages of certain types, but it was not considered acceptable for a private person to approach the deity through dreams and visions" (Oppenheim, 182).

Passages like this, and histories are full of them, make us wonder what was actually going on. Oppenheim probably does not believe that kings literally received divine messages—if that means communications from Marduk and his Ilk. Since the content of these alleged messages could be anything from a death sentence or a tip on wheat futures to a code of morality, it is tempting to conclude that Hammurabi and his fellow priest-kings claimed their divine connections solely to bolster their power and authority. They looked at the problem, figured out a solution, and then published it in the name of their god. It is also tempting to embrace similar explanations of the words of other ancient (and not so ancient) figures, who also claim to have received messages from divine sources. Moses, the prophets of the Old Testament, Muhammad, Zoroaster, Joseph Smith, and many others, claim to have communicated with, or to be speaking for, supernatural beings. It is *possible* that every one of these reports of visions and voices bringing messages from the beyond are outright fabrications, that Jeremiah was lying when he said, "The word of the LORD came to me," as was Ezekiel when he said, "These are the words of the LORD God." It may be hard to believe that these prophets, seers, and priest-kings were claiming supernatural contact in order to make sure their pronouncements, warnings, decisions, regulations, messages, and orders would be taken seriously, but without a better hypothesis what else can we think?

> So the child Samuel was in the LORD's service under his master Eli. Now in those days the word of the LORD was seldom heard,

and no vision was granted. But one night Eli, whose eyes were dim and his sight failing, was lying down in his usual place, while Samuel slept in the temple of the LORD where the Ark of God was. Before the lamp of God had gone out, the LORD called him, and Samuel answered, "Here I am," and ran to Eli saying, "You called me: here I am." "No, I did not call you," said Eli; "lie down again." So he went and lay down. The LORD called Samuel again, and he got up and went to Eli. "Here I am," he said; "surely you called me." "I did not call, my son," he answered; "lie down again." Now Samuel had not yet come to know the LORD, and the word of the LORD had not been disclosed to him. When the LORD called him for the third time, he again went to Eli and said, "Here I am; you did call me." Then Eli understood that it was the LORD calling the child; he told Samuel to go and lie down and said, "If he calls again, say, 'Speak, LORD; thy servant hears thee.' " So Samuel went and lay down in his place. (1 Samuel 3:1–9)

Joseph Smith . . . affirmed that during the night of September 21, 1823, he sought the Lord in fervent prayer, having previously received a Divine manifestation of transcendent import. His account follows:

"While I was thus in the act of calling upon God, I discovered a light appearing in my room, which continued to increase till the room was lighter than at noonday, when immediately a personage appeared at my bedside, standing in the air, for his feet did not touch the floor.

"He had on a loose robe of the most exquisite whiteness. It was a whiteness beyond anything earthly I had ever seen; nor do I believe that any earthly thing could be made to appear so exceedingly white and brilliant . . .

"Not only was his robe exceedingly white, but his whole person was glorious beyond description, and his countenance truly like lightning. The room was exceedingly light, but not so very bright as immediately around his person. When I first looked upon him, I was afraid; but the fear soon left me.

"He called me by name, and said unto me that he was a messenger sent from the presence of God to me, and that his name was Moroni; that God had a work for me to do." (Introduction to the Book of Mormon)

I swear by all that you can see, and all that is hidden from your view, that this is the utterance of a noble messenger. It is no poet's speech: scant is your faith! It is no soothsayer's divination: how little you reflect! It is a revelation from the Lord of all creatures. (The Koran, 69:40–45)

> During the period from +238 to +250 Ko Hsüan was the recipient of visions and revelations from the ruler of Heaven (who was now beginning to take on a distinctly more personalized character) . . . who sent him four celestial visitants with more than thirty divinely inspired texts. . . .
>
> In the +4th century the series of revelations continued. During the Chin dynasty, between +326 and +342, the woman Taoist Wei Hua-Tshun received all kinds of further information about the organisation of heaven and earth from a mysterious figure Wang Pao. (Needham, 157–58)

Explaining the Messages

It may be possible to explain messages from the gods without resorting to either polytheism or deceit. Perhaps Hammurabi and other inspired visionaries encountered their gods and muses in dreams or hallucinations. In *Five Stages of Greek Religion*, Gilbert Murray muses in a footnote about Émile Durkheim's analysis of religious emotions. Durkheim, he says, claimed that early humans may have felt the force of religious commands because "religion is the work of the tribe and, as such, superior to the individual." In dreams and hallucinations one might hear the voice of god, but really "the Voice of God is the imagined voice of the whole tribe, heard or imagined by him who is going to break its laws" (Murray, 6, fn. 1). Later Murray reminds us that "we must not forget the power of hallucination, still fairly strong, as the history of religious revivals in America will bear witness, but far stronger, of course, among the impressionable hordes of early men" (25). After mentioning some of the better known Greek, Roman, and Christian hallucinations, he adds that "even in daily life primitive men seem to have dealt more freely than we generally do with apparitions and voices and daemons of every kind" (26).

Without doubt, dreams and hallucinations were important to early humans, who had no reason to think they were not messages from another world. Perhaps it did us no great harm to believe that information provided and orders given in dreams and hallucinations had authoritative extraterrestrial sources. Many dreams and hallucinations do seem to encapsulate our own best advice to ourselves. Socrates said that a little voice always warned him when he was about to make some serious mistake. Early in the *Iliad*, Athena grabbed Achilles by the hair and dissuaded him from attacking Agamemnon the king, who had made him angry (Lattimore, 64).

The word from On High is frequently delivered in a forceful and dramatic way. Saul was knocked to the ground and temporarily blinded (Acts 9:1–9); Jacob wrestled with some supernatural being (possibly God) all night—and beat him (Genesis 32:24–31); and Muhammad was said to have been choked by the angel Gabriel until he lost his inhibitions and began to recite. The question is probably not "Did hallucinations occur to early prophets and people?" but rather "How much of what was reported was hallucination and how much was politically motivated fabrication?"

In *The Origin of Consciousness in the Breakdown of the Bicameral Mind,* Julian Jaynes takes hallucinations very seriously. In fact he argues that verbal hallucinations were common among early humans and were a side effect of the completion of language, which, according to his unorthodox account, occurred around 10,000 B.C. According to Jaynes, Achilles, Agamemnon and all the Greeks and Trojans, the Old Testament prophets, the village shaman, Hammurabi and his fellow Babylonians, and virtually all the *Homo sapiens sapiens* who lived before 1000 B.C. (and many who lived after that time) lacked consciousness. This means, among other things, that they did not have a concept of themselves as individuals in a situation with a structure and a history. They could not plan, imagine alternatives, or evaluate their performance. Much of their action was habitual, and sometimes (especially in situations of great stress) they experienced, and usually obeyed, auditory hallucinations issued by the right hemisphere of the brain.

Consciousness

Jaynes argues that language was not fully developed until around 10,000 B.C., which is roughly when humans began dabbling in agriculture and settling into villages. He says that hallucinated voices evolved as the first form of social control in the earliest agricultural communities. A worker, for example, might hear the "imagined voice" of a leader telling him to persevere, to work harder, or to come home. According to Jaynes, this system worked for thousands of years, and only after it failed did the hallucinations stop and the phenomenon of consciousness appear.

But what does he mean by 'consciousness'? Sometimes he uses the word 'conscious' as we would use 'aware'. The Zen archer, he says, is urged to release himself from "the consciousness of what he is doing" (34). Further, he notes that in playing the piano, "a complex array of various tasks is accomplished all at once with scarcely any consciousness of them whatever" (25). "Right at this moment," he says, "you are not conscious of how you are sitting, of where your hands are placed, of how fast you are reading, though even as I mentioned these items, you were" (26). In each of these remarks 'conscious' or 'consciousness' could easily be replaced by 'aware' or 'awareness'. But knowing that Jaynes sometimes uses two words in the same way does not tell us what he means by either of them.

Jaynes says that consciousness is a very special creation, and not necessary for a wide range of complex activities—like playing the piano or performing in some sport. Nevertheless, humans are (or are nearly) unique in having created, out of visual and spatial metaphors, an inner mental space in which ideas can be compared, arranged, and strung together to comprise a story, a version, or an interpretation of what has been going on. Jaynes calls the center of this metaphorical but imaginary inner mental space "The Analog 'I' " (Jaynes, 62–63). This is the imaginary being we imagine glancing down the corridors of our spatially interpreted minds. This is the knower, this is consciousness. What it is to be conscious is to have constructed this metaphorical mind-space, and to have learned to enjoy the simultaneously constructed point of view from which it can be explored.

There are three important aspects to this process: excerption, narratization, and the construction of a self. Just as we glance from one item to another in real space, so in the mental space that is consciousness we attend only to *excerpts* of events and items. When we recall some experience, we string together a few of these scenes and images, and then display them to ourselves. We place these snippets of our life in a *narratization*, which is a story in which they have a fixed place and meaning.

> New situations are selectively perceived as part of this ongoing story, perceptions that do not fit into it being unnoticed or at least unremembered. More important, situations are chosen which are congruent to this ongoing story, until the picture I have of myself in my life story determines how I am to act and choose in novel situations as they arise. (Jaynes, 64)

Finally, we *construct a self*. This self is not consciousness (which is the Analog 'I'), but an "object" of consciousness. It is constructed on the basis of what we are told about who we are, and what we can find out about it for ourselves. This "empirical" or "psychological" self has attributes, character traits, habits, a past, and, with luck, a future as well. It is the creation of the analog 'I' and the star figure and reference point in the ongoing story of what is happening.

The analogue 'I' and the empirical self have made it possible for us to reflect and remember, plan and verbalize, deliberate and explain. But anything can be overdone, and these activities are no exception. We must consider the possibility that the contributions of consciousness sometimes interfere with more direct and appropriate responses to problems.

Deliberation can interfere with action, planning can destroy spontaneity, and we often talk (to others or to ourselves) when we should be listening (to others or to ourselves). When we try to correct some of these excesses we are, in effect, trying to quiet our "minds." We want to reduce the leaping subvocalizations of consciousness that, like a flashlight in a trembling hand, jump from one object to another. By taking our inner monologue less seriously, we let go of stereotypes and hasty generalizations and arrive at a better version of events. This, in turn, makes it easier to respond appropriately and to solve problems. Perhaps the Buddhist and Daoist goal of an empty mind can be understood as advice to eliminate or neutralize this soundtrack that distracts us from what we are doing. Meditation may slow the activities of the analog 'I', and, by inhibiting the stringing together of excerpts of experience, it may lead us to accept the self we construct as the illusion it is.

Hallucinations

Even if we reject the conclusion that humans who lived between 10,000 and 1000 B.C. were unconscious automatons who hallucinated voices when traditional routines failed, we cannot deny that Jaynes's hypothesis is worth considering, or dismiss it as a groundless fantasy. We return to consciousness in later chapters, so now let us turn to Jaynes's account of the role of auditory hallucinations in the social configurations that developed after the start of the agricultural and urban revolutions.

Jaynes says that auditory hallucinations are produced by the speech center on the right side of the brain and "heard" by the other hemisphere. Today most human speech is controlled by the speech center on the left side of the brain, Wernicke's area, but it is possible that long ago "what corresponds to Wernicke's area on the right hemisphere may have organized admonitory experience and coded it into 'voices' which were then 'heard' over the anterior commissure by the left or dominant hemisphere" (Jaynes, 104).

Sometimes, when we are driving along a freeway, we are thinking about things and sometimes we are not thinking at all. In either case, a flat tire, an accident, or a funny noise from the motor will simply flip us into another mode, and we will sometimes form words to ourselves on the order of: "SHIT! A FLAT TIRE. PULL OVER. CHECK THE SPARE." These thoughts appear spontaneously and we spend no conscious effort formulating them or rejecting alternatives like driving the rest of the way on the flat or destroying the car.

According to Jaynes's story, if one of our unconscious ancestors had found himself in an analogous fix, rather than telling himself (thinking in words) what to do under the circumstances, he would hear an authoritative voice that would, more or less, have told him what we tell ourselves: "YOU HAVE A BROKEN WHEEL. PULL OVER. CHECK THE SPARE."

Maybe Jaynes is right when he says that our ancestors operated in this way, and maybe not. But hallucinations and dreams did and do occur, and when we realize that ancient people had more reasons to believe in gods than we do, and that many of them practiced austerities and took mind-altering drugs, we can understand how they might have believed that the voices and visions they experienced were sent to them from an external source.

Jaynes says that auditory hallucinations were part of a natural and elegant solution to a problem faced by the brain. If the right hemisphere (the gods) performs synthetic and constructive tasks, puts things together, sees things from the point of view of the whole, and if the left hemisphere is analytic and verbal, then the problem is that there are

> billions of nerve cells processing complex experience on one side and needing to send the results over to the other. . . . Some code would have to be used, some way of reducing very complicated processing into a form that could be transmitted through the . . . neurons of the . . . anterior commissures. And what better code has ever appeared in the evolution of animal nervous systems than human language? Thus in the stronger form of our model, auditory hallucinations exist as such in a linguistic manner because that is the most efficient method of getting complicated cortical processing from one side of the brain to the other. (Jaynes, 105)

The mechanisms for social control that existed in nomadic hunter-gatherer bands might have been enough to produce order in a close-knit and relatively small group of hominids, but the effectiveness of these methods decreases in proportion to the size of the group. In a village with a population of one thousand or more, something else was needed. Jaynes suggests what the first "something else" might have been: The ways of behavior encouraged by the community and the directives issued by those in charge were stored in our brains and then, when expedient, were delivered not by the internal "voice" that now delivers what we call thoughts but by the hallucinated voice of some major authority figure. Instead of saying to ourselves "I really ought to keep working," we might, when our energies are flagging, hear "YOU MUST KEEP AT YOUR WORK." If that happened, you can bet it was effective.

Jaynes tells us that this system worked reasonably well until a series of natural disasters turned the relatively stable and peaceful bicameral world upside down. Volcanos erupted; tidal waves demolished entire cities; earthquakes, floods, and massive migrations destabilized the world and created more turmoil than the bicameral mind could cope with; and consciousness was born.

If we suppose that Hammurabi, Moses, and other seers and prophets were individuals who retained some vestige of a once widespread ability to get hallucinated advice from the right side of the brain, then we can find a more charitable explanation for the widespread claims about the voices and commands of gods than the one that involves politically motivated deception.

Early Morality

All social animals develop methods to ensure stability within their clan, pack, group, or herd, which is to say that they manage to devise techniques to resolve conflicts. The world is filled with fascinating and usually non-lethal solutions to disputes about territory, food, and mating, but only animals with a language and the power of abstraction can exploit what I have been calling morality to head off conflict by requiring that we deal "correctly" with others.

If morality is seen as an objective and binding set of rules, rights, virtues, or values, then members of early hunting and gathering bands could have done well enough without it. Their customs and habits (their "ethics") were constantly enforced and reinforced. When such optimum conditions for "moral education" exist, abstract concepts of right, wrong, good, and bad are superfluous. When behavior preferred by the members of the group is so well-understood, rewarding, and inescapable, there is no use for the thought of an objective and binding morality. People are already bound, by custom and by one another.

The traits necessary for successful band-life were easily imparted to the band-members. But when social arrangements became more complex, people more reflective, and the opportunities for the unscrupulous more tempting and numerous, the old techniques of control were no longer adequate. One of the devices we developed to fill the need was morality.

Jaynes's suggestion about the character of life in the first towns makes no use of anything remotely resembling morality. The earliest farmers "unconsciously" experienced auditory hallucinations that expressed both their absent leaders' commands and their own best advice. After the breakdown of this system, consciousness, selfhood, and inner verbal thought replaced the voices. The silencing of the voices led to a belief in angry and sullen gods, and to a set of rules, laws, and practices thought to be warranted by the commands of these powerful but temporarily absent deities.

Stone's account of these early days is quite different from the story offered by Jaynes. Even before the time of the agricultural villages, perhaps as far back as 25,000 B.C., nomads worshiped a mother goddess. The mother, as sole known parent, was the center of the family or clan, the mysterious source of life. As the nomads settled into villages and the villages grew into towns, this religion flourished. The early villages did not war with each other, life was honored, sexual customs were not neurotic, and men who tried to take over were killed.

When the Indo-Europeans made their way into the lands where the Goddess was worshiped, dominance and inequality replaced egalitarian cooperation, and patriarchal authority was enforced with violence. New laws were established in the name of a god of great wrath and power who stood to his subjects as an owner to his slaves.

There is no way to say when "morality" finally appeared on the scene. Much happens on the way from a feeling of anger at something to the belief that such a thing ought not be, and morality emerges somewhere in the transition from feelings of dislike to apprehensions of obligation. Ideas basic to morality, bondage and objective value, appear only after we gain the ability to identify our rules and principles and to question them. Only in the face of a challenge is it necessary to bring in some concept of intrinsic value or moral obligation to shore up the tradition.

If Jaynes is right, morality came late because the tools necessary to think morally were absent in the bicameral era. If the history sketched by Stone and Gadon is accurate, we can wonder if the early female-dominated societies had something similar to what we are calling morality. Was something right because the Goddess commanded it? If not, then what, if anything, justified demands made on people? If these early societies had no morality, if morality was a male invention, then we must wonder what served the functions that (we think) morality now serves?

Let us leave these difficult questions about the origin of the concept of objective moral bondage and turn to a time when writing and morality (or something close to it) were features of everyday life. In some of the most ancient texts we know, there appear to be references to "justice," and to a "cosmic moral order" that even the gods must acknowledge. The Egyptians had a word, *ma'at,* that is translated sometimes as "justice." They believed in a judgment after death in which a person's character was weighed on the scales of justice. This procedure clearly indicates the existence of the moralistic notion that there are objective requirements and values, and that when we fall short we deserve to be punished. John A. Wilson says that *ma'at*

> is probably a physical term, 'levelness, evenness, straightness, correctness', in a sense of regularity or order. From that it can be used in the metaphorical sense of 'uprightness, righteousness, truth, justice'. (Wilson, 119–20)

According to Barbara Mertz, *ma'at* can be translated as "truth" or as "justice."

> The hieroglyph for *ma'at* is the feather, which was weighed against the heart of the dead man—the heart must be empty of evil to balance the feather weight on the other pan of the scales. But *ma'at* went beyond justice; it has been defined as the universal order, the divine system of correctness—the *right* way to do things. (Mertz, 218–19)

Finally, Stone mentions that *ma'at* was personified as a goddess who "symbolized the order of the universe, all that was righteous and good" (Merlin Stone, 92). Meanwhile in Mesopotamia, Enlil, the Sumerian "father of the gods" and "king of the universe," was given credit for creating the *me*, which, according to Samuel Noah Kramer, were "a set of 'universal laws' governing all existence—physical and moral." He adds:

> There were special *me* for deities and men, lands and cities, palaces and temples, love and law, truth and falsehood, war and peace, music and art, cult and ritual, as well as for all the crafts and professions. Enlil granted these *me* to guide the gods, spelling out their rights, duties, and privileges, bounds and controls, authority and restraint. (Kramer, 102)

It was by violating one of his own *me* by raping a young goddess that Enlil was eventually banished to the netherworld. Mircea Eliade interprets the *me* as the "decrees" on which the commands of the gods are based (Eliade, 60).

We can find many connections between the new patriarchal gods and the forms of morality that were then developing. We have seen how moral rules can apply to the gods as well as humans; but as the gods were awarded more power and authority, they came to be seen as the ultimate source of the rules, and as beings to whom we owe absolute obedience—no matter what they command. In the next three chapters we observe this interplay of morality and religion in the early societies of India, China, and Greece, and in Chapter 8 we directly confront the idea that morality depends on religion.

5

Moralism and Amoralism in India

> The disciplined in mental attitude leaves behind in this world both good and evil deeds.
>
> —Bhagavad Gītā

AFTER THE HUNTING and gathering bands evolved into farming villages, the early city-dwellers redesigned their myths to teach new moral lessons, and they picked rulers (or the rulers picked themselves) to make and enforce laws. They relied on supernatural beings to back up social customs, and on promises of reward and punishment in this life and beyond to encourage civility. Concepts of virtue and vice, duty and obligation, right and wrong, justice, honor, and goodness evolved to help express the idea (or the hope) that some ways of acting and being were in accord with objective requirements.

Greeks were among the first to speculate on the nature and rationality of these requirements. We turn our attention to them in Chapter 7 and in several other places, but while we need to know our Western roots, we miss much when that is all we know. People in India and China also lived in society, and had families, friends, enemies, debts, jobs, poverty, death, and taxes. Some of the ways they invented to cope with these complications mirror those developed in the West; others are different. Our discussions of morality, society, human nature, desires, and decisions can only be enriched if we include contributions of non-Western movements such as Hinduism, Buddhism, Confucianism, and Daoism. For this reason I devote this and the next chapter to a discussion of some aspects of Indian and

Chinese thought that enrich our understanding of the controversy between the moralist and the amoralist.

The Āryans

An advanced civilization flourished between 2500 and 1500 B.C. in the Indus River Valley in northwestern India. Excavations at Harappa and Mohenjo-daro have uncovered carefully designed cities, with wide streets, covered sewers, and houses with courtyards and plumbing. By 1500 B.C. these cities appear to have been suffering from pollution and overcrowding, but these were minor problems compared to the trouble caused by the herdsmen and chariot riders sweeping down from the north to subjugate them.

The city-dwellers of the Harappan civilization must have seen these invaders as ignorant, smelly barbarians. Joseph Campbell describes them as "polygamous, patriarchal, proud of their genealogies, tent dwellers, filthy, and tough" (Campbell, 176). When they first appeared in what is now India, they divided themselves into three classes: priests, warriors, and workers. After sacking the Harappan cities and enslaving the original dwellers (who are called Dravidians), they had four castes: *brāhmins* (priests), *kṣatriyas* (warriors), *vaiśyas* (merchants, farmers and other Āryan workers), and *śūdras*. The word 'caste' comes from the Portuguese, but the original Sanskrit word was *varṇa*, which means "color." Since *śūdra* means "dark," there is no doubt that this lowest slot was created for the dark-skinned Dravidians. The only thing worse than being a *śūdra* was being the child of a *śūdra* father and a non-*śūdra* mother. The *caṇḍāla*, a child of a *śūdra* father and a *brāhmin* mother, had the jobs of executing criminals and cremating corpses, but was forbidden relationships with live members of other castes.

There is a famous verse of Hindu scripture from the *Ṛg Veda* that rationalizes the caste system by talking about a primal division of a giant being, the *Puruṣa*.

> When they divided the Puruṣa, into how many parts did they arrange him? What was his mouth? What his two arms? What are his thighs and feet called?
>
> The *brāhmin* was his mouth, his two arms were made the *rājanya* (warrior), his two thighs the *vaiśya* (trader and agriculturalist), from his feet the *śūdra* (servile class) was born. (Radhakrishnan and Moore, 19)

We may find it strange that anyone would try to justify the existence of a class system by appealing to such a story, but remember that the story comes from writings that are considered Holy Scriptures, and that the Bible itself justifies the subjugation of women by pointing out that, because of her part in the Fall, God said to Eve: "You shall be eager for your husband, and he shall be your master" (Genesis 3:16).

When the Āryans entered India they brought their gods with them. Their pantheon included a sky god (Dyaus [cf. Zeus]), gods for wind, fire, water, and thunder, and gods who create, regulate, and destroy. They held that Varuna, a god of order and righteousness, discovers sinners, but that he also has the power to forgive. M. Hiriyanna speaks of him as the "guardian of all that is worthy and good" (Hiriyanna, 12). The most important god during the period of migration was Indra, a vain and boastful god who represents valor and victory. He is called "protector of the Aryan colour" and "destroyer of the dark skin" (11).

The *Vedas*

The hymns, prayers, rituals, spells, incantations, and reflections of the invaders and their descendants have been assembled in four vast collections called the *Vedas*. The word comes from a Sanskrit root associated with knowing and seeing, and is related to the Latin *video* which means "I see" and to the English word 'wit'. The oldest and best known of the collections is called the *Ṛg Veda*. Each *Veda* is divided into four parts, *Saṁhitās* (songs or hymns—mantras), *Brāhmaṇas* (religious documents and rules about sacrifices), *Āraṇyakas* (meditations for forest dwellers), and *Upaniṣads* (metaphysical reflections about reality). The songs and hymns are the work of poets, the *Brāhmaṇas* and *Āraṇyakas* are the work of priests, and the *Upaniṣads*, which were composed between 800 and 400 B.C., are the work of mystics and philosophers.

It was the job of the *brāhmin* priests to serve the gods and to make sure that the gods in turn served humans. They taught that it was difficult for a god to refuse a request if the appropriate (and often expensive) ritual had been performed correctly. Over the years these priests bent this ritualistic polytheism to their own purposes, and thereby attained great power and wealth. This religion of ritual and sacrifice reached its peak in the period of the *Brāhmaṇas* (1000–600 B.C.). In this same period the original polytheism evolved into monotheism. But Vedic monotheism was unstable; the name and even the identity of the "one" god kept changing, and there was a drift toward monism—the view that "all is one."

> Wise art thou, punisher of guilt, O Indra. The sword lops limbs, thou smitest down the sinner,
> The men who injure, as it were a comrade, the lofty Law of Varuṇa and Mitra.
>
> (*Ṛg Veda*, in Radhakrishnan and Moore, 6)

> Dawn on us with prosperity, O Uṣas, daughter of the sky,
> Dawn with great glory, goddess, lady of the light, dawn thou with riches, bounteous one.
>
> (*Ṛg Veda*, in Radhakrishnan and Moore, 13)

> What sin we have committed against an intimate, O Varuṇa, against a friend or companion at any time, a brother, a neighbour, or a stranger, that, O Varuṇa, loose from us.
>
> If like gamblers at play we have cheated, whether in truth or without knowing, all that loose from us, O God. So may we be dear to thee, O Varuṇa.
>
> (*Ṛg Veda*, in Radhakrishnan and Moore, 29)

The *Upaniṣads*

The evolution from polytheism to monotheism and then to monism, is a move from the concrete to the abstract, and from the naive to the subtle. This movement culminates in the *Upaniṣads*, where essential elements of the Āryan way and of the *brāhmin* religion of ritual and sacrifice are replaced or altered drastically. Although signs of change appear much earlier, by 600 B.C. many of the descendants of the Āryans had been transformed into world-denying ascetics. People turned away from the pleasures and the pains of the world and looked for inner peace. The practice of yoga and a belief in the non-Vedic doctrines of karma and reincarnation became common. How had these radical cultural changes come about?

One answer is that the "noble warriors" had been so attached to war that by 1000 B.C. they had destroyed each other in the civil war celebrated in the *Mahābhārata* and justified or rationalized in the *Bhagavad Gītā*. Heinrich Zimmer notes that after this mutual destruction the word for a hero (*vīra*) came to apply not to the man who mastered others with force (as it had originally) but to the sage who had learned, through the practice of yoga, to master himself (Zimmer, 74). Zimmer and his student Joseph Campbell argue that the introspective world-denying tendency that emerged in the first half of the first millennium B.C. was the result of a resurgence of pre-Āryan beliefs and practices that were never totally eliminated (see Campbell, 183).

Another factor that helps explain the rejection of the way of the *Vedas* is the growing silliness of the *brāhmin* priests, who came to believe, or claimed to believe, that the sun would not rise unless they performed the proper rituals. Only *brāhmins* were permitted to teach the *Vedas*, to perform sacrifices, and to drink soma in important rituals. Most writers claim only that soma was a powerful "intoxicant," but a scattering of scholars say that soma was a hallucinogenic mushroom (see Wasson). It was only a matter of time before people began to wonder about these wealthy priests, collecting money for taking drugs and mumbling over slaughtered animals, and thinking that their intricate charades made the earth turn and the gods bend to the selfish and trivial demands of humans. "Thinking sacrifice and merit is the chiefest thing," it says in the *Muṇḍaka-Upaniṣad*, "naught better do they know—deluded!" (Radhakrishnan and Moore, 52).

The decline of the power of the *brāhmins* and the rejection of the Vedic way can also be traced to the growing strength and influence of the *kṣatriya* caste. Powerful warrior kings found it difficult to appreciate the *brāhmins*' claims to be owed service by all, and the common people abandoned the belief that the *brāhmins* were able to compel the gods with their rituals and their sacrifices. The caste system came to be seen, even by some *brāhmins*, as a relic of the past, and teachers appeared who said that salvation is available to anyone. These teachers attracted students who had resolved to replace the struggle for power with a quest for *mokṣa*, understood variously as release from worldly cares, from the prison of the ego, and from ignorance and delusion. The sages, whose thoughts are collected in the *Upaniṣads*, tell us that the individual ego is an unreal and harmful construction, and that release comes with the discovery of the True Self. The great truth they had discovered, and the secret they were willing to teach, was that each individual self is a part of a great Self that is identical with the entire Cosmos, with God, with everything that is. Sometimes they allowed the *brāhmins* their claim to be dealing with knowledge, and then, as in this passage from the *Muṇḍaka Upaniṣad*, introduced a distinction between lower and higher knowledge: "Of these, the lower is the *Ṛg Veda*, the *Yajur Veda*, the *Sāma Veda*, and the *Atharva Veda*. Now, the higher is that whereby that Imperishable is apprehended" (Radhakrishnan and Moore, 51).

The higher knowledge enables us to "apprehend the Imperishable," but what can that mean? In our daily lives we are, it was believed, living in a false dream-world of our own construction, the product of *māyā* (illusion). Behind the illusion lurks a Reality that is stable and eternal. But this Reality, if grasped at all, is not known by any experience that depends on our bodily senses, and it is not describable in words and concepts, which were designed to work in and on the illusory world of experience.

The *Upaniṣads* teach that when we begin to see the world and our egos as "mere" illusions, we may find that we have lost track of the boundaries between our illusory world and our illusory self. At that point we may experience a feeling of dissolving into a larger consciousness. In the *Kaṭha Upaniṣad*, this "great, all pervading Self" is called *Ātman*.

> The wise one [i.e., the *Ātman*, the Self] is not born, nor dies.
> This one has not come from anywhere, has not become anyone.
> Unborn, constant, eternal, primeval, this one is not slain when the body is slain.
> If the slayer think to slay,
> If the slain think himself slain,
> Both these understand not.
> This one slays not, nor is slain.
> More minute than the minute, greater than the great, is the Self that is set in the heart of a creature here.
> One who is without the active will beholds Him, and becomes freed from sorrow—
> When through the grace of the Creator he beholds the greatness of the Self.
> Him who is the bodiless among bodies,
> Stable among the unstable,
> The great, all-pervading Self—
> On recognizing Him, the wise man sorrows not.
>
> (Radhakrishnan and Moore, 45–46)

This is a well-known verse. The part about the slayer and the slain was repeated in the *Bhagavad Gītā* and was used by Ralph Waldo Emerson in his poem "Brahma." Our bodies, and even our personal egos, may vanish, but the Larger Self, of which these little egos are but lost fragments, is eternal, unchanging, and all-pervading. This is the *Ātman*, the Self with a capital '*S*'.

This passage tells us that one sees the Self when one has "no active will," and it suggests that this is accomplished by "the grace of the Creator." Here are two of the traditional avenues to enlightenment: self-discipline and grace. The former is the way of the yogin, the way of work, of meditation and self-denial. Patañjali, who systematized the teachings of the School of Yoga around 200 B.C., defines yoga as the "restraint of mental modifications." He adds that this is brought about by persistent practice and desirelessness. With the mind stilled and desires abated, the "active will" disappears and one becomes supernaturally quiet. Only then, it is said, is it possible to attain complete understanding of Ultimate Reality and thereby to attain "absolute independence" (Radhakrishnan and Moore, 453–85).

The second path is easier on the seeker and may have developed out of the thought that no amount of activity on our part is going to prepare us to apprehend the Infinite, and that only an act of grace on the part of the Infinite is capable of bridging that gap. Those who favor this alternative spend their time in prayer and adoration, seeking, through grace, a state they despair of producing (or meriting) by anything they might do.

Arriving at the idea of *Ātman* and placing one's identity in this "great all-pervading Self" was certainly an achievement, but it was not yet to "apprehend the Imperishable." There is one more step. One must see and understand that *Ātman*, this True Self beyond all individual selves, is "really" identical with Brahman, the Absolute, the "Holy All." This knowledge is the key to salvation, to the end of suffering, and to release from bondage to the world of illusion. The unification with Brahman was not considered to be an extinction of awareness—that is a later Buddhist idea—rather, it is a blissful expansion. When we merge with the Absolute we lose our individual consciousness, but we gain cosmic awareness *and* bliss: We lose the point of view of a solitary drop of water and acquire that of the ocean.

The ascetic teachers who tried to convey this insight in metaphors, parables, and similes were the *ṛṣis*. The word 'maharishi' is derived from *mahā* (great) and *ṛṣis* (sage). These "great sages" specialized in mystical knowledge, unusual powers, and the attainment of extraordinary states of consciousness. They considered themselves beyond civil restrictions and conventional morality, and they scorned the power of the king and the magic of the *brāhmins*. What was real was Brahman, and their lives were dedicated to experiencing, comprehending, participating in, and guiding others to, this Ultimate Reality.

> All these rivers flow my son, the eastern toward the east, the western toward the west. But they really flow from the ocean and then back to the ocean once again. Flowing, they become the ocean itself, and becoming ocean they do not say, "I am this river" or "I am that river." In the same way, my son, even though all creatures here have come forth from Being, they know not that they have come forth from Being. Whatever a creature may be here, whether tiger or lion or wolf or boar or worm or fly or gnat or mosquito, they become that Being again and again. For that Being is the finest essence of all this world and in that Being every creature has its Self. That is reality. That is *Ātman*. *Tat tvam asi* [That Thou Art], Śvetaketu. (*Chāndogya Upaniṣad*, in Herman, 113)

Karma and Reincarnation

Reincarnation is the doctrine that the soul occupies a series of bodies and that death is followed by rebirth into a new physical, but not necessarily human, form. This belief was not part of the original Āryan world-view, but between 800 and 600 B.C. it spread over much of India. Karma and reincarnation work together. The word 'karma' means "deed" or "action," and the idea is that one's actions affect one's future happiness. In some respects this is only obvious—if one is nice to people they are likely to return the gesture. But karma goes beyond that naturalistic understanding by postulating a hidden causal network that guarantees that each agent gets exactly what he or she deserves. When it is combined with the doctrine of reincarnation, karma becomes a weight or stain that influences the quality of one's next birth. Enough bad karma and a person might come back as a dog or a pig. Enough good karma and a person might come back in a privileged house, or at least as a male.

> What we sow, we must reap. That is, the karma doctrine signifies not merely that the events of our life are determined by their antecedent causes, but also that there is absolute justice in the rewards and punishments that fall to our lot in life. . . . The *Mahābhārata* says that the consequences of what a man does will seek him out later, "as surely as a calf does its mother in a herd of cows." (Hiriyanna, 48–49)

> Those who are of pleasant conduct here—the prospect is, indeed, that they will enter a pleasant womb, either the womb of a *brāhmin*, or the womb of a *kṣatriya*, or the womb of a *vaiśya*. But those who are of stinking conduct here—the prospect is, indeed, that they will enter a stinking womb, either the womb of a dog, or the womb of a swine, or the womb of an outcast (caṇḍāla). (*Chāndogya Upaniṣad*, in Radhakrishnan and Moore, 66–67)

Heterodoxies

Interpretations of Vedic texts and practices based on the *Vedas* could diverge widely, but as long as a belief or a school is based on the *Vedas* it is considered "orthodox." World-views neither based on nor justified by the *Vedas* are called "heterodox." Heterodox schools of thought and practice flourished where the *brāhmin* religion had not penetrated, and when independent people began to think for themselves.

The three forms of heterodoxy we address are Cārvāka, Jainism, and Buddhism. Buddhists and Jains accept reincarnation and karma, and they acknowledge the value of both mental and physical discipline. All three forms reject the Upaniṣadic concept of a Self (*Ātman*), and the monism that sees everything to be one in Brahman. Only the Jains accept a personal or individual soul, a self that migrates from life to life and that, when purified of all karma, ascends to a state of blissful isolation. Buddhism purports to chart a middle path between the asceticism of the Jains and the materialistic hedonism of the followers of Cārvāk.

Cārvāka

Cārvāka was a sage of unknown date and uncertain origins who is identified as the founder of a school of materialists. The Cārvākins tell us to eat, drink, and celebrate because there is no soul, no afterlife, no payment to be made for the enjoyment we experience, and no punishment for the pain we cause. Everything is material, a mixture of the four elements—earth, air, fire, and water. When we die nothing migrates anywhere—we are extinguished and that is that. The Cārvākins despised the *Vedas*, which they described as "the incoherent rhapsodies of knaves" (Radhakrishnan and Moore, 230). They rejected anything that could not be seen or experienced—the gods, fate, causality, karma, and the soul. They were so out-of-step with their culture that none of their original texts has been preserved and we know of their beliefs only when they are quoted to be attacked. One standard summary of their system describes them as holding the following beliefs:

> Others should not here postulate [the existence of] merit and demerit from happiness and misery. A person is happy or miserable through [the laws of] nature; there is no other cause.
>
> There is no world other than this; there is no heaven and no hell; the realm of Śiva and like religions are invented by stupid impostors of other schools of thought.
>
> The enjoyment of heaven lies in eating delicious food, keeping company of young women, using fine clothes, perfumes, garlands, sandal paste, etc.
>
> The pain of hell lies in the troubles that arise from enemies, weapons, diseases; while liberation (*mokṣa*) is death which is the cessation of life-breath.
>
> Chastity and other such ordinances are lain down by clever weaklings.
>
> (Radhakrishnan and Moore, 235)

It is easy to see why Cārvāka was never popular—its naturalism, hedonism, and disbelief in chastity and liberation would have outraged the *brāhmins*, alienated any devout believer in the *Vedas*, and terrified simple people committed to conventional morality.

Jainism

The Jains recognize a series of yogic heroes who have achieved the highest goal and now reside "in a supernal zone at the ceiling of the universe, beyond the reach of prayer" (Zimmer, 181). These *jina* (victors) are called *tīrthaṅkaras* (those who have crossed the stream) and are described as "transcendent, cleaned of temporality, omniscient, actionless, and absolutely at peace" (182). The twenty-fourth, and so far the last, of these was Vardhamāna Mahāvīra (599–527 B.C.), a contemporary of the Buddha. Mahāvīra (the name means "great hero") was born a *kṣatriya* and raised as a prince. He married and started a family, but after his parents died he became a Jain monk. After twelve years of self-denial, self-mortification, and rigid asceticism, he achieved the Jain version of enlightenment, and then spent the next forty-two years preaching and teaching. Unlike the Buddha, Mahāvīra made no original discovery, offered no new truth, and founded no order. He entered the Jain system, mastered it, reformed and rejuvenated it, and became its greatest saint.

Zimmer claims that Jainism "reflects the cosmology and anthropology of a much older, pre-Āryan upper class of northeastern India—being rooted in the same subsoil of archaic metaphysical speculation as Yoga, Sāṁkhya, and Buddhism, the other non-Vedic Indian systems" (Zimmer, 217). The Jains not only believe in reincarnation and karma but take these ideas to their logical extreme. They believe that inanimate as well as animate beings possess souls, trapped by their desires and actions in the dance of birth, suffering, and death. These souls are non-material, distinct, eternal, and originally pure. But they pick up karmic matter that results in and determines the quality of rebirths: "The soul, owing to its being with passion, assimilates matter which is fit to form *karmas*. This is bondage" (Radhakrishnan and Moore, 259).

According to the Jain, even good karma is bad because it attaches one to the world and guarantees rebirth. The goal is to escape from this cycle of birth and death, but the only way to do this is to get rid of all your karma, which is about as easy as getting rid of your shadow. Jains see life as a disaster—both for the person living it and for all the creatures damaged in the process. They attempt to minimize the harm they do and go to great lengths to put the doctrine of *ahiṁsā* (non-injury) into practice. Jains are vegetarians and some even refuse to eat in the dark for fear that some small living thing might have found its way into their food. Other Jains carry brooms and gently brush away insects in their path and on their person.

Unfortunately the practice of *ahiṁsā* only minimizes the quantity of bad karma one builds up. It does not lead to the absence of all karma, nor will it by itself result in the ultimate liberation, which the Jains call *kaivalya* (isolation). To achieve *kaivalya* a Jain must practice *ahiṁsā*, engage in further acts of self-denial and positive good works, and eliminate *all* desires. The soul of the saint who eliminates all desires and burns off the old karma ascends to the highest heaven, and there, without consciousness or desire, without thought but aware of everything, it floats in eternal and perfect indifference.

Buddhism

If Cārvāka thinkers took one extreme (absolute indulgence) and Jains the other (radical asceticism), the third heterodoxy, Buddhism, explicitly identified itself as a "middle way" between these two (and other) extremes. We can organize our discussion of Buddhism around what the Buddhists call the "Three Treasures": the Buddha, the *Dharma* (the teachings of the Buddha preserved in the *sūtras*), and the *Saṅgha* (the order of monks).

The Buddha

Siddhārtha Gautama (560–480 B.C.), the son of a powerful *kṣatriya* leader, was born to a life of comfort in Kapilavastu, a busy commercial city in northern India. In this place, where the religion and philosophy of the *brāhmins* had never taken firm hold, a multitude of different systems of thought flourished, and the forests were stocked with dropouts, unimpressed by the rituals and claims of the *brāhmins*, and dissatisfied with responsibility, conflict, and the struggle for worldly power. These wanderers abandoned their homes and possessions, begged for their food, and carried out a determined quest for *mokṣa*. There were materialists, determinists, fatalists, dualists, monists, atomists, skeptics, theists, and atheists. Ascetics devoted themselves to feats of concentration and meditation, often attaining states of blankness bordering on coma. Some, influenced by the belief that we are unfree because our pure and perfect spirit is attached to our gross, impure, corrupt, and polluted bodies, tried to break that attachment by self-abuse. They might remain in uncomfortable positions for hours, lie on beds of thorns, or go without food for weeks.

It was in this environment that the Buddha lived and taught. In the twenty-five hundred years since the event, so many legends about the birth and life of the Buddha have grown up that it is impossible to take any story at face value. In what follows, we do not stray far from the agreed upon naturalistic elements, and we ignore the fantastic details that now embellish the story of a human life that, without any supernatural elaboration, can serve as a solid foundation for the basic beliefs and practices of the Buddhists.

Though his early life was carefree and comfortable, Gautama became aware of suffering and misery—of sickness, old age, and death. He also knew of the wanderers and renouncers, and of their strenuous efforts to achieve liberation. At the age of twenty-nine, having fulfilled his duty to his father and his wife by producing a son, he departed to join these exotic individuals in the search for the solution to the riddle of existence.

The Buddha-to-be first tried contemplation with a teacher called Āḷāra-Kālāma, who was reputed to have attained a very high state of consciousness through meditation—a state in which "nothing existed for him." Upon mastering this method, he realized that "this teaching does not lead to dispassion, to the fading of desire, to cessation, to peace, to direct knowledge in meditation, to awakening, to release; it leads only to the Meditative Plane of Nothingness" (Carrithers, 30–31). Consequently, he found another teacher, Udakka-Rāmaputta, who had achieved an even higher state, "the attainment of neither conception nor non-conception." Again he quickly mastered this discipline and attained the state his new teacher promoted, but, as before, he saw that this was not what he sought.

It is important to pause here and ask what these two teachers were offering. Many of those who turned to austerity and to the practice of contemplation were following ancient techniques developed by the Upaniṣadic sages in their search for the Self. They believed that by stripping away all the noticeable features of experience, by restraining the modifications of the mind, they could arrive at a core of pure experience, the True Self, which was empty of qualities, simple, changeless, and eternal. Āḷāra-Kālāma and Udakka-Rāmaputta were operating in this tradition and had attained trance-like states of great calmness and nearly pure consciousness. But not even the highest state attained by strenuous meditation lasts forever, and so the Self, the "Imperishable," the unchanging eternal *Ātman*, was not, the Buddha realized, to be found by placing oneself in an altered state of consciousness, or by temporarily inhibiting the modifications of the mind.

Abandoning this form of meditation, Gautama turned to asceticism and extreme austerities. "What if I now set my teeth, press my tongue to my palate, and restrain, crush, and burn out my mind with my mind?" "What if I now practice trance without breathing?" But, he reports, "such painful acts did not overpower my mind." He also tried fasting until "the mark of my seat was like a camel's footprint through the little food." But he still failed to attain "superhuman, truly noble knowledge and insight" (Hamilton, 16–17). After six years of this, Gautama realized that what he was seeking could not be attained by this method either, and he disappointed his companions in self-deprivation by starting to eat.

After reviving his body and recovering his health, he renewed his determination and vowed to sit by himself in quiet meditation until enlightenment should come to him. He found the legendary Bodhi tree and began his final quest for liberation. He passed through a series of states of consciousness, recalled his former lives, and saw "beings passing away and being reborn, low and high, of good and bad color, in happy or miserable existences according to their karma" (Hamilton, 22). He also saw the moral power of the doctrines of karma and reincarnation. Those who live "evil lives in deed, word, or thought," those "of false views, who acquire karma through their false views, at the dissolution of the body after death are reborn in a state of misery and suffering in hell." Beings who lead good lives, on the other hand, "are reborn in a happy state in the world of heaven" (22). Finally, he learned the cause of suffering, the way that leads to its destruction, and he came to understand how desire and ignorance bind us to suffering and to the world.

After some hesitation (for who was likely to understand these hard-won truths?) Buddha, like Mahāvīra, spent the rest of his life trying to help others find the path he had discovered. One characteristic feature of this path is the use of a unique form of meditation. Previously Buddha had been engaging in what can be called "mental concentration," but what he practiced (and perhaps discovered) under the Bodhi tree was a form of meditation called "insight meditation." One who engages in insight meditation is not trying to escape into nothingness or ecstatic states of consciousness. The goal is simply to become very aware of the aspects of experience in the here and now. The keys are mindfulness, attention, and awareness. In *The Foundations of Mindfulness Sūtra,* where this form of meditation is explained, the Buddha gives the following instructions:

> Here Bhikkhus [monks], a bhikkhu having gone to the forest, to the foot of a tree or to some empty place, sits down, with his legs crossed, keeps his body straight and his mindfulness alert.
>
> Ever mindful he breathes in, and ever mindful he breathes out. Breathing in a long breath, he knows "I am breathing in a long breath"; breathing out a long breath, he knows "I am breathing out a long breath". . . .
>
> And further, Bhikkhus, a bhikkhu knows when he is going, "I am going". He knows when he is standing, "I am standing". He knows when he is sitting, "I am sitting". He knows when he is lying down, "I am lying down". Or he knows just how his body is disposed.
>
> And further, Bhikkhus, a bhikkhu applies full attention either in going forward or back; in looking straight on or looking away; in bending or in stretching; in wearing robes or carrying the bowl; in eating, drinking, chewing or savouring; in attending to the calls of nature; in walking, in standing, in sitting; in falling asleep, in waking; in speaking or in keeping silence. In all these he applies full attention. (Rahula, 110–11)

Michael Carrithers suggests that when exhaustive attempts to find the Self by the traditional forms of mental concentration failed, the Buddha might have reasoned that "if it was impossible to find an enduring entity, a Self with a capital 'S', through and behind these mutable experiences, it was possible at least to have an insight into the nature of these evanescent psychophysical processes themselves" (Carrithers, 50). What Buddha discovered when he trained his sharpened and controlled mind on these evanescent mental processes constitutes the *Dharma*.

The Dharma

Of the many meanings of the word *dharma*, the one that concerns us now makes reference to the teachings the Buddha presented in his sermons and in discussions with his followers. While the recorded (and invented) pronouncements of the Buddha were many, the fundamental ideas of the *Dharma* are contained in the Four Noble Truths, the Three Marks of Existence, and the Doctrine of Causality.

No sect or person who denies the Four Noble Truths could fairly be called Buddhist. They are the message of the first talk the Buddha gave after his enlightenment, and they constitute the heart of Buddhism.

The first of the four is called the "Truth of Suffering" and points to the existence and the ubiquity of suffering. "Birth is suffering; decay is suffering; illness is suffering; death is suffering; presence of objects we hate is suffering; separation from objects we love is suffering; not to obtain what we desire is suffering" (Hamilton, 29). The word *duḥkha* (Pali: *dukkha*) is frequently translated as "suffering," but a long list of alternative translations have been suggested, including "evil," "unsatisfactoriness," "imperfection," "impermanence," "inadequacy," "incompleteness," "uncontrollability," "insubstantiality," "pain," "sorrow," "misery," and "uneasiness" (see Hiriyanna, 75; Kalupahana [2], 37; and Carrithers, 57).

But 'evil' is too vague and moralistic a word to be a good choice, and 'pain' is too limited, since its primary use is to refer to physical pain. The pain one feels when sitting in the Lotus position may be seen as merely another phenomenon—it need not cause us to suffer mentally. Both 'unsatisfactoriness' and 'imperfection' place the emphasis on the thing judged and not on the experiencing subject: The suffering the Buddha is interested in occurs not because things are imperfect, but because we are imperfect. 'Sorrow' is too specific, 'misery' too graphic and intense, and 'uneasiness' too mild. Inadequacy, incompleteness, and uncontrollability are things *we* complain about, but they need give rise to no distress. 'Impermanence' and 'insubstantiality' are needed in the translation of other Buddhist terms. So we will use 'suffering', but we should remember that 'suffering' is only an English word—no more and no less—and that interpretation is required no matter what words are used.

The second of the four truths is "The Noble Truth concerning the Origin of Suffering." Suffering "originates in that craving which causes the renewal of becomings, is accompanied by sensual delight, and seeks satisfaction now here, now there" (Hamilton, 29). *Taṇhā*, the word just rendered as "craving," literally means "thirst," and is frequently translated as "desire."

It is too simple to say that desire or craving is *the* cause of suffering. Craving is certainly *a* cause of suffering, but so are many other things—anger, fear, war, hunger, and boxing. When the word 'desire' (which is milder than 'craving') is used to render the word *taṇhā*, the second noble truth becomes more problematic. Some desires (real cravings) are intense and unabated, but others, like a casual desire for a drink of water, are hard to see as causing suffering.

The claim that desire is the cause of suffering is problematic in another way. No single thing can be said to be *the* cause of any other single thing—reality is the causal flow in which elements are connected in subtle and multifarious ways. Even ignorance, which Buddha sometimes placed at the head of his list of causes of suffering, is caused by other things. Even so, *taṇhā*, (craving, desire, greed) is often found in causal sequences leading to suffering. Desires are definitely implicated.

The third noble truth offers the remedy for the disease of suffering brought about by desire. It is "The Noble Truth concerning the Cessation of Suffering." If desire helps to bring about (causes) suffering, then suffering can be reduced when we reduce desire. According to the Buddha, we can eliminate our suffering by the "cessation without remainder of this very craving; the laying aside of, the giving up, the being free from, the harboring no longer of, this craving" (Hamilton, 29).

Some Buddhists say that this very thing, the cessation of craving and the resultant freedom from suffering, is the ultimate goal. They even call it "*nirvāṇa*," which allows them to say that a person can achieve *nirvāṇa* while still living in the world. David Kalupahana says that Buddha and the earliest Buddhists took *nirvāṇa* to be the elimination of *taṅhā*, but he observes that "the idea that nirvana represents a transcendental reality beyond any form of conceptualization or logical thinking has dominated Buddhist thought since the death of the Buddha" (Kalupahana [2], 82).

Some Buddhists declare *nirvāṇa* to be indescribable, and others describe it as everything from complete extinction to some extraordinary state of consciousness in this life or the next. But attainment of the end of suffering is the common element in all these characterizations of the ultimate goal. The method of eliminating suffering by eliminating desire is what this third noble truth offers.

Finally, there is the "The Noble Truth concerning the Path which leads to the Cessation of Suffering." This is not a series of steps so much as a series of reminders of what one must do if one wishes to eliminate suffering by eliminating desire. The reminders are included together as the "Noble Eightfold Path": right understanding (views), right thought (intent), right speech, right action, right livelihood, right effort, right mindfulness, right concentration.

Right understanding refers to the understanding and acceptance of the Four Noble Truths themselves, the doctrines of karma and reincarnation, and other elements of the *Dharma. Right thought* has to do with our intentions, and brings us close to moral territory. But right thought can be understood by the amoralist to refer to the thoughts and motives one should have if one wants to avoid unpleasant results, such as an unhappy and cramped consciousness, angry friends, or rebirth as a beagle.

The next three steps are explicitly said to deal with "moral conduct," but even here it is not obvious that 'right action', for example, means the same as "morally right action." *Right action*, which includes refraining from harming other living creatures, from stealing, and from "sexual misconduct," might simply be the right action to take if one's goal is to win freedom from suffering. *Right speech* includes most of what we would expect: abstention from lying, slandering, and divisive speech, from "harsh, rude, impolite, malicious and abusive language, and from idle, useless and foolish babble and gossip" (Rahula, 47). *Right livelihood* means taking up an occupation that does not require you to hurt others. The call for *right effort* is an expression of the insight that hard and appropriate work brings results. *Right mindfulness* and *right concentration* both have to do with paying attention, and while they can be traced to the pre-Buddhist yogic tradition, they must be understood in terms of what has been said above about "insight meditation."

The second aspect of the *Dharma* is a trio of notions Buddhists call "The Three Characteristics of Existence." They say that "conditioned things" (that is, all things) share these three characteristics: impermanence (*anitya*), not-self (*anātman*), and suffering (*duḥkha*).

To say that things are impermanent is to say that nothing is free from change. It is to take the position of Buddha's Greek contemporary Heraclitus, who immortalized his belief in the fluidity of reality by saying that no one can step into the same river twice. Many have felt that a world in which nothing is stable is unacceptable, or at least distressing. It was unacceptable to the Upanisadic seers who were looking for the eternal unchanging *Ātman*, and striving to apprehend the Imperishable. It was unacceptable to Parmenides, the rival of Heraclitus who believed change is an illusion, and to Plato who, unhappy with flux, postulated changeless Forms.

Of all the things that distinguish Buddhism from orthodox Hinduism, the doctrine of *anātman*—the non-existence of the self—may be the most important. The Vedic priests and the common people believed in the immortality of the soul, and the priests promoted morality by constructing graphic descriptions of sinners suffering in hell. The Upaniṣadic *ṛṣis*, who rejected much of Vedic thought, still believed that the *Ātman* as well as individual souls are all "real," whether they are different from Brahman. The Jains believed in a multitude of originally pure selves (or *jīvas*) that are stained by the karma produced by action. Only the Buddha rejected all views of the self and insisted that liberation is not liberation *of* the self, but liberation *from* the idea of a self.

According to the Buddha, the truth of *anātman* is gained by "insight meditation." When we look carefully at what transpires in our mental life, we simply fail to find any simple, abiding, unchanging soul, and no matter how long we look, no matter how deep our trance, no matter how great our austerity, we never will. What we find instead is a "stream of consciousness" containing an assortment of variously related mental contents: feelings, perceptions, and impulses.

John Locke claims that we "perceive our own existence so plainly and clearly that it neither needs nor is capable of any proof"; David Hume asserts, however, that we have no such perception, and hence no such idea. In *A Treatise of Human Nature* he offers an argument that mirrors one the Buddha gave to establish that no experience, no matter how Cosmic, could be an experience of an eternal, unchanging self.

> If any impression gives rise to the idea of self, that impression must continue invariably the same, thro' the whole course of our lives; since self is suppos'd to exist after that manner. But there is no impression constant and invariable. Pain and pleasure, grief and joy, passions and sensations succeed each other, and never all exist at the same time. It cannot, therefore, be from any of these impressions, or from any other, that the idea of self is deriv'd; and consequently there is no such idea. (Hume [1], 251–52)

In his search for the self Hume probably did not look as deep or as long as the Buddha did, but he found the same lack.

> For my part, when I enter most intimately into what I call *myself*, I always stumble on some particular perception or other, of heat or cold, light or shade, love or hatred, pain or pleasure. I never can catch *myself* at any time without a perception, and never can observe anything but the perception. (Hume [1], 252)

As a result of this argument and observation Hume ventured his famous suggestion that a person is "nothing but a bundle or collection of different perceptions, which succeed each other with an inconceivable rapidity, and are in a perpetual flux and movement" (252).

To say that things are *duḥkha* is to repeat the first of the Four Noble Truths, but it is worth bringing it up again now that we have had a chance to think about *anātman*. From the point of view of a single individual, it may seem that impermanence results in suffering only when one harbors a desire for permanence. If we just accept impermanence, we might think, we can end (at least some) suffering.

But when we think in this way we have failed to grasp the essence of *anātman*. If there is no self, then there is no escape from suffering no matter how much happiness "we" feel and no matter how reconciled "we" are to impermanence. The suffering of others is our own, or better, as long as there is suffering anywhere, existence must still be characterized as suffering. It is this realization that leads to, and helps shape, the Buddhist concept of compassion, which results in the "vow of the *bodhisattva*" (see below).

Causality has been called the "central philosophy of Buddhism," but the Buddha's remarks about causality are some of the most baffling he is reported to have made. The name the Buddhists use for causality is *pratītya-samutpāda*, which is sometimes translated as "conditioned origination." and sometimes as "dependent origination." The idea is found in the following formula:

> When this is present, that comes to be; from the arising of this, that arises.
> When this is absent, that does not come to be; on the cessation of this, that ceases.
>
> (Kalupahana [1], 90)

Causality was an important topic in Buddha's time. Buddhists describe their account as a middle way between those who deny causality altogether and those who hold determinism or even fatalism. Both fatalism and a complete lack of causality can lead to the feeling that we can accomplish nothing and that our efforts are useless. Among other things, the Buddha wished to overcome these paralyzing philosophies.

Early Buddhist texts characterize causality as a twelve-stage sequence, often represented as a wheel.

> From ignorance come the aggregates [elements of the individual]; from the aggregates consciousness; from consciousness name-and-form [mind and body]; from mind and body, the six organs of sense [the five senses and mind, or the inner sense]; from the organs of sense contact; from contact feeling; from feeling craving; from craving clinging to existence; from clinging to existence the desire of becoming; from the desire of becoming rebirth; from rebirth old age and death, grief, lamentation, pain, sorrow, and despair. Such is the origin of the whole mass of suffering. (Hamilton, 23–24)

Ignorance (*avidyā*) is the beginning of the entire chain, and the first step on the way to sorrow and despair. This may be seen even by someone not versed in Buddhism. It is also easy to see how contact leads to feeling, feeling to craving, and craving to clinging, and how rebirth brings old age and death. On the other hand, it is harder to comprehend how the elements of the person arise from ignorance. Details aside, the message of the teaching of causality is the interrelatedness of things in a vast causal network, with special attention to the connection between desire and suffering.

The Buddha accepted the ideas of karma and reincarnation, even though they appear at odds with the doctrine that there is no self. The Buddha did not want to get bogged down in philosophical discussions about the ramifications of his teachings. Once when he was asked if there was a self, he gave no answer at all, and later explained that any answer would only have led the questioner into greater confusion.

In one *sūtra*, the Buddha was asked if the world is eternal or not, if the soul is the same as the body, and if a Buddha exists after death. He replied that he never promised to answer these questions, and that a person who insists on answers is like a man who, shot by a poison arrow, will not consent to have it removed until he has been given detailed information about the arrow, the physician, and his assailant. That person would die, said the Buddha, without knowing all this (Hamilton, 54–55). Elsewhere, he described each of a number of philosophical opinions and its denial as "a jungle, a wilderness, a puppet-show, a writhing, and a fetter" that is "coupled with misery, ruin, despair, and agony" (Radhakrishnan and Moore, 289–90). Many Buddhists were unable to follow their master here and they took definite philosophical positions on portions of the *Dharma*, to which, as Buddhist *philosophers*, they had become attached.

Buddhists may have become attached to doctrines and to the rules of their order, but the pragmatic and flexible attitude of the Buddha is made clear by his use of the metaphor of the raft. A wise man who uses a raft to cross a river will discard that raft, rather than, in gratitude for its having got him across, carry it around for the rest of his days. The paradox here is that the belief that there *is* another shore is part of the *Dharma*, the raft, that the enlightened person will discard. This means that for one who has arrived, there *is* no other shore, no raft, no crossing, no arrival—no distinction between "*saṃsāra* and *nirvāṇa*." Buddhists through the centuries have been left to make of this what they can.

The Saṅgha

After his enlightenment, the Buddha taught anyone who would listen and sent out disciples to spread the *Dharma*. Soon after his death in 480 B.C., some five hundred of his followers met to recall his teachings and to agree on the doctrines and rules of their movement. By the time this First Council convened, two of the Buddha's strongest disciples had died, and no one else was considered worthy to lead the group. The Buddha had urged his followers to let the *Dharma* be their guide, so the disciples met to preserve that *Dharma*.

The number of Buddhists grew rapidly, but so did the variety of interpretations of the Buddha's teachings. A hundred years after his death, conflicts between conservatives and liberals led to a second council. The liberals wanted to eat after noon, depart from the established dress code, and accept offerings of gold as well as food. All these ideas were rejected, but before fifty years had passed a third council was called at which the liberals, now in the majority, relaxed some rules and modified some teachings.

Alexander the Great invaded India in 327 B.C., but when his army refused to advance, he returned to Babylon, where he died in 323. Chandragupta then drove Alexander's generals out of India and established his own empire. His son Bindusāra solidified his militaristic police state, and Bindusāra's son, Ashoka, who inherited the throne in 268, began by following the ways of his father and grandfather. Several years after taking the throne, Ashoka began to regret the violence and cruelty of his regime. He gave up conquest and promoted Buddhist ideas of non-injury, compassion, and tolerance. Many of his edicts, including ones expressing regret for the grief caused by his military campaigns, were carved in stone; and he sent missionaries to spread the *Dharma* to other lands.

Ashoka convened another council around 250 B.C. but the division was not healed. Meanwhile, a conservative form of Buddhism called Theravāda (the way of the elders) held out against the more liberal forms. Theravādins believed that the Buddha was a wise human who managed, by hard work and discipline, to reach enlightenment. They also believed that no one alive at their time was capable of reaching that level of attainment, and that only a few who were willing to abandon the world and undertake a rigorous program of training could become *arhats*—perfected but not perfect beings.

The need to keep the *Dharma* in focus led to distillations of its essence, commentaries, elaborations, and debates. Some of the conflicts arising from these reflections are recorded in the *Abhidharma* writings. *Abhidharma* means "about or above the dharma," and it covers questions of metaphysics and epistemology, that is, questions about the nature of reality and of knowledge. If, for example, the doctrine of impermanence is true, and reality is merely a stream of isolated and momentary elements, we must (or at least we *may*) ask about the nature of these elements, their connections with each other, and their relation to our experience of a world of objects and our belief in a self.

One group of Buddhist philosophers (the Sarvāstivādins) taught that the elements themselves were real, and that our perception of them was direct in the sense that nothing comes between us and them in the way that light mediates between a tree and a perception of a tree. Others held that there must be a substance in which the elements inhere. But it was the liberal Mahāsāṅghikas who began the process that transformed Buddhism from a monastic movement into a world religion. They accepted beliefs from popular religion, and they added new texts to the reported teachings of the Buddha. They encouraged belief in gods, heavens, hells, prayers, devotion, grace, and other trappings and comforts of religion. Thus, they introduced the benefits of meditation and self-discipline to many who would have been uninterested in strenuous training or the dry debates of the scholars. These liberals described their opponents as followers of the lesser vehicle, the Hinayāna, and they accused them of selfishly emphasizing individual salvation. They described themselves as followers of the greater vehicle, the Mahāyāna, the goal of which is salvation for all sentient beings.

We find no evidence of the Mahāyāna movement until around A.D. 100, but soon after that, this new form of Buddhism began to dominate India and to spread into China, Korea, and Japan. Unlike the conservative way of the Elders (Theravāda Buddhism), the Mahāyāna was for everyone. In contrast to the elders, who recommended retreat from the world and admitted that Buddhism was not for everyone, the advocates of the Mahāyāna insisted that "everyone has the Buddha-nature," by which they meant that each and every person can, in this life, reach the identical state of enlightenment attained by the Buddha. The *arhat* ideal of the elders was replaced by the *bodhisattva* ideal of the Mahāyāna. A *bodhisattva* is a being who has gained enlightenment, but has forgone *nirvāṇa* in order to assist in the liberation of other sentient beings. "However numerous sentient beings are," says the *bodhisattva*, "I vow to save them all."

This message of boundless love and universal compassion was expressed in writings said to be records of discourses of the Buddha; but the ideas found in these works were often highly critical of the teachings found in the collections of *sūtras* of the more conservative tradition. In the *Vimalakīrti Nirdeśa Sūtra*, for example, Vimalakīrti is a *bodhisattva* who lives the life of a wealthy merchant, a full life, utterly different from the withdrawn asceticism of the *arhats*. In this fanciful *sūtra*, the disciples of the Buddha all declare themselves unworthy to engage this Mahāyāna hero in conversation because they have all been bested by him in the past. Finally, the *bodhisattva* Mañjuśrī agrees to call on him, and even this "Bodhisattva of Supreme Wisdom" is awed by the depth of Vimalakīrti's understanding.

The Mahāyāna movement adopted many beliefs of popular religion to elaborate the concept of the Buddha. He was promoted from a human to a superhuman being, and ultimately to a "Cosmic Principle." As the Mahāyāna movement developed, schools of thought formed around some of the new *sūtras*, and a number of superhuman god-like *bodhisattvas* were recognized to be working constantly to aid humans in their spiritual quest.

One Mahāyāna tradition emphasizes "wisdom," the other stresses meditation and altered states of consciousness. The Wisdom tradition produced the *Prajñāpāramitā* literature, a group of Mahāyāna *sūtras* and *śāstras* (secular writings) written to express the teaching of *śūnyatā* or Emptiness. These include the *Diamond Sūtra* and the *Lotus Sūtra*, as well as the secular writings of Nāgārjuna and Kumārajīva.

The meditative orientation of the Trance school is expressed in the *Laṅkāvatāra Sūtra*. It is noteworthy that Bodhidharma, the first patriarch of Chan (Zen) Buddhism, relied on the *Laṅkāvatāra Sūtra*, and Hui Neng, the sixth, claimed to have been enlightened upon hearing a verse of the *Diamond Sūtra*, a brief distillation of the *Prajñāpāramitā* philosophy of emptiness. *Prajñā* means "wisdom," and *prajñāpāramitā* is the wisdom that takes one to the opposite shore. When one reaches the opposite shore, one discovers the emptiness of all names and distinctions, which includes the emptiness of the distinction between *saṃsāra* (this shore) and *nirvāṇa* (the other shore). This paradoxical insight is driven home again and again in the *Diamond Sūtra*, where the Buddha teaches that Buddhas, atoms, goodness, persons, and enlightenment are not really Buddhas, atoms, goodness, persons, and enlightenment, but only called such "As to any Truth-declaring system, Truth is undeclarable; so "an enunciation of Truth" is just the name given to it" (Price and Wong, 60). And, "Subhuti, though we speak of "goodness" the Tathagata [the Buddha] declares that there is no goodness; such is merely a name" (62).

The *Lotus Sūtra* contains a striking condemnation of the *arhat*-ideal, which is said to be suitable only for the mentally and spiritually slow, a doctrine taught by the Buddha to those who were not ready for the complete truth, which is that the Buddha is an infinite, superhuman, and transcendent being. True salvation is the attainment of "Buddhahood," which is available to all living beings.

In the *Pure Land Sūtra*, Amitābha (Amida), a powerful *bodhisattva*, vowed to assist those seeking enlightenment, if only they request it. Those who, at the moment of death, say his name will be delivered to his Western Paradise (the Pure Land) to abide in inconceivable luxury until the world has improved to such a degree that one more rebirth will yield *nirvāṇa*.

If the Hindu identification of *Ātman* and Brahman is a substantialist monism (something exists and it is one), early Buddhism rejected the monism for pluralism and rejected the substantialism for phenomenalism. Later forms of Mahāyāna rejected both substantialism and pluralism. The Consciousness-Only School taught that everything is mind, and the Mādhyamika rejected *all* views, embracing "emptiness" and the denial of all dualities. The Mādhyamika, literally "middle way," survived in China almost as long as Buddhism, and the movement is alive today in the major forms of Tibetan Buddhism.

In addition to the demanding philosophies of the Consciousness-Only School and the Mādhyamika, there flourished a warm and approachable religious tradition that offered the help of individual *bodhisattvas.* Maitreya is the Buddha to come, the successor to Siddhārtha Gautama. Avalokiteśvara, a synthesis of some of the gods of the Hindus, protects people against danger and grants requests and prayers. Mañjuśrī is the *bodhisattva* of wisdom and learning.

By the end of Ashoka's reign, Buddhism had begun to lose its secular and psychological slant and was taking on many of the features of popular religions. Both Mahāyāna Buddhism and Theravāda Buddhism made their way to China in the first century A.D., but the Theravādins were unable to adapt to Chinese needs. In a few hundred years Buddhism had disappeared from India, but Mahāyāna Buddhism dominated China throughout the Tang Dynasty (A.D. 618–907).

Persuasive Definitions

The caste system regulated life in a way that was advantageous to those lucky enough to be born *brāhmins. Brāhmins* alone were allowed to perform religious ceremonies and to study the "sacred knowledge" of the *Vedas.* But a story that turns up in the middle of the *Chāndogya Upaniṣad* suggests that not all *brāhmins* were content with this system. Satyakāma Jābāla was a young boy with a *śūdra* mother who admitted to him that she had no idea who, or of what caste, his father was. Yet the boy wanted to study the "sacred knowledge," and so his determined mother took him to a *brāhmin* named Hāridrumatra, where he asked the old man to take him as his student. The first question the *brāhmin* asked was "Of what family are you?" Satyakāma's reply was truthful:

> I do not know this, Sir, of what family I am. I asked my mother. She answered me: "In my youth, when I went about a great deal serving as a

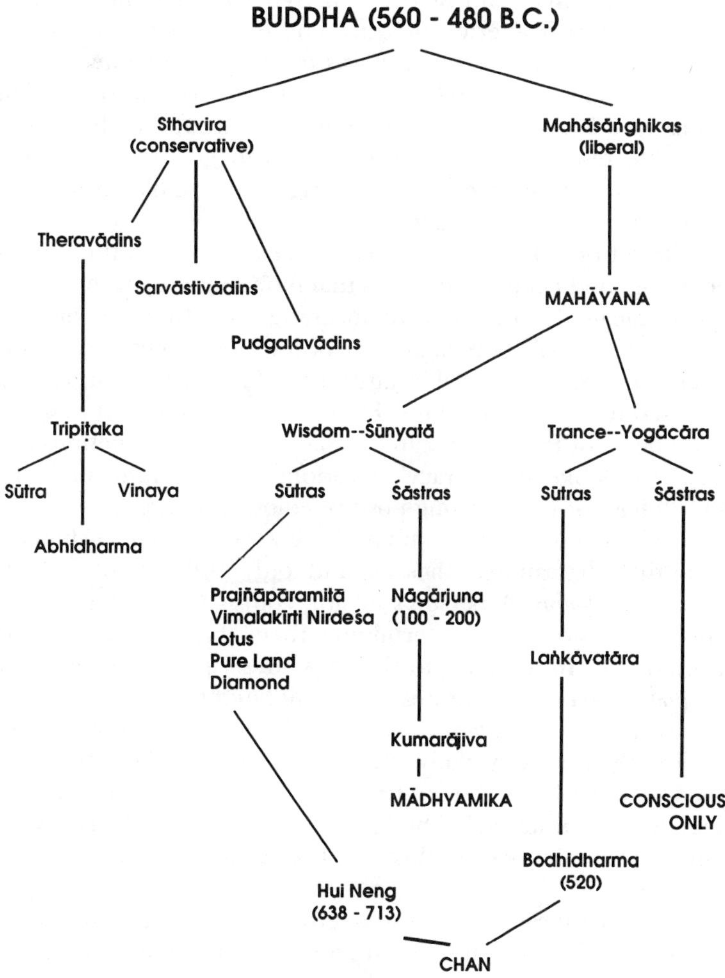

BUDDHA (560 - 480 B.C.)

Sthavira
(conservative)

Mahāsāṅghikas
(liberal)

Theravādins

Sarvāstivādins

Pudgalavādins

MAHĀYĀNA

Tripiṭaka

Sūtra

Vinaya

Abhidharma

Wisdom--Śūnyatā

Sūtras

Śāstras

Trance--Yogācāra

Sūtras

Śāstras

Prajñāpāramitā
Vimalakīrti Nirdeśa
Lotus
Pure Land
Diamond

Nāgārjuna
(100 - 200)

Laṅkāvatāra

Kumarājiva

MĀDHYAMIKA

CONSCIOUSNESS
ONLY

Bodhidharma
(520)

Hui Neng
(638 - 713)

CHAN

Figure 5-1

> maid, I got you. So I do not know this, of what family you are. However, I am Jābāla by name; you are Satyakāma by name." So I am Satyakāma Jābāla, Sir. (Radhakrishnan and Moore, 66)

This reply impressed Hāridrumatra, who answered the boy in a surprising way. A non-*brāhmin*, he said, "would not be able to explain thus. . . . I will receive you as a pupil. You have not deviated from the truth" (Radhakrishnan and Moore, 66). What is happening here is that Hāridrumatra is altering the meaning of the word '*brāhmin*' to suit his purpose, which in this case was to accept the young man as his student. "I only accept *brāhmins,* I want to accept this young man, so he must be a *brāhmin.* If he wasn't born a *brāhmin,* then birth is an inappropriate test to use in determining who gets to be called a *brāhmin.*" This shift of meaning challenges the whole caste-based system of privilege and servitude.

C. L. Stevenson, the author of *Ethics and Language* and the leading proponent of "non-cognitivism," says that moral judgments have both descriptive meaning and emotive meaning, but that the emotive meaning is "primary." The major function of moral judgments is to "create an influence," or to "alter attitudes." This emotive function is not restricted to moral judgments. Even in what look like straightforward statements of fact, words can be used to influence emotions and attitudes. Words like 'democracy', 'freedom', 'hero', 'humanity', and '*brāhmin*' all have or had a strong positive emotive charge.

The original descriptive meaning of the word '*brāhmin*' included a condition that determined that all and only children of *brāhmin* parents were *brāhmins.* A person's wealth, courage, and truthfulness were no more relevant to determining their "brahminhood" than their sandal size. In addition to this clear descriptive meaning, the word '*brāhmin*' carried strong positive connotations (at least for *brāhmins*). It was good to be a *brāhmin* because *brāhmins* were the highest, the best, and the most spiritually advanced of all castes. Hāridrumatra preserved that positive connotation, but changed the descriptive meaning. A *brāhmin* was still "the best," but birth was rejected as the criterion for brāhminhood. In this case it seems to have been replaced by truthfulness.

No single person can accomplish a reform like this because no one person can alter the language. But if enough people talk this way for long enough, the result may be a change in the way all people talk, and perhaps also in the way they feel and act. The change envisaged here involves two sub-changes: (1) no worthless and lying son of a *brāhmin* would get praised for being born of his mother, and (2) people who conform to a certain rather high code of conduct, or who meet a certain standard of behavior, get praised for their accomplishments and not condemned because of the facts of their birth.

A persuasive definition, says Stevenson, "is one which gives a new conceptual meaning to a familiar word without substantially changing its emotive meaning, and which is used with the conscious or unconscious purpose of changing, by this means, the direction of people's interests" (Stevenson [2], 32). One of Stevenson's favorite examples is the word 'freedom'. Suppose you love freedom and understand it as "being able to do what you want, as long as you don't hurt anyone." Now suppose I want you to accept some restraints, perhaps in the form of laws. One thing I might try to do is to get you to accept the idea that "true freedom is obedience to the laws." If I am successful, then the positive feelings you have about freedom might be transferred to the laws and to your obedience to them. If this is done slowly and subtly enough, it might work, and it is probably more effective than a direct approach. I cannot come up to you and say "I know you love freedom, but you see I've written these laws to take some of it away and I hope you will love my laws as much as you loved the freedom they are designed to restrict."

Buddhists enthusiastically supported Hāridrumatra in his attempt to redefine '*brahmin*' (or "brahman," as it is spelled in this translation of verse 136 of the *Sutta Nipāta*):

> No brahman is such by birth.
> No outcaste is such by birth.
> An outcaste is such by his deeds.
> A brahman is such by his deeds.
>
> (De Bary, Basham, et al., 140)

The same move is made repeatedly in the *Dhammapada*, a brief work from the Theravāda tradition that is said to contain the essence of Buddhist ethics.

> Not by matted hair, not by lineage, nor by caste does one become a *brāhmin*. He is a *brāhmin* in whom there are truth and righteousness. He is blessed. (Radhakrishnan and Moore, 323)
>
> Him I call a *brāhmin* who is free from anger, who is careful of religious duties, observes the moral rules, pure, controlled, and wears his last body. (Radhakrishnan and Moore, 323)
>
> Him I call a *brāhmin* who utters true speech, free from harshness, clearly understood, by which no one is offended. (Radhakrishnan and Moore, 324)
>
> Him I call a *brāhmin* who does not take, here in the world, what is not given him, be it long or short, small or large, good or bad. (Radhakrishnan and Moore, 324)

MORE PERSUASIVE DEFINITIONS

You shall not commit adultery. (Exodus 20:14)

If a man commits adultery with his neighbor's wife, both adulterer and adulteress shall be put to death. (Leviticus 20:10)

"You have learned that they were told, 'Do not commit adultery.' But what I tell you is this: If a man looks on a woman with a lustful eye, he has already committed adultery with her in his heart." . . . "They were told, 'A man who divorces his wife must give her a note of dismissal.' But what I tell you is this: If a man divorces his wife for any cause other than unchastity he involves her in adultery; and anyone who marries a divorced woman commits adultery." (Matthew 5:27–32)

C. L. Stevenson uses the following example from Aldous Huxley's *Eyeless in Gaza* as an amusing commentary on the use of persuasive definitions:

But if you want to be free, you've got to be a prisoner. It's the condition of freedom—true freedom.

"True freedom!" Anthony repeated in the parody of a clerical voice. "I always love that kind of argument. The contrary of a thing isn't the contrary; oh, dear me, no! It's the thing itself, but as it *truly* is. Ask any die-hard what conservatism is; he'll tell you it's *true* socialism. And the brewer's trade papers: they're full of articles about the beauty of true temperance. Ordinary temperance is just gross refusal to drink; but true temperance, *true* temperance is something much more refined. True temperance is a bottle of claret with each meal and three double whiskies after dinner. . . .

"What's in a name?" Anthony went on. "The answer is, practically everything, if the name's a good one. Freedom's a marvellous name. That's why you're so anxious to make use of it. You think that, if you call imprisonment true freedom, people will be attracted to the prison. And the worst of it is you're quite right." (Stevenson [3], 214–15)

Moralism and Indian Thought

As we see in Chapter 4, Sumerians express their moralism in the *me*—"universal" laws that Enlil willed and then was banished to the netherworld for disobeying. The Egyptian concept of *ma'at* (justice or true order), with its connotations of levelness, evenness, straightness, and correctness, is a sign that Egyptians believed in an objective standard of behavior. The order of nature contains orders for humans—things we must do, ways we must be.

We find similar ideas expressed in the most ancient writings of India. Vedic poets sing of an eternal cosmic order behind the changes in nature. They call this "cosmic law" *ṛta* (literally "the course of things"). In obedience to *ṛta* the seasons follow each other and the rivers run. At first even the gods were subject to these cosmic laws, but later the laws were attributed to the will of the gods. Kalupahana refers to *ṛta* as a "moral order," and adds that "the consciousness of right and wrong issuing out of a belief in the prevalence of a moral order is clearly expressed in the hymns addressed to Varuṇa" (Kalupahana [1], 4).

Violations of this cosmic morality are not only wrong and sinful, they produce evil consequences for the sinner. The first verse of the *Dhammapada* says that "if a man speaks or acts with an evil thought, sorrow follows him (as a consequence) even as the wheel follows the foot of the drawer (i.e., the ox which draws the cart)." The second verse says that if he "speaks or acts with a pure thought, happiness follows him (in consequence) like a shadow that never leaves him" (Radhakrishnan and Moore, 292).

The usual interpretation of *karma* is that good will be returned for good, and bad for bad, that sinners will suffer and virtue will be rewarded. But karma need not be given a moralist twist. One can interpret karma, with the Jains, as a simple case of similar causes producing similar effects.

Even though the law of karma *can* receive an amoralist interpretation, it is more frequently presented in the language of moralism. According to the *Chāndogya Upaniṣad*, those who "are of stinking conduct here" will "enter a stinking womb, either the womb of a dog, or the womb of a swine, or the womb of an outcast (*caṇḍāla*)" (Radhakrishnan and Moore, 67). Here 'stinking' clearly means "morally stinking," and that is just a fancy way of saying "objectively wrong from the moral point of view." Contrary to what the Cārvākins claimed, "chastity and other such ordinances" are not laid down by mere persons, but are demanded by an independent, objective, and authoritative source of moral requirements.

The idea that immoral behavior will be paid for in this or the next life is a useful conception, but it must be accompanied by a clear statement of the moral law so that we may know what specifically is required of us. *The Laws of Manu* is a collection of laws, social rules, and behavioral guidelines produced around 300 B.C. and attributed to a legendary Sage, Manu. In *The Laws of Manu* the rules of the caste system are elaborated, four stages of life (student, householder, hermit, and ascetic) are prescribed for the top three castes, and the *Vedas* are certified as the sacred foundation and fountain of law and morality.

The conservative, paternalistic thrust of the laws is highlighted by Manu's attitude toward women. He says that when they are honored "and adorned" the gods are pleased, but they must be kept under the control of a responsible male.

> By a girl, by a young woman, or even by an aged one, nothing must be done independently, even in her own house. In childhood a female must be subject to her father, in youth to her husband, when her lord is dead to her sons; a woman must never be independent. (Radhakrishnan and Moore, 190–91).
>
> Though destitute of virtue, or seeking pleasure (elsewhere), or devoid of good qualities, (yet) a husband must be constantly worshipped as a god by a faithful wife. (Radhakrishnan and Moore, 191)

Manu classifies sins and crimes, and he promises that no evil will go unpunished.

> Coveting the property of others, thinking in one's heart of what is undesirable, and adherence to false (doctrines), are the three kinds of (sinful) mental action.
>
> Abusing (others, speaking) untruth, detracting from the merits of all men, and talking idly, shall be the four kinds of (evil) verbal action.
>
> Taking what has not been given, injuring (creatures) without the sanction of the law, and holding criminal intercourse with another man's wife, are declared to be the three kinds of (wicked) bodily action.
>
> In consequence of (many) sinful acts committed with his body, a man becomes (in the next birth) something inanimate, in consequence (of sins) committed by speech, a bird, or a beast, and in consequence of mental (sins he is reborn in) a low caste.
>
> (Radhakrishnan and Moore, 173)

Buddhists did not have the *Vedas* to appeal to, and they were not about to appeal to the wisdom of legendary *brāhmins* like Manu. Yet they, too, needed a social morality for the world in which they found themselves, and so it is not surprising to find in the *Dhammapada* many of the same requirements mandated by Manu. The *Dhammapada* tells us to be earnest, serene, unconcerned with pleasure, and to put away lust, anger, impurity, and desire. It makes it clear what sorts of things count as good and evil, and that we are supposed to do good and to avoid evil, but it does not offer a ground or a foundation for the moral order. The reasons given for being moral are always based on self-interest. Verse after verse warns that evil deeds will bear bitter fruit. Moralistic notions of "good" and "evil" abound, but philosophical reflection on morality is absent. The Buddha claimed no divine source for his advice and his rules, and, as we have seen, we can give consistent amoralist interpretations of karma and enlightenment. Even if the average Buddhist would not feel comfortable with such a lean story, a mature understanding of Buddhism is quite compatible with amoralism. Buddhist teachers probably believed that morality was helpful to many people, but that, in the words of the *Diamond Sūtra*, 'goodness' is just a name.

6

Moralism and Amoralism in China

If you want to get the plain truth, be not concerned with right and wrong. The conflict between right and wrong is the sickness of the mind.

—*Seng-Ts'an*

'Does our own nature include evil?'
'It does not even include good.'
'If it contains neither good nor evil, where should we direct it when using it?'
'To set your mind on USING it is a great error.'
'Then what should we do to be right?'
'There is nothing to do and nothing which can be called right.'

—*Hui Hai,* The Zen Teaching of Hui Hai

THINKERS FROM INDIA who were searching for the answer to the riddle of existence turned their attention inward. Upaniṣadic seers hoped to identify with, and in this way comprehend, reality by finding the Self within. Buddhists, who rejected the very idea of a self, taught "insight meditation," which involved concentration on mental events as they passed from an unreal future to an unreal past. In China, at least before Buddhism appeared, there was more interest in the operations of nature and society than in questions about the self and experience.

The transition from hunting and gathering to farming was made in China before 5000 B.C. Farmers in the Yellow River valley developed weaving, carpentry, pottery making, and metalworking. The rough date for the beginning of the first recorded dynasty, the Xia (Hsia), is 2200 B.C. Legends say that the Xia rulers became corrupt and that around 1700 B.C. they were overcome by the founders of the Shang dynasty.

What we know about life in the Shang dynasty comes from inscriptions on bronze artifacts and on bones and shells used in divination. Since 1899, when this "oracle-bone writing" was discovered, scholars have examined more than one hundred thousand inscribed bones and shells. They have learned that, like their *brāhmin* counterparts in India, the Shang priests performed ceremonies of worship, thanksgiving, supplication, and divination. They differed from the *brāhmins,* however, in that their sacrifices, prayers, and questions were directed to the deceased ancestors of aristocrats, who were thought to hold important positions in the bureaucracies of Heaven.

The Shang diviners sought information about the weather, farming, hunting, travel, religion, and war. They asked about the outcome of childbirth, the future course of headaches, and even the meaning of dreams (Chou). The priest would inscribe a question on an animal bone or a tortoise shell, drill holes in the other side to promote and probably guide cracking, and then apply heat. The answer to the question (usually yes or no) would appear in the design of the cracks that resulted from the heat (and from the strategically drilled holes).

Legends say the Shang rulers became corrupt, and that in 1122 B.C. the "Mandate of Heaven" passed to the founders of the third dynasty, the Zhou (Chou). Initially the Zhou conquerors treated the people well and won their loyalty. But, driven by their struggle for power and luxury, these aristocrats raised taxes and drafted young men to fight in their armies and to work on vast domestic projects. As the years passed, the lords became stronger, the Zhou ruler weaker, and the people more miserable. At last the bonds of feudalism dissolved and a furious struggle for power broke out, both among the feudal lords and between the lords and the Zhou king. In 771 B.C., the king was killed and China was left without a central authority. It took more than five hundred years to resolve the question of succession, and in the process, provinces were destroyed and countless thousands of people were killed. This period is aptly called the "Warring States Period," and the social realities of the time gave birth to the major schools of thought: Confucianism, Moism, The School of Names, The Yin-Yang School, Legalism, and Daoism.

> A number of different ways and means were used to forge links between the gods and the members of the Shang clan. There are, to begin with, a series of fragments of oracle texts which can only be interpreted as meaning that the gods moved about in person among men. One says, for example, "Question to the oracle: Will Ti come down into the capital . . ." or "Oracle of the day Kuei-ssŭ. Reception (of the gods). When the sacrifice had ended the Ti-mother entered the town. Misfortune." This misfortune may have been the outbreak of an epidemic. It is uncertain what in fact is meant here. There is a hint, however, in the *Kuo-yü* (*Conversations from the States*), a work written some thousand years later, of the belief that in early antiquity there had been a period of decadence of some kind, in which men and gods had intermingled. (Eichhorn, 36–37)

Confucianism

Confucius (551–479 B.C.) grew up in a society deranged by war, greed, and corruption. It was to set this world right that he developed ideas about good and humane government, but none of the aristocrats he approached was willing to take him seriously. The only education they wanted was one that would show them how to win wars and raise taxes. Confucius was discouraged by his encounters with these aristocrats, but he persevered. He never attained a post of importance, but some of his students did, and finally, through a fantastically complex historical process, he came to be seen as China's most influential thinker. Many writings that have been ascribed to him were written after his death, but some of his own sayings are preserved in the *Analects*.

The actual facts of Confucius's life are unrecoverable, and depending on the needs of the day, he has been deified and vilified, emulated and mocked. The majority opinion seems to be that he was responsible for moral reform, educational excellence, and philosophical profundity, that he was China's first and best moral teacher and the wisest of her sages. That is why his name is attached to so many writings he did not write and thoughts he did not think.

Jun zi (chün-tzu)

In and before Confucius's time, when power was concentrated in the hands of a feudal aristocracy, the term *jun zi* (translated gentleman, superior man) applied only to those who were born into aristocratic families. The word *jun* denoted a "member of the ruling nobility," and *zi* meant "son". Herrlee G. Creel says that "no gentleman could ever become less than one, no matter how vile his conduct might be." But then he adds:

> Confucius changed this usage completely. He asserted that any man might be a gentleman, if his conduct were noble, unselfish, just, and kind. On the other hand, he asserted that no man could be considered a gentleman on the ground of birth; this was solely a question of conduct and character. (Creel, 27)

If Confucius had merely asserted that being a *jun zi* was not a matter of birth, he could be charged with making a plainly false statement. Officially and literally, sons with *jun zi* fathers were *jun zi*. Confucius knew this, but his interest in reform led him to disregard it. When, for example, he said that "the superior man (*jun zi*) is ashamed that his words exceed his deeds" (Chan [1], 42), we can read him as urging the *jun zi* not to brag and exaggerate. He knew how he wanted the ruling class to behave, and he knew that aristocrats craved the prestige that comes from being called *jun zi* (gentlemen, nobles, superior men), so he tried to make the application of the label depend on the possession of the virtues he wanted to encourage. He held the positive tone of the term '*jun zi*' steady while promoting a change in its grounds of application. He tried, that is, to get across a persuasive definition.

This shift stands out clearly when the word used to render '*jun zi*' is the openly evaluative expression 'superior man'. Wing-tsit Chan translates '*jun zi*' this way and says that Confucius used it "to denote a morally superior man." He remarks, as did Creel, that to Confucius "nobility was no longer a matter of blood, but of character—a concept that amounted to a social revolution" (Chan [1], 15).

In the *Analects*, Confucius says that the *jun zi* "extensively studies literature (*wen*) and restrains himself with the rules of propriety" (Chan [1], 30), and that while the *jun zi* understands righteousness (*yi* [*i*]), the inferior man understands profit (28). In addition to restraining himself with the rules of propriety (*li*) and exhibiting righteousness, the *jun zi* has many other virtues:

ren (*jen*)	humanity/benevolence
shu	altruism/reciprocity
jung (*chung*)	conscientiousness/doing one's best
zhi (*chih*)	wisdom/knowledge

xin (*hsin*)	sincerity/reliability/truthfulness
rang (*jang*)	deference/yielding
yi (*i*)	justice/righteousness

Li

The *li* was a code of rules and rituals Shang and Zhou priests used when they tried to interact with and influence their ancestors. It was also a code of rules regulating the behavior of the aristocrats in their dealings with one another. Of the many phrases used to translate this term, one of the most frequent is "(the rules of) propriety." Fung Yulan gives the widest possible meaning to *li*, which, he claims, signifies "the entire body of usages and customs, political and social institutions." "In short," he adds, "all the rules for everything pertaining to human conduct may be included under the term *li*" (Fung, vol. 1, 68)

Confucians saw the past as a Golden Age in which rules determining the proper relationships between ruler and subject, father and son, husband and wife, master and slave, were clear and universally respected. One of Confucius's main ideas is that names should be "rectified." "Let a father be a father, a son be a son, and a wife be a wife." By saying this, he meant that fathers, sons, and wives, should, without complaint or deviation, conform to the conventions of behavior, speech, and even dress that were established in antiquity.

Because Confucius advocated a return to the "ways of the ancient kings," he has been accused of being a reactionary advocate of feudalism. But if he was "guilty" of looking to the past as a model for society, that past was more idealized than actual. He appealed to the ways of the past because he had to appeal to something. As we have seen, no matter who urges you to change your familiar ways—be it Confucius, a total stranger, or your best friend—you are likely to ask for some reason. That reason will only work if it gets help from some principle, belief, or desire you have. The Chinese lacked an unequivocal religious tradition capable of dictating the rules of propriety, but they respected antiquity, age, and history, and they believed that in former times people were happy and the government was good. It was natural for Confucius, those who followed him, and even those who disagreed with him, to appeal to the "ways of the ancient kings."

What Confucius really wanted to do was to find a ruler of a small state who would let him "reestablish" the ways of the ancient kings. He believed that when other rulers saw how well his plan was working they would adopt his methods out of sheer self-interest. When he had no luck with this dream, he turned his attention to preparing younger men to succeed where he had failed. He taught them how to act like "gentlemen" both in the literal sense, which involved knowing how to behave at the courts of the aristocrats, and in the extended sense, which involved developing and manifesting the kind of "superior" character he wanted to promote. Creel tells us that the meaning of *li* had already been extended from its original meaning of 'sacrifice' to "cover every sort of ceremony and the 'courtesy' that characterized the conduct of those that made up a ruler's court." Confucius, he says, "started from there."

> If rulers were gravely serious in sacrificing to their ancestors, why should they not be equally so in attending to the government of the realm? If ministers treated one another with courtesy, in the daily intercourse of court, why should they not be equally considerate toward the common people, who were the backbone of the state? Thus he said to one of his disciples that, wherever he went in the world, he should treat all those with whom he came in contact as if he were "receiving an important guest"; and if he became an official of the government, he should deal with the people as if he were "officiating at a great sacrifice." Such conduct would, of course, contrast sharply with the careless conduct of most of the aristocrats. (Creel, 30)

The point of extending the term *'li'* to cover new forms of behavior is to modify the way the Chinese treated each other. Confucius wanted aristocrats and officials to care about the welfare of the people, and he wanted the people to be more considerate. Confucians believed that many difficult human interactions could be navigated if people had a clear and definitive set of protocols. They urged, more than Confucius did, that daily life take on a ritualistic and ceremonial aspect, and it is hard to overemphasize the importance they placed on dress, paraphernalia, and the respect and obedience due to parents, living and dead.

> When the elder asks a question, to reply without acknowledging one's incompetency and (trying to) decline answering, is contrary to propriety. . . . A son, when he is going abroad, must inform (his parents where he is going); when he returns, he must present himself before them. . . . In ordinary conversation (with his parents), he does not use the term 'old' (with reference to them).
>
> . . . When two men are sitting or standing together, do not join them as a third. When two are standing together, another

> should not pass between them. (*The Book of Rites*, in Legge [2], vol. 1, 67–68, 77)
>
> When he sees anyone in mourning, even if he knows him well, he must change countenance; and when he sees anyone in sacrificial garb, or a blind man, even if he is in informal dress, he must be sure to adopt the appropriate attitude.
> . . . When he is given a dish of delicacies, he must change countenance and rise to his feet. At a sudden clap of thunder or a violent gust of wind he must change countenance. (*Analects* 10:16, in Dawson, 28)

Ren (jen)

There is no standard translation of '*ren*', but it is clear that the word is a key one in the moral and social thought of Confucius and the Confucians. Raymond Dawson gives a daunting list of terms that have been used to express this elusive concept: "benevolence, love, altruism, kindness, charity, compassion, magnanimity, perfect virtue, goodness, human-heartedness, humaneness, humanity, and man-to-manness" (Dawson, 37–38). Some of these can be dismissed on the grounds that they are needed to render other Chinese terms, but 'goodness' expresses the evaluative aspect of '*ren*', and 'humanity' brings out its social side.

The Chinese write the character for '*ren*' by placing a picture of a human being next to the sign for the number two, suggesting thereby that 'ren' has to do with relationships among people. Dawson says that the word "may be defined as dealing with other human beings as a man ideally should" (Dawson, 38). Charles Wei-hsun Fu says that while Confucius does not "give a conclusive definition of *jen* as an all-pervading virtue," what he does say implies "that *jen* is what constitutes the necessary and sufficient moral nature of man; it is moral perfection as such" (Fu, 378–79). D. C. Lau, in his introduction to his translation of the *Analects*, says that *ren* "is the most important moral quality a man can possess" (Lau, 14). Clearly, no one who lacks the virtue of *ren* can be a "true" *jun zi* (see *Analects* 4:5, in Chan [1], 26). *Ren* is also linked with the rules of propriety (*li*). In *Analects* 12:1, when Confucius's favorite disciple, Yen Yuan, asks him about *ren*, Confucius answers that "to master oneself and return to propriety is humanity" (38).

In another well-known passage from the *Analects* (12:2), Confucius gives the following answer to a disciple who has asked him about *ren*:

> When you go abroad, behave to everyone as if you were receiving a great guest. Employ the people as if you were assisting at a great sacrifice. Do not do to others what you do not want them to do to you. Then there will be no complaint against you in the state or in the family (the ruling clan). (Chan [1], 39)

The first two sentences link *ren* to the *li*, but in the third we get something different—a version of what is called the "Silver Rule." This idea appears again in *Analects* 15:23 when Confucius is asked for the "one word that can serve as the guiding principle for conduct throughout life." His answer is that "it is the word altruism (*shu*). Do not do to others what you do not want them to do to you" (44). Though this is called the "Silver Rule," it is in no way inferior to the "Golden Rule," which, taken literally, asks many things of us which others might wish us to leave undone.

Ren and *shu* may, by showing up as the Silver Rule, be similar, but since 'altruism' suggests actively contributing something positive to the welfare of another at some personal expense, it may not be the best choice for '*shu*'. Dawson (51) and James Legge ([3], 301) use 'reciprocity', and there are other possibilities. In his introduction to the *Analects*, Lau makes explicit the connection between '*shu*' and '*ren*' (which he renders as "benevolence"). He says that *shu* is a part of *ren*: It is "the ability to take as analogy what is near at hand." It is the method of finding out what other people wish or do not wish done to them, by "taking oneself—'what is near at hand'—as an analogy and asking oneself what one would like or dislike were one in the position of the person at the receiving end" (Lau, 16). But there is more to *ren* (benevolence) than this, because after we have discovered what a person desires, we still must determine what to do with that information. Since Confucius says that his way (the "one thread" running through all his teaching) consists of *jung* (*chung*) and *shu*, Lau suggests that *jung* is the other component of benevolence (*ren*). "Chung," he says, "is the doing of one's best and it is through *chung* that one puts into effect what one has found out by the method of *shu*" (16). Dawson agrees, and notes that while the original meaning of *jung* was "loyalty", the Confucians took this to include the responsibility to criticize one's superior. "In the *Analects*, *chung* [*jung*] certainly meant 'doing one's best for' rather than blind obedience to the dictates of one's superior" (51). "True loyalty," they might have said, "may require disobedience."

Other Virtues

In addition to *li* and *ren*, several other virtues are attributed to the *jun zi*, and recommended to everyone. We can fill in our picture of the *jun zi*, and further prepare ourselves to discuss moralism in Chinese thought, by glancing briefly at four such virtues: wisdom (*zhi* [*chih*]), sincerity (reliability or truthfulness) (*xin* [*hsin*]), deference or yielding (*rang* [*jang*]), and righteousness (*yi*).

Socrates said that wisdom (*zhi*) consists in knowing yourself, and Confucius would have agreed, but would have added that it also involves knowing others. (12:22) Confucius also said in two places (9:29 and 14:28) that "the man of wisdom is never in two minds" (Lau, 100 and 128). Lau reads this as meaning that "a man of wisdom is never in two minds in his judgments about right and wrong" (22). This seems to imply that Confucius believed in an objective morality that can be known by a "man of wisdom," but he may only have meant that a man of wisdom is not perplexed by complex cases and knows what to do.

Another word sometimes used to render *zhi* is "knowledge," blurring a distinction we make between an accumulation of information (knowledge) and something considerably more grand and difficult to define (wisdom). According to Confucius, *zhi* is not a natural endowment, but something acquired through learning, but in the end we do not have a helpful definition of *zhi* from Confucius. In *Analects* 2:17, he is reported to have said: "To say you know when you know, and to say you do not when you do not, that is knowledge" (Lau, 65). While this is good advice, it is neither a definition nor an explanation of knowledge, as Chan indicates when he interpolates a phrase into his translation of the passage that makes the saying an insightful remark not about knowledge, but about "the way to acquire knowledge" (Chan [1], 24).

The character for *xin* pictures a man standing next to his words. Legge ([3] 129–30) uses "sincerity" as a translation, and Lau speaks of being trustworthy (and reliable) in what one says. One of Confucius's disciples said that being trustworthy in one's words is "close to being moral," and Lau interprets the qualification "close to" as evidence of sensitivity to the fact that "there are bound to be cases where an inflexible adherence to the principle of trustworthiness in word will lead to action that is not moral" (Lau, 25). But this qualification does not diminish the importance of this notion, or displace *xin* from its place among the Confucian virtues.

Next we can look at the virtue of deference (*rang*). In *Analects* 4:13 we read: "If a man is able to govern a state by observing the rites and showing deference, what difficulties will he have in public life?" (Lau, 74). Dawson says that this virtue, which is associated with ritual, "could also be used in ordinary social intercourse, to mean 'yielding precedence' " (Dawson, 26). Joseph Needham says it denotes "the feminine yieldingness of masculine ownership," and mentions the possibility that it may be related to the tribal custom of *potlach* (Needham, 61–62).

While it is hard to deny that an increase in the practice of deference would result in a more peaceful environment, we can have trouble figuring out how much deference is enough. Confucius saw that its cultivation and ritualization would be a strong antidote to egoism and selfishness, and he left the details vague. He was certainly wise enough to realize that we can know that more is needed, without knowing how much more is needed.

This brief discussion of Confucius and of Confucian moral concepts would be incomplete if we found no place for *yi*. Once again we are confronted with alternative translations. Dawson says that originally *yi* meant "natural justice," or "what seemed just to the natural man before concepts like law and ritual were evolved," and that it was "regarded as the ultimate yardstick against which matters of law and ritual must be judged" (Dawson, 52). Lau says:

> *Yi* is a word which can be used of an act in which case it can be rendered as 'right', or it can be used of an act an agent ought to perform in which case it can be rendered as 'duty', or it can be used of an agent in which case it can be rendered as 'righteous' or 'dutiful'. When used in a general sense, sometimes the only possible rendering is 'moral' or 'morality'. (Lau, 26)

He adds that *yi* is involved primarily in assessments of acts rather than agents, and that "the rightness of acts depends on their being morally fitting in the circumstances" (Lau, 27).

By now it should be obvious that either Confucius was a moralist, or those who translate and interpret him are, and that they cannot imagine him either beyond (or before) morality. "Morality" becomes a part of the essence of the superior man, and one who is moral does the right thing—which, of course, means that there is a right thing, an objectively "fitting" act or choice.

> The enormous importance which Confucius ascribes to ceremony by no means implies that he identifies the ritual with the

> moral. He has a different word, *yi* . . . for the right, which is conceived as the conduct fitting to one's role or status, for example as father or son, ruler or minister. (Graham, 11)
>
> An important feature of the cultural unity inspired by the Confucian writings was the role of *li* (ritual), the rules of which, as we have seen, were thought of, not as the mores of a particular society, but as a universally valid system. Similarly the filial piety associated with the name of Confucius was universalized in the *Book of Filial Piety* and regarded as a cosmic principle. (Dawson, 82)

Moism

The first and most vocal opponent the Confucians faced was Mo Zi (Mo Tzu) (479–438 B.C.). Mo Zi complained that Confucian rituals and funerals were extravagant, that their music was a waste of time, and that their emphasis on love for parents and family loyalty drove members of *different* families further apart. He condemned offensive war, but studied defense. His answer to the problems of his war-torn country was "universal love," or "love without distinction," an extension to all humanity of the love we feel for our kin.

> When all the people in the world love one another, the strong will not overcome the weak, the many will not oppress the few, the rich will not insult the poor, the honored will not despise the humble, and the cunning will not deceive the ignorant. Because of universal love, all the calamities, usurpations, hatred, and animosity in the world may be prevented from arising. Therefore the man of humanity praises it. (Chan [1], 214)

Mo Zi thought people could be led to universal love by argument and by intimidation. The above passage is a sample of his utilitarian defense of universal love. He also promised that the gods and spirits will reward universal love and punish those who fall short or do evil. Confucius had almost nothing to say about the gods, and the Daoists were in awe of nature, but not of gods. Beliefs in divine retribution existed among the Chinese, but of the great social thinkers of the late Zhou dynasty, only Mo Zi would have said that "even in deep gorges and great forests, where there is no man, one may not act improperly. There are ghosts and spirits who will see one!" (Creel, 61).

Daoism

The most dramatic alternative to Confucianism is the Daoism of Lao Zi (Lao Tzu) and Zhuang Zi (Chuang Tzu). Many scholars doubt that there ever was a person called Lao Zi (the words mean "old master"), but here I will follow the tradition and speak of Lao Zi as the author of *Dao De Jing* (*Tao Te Ching*), and as one of the most eloquent exponents of the distinctive approach to life it expresses. It is more likely that Zhuang Zi was real. He probably lived between 400 and 300 B.C. and his thoughts are found in the early chapters of the work called by his name.

The conservative Confucians looked fondly on the stability of early Zhou feudalism, which had promoted a system in which everyone had a place, and in which manners and protocol were clearly defined and carefully observed. They cared about propriety in manners, morals, and even clothes, and, as a result, they often came across as rigid and pompous snobs. Lao Zi and Zhuang Zi mocked the Confucian virtues of *ren* and *yi*. Where Confucians promoted the rules of propriety (*li*), Daoists recommended naturalness and spontaneity; where Confucians promoted study and learning, Daoists urged that learning be abandoned. The Confucians spoke for the feudal system, its ranks and duties, its allocation of power, its stratification, and its attempt to impose an artificial order on many aspects of daily life. The Daoists attacked this feudal system and took the presence, not the absence, of the Confucian virtues to be a sign of disorder in the world:

> 18 When the great Tao declined,
> The doctrines of humanity [*jen*] and righteousness [*i*] arose.
> When knowledge and wisdom appeared,
> There emerged great hypocrisy.
> When the six family relationships are not in harmony,
> There will be advocacy of filial piety and deep love to children.
> When a country is in disorder,
> There will be praise of loyal ministers.
>
> (Chan [1], 148–49)

The Dao and Deregulation

When Confucians talked about "The Way" (*dao*), they meant the correct "way" to live and to organize society. Confucius believed he had discovered this, and that it was an improved and reformed version of the feudal system crumbling around his ears. He said the *li* should be extended to daily life, but he left vague many details that generations of Confucians then tried to fill in. Rituals have a place in any society, but as they increase in number and importance, their spirit fades. When propriety asks us to exhibit a "change of countenance" upon being given a dish of delicacies or when experiencing a gust of wind, it promotes affectation rather than order.

The Daoists had no use for the Confucian "Way" of feudal authoritarianism, codes of dress and behavior, aristocratic refinement, and edifying music. And they had even less use for the Confucian way of using the word 'dao'. For the Daoist, the Dao is eternal, nameless, and indescribable—the totality of being and nonbeing in all its spontaneous activity. Needham characterizes this Dao as "The Order of Nature" and describes Daoism as "a naturalistic pantheism, which emphasizes the unity and spontaneity of the operations of Nature" (Needham, 36, 38).

In contrast with the Confucians, who wanted life to be regulated by the *li*, the Daoists were for deregulation. Regulations impose an artificial order on the natural one, and the Daoists favored the natural one. In verse 38 of the *Dao De Jing*, Lao Zi says that virtue arises only when the Dao is lost, and that humanity (*ren*) arises only when virtue is lost. When humanity is lost, righteousness (*yi*) arises, and when that is lost, we get propriety (*li*). Then he adds: "propriety is a superficial expression of loyalty and faithfulness, and the beginning of disorder" (Chan [1], 158). So much for the Confucian virtues—none of them is necessary if we can figure out how to harmonize with the Dao.

> 32 If kings and barons would hold on to it,
> all things would submit to them spontaneously.
> Heaven and earth unite to drip sweet dew.
> Without the command of men, it drips evenly over all.
> As soon as there were regulations and institutions, there were names (differentiations of things).
> As soon as there are names, know that it is time to stop.
> It is by knowing when to stop that one can be free from danger.
>
> (Chan [1], 156)

The '*De*' (*te*) of the *Dao De Jing* is usually translated as "virtue," but it also means "power." One who "holds on to" the Dao gains access to its *de*, its power, and no longer needs to struggle, or even to do anything, to succeed.

Daoist Symbols

Symbols and metaphors play a larger role in the writing of Lao Zi and Zhuang Zi than do arguments and reasoning. Needham says that "if it were not unthinkable (from the Chinese point of view) that the Yin [negative, female, passive] and the Yang [positive, male, active] could ever be separated, one might say that Taoism was a Yin thought-system and Confucianism a Yang one" (Needham, 61). In theory the *yin* and the *yang* are pervasive, complementary, and equal forces, but those who evaluate (a *yang* activity) tend to rank items from the *yin* side as inferior. One need only consider the historical position of the (actual) female in China to see that she has not been afforded the equality granted her metaphysical counterpart. The lists below indicate how encompassing the distinction between *yin* and *yang* can be.

YIN	YANG
negative	positive
female	male
dark	light
weak	strong
night	day
curved	straight

The Daoist speaks of harmony but favors the *yin*. One explanation for this emphasis on the feminine is that Daoists were reacting to the more "masculine," active, and domineering mind-set of the Confucians. Another, which Needham advocates, is that the Daoists were looking back to a time when society was matriarchal. This is supported by a remark in the Zhuang Zi that refers to the time of "perfected virtue" when the people were innocent, peaceful, cooperative, and "knew their mothers, but did not know their fathers" (Needham, 108).

Water is another important Daoist symbol. Water has many virtues and much power. It occupies low places, so things come to it. It overcomes obstacles by gentle perseverance. It nourishes and yet has no shape of its own.

78 There is nothing softer and weaker than water,
And yet there is nothing better for attacking hard and strong things.
For this reason there is no substitute for it.
All the world knows that the weak overcomes the strong and the soft overcomes the hard.
But none can practice it.

(Chan [1], 174)

The Political Character of Daoism

The Confucians justified their recommendations for society by appealing to the past, but the Daoists based their recommendations on an even older precedent. They spoke of a time when there was no need for the Confucian virtues because people were simple, natural, and spontaneous; a time when there was no feudalism, no slavery, and no aristocrats to demand an ever-increasing share of the farmers' harvest. The Confucian wanted to govern society, but the Daoist pointed out that governments cause wars, poverty, and misery, they collect taxes, and in almost every way make things worse than they were before the aristocrats and their henchmen took over.

Needham roots Daoist attitudes in the lives of passive agriculturalists and finds the source of the habit of domination in the ways of the "shepherd and the cowherd," who "beat their beasts, and take up an active attitude of command over their flocks and herds." He mentions God as a "good shepherd" and concludes that "the shepherd is not far from the legislator." On the other hand,

> when man has to do primarily with plants, as in predominantly agricultural civilisations, the psychological conditions are quite different—often the less he interferes with the growth of his crops the better. Until the harvest he does not touch them. (Needham, 576)

The Confucians saw that trouble was caused by bad government, government by the ignorant and greedy stooges of the aristocrats. But they knew that there was no path back to primitive collectivism, so they hoped to improve the system by working within it. At their best they sought public office to bring good government to the people, and many of them were tortured or executed for their integrity.

Confucians criticized Daoists for refusing to participate in the affairs of state, but given the danger of associating with headstrong aristocrats, and given the special message of the Daoists, it is easy to understand why most of them choose to contemplate nature in remote mountains. No flourishing aristocrat was likely to listen calmly to praise of pre-feudal collectivism. The average ruler was doubtless annoyed when the Confucians urged him to clean up his act, but Daoists went well beyond the call for reform. Chapter 9 of the *Dao De Jing* says that "wealth and place breed insolence, which brings ruin in its train" (Needham, 100), and Zhuang Zi makes one of his characters say this: "The shameless become rich, and good talkers become high officials. . . . Small robbers are put in prison, but great robbers become feudal lords, and there in the gates of the feudal lords will your 'righteous scholars' be found" (102).

Not everyone goes along with Needham's interpretation of Daoism. Scholars continue to describe the Daoists as less than admirable anti-social dropouts. Even when scholars recognize that Daoists were protesting against political injustice, slavery, oppression, patriarchy, and the rule of the strong, they are rarely willing to go as far as Needham. Chan, for example, says that "there is no evidence whatsoever in the *Lao Tzu* of collectivism, antifeudalism, or opposition to merchants, nor is there any condemnation of kings and barons." It is not, however, renunciation and a return to primitive simplicity that Daoism recommends but simplicity and a "life of plainness in which profit, cleverness, selfishness, and evil desires are all forsaken" (Chan [2], 14).

Wu Wei

The best phrase with which to summarize Daoist advice on all fronts—political, social, and personal—is *wu wei. Wu* is a word used for negation, and *wei* means "activity" or "action." It is not wrong to translate *wu wei* as "non-action," but this should not be taken literally. In his commentary on the Zhuang Zi, Guo Xiang (Kuo Hsiang) says that when some people hear of *wu wei,* they think they are being told that lying down is better than walking. But the proponent of *wu wei* does not recommend lying down, sitting still as a stone, or meeting all stimuli with motionlessness. It has always been relatively clear what *wu wei* is not; but it is hard to say just what it is. According to Creel, *wu wei* is "doing nothing that is not natural or spontaneous." "The important thing," he says, "is not to strain in any way" (Creel, 106). But this explanation neglects the possibility that there are times when it is natural to exert a great amount of energy. The emphasis on natural spontaneity, however, points in the right direction.

Needham also sees *wu wei* as refraining from "activity contrary to Nature," which he characterizes as refraining from

> going against the grain of things, from trying to make materials perform functions for which they are unsuitable, from exerting force in human affairs when the man of insight could see that it would be doomed to failure, and that subtler methods of persuasion, or simply letting things alone to take their own course, would bring about the desired result. (Needham, 68)

Needham's interpretation of *wu wei* is influenced by his vision of Daoism as reflecting primitive agriculturalism. He says that "one of the deepest roots of the concept of *wu wei* may lie in the anarchic nature of primitive peasant life; plants grow best without interference by man; men thrive best without State interference" (70).

Creel introduces a distinction between two forms of Daoism—contemplative and purposive. "Contemplative Daoism" emphasizes a passive, detached, inactive approach to reality. Daoists of the contemplative sort are not inert, but they tend to avoid political activity, high-stress situations, and life in the city. "Purposive Daoism" is Daoism for the ruler, or the individual unable to avoid responsibility. The purposive Daoist realizes that one can accomplish many things by doing very little, if one understands the Dao well enough to see what small step can bring about a desired outcome (Creel, 109–11). In the following passage from the *Dao De Jing*, Lao Zi offers a clear statement of purposive Daoism:

> 64 What remains still is easy to hold.
> What is not yet manifest is easy to plan for.
> What is brittle is easy to crack.
> What is minute is easy to scatter.
> Deal with things before they appear.
> Put things in order before disorder arises.
> A tree as big as a man's embrace grows from a tiny shoot.
> A tower of nine storeys begins with a heap of earth.
> The journey of a thousand *li* starts from where one stands.
>
> (Chan [1], 169–70)

Confucians, looking for an easy mark, focus on the most senseless interpretations of *wu wei* and on practitioners of literal inactivity. A deeper interpretation of *wu wei* is defended by David Loy, who identifies *wu wei* as "non-dual action," and relates it to both karma yoga and Zen Buddhism. Non-dual action is action without a distinction between subject and object, spontaneous action with no thought of the "fruits" (Loy, 73–86). To achieve it, one cultivates "emptiness" and what Daoists and Buddhists alike refer to as a "mirror mind," a mind so pure that it does not filter what is experienced through misleading concepts or distort it with neurotic self-concern.

> The mind of the perfect man is like a mirror. It does not lean forward or backward in its response to things. It responds to things but conceals nothing of its own. Therefore it is able to deal with things without injury to [its reality]. (Zhuang Zi, in Chan [1], 207)
>
> The Perfect Man uses his mind like a mirror—going after nothing, welcoming nothing, responding but not storing. Therefore he can win out over things and not hurt himself. (Zhuang Zi, in Watson, 97)
>
> When the perfect man employs his mind, it is a mirror. It conducts nothing and anticipates nothing; it responds to (what is before it), but does not retain it. Thus he is able to deal successfully with all things, and injures none. (Zhuang Zi, in Legge [1], vol. 1, 266)
>
> As a mirror impartially reflects green and red, black and white, without being to the smallest extent affected by any of them; as the spray of a waterfall reflects all the colours of the rainbow without losing its colourless purity; as dreamers behold acts of love and violence without moving so much as a hand; so does the mind of an Enlightened One react to the ceaseless play of phenomena. (Hui Hai, in Blofeld [2], 33)

Mencius

After the death of Confucius, various new "ways of thought" emerged, some within Confucianism itself, and some in opposition to Confucianism. The Chinese world continued to deteriorate, and philosophies of egoism and exploitation better expressed the mood of the day than the ritualism and moralism of the Confucians, who seemed to have lost faith in their own mission. According to Benjamin Schwartz, "They no longer seem to believe in the noble man's ability to influence the world through the power of his moral suasion. The noble man's function seems to have shrunken in their view to the modest role of the custodian of 'holy rites,' music, and learning" (Schwartz, 256).

Mencius (371–289 B.C.) was different. He had a simpler and clearer moral vision than Confucius, and he held to it steadfastly in a world that was either hostile or indifferent to his message. Like Confucius, he traced his good ideas to the early Zhou rulers, but many of the ideas he attributed to the ancient kings were in fact radical and new. He supported the ranks and privileges of Zhou feudalism, but then said that the whole system should be for the good of the people.

Both Confucius and Mencius were teachers, both sought authority in the past, and both promoted their conception of "good government"—in person and to little avail. Mencius offered a more popular form of Confucianism, but one with teeth. He insisted, for example, that prosperity following upon the removal of an inadequate ruler is a sign of Heaven's approval of the revolution. Over the years his support of the "right to revolution" has inspired many attempts to overthrow corrupt (and not-so-corrupt) rulers.

Mencius spent much time seeking out and lecturing rulers on their duties, trying, as did Confucius, to institute reforms from the top down. He demanded, and often received, the high respect and ceremonious treatment he believed himself to deserve. This sometimes forced him to be circumspect about his radical beliefs. He said that the *jun zi* does not insist that his words always be truthful, and he was not above playing word games to stay out of trouble. Once when he and the king of Qi (Ch'i) were having a conversation, the king asked him if a subject may kill a sovereign. Anticipating the uncomfortable results of an unqualified affirmative, Mencius resorted to a persuasive definition.

> He who outrages humanity is a scoundrel; he who outrages righteousness is a scourge. A scourge or a scoundrel is a despised creature [and no longer a king]. I have heard that a despised creature called Chou was put to death, but I have not heard anything about the murdering of a sovereign. (De Bary, Chan, and Watson, 97)

The parenthetical addition to the above passage is provided by the translator, and it highlights Mencius's drift: No genuine sovereign may be killed, but a bad sovereign (or a despised sovereign?) is not a genuine sovereign.

Confucius is not definite about the goodness or badness of human nature—perhaps he realizes the pitfalls that accompany such a way of talking. But Mencius has no aversion to moralism, and one of his distinguishing ideas is the claim that human nature is "originally," that is, innately, good. Evil is brought about by external influences, and learning can return us to our original innocence and goodness.

> Mencius said, "If you let people follow their feelings (original nature), they will be able to do good. This is what is meant by saying that human nature is good. If man does evil, it is not the fault of his natural endowment. The feeling of commiseration is found in all men; the feeling of shame and dislike is found in all men; the feeling of respect and reverence is found in all men; and the feeling of right and wrong is found in all men. The feeling of commiseration is what we call humanity; the feeling of shame and dislike is what we call righteousness; the feeling of respect and reverence is what we call propriety (*li*); and the feeling of right and wrong is what we call wisdom. Humanity, righteousness, propriety, and wisdom are not drilled into us from outside. We originally have them with us. (Chan [1], 54)

Here the four Confucian virtues—humanity, righteousness, propriety, and wisdom—are traced to natural instincts we all have. This is what makes human nature good.

In the face of what must have been overwhelming contrary evidence, Mencius insists that "All men have the mind which cannot bear [to see the suffering of] others" (Chan [1], 65). When people see a child about to fall into a well, he observes, they feel alarm and distress, and leap to help—not for selfish motives, but from their natural desire not to see another suffer. When this impulse is extended, it becomes humanity. What makes Mencius a moralist is the fact that he believes that the initial aversion to suffering and the developed virtue of humanity are both good, that we ought to develop the first into the second, and that when we do, we will then be disposed to do what is morally right.

The School of Names

The adherents of this, the least influential of the six schools, are called "dialecticians" or "logicians." This is not because they developed any form of dialectical reasoning, or made any contribution to logic as we understand it, but because they liked to argue, and to exploit language to produce paradoxical utterances and baffling dialogues. Gong-sun Long (Kung-sun Lung) and Hui Shi (Hui Shih), both born around 380 B.C., are two important figures of this school.

Gong-sun Long is best known for his famous pronouncement; "A white horse is not a horse," and for his discussion of qualities like whiteness and hardness. His problems have to do with properties, and he generates his paradoxes by playing with language about properties. His thoughts are of some interest to contemporary Western philosophers, but few Chinese have taken him seriously.

Hui Shi is best known for his odd sayings, and for his ability to defend them. He is reported to have asserted and defended all of the following:

> An egg has hair.
> A chicken has three legs.
> Fire is not hot.
> The eye does not see.
> A white dog is black.
>
> (Chan [1], 234–35)

These are more like riddles than problems in logic, and they may have been meant to be solved as riddles are. So, a white dog is black at midnight, the eye that is asleep does not see, and fire that burns at a distance is not hot. As for the egg and the chicken, your guess is as good as mine. Zhuang Zi, who was a friend of Hui Shi, criticized him severely:

> Hui Shih was a man of many ideas. His writings would fill five carriages, but his doctrines were contradictory and his sayings missed the truth. . . . Actually he merely contradicted people, but wished to have the reputation of overcoming them. Therefore he was never on good terms with others. Weak in the cultivation of virtue, strong in the handling of things, his way was a narrow one indeed! (De Bary, Chan, and Watson, 84)

The Yin-Yang School

Yin signifies clouds and *yang* the sun. They occur as symbols for a truly primal division that pervades Chinese thought. Zhuang Zi tells of a time when Confucius came upon Lao Zi, who was meditating. When he finished his meditations Confucius asked him what he had experienced. This was his answer:

> I saw Yin, the Female Energy, in its motionless grandeur; I saw Yang, the Male Energy, rampant in its fiery vigour. The motionless grandeur came up out of the earth; the fiery vigour burst out from heaven. The two penetrated one another, were inextricably blended and from their union the things of the world were born. (Waley, 16)

Even before Confucius, the operations of nature had been explained in terms of opposition between, and harmonization of, positive (*yang*) and negative (*yin*) forces. The origin of this idea is lost in antiquity, but a text from 644 B.C. attributes an earthquake to a repression of the *yin*. During the Han dynasty the yin-yang theory was combined with a theory of "Five Elements" (wood, fire, earth, metal, and water) to form a complicated and ultimately fantastic metaphysical system that correlated each of the five elements with its own direction, color, flavor, animal, dynasty, day, and so forth.

Both the concepts of *yin* and *yang* and the five-element model of change seem to be steps in the direction of a "scientific" account of nature. If Needham is right to say that the Daoists were deterred from scientific investigation by Confucians who insisted on attending to things human and social, the yin-yang thinkers may have suffered a similar fate. But it is also possible that they were diverted from the path of science by external requirements placed on their theories. Rulers needed (and supported) philosophers who provided theories that could justify their regimes. Divorced from the world of experience and co-opted by politics, the yin-yang philosophers floated in realms of pure speculation.

Legalism

Confucius had (wisely) neglected to take a stand on the question of whether humans are basically good or evil. But Mencius said that human nature is "endowed with feelings which impel it toward the good," and added, "that is why I call it good" (Creel, 88). Other Confucians developed the opposite opinion. This debate between Chinese "hard-liners" and "soft-liners" mirrored (and antedated by two thousand years) the debate between the followers of Hobbes and the followers of Rousseau (see Chapter 4).

The Confucian who first took the "Hobbesian" position was Xun Zi (Hsün Tzu), who, from his belief that "the nature of man is evil," concluded that we need "the civilizing influence of teachers and laws and the guidance of propriety and righteousness" (Chan [1], 128). It is his emphasis on teaching and on propriety (*li*) and righteousness (*yi*) that made Xun Zi a Confucian. But Xun Zi had two famous students who accepted his belief that human nature is evil, and then rejected both the Confucian emphasis on the influence of teachers and the Confucian virtues of propriety and righteousness, opting instead for the civilizing influence of laws and punishments.

Xun Zi's most famous pupil, Han Fei Zi (Han Fei Tzu) (*d.* 233 B.C.), was a member of the ruling family of the state of Han, but his ideas were too un-Confucian to be heard in Han. He stressed discipline and punishment, laws and penalties:

> The severe household has no fierce slaves, but it is the affectionate mother who has spoiled sons. From this I know that awe-inspiring power can prohibit violence and that virtue and kindness [the alleged qualities of the Confucian ruler] are insufficient to end disorder. (Chan [1], 253)

The ruler of the state of Qin (Ch'in), a semi-barbaric state in the west, heard of the writings of Han Fei Zi, praised them, and invited this thinker to visit Qin. Xun Zi's other famous student, Li Si (Li Ssu), was already an official in Qin, and when Han Fei Zi arrived, Li Si had him thrown into jail, and eventually forced him to commit suicide. Here is a demonstration of Legalism in action. Han Fei Zi may have been a superior pupil and a stronger thinker, but Li Si was, in a sense, a better Legalist.

One of the main differences between the Legalists and the Confucians can be found in their views about laws and penalties. Confucians hoped to infuse people with a love of ceremony and an appreciation of etiquette, and they wanted the government to be run by virtuous and pragmatic administrators trained in the Confucian tradition. Legalists saw this as an impossible and dangerous dream. They thought that when the laws are explicit, and punishment certain and harsh, people quickly fall into line.

The Legalists despised the Confucians and the Daoists, and considered them to be useless, soft, and lazy. Han Fei Zi thought they should all be put to work, and he argued that the ruler should pay no attention to their suggestions. The only thing a ruler needs, he believed, is complete control of the "two handles" of power.

> The empire can be ruled only by utilizing human nature. Men have likes and dislikes; thus they can be controlled by means of rewards and punishments. On this basis prohibitions and commands can be put in operation, and a complete system of government set up. The ruler need only hold these handles [rewards and punishments] firmly, in order to

> maintain his supremacy. . . . These handles are the power of life and death. Force is the stuff that keeps the masses in subjugation. (Creel, 149)

It was with the aid of this harsh philosophy that Qin was finally able to eliminate the other states and to unify China, putting an end to more than five hundred years of civil strife. The *Historical Records* say that the ruler of Qin

> secretly sent out agents well-supplied with gold and gems, which they were to use to persuade the various feudal lords to ally themselves with Ch'in. Thus they bought the adherence of those rulers and statesmen who could be bribed. Those who could not be bribed were cut down by the assassin's sword. Thus they divided the rulers and their subjects. After these conspirators had done their work, the king of Ch'in sent his excellent generals to reap the harvest. (Creel, 156)

Finally, in 221 B.C., the last of the opposition was eliminated and the ruler of Qin became the First Emperor of China. This energetic and ruthless emperor got right to work. He encouraged agriculture, standardized the weights and axle sizes, improved the roads, established a uniform writing system, promulgated countless laws, and actually started to get the country organized. The old feudal system was demolished, and spies and informers were everywhere. Anyone who broke a law, botched a job, or even complained, was punished. Confucian books, indeed all books except those that dealt with agriculture or medicine, were ordered burned.

Eleven years after the unification, the First Emperor of China died—some say of overwork. Before two years had passed, his eldest son was killed by Li Si, who was himself murdered shortly after that. The dynasty that was supposed to last ten thousand years collapsed after fourteen.

Confucians emerged from hiding to join a peasants' revolt and after a relatively short struggle, a new dynasty, the Han, was established in 206 B.C. Han emperors inherited a strengthened and still unified China, which they ran by employing Legalist administrators and methods, while promoting "yin-yang Confucianism," a mixture of mysticism and metaphysics that Confucius would not have recognized. Arthur Wright explains how the thoughts and the name of Confucius were exploited for political ends.

> Confucius, the modest teacher of the state of Lu, was dehumanized and transformed into the prophet and patron saint of a united empire of

> which he had never dreamed. The old books were pushed, forced, interpolated, and "interpreted" to give them a consistency which their differing ages and authorships belied. . . . *The Book of Poetry*, in which the people of an earlier day had sung of their hopes and fears, was tortured to provide authority for approved moral principles. New "classics" such as the Classic of Filial Submission . . . went far to transform Confucius into what Granet called the patron saint of a conformist morality. (Wright, 16–17)

The last fifty years of the Han were marked by struggle among entrenched families, court eunuchs, the *nouveaux riches*, and the intelligentsia. In A.D. 166 the struggle erupted into a bloody conflagration that undermined the authority of the government. Two forms of "Neo-Daoism" moved to fill the void, a religious Daoism for the people, and a literary and artistic escapist form for the intellectuals. Religious Daoism was highly organized, emotionally satisfying, and very popular. Many of its texts were based on visions of and visitations from celestial messengers (Needham, 157). It was also intensely political, and as the strength of the Han ebbed away, Daoist popular leaders (still believing in "primitive collectivism" if Needham is right) occupied roles the central government was no longer able to fill. This led to challenges to that government and eventually to the cataclysmic Yellow Turban rebellions, the crushing of which in A.D. 184 and 189 was the final act of the enfeebled Han dynasty.

Buddhism in China

At first the Chinese believed that Buddhism was a form of religious Daoism, but a less Chinese system of thought could hardly have been imagined. Unlike the Chinese, the Buddhists were devoted to introspection. Indian philosophy is abstract and revels in the cosmic, and the Buddhist philosophy that first found its way to China was no exception. Chinese thought, on the other hand, is concrete and this-worldly. Sanskrit and Chinese are radically different languages, and the literary habits of the Indian Buddhists and the Chinese were as different as their languages.

Chinese monks made epic journeys to India to learn from Buddhist teachers and to bring back Buddhist texts. It took Xuan Zang (Hsüan-tsang), the most famous of the pilgrims, seventeen years to complete his journey to India. Upon his return, he spent the remainder of his life working with teams of translators to render the puzzling documents into Chinese. Kumārajīva (350–413) established a state-sponsored translation bureau at Chang-an (Ch'ang-an), where monks translated or retranslated the great Mahāyāna *sūtras*, and clarified Buddhism by distinguishing it from Daoism.

The more Buddhism took on its own character, the more criticism it received from the Confucians and the Daoists. Confucian moralists, who stressed filial piety, criticized the Buddhists for urging their followers to forsake their families. They also objected to the Mahāyāna emphasis on *bodhisattvas*, relics, and other religious trappings. They saw the Buddhist practice of shaving one's head as a form of self-mutilation. These objections were answered in various ways by Buddhist apologists, who argued, for example, that by abandoning his home, the Buddhist takes all parents for his own, and so exercises a superior brand of filial piety—*true* filial piety.

Many varieties of Buddhism made their way to China, but only those of the Mahāyāna strain survived. Chinese Buddhists, unaware that Mahāyāna had already fragmented into countless sects, were at their wits' end trying to reconcile the various doctrines alleged to have been taught by the Buddha. This led some Chinese Buddhists to cling to a single *sūtra* or doctrine, and it led others to a form of syncretism in which superficially conflicting doctrines are arranged in order of increasing subtlety.

The Three Treatise School is a Chinese version of Nāgārjuna's Mādhyamika, and the Consciousness-Only School taught a form of idealism based on Yogācāra. But Nāgārjuna's subtle dialectics found little favor with the Chinese, who were also unprepared for the Yogācāra thought that reality is mental. Other versions of Mahāyāna Buddhism were more successful. Tien Tai (T'ien T'ai) and Hua Yen made elaborate arrangements of all the forms of Buddhism in order to show how all views lead naturally and inevitably to their own teachings. Both of these forms of Buddhism came with impressive rituals and devotional observances. The *Lotus Sūtra* itself was considered to have so much magical power that the mere recitation of its name guaranteed salvation.

Two popular forms of Chinese Buddhism, both adaptations of Indian Māhāyana, were Pure Land Buddhism and Chan (Ch'an). The Pure Land School is grounded in a belief in the Bodhisattva Amitābha and his Western Paradise, entrance to which is attained by chanting his name and keeping him in mind, especially at the moment of death. While the Pure Land School offered salvation through divine grace and devotion, Chan offered meditation, monasticism, and a down-to-earth approach spiced with a sense of humor. Bodhidharma, the First Patriarch of Chan, spent years staring at a wall, thereby promoting unrelenting meditation. By the time of Hui Neng, a system of monasteries had developed and Chan had fragmented into different factions, each with its own idea of the path to enlightenment. Hui Neng, for example, favored the *Diamond Sūtra*, according to which 'truth', 'goodness', and 'self' are only names, referring to no reality at all.

Some say that of all the types of Buddhism, Chan is closest to the Buddha's original teaching. In Chan, the Buddha is seen as just another person, not a supernatural being. What he offered was meditation, and with it the capacity to appreciate the present. Features that found their way into Buddhism just to attract converts (or philosophers) are either disregarded or not taken literally.

Buddhism did not survive in China. It was eventually overcome by "Neo-Confucianism," a general term for a variety of movements acknowledging the authority of Confucius and Mencius, but reacting to and adopting many later ideas. Ju Xi (Chu Hsi) (1131–1200) blended elements of Daoism, Buddhism, and Confucian thought and produced a definitive and basically naturalistic synthesis, which established the character of all later Chinese thought.

Buddhism migrated from India to Korea, and from Korea and China to Japan, where a number of the Mahāyāna forms developed characteristic Japanese versions. The Japanese Buddhists distinguish between *jiriki*, the attempt to gain enlightenment or some other spiritual goal by works, and *tariki*, the reliance on the power of another. Zen (the Japanese term for Chinese Chan Buddhism) adopts a radically *jiriki* approach. The Pure Land School (or in Japan, the Jōdo Sect) is *tariki* because its members seek rebirth in the Pure Land through the grace of the Bodhisattva Amitābha. The emphasis on the magical power of the *Lotus Sūtra* is another instance of a *tariki* approach. According to Nichiren (1222–1282) one did better calling on the power of the *Lotus Sūtra* than on any *bodhisattva*, and he offered a saying his followers use to this day: "Namu myōho renge-kyō" (Reverence to the wonderful law of the Lotus).

Theravāda Buddhism spread to Southeast Asia, and the forms there preserve some of the oldest Buddhist traditions. In Tibet, the Mādhyamika coalesced with the local shamanistic religion to flower into several different forms of Tibetan Buddhism, some of which are now being taught in the West because of the diaspora of Buddhists brought about by the Chinese invasion of Tibet in 1949.

Moralism and Chinese Thought

Our ways of satisfying our biological and personal needs are selected from a limited range of strategies. As long as there are families, homes, possessions, desires, and work to be done, our forms of life will be mutually intelligible. We start with the same problems, and we are capable of appreciating and understanding each others' solutions.

In the introduction to his translation of the *Analects*, Lau says that even before Confucius, two moral concepts were current in Chinese society, "The Way" (*Dao*) and "Virtue" (*De*), and that both "in some way, stem from Heaven" (Lau, 12). It is significant that Lau qualifies his claim with the words "in some way." It would be a mistake to think of Heaven as a personal God like Jehovah, laying down a moral law. Although supernatural beings were not unknown in China, the Chinese did not (with the exception of Mo Zi) back their moral notions with divine authority or enforce them with threats of supernatural punishment. Dawson makes this clear, "The importance of ritual in Chinese society may partly be due to the fact that the Chinese did not share our concept of a divine law-giver, so that human conduct had to depend much more on codes of behaviour based on precedent" (Dawson, 27).

The Chinese may not have appealed to a divine lawgiver, but they provided moral guidelines for behavior, and they promoted their virtues and values. Dawson says that the Chinese, "being unfamiliar with other advanced societies, considered *li* to be universally valid" (Dawson, 27). He adds that Xun Zi "took the matter a stage further and elevated *li* to the status of a cosmic principle. 'Heaven and Earth gave birth to the *li*', he declared" (31). In his book on Confucius, Herbert Fingarette says that in seeking the "Way" the Confucians were attempting "to characterize some object or action as objectively right or not" (Fingarette, 22). In learning the *li* "one's own effort provides the 'push', but it is the intrinsic nobility of the goal that provides the 'pull' " (27).

Assuming that the Chinese were in the business of moralizing, what would the Confucians, for example, have said to someone who wondered why anyone should bother to acquire *ren*, or conform to the *li*? What they did say was not very different from what moralists the world over have said in answer to similar questions.

First, in *Analects* 4:2, Confucius says that "the man of wisdom cultivates humanity for its advantage" (Chan [1], 25), which suggests that *ren* is in one's self-interest. The idea that crime does not (or should not) pay lies behind Mo Zi's stories of angry gods: the concept of karma; the Hindu, Buddhist, Christian, and Islamic doctrines of hell; and the Legalist's promise of punishment for the disobedient. Self-interest may seem an unworthy motivation for good behavior, but there is no doubt that, unlike abstract arguments, it will be taken seriously. Even so, the Confucians did not praise self-interest as a motive. In a famous passage, Mencius condemns profit and recommends humanity and righteousness on their own merits (60–61).

Second, when discussing the uses of '*jun zi*' and '*ren*', we saw how the Confucians hoped to exploit persuasive definitions of these highly charged moral terms. If enough people want to be called "superior," if they accept the claim that a superior man (*jun zi*) is humane, and if they accept what Confucius says about what is involved in being humane, then there may actually be some change in the way they treat others. That does not alter the fact that the pleasant result was accomplished by a persuasive definition, a trick of language to change attitudes and behavior. Mencius was especially given to offering persuasive definitions. Recall his remark that the "despised creature called Chou" was a scoundrel, and so his murder was not the murder of a sovereign.

Third, Confucius appealed to the respect the Chinese felt for the past—a respect that led many of them to count the fact that something was done in the past as a reason for doing it in the present (and for continuing to do it in the future). Sometimes this appeal was coupled with a "creative interpretation" of an ancient text. Some line from an old song or poem would be adopted to express or support a new value. Dawson reminds us how Confucius turned a passage from a song about horses "not swerving" into a general moral maxim: "let there be no depravity (swerving) in your thoughts" (Dawson, 23).

It was not only Confucius who made this appeal to the past. When Mencius proposed an utter novelty, like a public school system or a plan for agriculture, he would identify it as part of the "ways of the ancient kings." He said that in all things the rulers should imitate the ways of the ancient Kings Yao and Shun, and that "in levying taxes, it would be wrong either to tax more or to tax less than Yao and Shun did" (Creel, 85). Creel notes that while Mencius frequently recommends righteousness on grounds of self-interest, "he does speak of the doctrines of Yao and Shun as having authority in themselves" (87).

Finally, when the Confucians gained control of the educational system, they were able to see that everyone was indoctrinated with stories and slogans promoting traits and behavior they wished to produce in the people. Children were told of little Wu Ming, "who let himself be eaten by mosquitoes in order to divert them from his parents, and Lao Lai-tzu, who in adult life still dressed as a child and played with his toys to make his parents happy" (Dawson, 49).

Mencius claimed that the emperor Shun appointed a minister of education to instruct the people who were failing in their moral duties. As Dawson notes, "in the nineteenth century it was still widely believed that such moral training was the cure for the ills which had beset the country, so it was urged that colleges should be established in troubled provinces to educate the people in Confucian principles" (Dawson, 11).

Confucius and Mencius were moralists, but the Daoists and the Legalists were amoralists. What they offered in place of Confucian morality were two alternative amoralist political systems: the Legalists advocated a system of oppressive authoritarianism and the Daoists one of permissive cooperation. Chan tells us that the Legalists "rejected the moral standards of the Confucianists and the religious sanction of the Moists in favor of power" (Chan [1], 251). The same could be said of the Daoists, as long as 'power' is understood in a Daoist (*yin*) rather than a Legalist (*yang*) way. But even if the Daoists and the Legalists were amoralists, this does not mean we will find no moralistic utterances in their writings. We have already seen that amoralists can lapse (intentionally or unintentionally) into moralist discourse, and we know that translators often project their own moral assumptions (which are built into the language they speak) onto the texts they translate.

Still, even given such real or projected lapses into moralism, the Daoists and Legalists do not make the kind of moralist assumptions we find in the writings of the Confucians, and they are often critical of moral distinctions as such. Lao Zi saw the rise of Confucian virtues as a sign of disorder, and Zhuang Zi asked: "How can speech be so obscured that there should be a distinction of right and wrong?" (Chan [1], 182). "From my point of view," he said, "the principle of humanity and righteousness and the doctrines of right and wrong are mixed and confused. How do I know the difference among them?" (188).

According to Verse 5 of the *Dao De Jing*:

> Heaven and earth are not humane (*jen*).
> They regard all things as straw dogs.

> The sage is not humane.
> He regards all people as straw dogs.
>
> (Chan [1], 141)

Nature does not exhibit the Confucian virtue of *ren*, and neither does the sage. Straw dogs were used in religious ceremonies, dressed up and placed on the altar. During the ceremony itself they were treated with the greatest respect, but when the ritual was finished, they were tossed aside and forgotten. We can expect little more from nature, but that a *sage* should be as neutral and uninvolved as nature itself has struck many Confucians as nothing short of scandalous. Creel replaces the line about "straw dogs" (which is actually there in the original) with the claim that the sage treats the people "ruthlessly." Then he says that since the "enlightened Taoist is beyond good and evil" this conception can result in terrifying consequences "if it falls into the wrong hands."

> For the enlightened Taoist is beyond good and evil; for him these are merely words used by the ignorant and foolish. If it suits his whim, he may destroy a city and massacre its inhabitants with the concentrated fury of a typhoon, and feel no more qualms of conscience than the majestic sun that shines upon the scene of desolation after the storm. After all, both life and death, begetting and destruction, are parts of the harmonious order of the universe, which is good because it exists and because it is itself. (Creel, 112)

In his eloquence Creel forgets that he is talking about an *amoralist*, and he makes his "Taoist monster" judge that the universe (or its harmonious order) is intrinsically good. Creel's slip is a sign of how difficult it is for someone who is a moralist to keep focused on what the amoralist is saying.

This lack of sympathy with amoralism leads to another misunderstanding. Creel subscribes to the popular assumption that one who is beyond good and evil is more likely than the moralist to tear things apart. He never explains why an "enlightened Daoist" would conceive a whim to destroy a city—an act that hardly seems to exemplify *wu wei* in any of its interpretations.

7

Moralism and Amoralism in Greece

A man who is good for anything . . . ought only to consider whether in doing anything he is doing right or wrong—acting the part of a good man or of a bad.

—*Socrates, in Plato's* Apology

Minoans and Mycenaeans

BY 4000 B.C., settlers from Greece had migrated to the Cyclades, small islands in the Mediterranean. Pottery and other artifacts tell us that a civilization flourished there between 3000 and 2000 B.C. The fall of this culture was followed by the rise of the Minoans of Crete who, by 2000 B.C., were living in colossal palaces and writing in a language we have not yet deciphered. By 1700 they were the undisputed masters of the Mediterranean and had put an end to the piracy that was flourishing there.

The Minoans were gifted artists with an eye for beauty and grace, but until Sir Arthur Evans uncovered the ruins at Knossos in 1900, they were nearly forgotten. In 1952, one of the two types of writing found in those ruins was deciphered. It was called Linear B and it turned out to be a form of Greek. This led to the hypothesis that somewhere around 1400 B.C. Greek invaders overran Knossos. Spyridon Marinatos has concluded that the Cretan civilization was destroyed around 1450 B.C. by tidal waves and the fallout from the eruption of Thera (Marinatos).

Civilization came more slowly to the mainland than to the small islands and Crete, but by 3000 B.C. the mainlanders had begun to develop a distinctive culture, stimulated by the wine and olive industries. Then, around 2000 B.C., Indo-Europeans in horse-driven chariots overwhelmed the more peaceful inhabitants, much as their relatives did when they invaded the Indus valley and ended the Harappan civilization.

The result of this invasion was a cultural setback followed by a period of vitality and growth. By 1600 B.C. the people we now call the Mycenaeans had done very well for themselves by combining the arts of trade and piracy. Though the Cretans remained the dominant power, the competition was definitely on. Before the situation could erupt into an all-out war, the eruption of Thera changed everyone's plans. The resulting tidal waves destroyed ports, palaces, and ships, and the fallout of ash ruined agriculture. Crete was defenseless and the Mycenaeans, untouched by the cataclysm, occupied the palace at Knossos and destroyed the other ones. Linear B is the form of Greek used by the Mycenaeans, and that is why it was found at the palace at Knossos.

Mycenaean society was organized into states of varying size, power, and importance. Each state was controlled by its king, who resided in one or more strategically located palaces. By 1300, Mycenae had become the most important state in Greece, and by 1250, extensive fortifications were being built by all the palaces that could afford them. If there was a Trojan war, it probably took place around 1220, but whatever the truth about *that*, there is no doubt that the Mycenaeans developed an appetite and a knack for sacking cities. This, along with their fondness for piracy, was ruining trade in the Mediterranean and unraveling a civilization that had been developing for hundreds of years. The shipping lanes were closed, with ironic and disastrous results for the Mycenaeans, who depended on imported grain.

Thucydides tells us that the Greeks were away at Troy for ten years, and that in their absence the situation at home deteriorated rapidly. Many heroes who returned from their raids and wars may have found as unwelcome a situation as did Agamemnon, who was killed by his wife and her lover, and Odysseus, whose palace was filled with young heroes eating his food, drinking his wine, and contending among themselves for the hand of his wife, Penelope.

The Āryan Harvest

Around 1200 B.C., the palace at Pylos was sacked and leveled so thoroughly that its ruins lay undiscovered until 1939. Palaces at

Tiryns, Iolkos, Gla, and Mycenae were also destroyed, looted, and abandoned at about the same time. The Mycenaeans, with their pirate philosophy and their murderous heritage, had no more chance of survival than any group of city-states (or countries) led by killers dedicated to conquest and intoxicated by honor and pride.

After the collapse of the Mycenaean palace system, order vanished and refugee camps dotted the ruins of the former citadels. Those who could fled across the Aegean Sea to Ionia (Asia Minor), where they tried to reorganize their shattered lives. They developed a system in which the fundamental economic and political unit was the aristocratic *oikos* (household). Strength, ruthlessness, courage, and skill in battle were still valued in the new society, and there was little room outside one's own family or clan for mercy, compassion, kindness, or cooperation. Within the *oikos*, duties were determined by status and kinship and by rules retained or restored from tribal days. Crimes were dealt with at the family level and "avenged by kinsmen according to the ancient customs of blood-vengeance" (Wood and Wood, 18). The honor and status of the aristocrat (or *agathos*) at the head of an *oikos* was determined in large part by his *time*, a word that, according to A.W.H. Adkins, "denotes the possessions of which the *agathos* has more than any other human being" (Adkins [2], 14). He adds that the word carries a high emotive charge, and that "to defend one's own *time*, if possible to acquire more, and at all events not to lose any of what one has, is the principal motivation of Homeric man" (15).

As the independent *agathoi* evolved into an aristocratic ruling class, the difference between the aristocrats and the common people, who farmed the land, grew, and the *aristoi* (the "best") were seen, even by the farmers, as natural and inevitable owners and rulers. With the growth of centers of trade and handicraft, there developed a class of merchants and workers no longer dependent on the aristocracy for their livelihood, and the *polis* (city-state) began to replace the *oikos* as the center of power. As the aristocrats held more closely to the tribal principles on which their inheritance of wealth and power depended, the independent laborers, farmers, merchants, and seamen developed the concepts of democracy (rule by the *demos*, the people) and political equality. Yet even in this new situation, the workers often found themselves bound in servitude to the aristocrats.

'*Agathos*' and Its Persuasive Definition

The chief word of commendation in ancient Greece was '*agathos*'. Homer used it to "denote and commend men who are effective and successful fighters," and who "unite in themselves courage, strength, wealth and high birth" (Adkins [2], 12–13). By a familiar twist, the word came to denote those who were *supposed to be* effective and successful fighters—the military aristocracy—and it came to denote them no matter what characteristics they actually had. Thus, '*agathos*' takes its place next to '*brāhmin*' and '*jun zi*' in our lexicon of important and powerful words from the ancient world. In India, the word '*brāhmin*' stood for someone born into the highest caste; in China, '*jun zi*' denoted a member of the hereditary nobility; and now we learn that in Greece, '*agathos*', a strongly positive word, was used to denote people of an upper class without regard for whether they possessed the qualities implied by the word.

An *agathos* was supposed to display the virtues of boldness, courage, strength, and dominance. Kindness, consideration, and justice, or *dikaiosunē*—"the quiet co-operation of one citizen with another" (Adkins [2], 42)—were not in serious competition with the bloody and violent Homeric virtues. Nevertheless, a few reformers, bent on softening the ways of the aristocrats, and perhaps of the common people as well, suggested that anyone who is "really" *agathos* will manifest some of the cooperative virtues. We find this claim in the Theognid poems from the sixth century B.C.

> Be willing to be a pious man and dwell with little wealth rather than be wealthy with possessions unjustly acquired. The whole of *arete* is summed up in *dikaiosunē*: every man, Cyrnus, is *agathos* if he is *dikaios*. (Adkins [2], 42)

Adkins remarks that this verse "must have amazed the writer's contemporaries," for its effect is to smash "the whole framework of Homeric values" (42). If, that is, it had been accepted. But in the post-Mycenaean world sung about by Homer, *dikaiosunē* and other traits *we* call virtues—kindness, gentleness, compassion, and cooperativeness—were not parts of the excellence of an *agathos*.

Hesiod

Hesiod's *Works and Days* (written around 700 B.C.) is a collection of agricultural and moral advice addressed by Hesiod to his brother, "Foolish Perses." It contains information about planting, harvesting, the seasons, and the weather; and it includes advice about how to survive in the society that was then coming into being. The competitive traits of the *agathoi* were still applauded, but there was a move afoot to focus those traits on something other than combat. Hesiod told them that hard work was no disgrace, and that those who work hard and grow rich will be loved by gods and by humans. He also told them that crime, injustice, and unfairness do not pay. As he says to "foolish Perses": "He who does *kaka* (harm) to another does *kaka* to himself, and a *kakē* (harmful) plan is *kakistē* (most harmful) for the person who made the plan" (Adkins [2], 27). Sometimes the harm is returned by other humans, but in *Works and Days* (ll. 321–33) Hesiod makes it clear that human retribution is supplemented "in the end" with divine justice.

> If a man gets wealth by force of hands or through his lying tongue, as often happens, when greed clouds his mind and shame is pushed aside by shamelessness, then the gods blot him out and blast his house and soon his wealth deserts him. Also he who harms a guest or suppliant, or acts unseemly, sleeping with his brother's wife, or in his folly, hurts an orphan child, or he who picks rough quarrels, and attacks his father at the threshold of old age, he angers Zeus himself, and in the end he pays harsh penalties for all his sins. (Wender, 68–69)

Retribution-minded moralists often find it hard to restrict the rewards and punishments to this life, this world, or even to the perpetrator of the deed. It was once believed that misfortune falls on the children (or even the countrymen) of those who do wrong, though, as Adkins suggests, the Greeks' growing sense of individualism may have led them to reject this displacement of *kaka* (Adkins [2], 43–44).

> In Aeschylus we find two uses of the belief [in postmortem retribution] to deter from injustice. In the *Suppliant Women* Danaus maintains that no man who forced marriage on his daughters would be pure, but that even when dead he would have to pay a penalty:
>
> > In the next world, it is said, another Zeus pronounces final judgment among the dead for wrongdoing.
>
> In the *Eumenides*, too, the Furies threaten that they will wither Orestes and carry him off to Hades to be punished for his matricide. They add:
>
> > There you will see all other mortals who have impiously wronged a god, some guest-friend or their dear parents, each receiving his deserved punishment. For Hades is a

> mighty judge of mortals beneath the earth, and he watches with faithfully recording mind.

> In such passages as these Hades, the 'other Zeus', is believed to punish in the next world the injustices which it is hoped that Zeus will punish in this, and which he all too frequently fails to punish. In the next world, however, there can be no escape, and punishment falls, not upon the descendents, but upon the wrongdoer himself. Insofar as it is held, surely this belief must be a powerful inducement to be just. (Adkins [2], 96–97)

Government and War

These first efforts to bring more cooperation and gentleness into the Greek world were unsuccessful. City-states flourished and dissolved, and wars, broken alliances, and revolutions were common. Sparta and Athens, both in out-of-the-way locations, avoided the worst of these troubles, and each developed a distinctive form of government. Slavery was a pervasive feature of the Greek world, but while Athens had slaves, Sparta was built on the institution of slavery. The Spartan aristocrats had conquered and enslaved the original inhabitants of their domain, creating a class of slaves ("Helots"). In order to preserve their way of life and to prevent other city-states from inciting rebellion among their Helots, the Spartans developed a closed militaristic society characterized by what they called "law and order."

In Athens, the tribal institutions that developed after the collapse of the Mycenaean palace civilization paved the way for the growth of a feudal aristocracy. In a process that has been repeated so often that one is tempted to think of "historical necessity," the hereditary nobility and large landowners began to accumulate more land and to enslave the peasants and landless craftsmen. According to Aristotle, "the people were in revolt because the many had become slaves to the few" (Wood and Wood, 31).

In 594 B.C., Solon, who had been selected to deal with this problem, eliminated debt-slavery and freed those who had already become slaves because of their debts. He gave political power and full citizenship to many non-aristocrats and introduced a "people's court," in which anyone could introduce litigation, and a court of appeals, where common people could appeal decisions rendered by aristocratic magistrates. Then, leaving no doubt at all about his legendary wisdom, he left town.

Solon's reforms, being equitable, satisfied no one; conflict, intrigue, and violence flourished as aristocrats resisted the reforms and radicals tried to push them even further. In 561 B.C. the Assembly voted to give a bodyguard to Peisistratus, a popular general, who promptly used it to make himself tyrant. Though he was exiled twice, he was twice restored to power, and his relatively moderate tyranny lasted until his death in 528. His sons Hippias and Hipparchus ruled until 514, when Hipparchus was murdered. Hippias, becoming suspicious and vengeful, killed many Athenians until he was forced into exile by aristocrats who were aided by the Spartans. Two groups of aristocrats then struggled for power, but in 508 Cleisthenes reestablished democracy, introduced additional democratic reforms, and further weakened the power of the aristocrats.

The struggles between the classes and conflicts about the emergence of democracy were soon dwarfed by a monumental external danger. By 540 B.C., Darius of Persia had seized the Greek colonies in Asia Minor. In 499 some of these colonies revolted, and when Darius set out to reclaim them, they appealed to their homelands for help. Sparta refused, but Athens and a few others offered some aid—enough to anger Darius, but not enough to do any good. After he squelched the revolt, Darius decided to punish the Greeks who had opposed him. In 490 he sent an expedition that destroyed Eretria and then landed at Marathon, where a unified force of Greeks met and, to everyone's surprise, demolished the Persians. This led Darius to assemble a much larger expedition in order to wipe the Greeks off the map, but he died before this invasion could get under way. In 481 his son Xerxes assembled a great army on the coast of Asia Minor. Most of the Greek states went over to Xerxes' side, or at least promised to remain neutral, but a small group, including Athens and Sparta, banded together and, by a combination of good fortune and bravery, again succeeded in destroying the Persians.

After the victory, Sparta advised Athens and the other Greek states to bring their colonists back home and to stay out of the Persians' hair. But Athens formed the Delian League, which enjoyed military success at the expense of the Persians for the next thirty years. This "defense league" was gradually converted into the Athenian Empire.

Democracy had been introduced in Athens in 508 B.C., and by 440 all male Athenians over age eighteen were welcome to attend a meeting of the Assembly, held every ten days. This Assembly had a steering committee of five hundred, chosen by lot for one-year terms.

There was also a powerful Council of Generals elected by the people and led for many years by Pericles, who could usually count on the Assembly to support his program of domestic improvement and foreign imperialism.

This policy troubled the Spartans and it troubled the aristocrats in Athens, who often found more to like in the orderly totalitarian slave state to their south than in the brash and erratic democracy that allowed the people to express their dissent. Despite intense political activity and extensive negotiations, the two states drifted into the Peloponnesian War, which lasted from 434 till 404 B.C. and ended with a Spartan victory over a starving and plague-ridden Athens.

In 411 Alcibiades and other opponents of democracy instigated a transfer of power to "The Four Hundred," who, after failing to negotiate peace with Sparta, conducted a reign of terror for several months until democracy was restored. In 404, in the wake of the loss of the war, a group of aristocrats called "The Thirty" ran Athens. This was a group of pro-Spartan exiles led by Critias and Charmides, associates of Socrates and relatives of Plato. For all his ruthlessness, Critias was able to stay in power only with the help of a Spartan garrison.

Neither Plato nor Socrates opposed these attempts to overthrow the democracy, and a number of the youthful disciples of Socrates supported the Spartans. According to Aristophanes, Socrates was "the idol of the pro-Spartan malcontents in Athens" (I. F. Stone, 121). The hostility of Socrates and Plato to democracy is well-known and clearly documented, and Plato's fondness for Spartan institutions can be seen in his attempts to describe the perfect state.

After their victory, the Spartans made the mistake of trying to run the empire Athens had assembled. They failed, and were beaten by Thebes in 371 B.C. Plato was born in 428 B.C., six years after the start of the war with Sparta, and he was twenty-four years old at the time of Sparta's victory. Five years later, Socrates was executed, giving Plato another reason to despise democracy.

The Philosophers

In the sixth and fifth centuries, Greek colonies on the coast of Asia Minor were flourishing in relative independence from a weak Persian empire to the east and from their native cities westward across the sea. After a time, the colonists began to neglect the gods they had brought from Greece and devised their own alternatives to traditional mythological explanations of the features and acts of nature. They tried to figure out things for themselves, and in the process they developed the naturalism and science that is often cited as the hallmark of the Western mind.

Thales of Miletus (*c.* 625–547) is considered the first philosopher of the West. He said that everything is made of water, and that change occurs because things are full of gods. Scholars have speculated about what he meant by his answers, but his questions seem clear enough. He wanted to know what things are made of and why they change, and he simply assumed that there is one basic substance.

Anaximines (*fl. c.* 545), also of Miletus, substituted air for water, and naturalized change by replacing gods with condensation and rarefaction. His world is a world of expanding and contracting gas. A third Milesian, Anaximander (610–*c.* 547), argued that nothing like earth, air, fire, or water could be the original material of everything else because things cannot come from their opposites. How can fire be made out of water? So he said that there was one basic substance, and he called it *aperion*, a word that has been translated as "the boundless" or "the limitless."

These thinkers were looking for a story they could tell that would help them make sense of their experience. Thales noticed that water can be a solid, a liquid, or a gas, and took it from there. Even the *aperion* was postulated because of the apparent incompatibility of opposites. The questions these early thinkers asked set the pattern for a wide variety of alternative answers. Heraclitus said that everything was fire, Xenophanes said it was earth, and Empedocles analyzed things into four basic "roots"—earth, air, fire, and water.

In time, the answers became more speculative and removed from common sense. The Greeks had discovered the many ways the senses can mislead, and this affected their theories. The new approach is best illustrated by Parmenides of Elea (*b.* 515). "Ply not eye and ear and tongue," he said, "but judge by thought." What *his* thought told him was that, despite appearances, nothing ever moves. He began with what seem to be two empty and undeniable truisms: (*a*) What is, is, and (*b*) What is not, is not. But he took (*b*) to mean that there is no empty space (what is not, i.e., nothingness, is not). Since there is no empty space, he reasoned, there is no empty place into which anything can move. Therefore, despite what our eyes tell us, there is no motion.

Greek atomism is sometimes characterized as an attempt to integrate the Heraclitean insight that things are in motion with the Parmenidean insight that they are not. What the atomists thought to be unchangeable were minute atoms, indivisible particles of matter. The change we see is due to the motion of large collections of these tiny items. Atoms themselves come in various sizes and shapes, and some atomists even equipped them with hooks and eyes to facilitate combination. The various tastes and textures of food were explained by postulating atoms of different shapes—jagged ones for vinegar and other sharp-tasting food, and smoother ones for water and fine wine. The world of the atomist is as naturalistic as a world can be. Reality is absolutely nothing but atoms combining and separating in the void. Even the soul was thought to be composed of the very smallest atoms, which are expelled at death and scattered by the wind.

The Greek term *sophia* meant "wisdom," and *philos* meant "love." Hence a philosopher is, in name at least, a lover of wisdom. But the Sophists were not so much lovers as they were teachers of (what they called) wisdom. They roamed the Greek world of city-states and colonies, offering their services to those who could afford the tuition. While they regularly debated the nature of wisdom, another item rarely absent from their curriculum was rhetoric: the art of speaking in public. This ability was the key to power and influence in the democratic assemblies and courts in the cities, and especially in Athens. A good Sophist, it was said, could argue the case of either side and could always make the weaker side appear the stronger.

The fathers of powerful families hired Sophists to teach their sons, but the fact that Sophists took money for their lessons led many Greeks to look down on them. Plato always insisted that Socrates *never* accepted money. But Socrates was not actively engaged in teaching people how to win arguments so much as deflating those who claimed to know things. Not many wealthy fathers were likely to pay him for that.

As they moved from city to city, the Sophists saw how the laws and customs of each city were relative to specific circumstances. Their instruction in debate was welcome, but their relativism was distressing to the aristocratic members of the *polis,* who were inclined to look upon the laws and customs that supported their way of life as objective and eternal. One of the ways the Sophists were said to "corrupt the youth" was by teaching them that law, custom, and morality are conventional and, for this reason, open to revision.

Perhaps the best known and most highly regarded Sophist in Greece was Protagoras, an older contemporary of Socrates. We met him in Chapter 2, where he was advocating relativism and defending the view that virtue, like language, is conventional and taught by all to all. According to Ellen Meiksins Wood and Neal Wood, "He viewed the democratic polis as a great school for moulding the citizenry from the cradle to the grave into cooperative, law-abiding, cultured, and virtuous human beings" (Wood and Wood, 90).

Socrates and Plato

Everyone knows the question to the answer: "The philosopher who drank hemlock." And almost everyone believes some version of the following story. Socrates was a wise and disputatious Athenian who made a practice of engaging the citizens of Athens in his version of philosophical conversation. These discussions all had the same pattern: The victim would begin by confidently asserting something or by offering a definition; inevitably he would be forced to admit that he did not really know what he was talking about. Because he antagonized the wrong people in this way, the story continues, Socrates was brought to court on trumped-up charges. Despite a masterful defense (the *Apology*), Socrates was convicted. Faced with the option of exile or death, he chose death. After arguing that it would be wrong for him to try to escape (the *Crito*), and after drinking the cup of hemlock, he became philosophy's first martyr (the *Phaedo*). This event, which occurred in 399 B.C., activated Plato, a young aristocrat under the spell of Socrates' penetrating intellect and forceful personality. In order to preserve Socrates' wisdom for posterity, Plato began to write dialogues, the earliest of which are dramatically enhanced records of Socrates' debates. Eventually Plato developed his own ideas, but he continued to write dialogues in which Socrates played the starring role. Only in his last dialogues did he stop using Socrates' name.

But, as we all know, the future is uncertain and the past is subject to change. The above story only gives us the bare bones version of the Socrates story, and historians do not even agree about that. When it comes to the details, the explanations, and the philosophy, there is no end to the questions and the answers. We do not know whether Socrates was as opposed to democracy as Plato was; we do not know why he was brought to trial or what he hoped to gain by choosing death; and—thanks to the intrinsic ambiguity of the dialogue form—

we do not know how to interpret our main source of evidence, Plato's dialogues.

Democracy takes heavy criticism and low blows in Plato's dialogues, and both come from Socrates. But since we do not know how to tell where Socrates stops and Plato begins, it is possible that only Plato thought democracy was a terrible form of government. Socrates may have been willing to put up with the equality for the sake of the liberty. On the other hand, he may have taken advantage of the liberty but despised the equality so much that he rejected the democracy that provided both. Or, it is possible that Socrates conspired against the Athenian democracy with his associates, who were in fact plotting their oligarchic revolts, even though he denied this at his trial.

Karl Popper characterizes Socrates as an egalitarian individualist, an opponent of the oligarchs, and a supporter of democracy who only criticized it to make it better. He says that Plato betrayed his old teacher twice: first when he abandoned egalitarianism for class-rule, individualism for collectivism, and democracy for rule by philosopher kings, and second when he put his un-Socratic reactionary ideas into the mouth of Socrates.

I. F. Stone bases his portrait of Socrates on Xenophon's *Memorabilia* as well as Plato's dialogues. His Socrates favored neither democracy nor oligarchy but was a totalitarian who supported rule by the one or several who "know"—a "monarchist" who was totally out of step with his times. Plato was even worse. In the fourth century B.C., Stone says, Plato "carried on the same intellectual assault against Athenian freedom and democracy that his master had launched in the fifth" (I. F. Stone, 129).

Stone emphasizes both the anti-democratic attitudes of Socrates and Plato and the animosity between the aristocrats and the common people. He thinks that at the time of the trial, Socrates' friends and disciples may have posed a genuine threat to the democracy. They had, after all, been involved in oligarchic takeovers in 411 and 404. The trial may have begun as an effort to quiet the old man down or get him out of town, but Socrates took charge of the situation and used it to achieve his own end, which, according to Stone, was to be convicted and executed.

To support his claim that Socrates' "apology" was in this way suicidal, Stone argues that not only did Socrates fail to conduct a masterful defense at his trial, but he passed up his best argument (the "free-speech" defense) without a word and adopted a boastful and arrogant tone with the jury. As Stone sees it, he "looks more like a picador enraging a bull than a defendant trying to mollify a jury" (I. F. Stone, 186). After Socrates was found guilty, a second trial was held to determine the penalty. In this trial Socrates made it impossible for the jury not to condemn him to death. Stone says that Socrates wanted to die; his "defense" guaranteed that this last service would be performed for him by the state.

But why did he want to die? Stone does not speculate, but here is a thought. Perhaps he hated democracy so much he thought that by getting it to kill him he would have revealed it to be no better than the ill-fated oligarchies his beloved students had embraced. Perhaps this was his final, kamikaze, passive-aggressive criticism of democracy, his way of getting it to cast eternal disrepute on itself. "Look," he might be saying, "at these lovely democratic laws that permit a mob of ignoramuses to condemn the wisest man in Athens to death." Perhaps he was just a stubborn old coot who decided to play "chicken" with the Athenians, who were, for whatever reason, tired of having him around. They said, "Shut up or get out." He replied, "Support me or kill me," thereby pushing enough of them over the line one last time.

Popper sees Socrates as a democratic saint and Plato as a totalitarian devil; Stone sees them both as totalitarian devils. Richard Kraut adopts a third stance. He argues that both Socrates and Plato believed that if there are any moral experts then they should be given the reins of government and unquestioning obedience. Moral experts know what true justice is, and they know how people ought to act. With the true pattern of justice before them, they can spot *and correct* deviations. What Plato inherited from Socrates, says Kraut, was the belief that "moral experts should rule" (Kraut, 234).

Because Socrates thought there probably never would be any moral experts, he avoided politics and continued his futile search for real definitions. He was convinced that the common citizens of a democracy, distracted by rhetoric and made stupid by hard work, will never understand the truth about the good life, and since even he, the wisest man in Athens, failed to attain knowledge and true definitions, he was pessimistic about the ability of any person or group to rule. At least the Athenian democracy allowed him to choose his style of life and speak his mind. Seeing both its good points and its problems, Socrates "was neither entirely opposed nor entirely friendly to Athenian democracy" (Kraut, 9).

Plato, however, shows no friendliness at all to democracy. Where Socrates' skepticism made him withdraw from civil life, Plato's epistemic optimism and his belief in the power of his style of moral education led him to seek political influence and to look to the day when some despot would take him seriously.

There is one more interpretation of the Socrates story to be heard. According to Gilbert Ryle, the story of Socrates' annoying habits and of his consequent martyrdom disguises the truth, which is that during the 370s (twenty-five or thirty years after the death of Socrates) Plato got into trouble with the politicians in Athens for teaching young men the art of "eristic."

> By the end of the 370's Plato had written and recited to Athenian audiences about a dozen dialogues in which Socrates debates with his interlocutors according to the Socratic Method. He plies his interlocutors with chains of questions, their successive replies to which entrap them in self-contradictions. The theses which they had begun by championing are by their own admission demolished by answers voluntarily given by themselves to interrogations strategically deployed by Socrates. . . . Dialogues of this structure can be called 'eristic dialogues'. (Ryle, 193)

Ryle thinks these early eristic dialogues were not transcriptions of arguments conducted by Socrates on the streets of Athens but revisions of debates—Ryle calls them "eristic moots"—that were held in Plato's school. A "Socratic dialogue" was then "compiled out of a run of fresh Moot-memoranda, supplemented by the memories of the composer and of his fellow-participants" (Ryle, 202). Ryle argues that Plato was blamed when his students used these powerful techniques on their fellow Athenians. It was Plato himself who was charged with "corrupting the youth," and he was ordered to stop teaching eristic in his Academy. Ryle concludes that this insult to Plato, rather than the death of Socrates, led to the writing of the *Apology*.

> Plato was not writing even a romantic history of the trial of the real Socrates in the *Gorgias*, the *Meno* or even the *Apology*. . . . The bulk of Socrates' defense is no more historical than Thucydides' speeches are historical. The *Apology* is for the most part a defense of the Socratic Method against an attack which was not made in 399, but was made well on in the 370's. The martyr's name was not 'Socrates' but 'Plato'. . . . The *Apology* is Plato's protest against the suppression of Plato's practice of the Socratic method. (Ryle, 151–52)

If we follow the sound policy of not rashly rejecting the argued positions of knowledgeable and sincere people, we can allow the versions of Popper, Stone, Kraut, and even Ryle to thrive as more or less likely alternatives. Each of the versions, and others too, may be taken seriously but held in epistemological quarantine. The ability to do this is a mark of someone who represents reality in a healthy way. When we cannot decide between two (or more) versions of events, we just have to learn to live with the ambiguity and the uncertainty. Sometimes things clear up.

Justice and the *Republic*

Ryle sees Plato's *Republic* as a combination of two works, joined because of their common subject—justice. The first is a short and incomplete eristic dialogue in which Socrates attacks the proposition, maintained by Thrasymachus, that justice is what is in the interest of the strongest party: Might makes right. The second and larger part of the *Republic* was, Ryle claims, designed to be read in private to a circle of elderly, conservative, and decidedly anti-democratic Athenian men. There Plato offers his own answer to the question "What is justice?" and tries to show that justice is superior to injustice.

In the introduction to his translation of the *Republic*, Francis Cornford observes that the Greek words we translate as 'just' and 'justice' are among the most ambiguous and flexible words in the Greek vocabulary, and nowhere more so than in the writings of Plato.

> The Greek word for 'just' has as many senses as the English 'right'. It can mean: observant of custom or of duty, righteous; fair, honest; legally right, lawful; what is due to or from a person, deserts, rights; what one ought to do. Thus it covers the whole field of the individual's conduct in so far as it affects others—all that they have a 'right' to expect from him or he has a right to expect from them, whatever is right as opposed to wrong. A proverbial saying declared that justice is the sum of all virtue. (Cornford, 1)

Such an all-purpose use was foreign to earlier understandings of 'justice'. But when the question changes from "What is most useful for the *oikos*?" to "What is most useful for the *polis*?" it is easy to see why justice—which had to do with fairness and getting along with one's associates—was valued more highly than aristocratic pride and a short fuse.

The Argument in the Republic

Early in the *Republic*, Socrates asks an elderly well-to-do Athenian gentleman, Cephalus, some rather personal questions about his wealth. Cephalus replies generously and not without wisdom. Old age is "no intolerable burden," he says "if you have a contented mind at peace with itself" (Plato [4], 5). Eventually Socrates asks Cephalus to tell him what he has found to be the greatest advantage of wealth. Cephalus replies by confessing that he has recently begun to feel some alarm about things that never troubled him when he was young. A man who has begun to grow old, he says,

> may have laughed at those stories they tell of another world and of punishments there for wrongdoing in this life; but now the soul is tormented by a doubt whether they may not be true. . . . If he finds that his life has been full of wrongdoing, he starts up from his sleep in terror like a child, and his life is haunted by dark forebodings; whereas, if his conscience is clear, that 'sweet Hope' that Pindar speaks of is always with him to tend his age. . . . Now in this, as I believe, lies the chief value of wealth, not for everyone, perhaps, but for the right-thinking man. It can do much to save us from going to that other world in fear of having cheated or deceived anyone even unintentionally or of being in debt to some god for sacrifice or to some man for money. (Plato [4], 6–7)

This is a thoughtful, honest answer. Cephalus has come, with age, to reconsider the possibility of punishment in the next world for harm done, perhaps even unknowingly, in this one. The advantage of wealth is that it has minimized this danger, and the attendant worry, by allowing him to treat other people well, to serve the gods properly, and to pay his bills.

Note that Cephalus never tries to define justice, that he does not say that cheating, deceiving, and being in debt are the only things we have to avoid, and that he does not say it is always wrong to lie. Nevertheless, Socrates, in his very next remark, attributes a definition to Cephalus that he never gave and then smashes this definition with a counterexample that has become a model for those who hope to learn to argue like philosophers.

> You put your case admirably, Cephalus, said I. But take this matter of doing right [justice]: can we say that it really consists in nothing more nor less than telling the truth and paying back anything we may have received? Are not these very actions sometimes right and sometimes wrong? Suppose, for example, a friend who has lent us a weapon were to go mad and then ask for it back, surely anyone would say we ought not

> to return it. It would not be 'right' to do so; nor yet to tell the truth without reserve to a madman. (Plato [4], 7)

But Cephalus never said that doing right "really consists in nothing more nor less" than anything, and Socrates' example of the madman has nothing to do with anything he did say.

When Cephalus understandably declines to get into an eristic struggle with Socrates, Polymarchus offers to defend the definition Socrates has attributed to his father. Before long Polymarchus has been forced to redefine justice as "helping friends and harming enemies." This was the aristocratic notion of proper behavior—an idea based on the *oikos*, where "friends" are those who fall within the narrow sphere of the family, the clan, or those owed special obligations because of their actions or their status. Socrates also demolishes this definition.

Socrates' easy victory is more than Thrasymachus can stand, and he bursts in to demand a precise definition of justice. When Socrates says he does not have one, Thrasymachus offers his own: " 'Just' or 'right' means nothing but what is to the interest of the stronger party" (Plato [4], 18). With an explicit definition before him, Socrates can get to work. With the help of some clever sophistry, he gets Thrasymachus to contradict himself by admitting that a *real* ruler (watch out for the persuasive definition) is as concerned about the good of his people as a shepherd is about the good of his sheep, and will never work for his own benefit.

Thrasymachus, by the rules of eristic argument, should admit defeat. Instead, he breaks in with an insult—Socrates, he says, you are as naive as a child whose nose needs to be wiped by a nurse! You don't even know that a shepherd is only concerned about the well-being of his sheep because he expects to sell them to be slaughtered. Likewise, he continues, "in politics, the genuine ruler regards his subjects exactly like sheep, and thinks of nothing else, night and day, but the good he can get out of them for himself" (Plato [4], 25). The "just man," like the shepherd who takes a benevolent attitude toward his sheep, "always has the worst of it" (25).

This move shifts the topic from the definition (or redefinition) of 'justice' to the question of whether justice pays. Thrasymachus simply insists that the just person is always the loser—he walks away with the smaller share, he pays more tax, and he emerges from public office poorer than when he entered it. He is convinced that injustice, when practiced on a grand enough scale, pays better dividends than justice.

Socrates, however, is firmly convinced that justice is the more "profitable."

> I will make no secret of my own conviction, which is that injustice is not more profitable than justice, even when left free to work its will unchecked. No; let your unjust man have full power to do wrong, whether by successful violence or by escaping detection; all the same he will not convince me that he will gain more than he would by being just. (Plato [4], 26)

Having stated their positions, Socrates and Thrasymachus launch into another eristic debate with Socrates asking more questions and Thrasymachus grudgingly giving the answers. The details of this stretch of the argument are so obscure and complicated that Cornford finds it unrewarding to translate the entire passage. Basically, Socrates gets Thrasymachus to admit that in the art of living, as in all the other arts, there is "a measure which is absolutely right, whether we recognize it or not" (Plato [4], 33). The amoralist will not be surprised that the argument lapses into obscurity at precisely this point. Here, shining as a jewel by its own light, is the essence of the moralist's claim—there is some objective limit, some absolute demand, some recognition–independent requirement, some prescribed pattern of conduct and being.

The eristic part of the *Republic* concludes with the rout of Thrasymachus, but it is clear that the audience is no more convinced than Thrasymachus. The point is made by Glaucon, who accuses Socrates of having "made a show of proving that justice is better than injustice," and then asks: "Is that enough, or do you want us to be really convinced?" (Plato [4], 42). If, as Hesiod and Socrates believed, justice is "more profitable" than injustice, then some *agathoi* may be motivated to act justly, but this has nothing to do with morality. The moralist is in business because a set of different questions can be raised, questions about the "intrinsic" worth of justice—moralists' questions. We can formulate them either as questions about what we *ought* to do, or as questions about what is *valuable*. Do we have an obligation to treat other people, even strangers, justly when it is not in our interest to do so? Is justice good in itself, apart from the consequences of being just? Is it *so* good that anyone who understood *how* good would choose it no matter what?

Glaucon wants Socrates to tell him "what is to be said in praise of justice in and for itself" (Plato [4], 43), so he offers to state the case for injustice so that Socrates can answer it. Civil behavior, he says, is a vexing compromise between what is best (the ability to do whatever we want to do) and what is worst (being trampled by others). Society is built on a "compact neither to do wrong nor suffer it," and justice is practiced unwillingly. Everyone, he said, is like Gyges, the shepherd who found a ring that made him invisible and immediately proceeded to seduce the queen, kill the king, and take over the kingdom. We all jump at the chance to perform undetected injustice. Finally, a perfect practitioner of injustice—one who manages to be unjust but to appear just—will "hold offices of state, ally himself by marriage to any family he may choose, become a partner in any business, and, having no scruples about being dishonest, turn all these advantages to profit" (47).

After this formidable challenge, Glaucon's brother Adeimantus adds to Socrates' task by asking that future rewards and punishments in the afterlife be excluded from consideration. Justice, according to the brothers, should be praised apart from any reputation, honor, or rewards it brings, in this world or the next: "You must not be content merely to prove that justice is superior to injustice, but explain how one is good, the other evil, in virtue of the intrinsic effect each has on its possessor, whether gods or men see it or not" (Plato [4], 53). If Glaucon and Adeimantus are not here asking Socrates to prove that justice is intrinsically valuable, they are at least asking him to prove that its intrinsic effects are.

Two Conceptions of Justice

According to David Sachs, Plato is actually working with two different notions of justice. There is, first, *conventional justice*, which one attains by conforming to the local, conventional, moral rules. A long list of conventionally unjust actions can be extracted from the *Republic*: embezzling, sacrilege, theft, betrayal, breaking agreements, adultery, neglecting parents and the gods, temple robbing, kidnapping, swindling, and killing.

The second kind of justice, which Sachs calls *Platonic justice*, is based on an analogy between the state and the soul. He says that each consists of three components: The state is made up of rulers, soldiers, and workers; the soul of reason, will, and desire. A state has Platonic justice when the wise rule, the soldiers fight, and the rest work at their assigned jobs without giving in to their potentially raging desires. Plato is thinking of Platonic justice when he has Socrates say, "Everyone ought to perform the one function in the community for which his nature best suited him. Well, I believe that that principle, or some form of it, is justice" (Plato [4], 127). Platonic justice in the individual soul is characterized in an analogous way—it occurs when desires are kept in check by the will in obedience to the dictates of reason. A soul lacks Platonic justice when

> some one part of the soul rises up in rebellion against the whole, claiming a supremacy to which it has no right because its nature fits it only to be the servant of the ruling principle. Such turmoil and aberration we shall, I think, identify with injustice, intemperance, cowardice, ignorance, and in a word with all wickedness. (Plato [4], 142)

Is Justice More Profitable Than Injustice?

When we ask whether the "just" person will always be happier than the "unjust" person, we face two separate questions, depending on whether we have conventional justice or Platonic justice in mind. Let us begin with conventional justice. It is all too obvious that people who commit acts listed as unjust in the *Republic* are sometimes happy. Some embezzlers, adulterers, and swindlers do live lives that are happier than most, and happier than their lives would have been if they had followed the rules of conventional morality. It is also well-known that paragons of conventional justice can have relatively unhappy lives. So, unless we postulate an afterlife or a next life where "justice is served," which is what Adeimantus asked Socrates not to do, we may have to admit that conventional injustice *can* be more profitable, or result in more happiness, than conventional justice.

What about the claim that a person who is just in the Platonic sense will be happier than the person who is not? If we spell out what Platonic justice involves, the question becomes: "Will the person who makes choices on the basis of rational deliberations always be happier than the person who is less rational?" Put this way, the answer again seems to be that the Platonically *unjust* person, the person not ruled by reason, may, with a little bit of luck, end up happier than the Platonically just person, who always follows reason.

Is Justice Good in Itself?

Glaucon thought that Socrates may have been the only person capable of telling him "what is to be said in praise of justice in and for itself." But what, exactly, was Glaucon asking for, and did Socrates ever satisfy him? Sachs argues that Plato never even *tried* to prove that

Platonic justice was good in itself, that he "consistently viewed his defense of justice as one made solely in terms of justice's effects" (Sachs, 66). But if Plato never tried to show that Platonic justice is good in itself, he nevertheless puts into the mouth of Socrates many things that suggest he did believe that it was valuable in some special way, and that it would be chosen over mundane happiness by anyone who understood what it was. In *Socrates and the State*, Richard Kraut has no doubt about the moralism in Socrates and Plato. He takes it "to be an uncontroversial matter that Socrates has an objective conception of ethics," that he "thinks there is an objective standard of justice" and "assumes that there are independent truths about the good" (Kraut, 11, n. 20).

Another Conception of Justice

When the aristocrats spoke of justice, they tended to think of it as harmony. This is reflected in the *Republic* when justice is defined as "everyone minding his own business," which amounted to allowing the few to make the rules, and requiring the many to harmonize with that. As it happened, the merchants, workers, and sailors did not buy this aristocratic arrangement. Instead, they proposed their own persuasive definition for the power-word 'justice'. They said that justice is equality, and they argued that in a *truly* just state the same laws will apply to everyone and all citizens will have the right to participate fully in the political process. Platonic justice, by contrast, is anti-democratic and involved with moralist assumptions about the intrinsic superiority of some people. The idea that justice is equality needs no moralist assumptions to put everyone on the same level: A citizen is a citizen.

When discussing degenerate forms of government, Plato ranks democracy as superior only to tyranny and worse than oligarchy. In such a government, he says, you are not obliged to be in authority, however good you are, nor to submit to authority if you do not want to. In a democracy all standards are gone, and anyone who calls himself "the people's friend" can be promoted to office. He continues with a venomous but amusing anti-democratic tirade that must have had his aristocratic admirers rolling in the agora. Plato blames disobedient children, fawning parents, impudent slaves, and the equality of the sexes on democracy, and concludes by saying that in a democracy even the animals walk down the street like freemen and the dogs behave like their owners (Plato [4], 289).

But democracy was not the absurd thing Plato suggested, and there were many honorable Athenians who understood what they had achieved by instituting the notions of self-government, freedom, and equality. It is these anonymous Athenians who discovered, and sometimes died for, the principles by which most people alive today either live or aspire to live.

I do not say that amoralists necessarily support democracy, but one way (and by far the easiest) to make sure that everyone is considered equal in value is to stop taking the idea of value seriously. If people have no value, there are no inferior or base people. Humans and other animals, and even plants, rivers, and mountains, can be respected, admired, appreciated, and cared for without addressing the topic of value at all. Amoralists who are democrats know everything they need to know—they know how to ask questions and how to count noses. It is only when someone begins to insist that some noses "are more equal than others" that indefensible forms of moralism emerge to rationalize the discrimination.

The Theory of Forms

While the ordinary citizens of Athens approved of the idea of justice as equality, others looked for an explanation of justice that would make it clear that power should not be in the hands of the people. It is here that Plato's Theory of Forms enters the picture.

Forms

Plato was not a skeptic, but he did accept Heraclitus's idea that our world is in a state of eternal flux. "You can't step into the same river twice," said Heraclitus—and Plato agreed. But Plato not only believed that the objects of our experience are constantly changing, he also knew that our senses introduce limitations and distortions of their own. He concluded, as some before and many after him have, that knowledge about the world of experience is impossible. Since he wanted knowledge, he had to find more stable "objects of knowledge," ones that did not change and that did not have to be known by the (finite and deceptive) senses. Since nothing in *this* world is like that, these objects, the Forms, had to "reside" in another world.

> First we must come to an understanding. Let me remind you of the distinction we drew earlier and have often drawn on other occasions,

> between the multiplicity of things that we call good or beautiful or whatever it may be and, on the other hand, Goodness itself or Beauty itself and so on. Corresponding to each of these sets of many things, we postulate a single Form or real essence, as we call it. . . . Further, the many things, we say, can be seen, but are not objects of rational thought; whereas the Forms are objects of thought, but invisible. (Plato [4], 217–18)

Rather than realizing that words like 'straight', 'circle', 'dog', 'bed', 'just', and 'good' have various roles and functions that we learn, as Protagoras said, from all those who speak the language, Plato assumed that each of the many things that are straight, or dogs, or just, or beautiful, merits one of these labels because it matches, or partakes of, or mirrors a "Form."

Did Plato really believe in a world of items open to inspection only by those who have somehow escaped the physical limitations of bodily experience? Or is this a "convenient fiction," a myth designed for people who insist on having answers? What *was* Plato supposed to say when people asked him how Socrates (or, closer to home, how he himself) differed from the Sophists? What justification was there for teaching eristic in his Academy? What could he say to justify his aristocratic beliefs and recommendations? Why was the rule of philosophers to be preferred to rule by the wealthy, the strong, or even the people? Plato could appeal to his Theory of Forms to answer all of these questions.

Everyone knew that the Sophists aimed at victory, and many were bothered by the fact that clever Sophists were able to argue either side of a case and win. Plato could distinguish Socrates from the Sophists by pointing out that Socrates accepted no pay, and that he never claimed to know the truth about anything. But he could not use the same characteristics to distinguish himself for he did accept pay and he claimed to know and to be able to teach.

Plato separated himself from the Sophists by opposing their relativism and conventionalism, and by postulating an absolute truth that he, but not they, had a way of apprehending. The sequence of studies followed in his Academy was supposed to involve a gradual and guided ascent to knowledge of the Forms, the true essences of things. No Sophist ever promised anything that grand. Eristic was a preparation for this more advanced study, and not an idle pointless game or an end in itself. It was the logical solvent that dissolved false notions and cleared the mind for the positive search for Truth. 'Dialectic' was the name Plato gave to this more positive investigation.

> So here, the summit of the intelligible world is reached in philosophic discussion by one who aspires, through the discourse of reason unaided by any of the senses, to make his way in every case to the essential reality and perseveres until he has grasped by pure intelligence the very nature of Goodness itself. This journey is what we call Dialectic. (Plato [4], 252)

Knowledge of the highest Form, the Form of the Good, is the "highest" knowledge possible. One who has arrived here understands everything worth understanding. Plato writes of coming to "grasp" the Form of the Good in terms usually reserved for describing mystical experiences. Even those who have the necessary mental equipment and who study hard cannot expect to reach this ultimate understanding until they approach fifty years of age. But then, when "they have seen the Good itself," they will "take it as a pattern for the right ordering of the state and of the individual, themselves included" (Plato [4], 262).

If we assume the existence and knowability of Forms, then (contrary to what the Sophists say) there is a right way to organize society and our own lives, a standard of justice by which actual institutions can be judged, and a right and wrong side of any argument about what to do. If the Forms can be discovered by Dialectic, and if a lover of wisdom has completed this "journey" and has "grasped by pure intelligence the very nature of Goodness itself," then it would be absurd to allow anyone else to make fundamental decisions.

Doubts about Forms

Plato appeals to Forms to answer such questions as "Why is this thing a bed?" and "Why will the wise choose the path of justice?" but his answers to these questions are as curious as the questions themselves. This thing is a bed, he said, because it stands in a certain relationship to Bedhood, a pattern existing in "another world, out of space and time." The beds we sleep in are, one and all, merely imitations, reflections, pale shadows, of the Perfect Bed. Plato even proposed to exile painters from his state on the grounds that when they paint pictures of beds and other things, they mislead people because they create imitations of things that are already imitations. Their painted beds were twice removed from Reality—from Bedhood. We do not get *knowledge* about beds from sleeping on them, making them, looking at them, or doing structural analyses of them, we get knowledge of beds by recalling the Form of Bedhood that each of us experienced in this other world before our souls were joined to a body. And so with every object or property that has a name.

The problem with this answer is that there is very little reason to suppose that, and no way to know if, it is correct. It is a wildly imaginative attempt to provide a solution to a host of problems, and it appeals to the imagination on many levels. We can all make correct sentences using the word 'Form' and enter into debates about the proper relationship between the Forms and things. But when (and if) we do this, are we doing anything more than mindlessly following "correct philosophical syntax"? We know that it makes sense to talk about things existing out of water, and so we just take it for granted that it makes sense to talk about things existing out of space, or out of time, or out of both. Rather than saying: "Forms existing outside space and time, what a curious philosophical fantasy," we are willing to blame ourselves when we do not understand how such things can be.

Plato's Theory of Forms was a brilliant solution to a number of problems, and we can see how someone in Plato's position would have been tempted to adopt it. But even Plato gave it up, and with it all his answers that depend on it. Today it is hard, though not impossible, to find a philosopher who would admit to believing in the Theory of Forms. It is a true philosophical antique, but like many of our antiques, not something we are inclined either to use or to throw away.

> Hsün Tzŭ's next question is: "What is the basis of similarity and difference?" At first sight, this may seem a queer or even a foolish question, but in fact it is quite profound. Why *are* dogs dogs, and horses horses? Plato would presumably have said that they are so because they are copies of the ideal dog and the ideal horse, in the same way that all shuttles used in weaving are patterned after "the true or ideal shuttle," an unchanging metaphysical pattern. Similarly, Plato says that beds and tables are what they are because they are copies of the ideal bed and the ideal table. And beautiful things are beautiful only because they "partake of absolute beauty." (Creel, 117–18)

> Plato tells us that beyond this ephemeral and imperfect existence here below, there is another Ideal world of Archetypes, where the original, the true, the beautiful Pattern of things exists for evermore. Poets and philosophers for millennia have pondered and discussed his conception. It is clear to me where Plato found his 'Ideas'; it was clear to those who were initiated into

> the Mysteries among his contemporaries too. Plato had drunk of the potion in the Temple of Eleusis and had spent the night seeing the great Vision. (Wasson, Ruck, and Hofmann, 19–20)

Aristotle

Although Aristotle studied at Plato's Academy, there is no evidence that he was actually Plato's student or associate. He rejected the otherworldly mysticism that infected (or graced) Plato's account of reality and offered a more naturalistic story, though one less naturalistic than that of the atomists.

Purpose

Aristotle did not see how to make sense of the world without attributing purpose to nature. Things have a natural order, a design, a way they should be. This purpose is not imposed on things from outside but is written into their nature. An acorn becomes an oak and not an apple tree because of its inner nature. Everything that changes becomes only what it has the potential to become. We know far more now about how this works than Aristotle did, but he knew enough to emphasize the fact that the fundamental design of a living thing is contained in the thing from the start.

Aristotle would have said that we can sometimes discover what the purpose of a thing is by noticing what is special about it. What is special about humans, he thought, was reason, and so our purpose, and in a sense our obligation, is to exercise and perfect that capacity—to become all we can and should be.

The Mean

Since we are social beings as well as intellectual beings, Aristotle distinguishes between intellectual virtue (being rational) and moral virtue (being good). In action as well as in thought, there is a right measure, a choice that falls between the extremes of too much and too little. A person with moral virtue will choose the action that is right in the circumstances.

Is this the answer of a moralist? Moralists read Aristotle as saying that in most circumstances there is an objectively right course of action for each of us. They fasten on his remark that the choice of the mean is a matter of perception, and they speak of *apprehending* the mean rather than *choosing* it. We do not choose a midpoint, we find it. If we apprehend something, it is there to be apprehended.

But it is easy to give an amoralist interpretation of Aristotle's remarks about the mean. Amoralists realize that we have to make decisions, and that our decisions had better be a function of what we know about the situation. We do not need a moral intuition to realize that an athlete needs more food than a librarian, and a sick person needs more attention than a well one. It should not be hard to purge moralistic assumptions from our thoughts about the mean, and to see Aristotle as advising us to avoid excess and seek balance.

The Good

In the *Nichomachean Ethics* Aristotle asks, "What is the good?" and answers, "happiness," but that takes some explaining. By 'the good' he seems to have meant 'the thing that everyone does desire' (not 'the thing everyone should desire'). This opens up the possibility that he does not have an objective account of value and is simply replacing talk about what is desirable with talk about what is desired. Unfortunately, when happiness has been described more fully (as a disposition to choose what is appropriate in the circumstances), it is not clear that everyone does desire this, and it is also possible that value sneaks back in with the word 'appropriate'.

Society

Socrates was probably, and Plato certainly, an enemy of democracy. They insult it, offer up bad arguments against it, and never cease yearning for something different. They divide humans into those who should rule and those who should be ruled, and they mistrust the original social impulses of human beings. Aristotle was considerably friendlier to democracy, and even allowed that "the principle that the multitude ought to be supreme rather than the few best . . . , though not free from difficulty, yet seems to contain an element of the truth" (Aristotle [2], 1281 a 40). His point is that while each individual is limited in virtue and information, the combined judgments of the many may be as good as, or better than, the judgments of their "betters." But while Aristotle lays this argument out as a point for democracy, he concludes that all forms of government have their difficulties and that "none of the principles on which men claim to rule and to hold all other men in subjection to them are strictly right" (1283 b 26). Then he provides a puzzling hypothetical support for rule by one or a few "whose virtue is so pre-eminent that the virtues or the political capacity of all the rest admit of no comparison with his or theirs." Such a person, he says, "can be no longer regarded as part of a state" and "may truly be deemed a God among men" (1284 a 3–11). He should be placed in charge, and "all should joyfully obey such a ruler, according to what seems to be the order of nature." "Men like him," he concludes, "should be kings in their state for life" (1284 b 33–34).

> A *śūdra*, though emancipated by his master, is not released from servitude; since that is innate in him, who can set him free from it. (*The Laws of Manu*, in Radhakrishnan and Moore, 189)

> But is there any one thus intended by nature to be a slave, and for whom such a condition is expedient and right, or rather is not all slavery a violation of nature?
>
> There is no difficulty in answering this question, on grounds both of reason and of fact. For that some should rule and others be ruled is a thing not only necessary, but expedient; from the hour of their birth, some are marked out for subjection, others for rule. (Aristotle [2], 1254 a 18–23)

Moralism and Greek Thought

One might have thought that after the fall of the Mycenaeans, the aristocrats would have learned a lesson. Perhaps some did, but others retained their pirate morality. The *Iliad*, which took shape a couple hundred years after the events it describes, opens with the story of an argument between Achilles and Agamemnon over a woman who was captured by the former and appropriated by the latter after a raid on Thebes. That was the sort of behavior the ethics of the Greeks permitted and encouraged, and the Trojans were not very different. Hector, the best of them, going out to die, prays that his boy will grow up to "kill his enemy and bring home the blooded spoils, and delight the heart of his mother" (Lattimore, 166). Whether the *Iliad* is a story of a Mycenaean raid on Troy, an account of a raid by post-Mycenaean exiles, or a fabrication based on stories of such raids, the ruins of heroically sacked and demolished Mycenaean cities proves that the ideals sung about by Homer were no poet's invention.

Like many early people, the Mycenaeans believed the gods enjoyed and responded positively to sacrifices. Cows, sheep, goats, and oxen—domestic beasts of considerable value—were slaughtered for the benefit of the gods (and the priests), but sometimes humans were chosen to be "given" to the gods. The troubles Aeschylus writes about in the *Oresteia* trilogy, which included the murder of Agamemnon by Clytemnestra and her own death at the hand of her son Orestes, began when Agamemnon sacrificed their daughter Iphigeneia before setting out on the Trojan expedition. After Orestes had killed his mother, there was no one left to avenge his mother's murder, so the Furies pursued him themselves. It did not matter that he had been divinely encouraged to perform his deed of revenge, he was still guilty of matricide and subject to torment.

Here we see the familiar presumption of objectivity—of "ought-to-be-ness." A murder, and particularly a murder of a relative, is not just an objectively neutral event that others, wanting to discourage, have agreed to forbid. A murder befouls the murderer, and introduces a pollution that can affect an entire city—as it did when Oedipus's killing of his father polluted Thebes. Pollution can sometimes be cleaned up, but in the *Oresteia*, even Apollo was unable to detoxify Orestes, who had killed his mother, and that is where Aeschylus introduces a new idea—the rule of law.

People cannot live together without mutually understood and generally observed customs. Social beings develop, almost from the start, the idea of fairness and an understanding that some things are required and others forbidden. Here are the roots of morality—one's share becomes one's right, what is required becomes one's duty, the qualities we want to see become virtues, and the ones we do not want to see become vices. What we value is taken to be valuable, and our valuing is seen as apprehension of an objective aspect of the world.

In the days of the *oikos*, the virtues of the *agathoi* included those qualities on which the survival of the *oikos* depended. These did not include what Adkins calls "the quieter co-operative excellences" because "it is not evident at this time that the security of the group depends to any large extent upon these excellences" (Adkins [1], 36). As soon as people began to see that many of the old Homeric virtues were obsolete in the *polis*, efforts to link *arete* (virtue) with *dike* (justice) began.

Moralist assumptions lie behind the religious beliefs of the elder

Cephalus, Polymarchus's *oikos*-based idea that it is just to help friends and harm enemies, and even Thrasymachus's belief that the strong ought to rule and the weak to obey. When Socrates asked these people questions, they were caught in the contradictions contained in their own moralisms. Cephalus, who was wise enough not to argue with Socrates, did not propose the rules Socrates criticized, but what he says makes it clear that he would have offered rules of conduct backed by a pious attitude toward the commands of the gods. These beliefs, if expressed, would have been open to attack by Sophists less skillful than Socrates for, as we see in Chapter 8, religion is a popular but ultimately flawed foundation on which to erect a moral system.

8

Gods and Religious Morality

> The attempts to found a morality apart from religion, are like the attempts of children who, wishing to transplant a flower that pleases them, pluck it from the roots that seem to them unpleasing and superfluous, and stick it rootless into the ground. Without religion there can be no real, sincere morality, just as without roots there can be no real flower.
>
> —*Leo Tolstoy, "Religion and Morality"*

THE STORY of the personal and political forces that eventually resulted in a near-universal belief in deities is a story of ignorance, superstition, greed, lust for power, good intentions, altered states of consciousness, hopes, fears, dreams, delusions, and lies. Early humans understood next to nothing about the way nature works. Birth, death, the seasons, fire, storms, animals, and eclipses were all shrouded in mystery and interpreted by myth. Goddesses and gods create worlds, weep rain, breathe life, eat sacrifices, and speak to mortals. They cause disasters, send prodigies, and make it possible to give simple, comprehensive, and sometimes satisfying answers to countless puzzles.

Thanks to their fertile imaginations and to mind-altering substances (soma, sacred mushrooms, Greek wine, Mesopotamian beer) and practices (yoga, meditation, and fasting), our ancestors enjoyed a variety of altered states of consciousness about the causes of which they were completely in the dark. When even the ordinary is a mystery, what is *extra*-ordinary—dreams, visions, hallucinations, powers—is either explained supernaturally or not explained at all.

Religious beliefs were reinforced by rulers and priests, who promoted the deities from whom their authority was supposed to flow. Hammurabi named Marduk as the source of the laws he promulgated, and in Exodus 32:15–16, Moses was said to have brought down tablets inscribed on both sides in the "handwriting" of God himself. In Egypt the pharaoh was believed to *be* a god. Chinese emperors claimed the Mandate of Heaven, and *brāhmin* priests cited the *Vedas* to support their privileges. Clearly, a religious backing was valuable to have, easy to claim, difficult to refute, and available to anybody. Without it the word of a prophet, king, priest, or reformer carried no more weight than that of the next person.

The Enforcers

In the West we rarely mention karma or reincarnation: we seem to prefer to leave the enforcement of morality (beyond what we manage to do ourselves) to supernatural beings. These beings can punish or reward anyone at any time, but they also preside at a final assay of the soul, and then oversee the distribution of punishments and rewards in their heavens and hells. But while Western moralists make no use of karma, Eastern moralists freely exploit belief in heavens, hells, and other extraordinary postmortem resorts. Indian, Chinese, and Japanese thinkers have imagined hells as horrible as (and heavens as delightful as) anything conceived in the West.

The god who gave the laws to Moses made it clear that he would handsomely reward those who obey him: rain at the proper time, peace in the land, victory over enemies, lots of children, and, as he said in Leviticus 26:12, "I will walk to and fro among you." But he also explained what was going to happen to those who "do not listen."

> But if you do not listen to me, if you fail to keep all these commandments of mine, if you reject my statutes, if you spurn my judgements, and do not obey all my commandments, but break my covenant, then be sure that this is what I will do: I will bring upon you sudden terror, wasting disease, recurrent fever, and plagues that dim the sight and cause the appetite to fail. You shall sow your seed to no purpose, for your enemies shall eat the crop. I will set my face against you, and you shall be routed by your enemies. Those that hate you shall hound you on until you run when there is no pursuit. (Leviticus 26:14–17)

Isaiah speaks of sinners who "have earned their own disaster," and adds that all will go well with the righteous, who will "enjoy the fruits of their actions" (Isaiah 3:9–10). Jeremiah promises disaster if the "apostate children" do not return to the Lord. "Mend your ways and your doings," he says, "deal fairly with one another, do not oppress the alien, the orphan, and the widow, shed no innocent blood in this place, do not run after other gods to your own ruin" (Jeremiah 7:5–6).

The deities of Greece were more capricious and human-like than Yahweh, but they were capable of equally stinging retribution and ferocious anger. They were distinguished from humans only by having more *arete* and *time* than even the greatest *agathos*, and by being immortal. In Heaven, as on earth, an excess of Homeric virtue can lead to destructive outbursts at what may seem to be slight infractions.

Although Homeric deities punished offenses, they usually did so only when they were offended by the offenses. There was no question of a consistently enforced law. After Hesiod it came to be believed, or at least asserted, that the gods punish acts of injustice. But because the distribution of good and ill fortune so often appears unrelated to what we do, this idea is easy to question and hard to defend. If one is to believe it, something must be done to explain the bad fortune of the good and the good fortune of the bad. One solution is to make the punishment reach beyond the grave to the agent in some future life here on earth or elsewhere. Another is to extend the punishment to someone "the evildoer" does not wish to see punished.

The Greeks and Hebrews believed in a divinely ordained punishment that falls on relatives, present associates, and future generations. The belief that God "punishes sons and grandsons to the third and fourth generations for the iniquity of their fathers" shares with the belief in karma an all-encompassing explanatory power (Exodus 34:7; see also Exodus 20:5; Numbers 14:18; Deuteronomy 5:9). The Greeks placed the limit at five generations, but even three would give us material to construct an explanation for the most dramatic cases of the suffering of the just.

This is a truly terrifying concept, but there is something paradoxical about using such an unjust device to promote justice. Laws designed for *humans* came to discourage punishing children for the sins of their fathers, and eventually this higher standard filtered up to the gods. After mentioning the proverb that "The fathers have eaten sour grapes, and the children's teeth are set on edge," Ezekiel, speaking for God, says, "This proverb shall never again be used in Israel" (Ezekiel 18:1–4).

> It is the soul that sins, and no other, that shall die; a son shall not share a father's guilt, nor a father his son's. The righteous man shall reap the fruit of his own righteousness, and the wicked man the fruit of his own wickedness. (Ezekiel 18:20)

By 2000 B.C. in Egypt it was believed that those who passed the judgment of Osiris, in which their hearts were weighed against the feather of *ma'at* (justice), could look forward to an eternity of luxury in "a delectable paradise with rivers, lakes, and islands, and fertile land ploughed by heavenly oxen and bringing forth its fruits in ever-increasing abundance and perfection" (E. O. James, 177). For the rest, at the foot of the scales there lurked a "hybrid monster in the form of a crocodile, hippopotamus and lion" (174).

The Mesopotamians had no such conception of a pleasant paradise after death, and so their hope was to avoid death. This was made difficult by the fact that the gods had reserved immortality for themselves. *The Epic of Gilgamesh* is the story of Gilgamesh's search for immortality and his ultimate failure. Yet the Mesopotamians did not see death as the complete end of consciousness. The dead, no matter how moral or immoral their lives had been, spend eternity in a shadowy and gloomy land of no return. "There, huddled together amid dust and dismal shadows in a semi-conscious condition, they were destined to wither away like the vegetation in the devastating heat of a Mesopotamian summer" (E. O. James, 179).

The Hebrews had a similar conception of the afterlife, but this changed under the influence of Iranian thought, and by 170 B.C., Sheol (the place of the dead)

> had been sub-divided into departments for particular cross-sections of the community with appropriate rewards and punishments respectively for the righteous and the wicked, and located in the far west, as in the Babylonian, Egyptian and Greek eschatologies [and as in Indian and Chinese legend as well]. (E. O. James, 191)

Heaven became the dwelling place of God and his angels. By the first century A.D., it was divided into seven heavens, the seventh being the pleasant destination of the righteous. Corresponding places of punishment evolved for the sinner.

A widespread belief (by no means restricted to primitive people and horror movies) is that spirits of the dead return and affect the lives of the living. There are benevolent spirits, but there are also malevolent ones who have been neglected after death or wronged while alive. A tremendous amount of effort and energy is expended in order to quiet these harmful beings. Mediums are consulted to discover what is bothering them, and invocations, charms, gongs, firecrackers, and incense are used to drive them away.

The undesirable consequences that now threaten the unjust person have begun to multiply. A violation can bring undesirable consequences for the agent, his family, or his children and grandchildren for generations. And the harm that comes to the agent can come in this world through the agency of other humans, gods, ghosts, or spirits; in another life on this earth; or in some suitable hell.

There are other possibilities, but even these are a winning combination. If a person does something wrong and something bad then happens to him, we can take this as evidence that the system is working; if nothing bad happens to him, we can say that he will pay in the next world, or that his descendants will pay in this one. If a good person suffers, or fails to prosper, the explanation will be that he had a secret crime, or that in another life he broke the rules, or that some ancestor of his did. When good people are rewarded with good luck, this is taken as proof of the justice of whoever or whatever is passing out the rewards.

> The evil-doer grieves in this world, he grieves in the next; he grieves in both. . . . The righteous man rejoices in this world, he rejoices in the next; he rejoices in both. (The *Dhammapada*, in Radhakrishnan and Moore, 293)
>
> Whoever does wrong to an innocent person or to one who is pure and sinless, evil recoils on that fool even as fine dust thrown against the wind (recoils on the person throwing it). (The *Dhammapada*, in Radhakrishnan and Moore, 302)
>
> Some enter the womb; evil doers go to hell; the good go to heaven; those free from worldly desire attain *nirvāṇa*. (The *Dhammapada*, in Radhakrishnan and Moore, 302)
>
> He who inflicts punishment on those who do not deserve punishment and offends against those who are without offense soon come to one of the ten states. He may have cruel suffering, infirmity, injury of the body, heavy afflictions (dread diseases), or a loss of mind, or a misfortune proceeding from the king or a fearful accusation, loss of relations, or destruction of treasures, or lightning fire burns his houses and when his body is dissolved

> the fool goes to hell. (The *Dhammapada*, in Radhakrishnan and Moore, 303)
>
> Those that deny Our revelations We will burn in Hellfire. No sooner will their skins be consumed than We shall give them other skins, so that they may truly taste Our scourge. Allah is mighty and wise.
>
> As for those that have faith and do good works, We shall admit them to gardens watered by running streams, where wedded to chaste virgins, they shall abide forever. We shall admit them to a cool shade. (The Koran, 4:54)

Some Unfamiliar Deities

Most of our examples have been from the Judeo-Christian tradition, but there are other traditions we might mention to fill out the picture. Goddess worship is discussed here because so much of our current religion seems to have been formed in opposition to it, and because it is undergoing something of a revival. We shall also briefly explore Zoroastrianism and Islam, two religions that take morality so seriously that in neither is there a question of erecting a wall between religious and moral beliefs.

The Goddess

When agriculture spread from the Middle East to other parts of the world, so did the myths that make sense of birth, growth, decay, death, and rebirth. These myths emphasized the role of the female as creator and provider, and there is every reason to believe that religion was matrifocal and society matrilocal. In *When God Was a Woman*, Merlin Stone claims that goddess worship was extensive in Neolithic Europe and in "the areas known today as Iraq, Iran, India, Saudi Arabia, Lebanon, Jordan, Israel (Palestine), Egypt, Sinai, Libya, Syria, Turkey, Greece and Italy as well as on the large island cultures of Crete, Cyprus, Malta, Sicily and Sardinia" (Merlin Stone, 23–24).

In the third millennium B.C., males began to replace females in places of power—both in heaven and on earth. Sometimes a new god would take a local goddess for a wife, but there are stories of a slaughter of the goddess (often depicted as a snake or a dragon) by a young god, who thereby becomes the supreme god. Versions of the story can be found in Yahweh's victory over the serpent Leviathan

(Job 41:1–8; Psalm 74:13–14), in the way Marduk of Babylon won authority over the other deities by slaying the dragon Tiamat, in the battle between "Indra, Lord of the Mountains, and the Goddess Danu and Her son Vritra," and in Zeus's struggle with the serpent Python (Merlin Stone, 68). It is likely that these legends reflect and symbolize the effort of the patriarchal invaders to crush both the worship of female deities and the political power of the females.

The activities of the goddess-followers are not well known because by the time writing came into serious use, goddess-worship was under attack and on the wane. Temples and records were frequently destroyed, goddess statues mutilated or ground into dust, and priestesses and priests killed. In the minds of the patriarchal monotheists, goddess-worship was one of the worst abominations on the face of the earth. Feelings ran high because what was at issue was power, pride, and paternity.

Zoroastrianism

Physical, linguistic, and religious traces of the Āryan invasions can be found from India to Ireland. The myths of the early Āryans tell of victory and conquest, and of gods who love war, dwell on high mountains and volcanos, and are associated with light, thunder and lightning, fire, and storms (Eliade, 187ff.).

One of the most fertile developments of the Āryan invasion took place in Iran and Persia. By 1000 B.C., the inhabitants of that area spoke an Indo-European language akin to Sanskrit and held to the three-class system of priests, chiefs, and herders so common in the Āryan world. Into this culture came Zoroaster, who, like the Buddha, Mahāvīra, and the writers of the *Upaniṣads*, criticized the priestly practices and rituals. At the age of thirty he had a powerful religious experience. He encountered an angel (Vohu Manah, or Good Thought), and his opposition to the Vedic-like polytheism of the Persians and to the practices of the priests was initiated by the revelations he received in this and other divine interviews.

Details of the life of Zoroaster as well as songs and revelations attributed to him, are collected in the Iranian *Avesta*. Ahura Mazda, a god of light living on a mountaintop, created the world out of nothing by thought. He also created the twin beings Spenta Mainyu (the Beneficent Spirit) and Angra Mainyu (the Destroying Spirit), one of whom chooses good and the other evil. The world does not exist on in sublime neutrality but is the scene of an all-pervading war between good and evil. Zoroaster preached that good will eventually triumph over evil, and that the world will be "transfigured" by this victory. The fire that ends civilization as we know it will consume the wicked and purify the earth. Until then it is important for all good people to unite under the banner of good and to fight evil with all their might. This religion became the religion of the Persian Empire, though it was greatly affected by the Greek occupation after the victory of Alexander. It was finally swamped by Islam.

Islam

In the seventh century A.D. the Arabian peninsula was sparsely populated with nomads who lived by tribal laws and the harsh ethics of revenge. They were polytheists who worshiped trees, rocks, and spirits. Muhammad, born in A.D. 571, was a man, not a god, and has never been thought of in any other way. He was chosen, by the god of the Jews and Christians, the *only* god, to be the last in the series of prophets stretching back to the Old Testament and including Jesus, who was only a mortal prophet, misunderstood and foolishly worshiped as a god by his apostles.

Little is known about Muhammad's early life, but by the time he was forty he had developed a strong religious inclination, and would sometimes retreat to a cave for prayer and meditation. The tradition says that one night Gabriel appeared to him and forced him to recite the message of God. After he began to preach, what he recited was taken down and grouped together in *suras* (chapters). The Koran is the collection of these recitations, and is said to contain the very words of God. Its message was one of uncompromising monotheism, featuring a final judgment between good and evil, a sensuous paradise, and a terrifying hell for sinners *and unbelievers*.

In 622 Muhammad and his followers moved to Medina and developed a political community. When war broke out with Mecca, he led his troops to victory. When he died in 632, Abū Bakr, rather than Ali, the husband of his daughter, was chosen to succeed him. The Arabs expanded rapidly under Abū Bakr and his successor Omar, who was assassinated in 644. In 656 Omar's successor was also murdered, and for a time it seemed as if Ali was finally to be allowed to lead the Arab world, but he was outfoxed by his rivals and eventually assassinated. Those who believe Ali and his descendants are the true heirs to the leadership are the *Shia*, or "party" of Ali.

The *Sunna* are the "orthodox" majority, who accept Ali's rival Muawiya and his successors.

Daniel Pipes observes that while Christianity provides general moral instructions, Islam specifies exact goals for all Muslims to follow as well as the rules by which to enforce them (Pipes, 11). The Koran forbids intoxicants, games of chance, and usury. It proclaims dietary laws, provides penalties for some crimes, condemns anti-social traits, and encourages repentance.

> You shall not kill one another. Allah is merciful, but he that does that through wickedness and injustice shall be burnt in
> Hell-fire. That is no difficult thing for Allah. (4:29–30)

> As for the man or woman who is guilty of theft, cut off their hands to punish them for their crimes. That is the punishment enjoined by Allah. He is mighty and wise. But whoever repents and mends his ways after committing evil shall be pardoned by Allah. Allah is forgiving and merciful. (5:37–39)

But not all situations are covered in the Koran, and so even though it is taken as the totally binding and utterly sacred word of Allah, its laws are supplemented with rules derived from several other sources. One major source is the *hadith* (traditions), the orally transmitted sayings and actions of the prophet. But in the years after Muhammad's death, proliferation of alleged *hadith* gave birth to a science of *hadith* criticism. Eventually, putative *hadith* were classified and by the end of the ninth century several collections of "sound" ones had been assembled. W. Montgomery Watt suggests that the principle of authentication was not so much historical accuracy but whether a particular *hadith* fit well with "the values on which the life of the Islamic community was founded" (Watt, 93).

The proclamations of the Koran, the sound *hadith,* and some other inspired moral, social, and legal teachings make up the *sharia*—the Islamic Law—which, according to the orthodox Muslim, is the ultimate, divinely dictated, and totally unquestionable basis for all conduct.

One of the main questions in Islamic countries today is whether to "institute" the *sharia* as law in fact as well as in theory. Pipes quotes the late Imam Ruholla Khomeini as having said that "Islamic government is rule by sacred law," and then he argues that this proposal is unrealistic, even contradictory (Pipes, 29). The rules of the Koran were written for desert nomads in the first millennium A.D. If they were to be instituted and taken literally today, they would make government impossible. The only way even a semblance of Islamic law could be instituted in many Muslim countries is by force, and the Koran insists that violence not be used by believers in Islam against other believers in Islam. Here, as elsewhere, theory and practice do not always walk the same road.

Revelation and Divination

If the gods have issued laws and determined penalties for offenses, then it is only fair for them to inform those subject to the laws and penalties. Richard Swinburne, in his book *Revelation*, asserts that it is "quite likely" that an all-powerful and all-good creator God would "intervene in human history to reveal things to us" (Swinburne, 70). Revelations come many forms. Some arrive in dreams and visions as commands and assertions from a deity or angel. God spoke *to* Moses and *through* the prophets; Jesus addressed his disciples and those who would listen; Marduk presented the laws to Hammurabi; Vohu Manah communicated with Zoroaster, Gabriel with Muhammad, and Moroni with Joseph Smith.

Even when commandments have been delivered in visions to people in authority, there remain daunting questions of interpretation and nagging suspicions of fraud. Further problems emerge when the gods do not choose direct forms of communication. Some believers think divine direction comes through subtle signs and portents; they think that it would deprive us of something valuable if God were revealed to the world in completely unambiguous terms. But the problem with this sort of revelation is that a believer can take just about any phenomenon at all—a breath of wind on the cheek, a sudden chill, a bolt of lightning, or the appearance of an animal—as a revelation. The recipient is (relatively) free to interpret one of these messages as he or she sees fit.

Most direct and indirect revelations arrive at the pleasure of the divinity rather than the recipient. Divination is a more active attempt to elicit some advice or information about the future—either from a supernatural being or by some non-standard process of information gathering. In the Old Testament both Saul and Ahab visited seers, and at Delphi "the framing of laws, the founding of colonies, the launching of wars, the fortunes of dynasties, the healing of disease and the legal suits of individuals, were referred to the judgment of the Pythian Apollo from the seventh century BC, and probably the famous shrine had been an oracular centre long before this time" (E. O. James, 232).

Merlin Stone extends this point by adding that long before Apollo issued the oracles, the temple at Delphi was the center of goddess-worship.

> The woman who brought forth the oracles of divine wisdom was called the Pythia. Coiled about the tripod stool on which she sat was a snake known as Python. Though in later Greek writings Python was male, in the earliest accounts Python was described as female. (Merlin Stone, 203)

The snakes are important. They are a major symbol of the goddess religion in Babylon, Egypt, Crete, Greece, and Canaan; and Stone explains how they were used in divination. People who have been immunized and then bitten "by krait, cobra or other elapids," she says, often experience "an emotional and mental state that has been compared to the effects of hallucinogenic drugs" (213).

Three kinds of divination were used in the ancient world: omens, sortilege, and augury. Omens are based on the principle that if B follows A once, it is likely to do so again. Important discoveries have been made by following this principle, but all too often the connections are arbitrary and the correlations a result of fear or wishful thinking. The Mesopotamians seem to have been addicted to omens.

> If a horse enters a man's house, and bites either an ass or a man, the owner of the house will die and his household will be scattered.
>
> If a man unwittingly treads on a lizard and kills it, he will prevail over his adversary. (Jaynes, 237–38)

Perhaps these things happened once, or even twice, and thereafter the stories were repeated and eventually written down on one of the thousands of omen tablets found in the ruins of the library of King Ashurbanipal at Nineveh.

The use of omens is passive and simple. One notices a configuration and expects it again. The use of sortilege (or the casting of lots) is different. It is an active attempt to elicit information from the gods, and it is a neat trick. One way to explain how it works is this: Since the gods control everything, they also control the fall of the lots. This means that they will not let a "no" come out if the answer is "yes," unless they want us to be fooled. By throwing dice, sticks, or coins one forces the silent spirits to speak, but in the language of sortilege.

The use of oracle bones in ancient China is a form of sortilege—

the Shang priests wrote their questions on the bones and then examined and "read" the shape of the cracks caused by heating. When the results of some divination were impressive—the prediction correct, the advice sound, the warning timely—it must have been nearly impossible to resist an explanation in terms of the supernatural. Failure, on the other hand, could be explained as a botched reading.

Another form of divination, augury, is more complex because the answer sought is more than a simple yes or no. Augury is described in cuneiform texts from Mesopotamia, where one technique was to pour oil into a bowl of water and then "interpret" the result as an answer to a question about war, the weather, illness, or any other thing of importance. Since reading the meaning of puddles of oil on water is not a skill possessed by everyone, a special priestly class of augurers developed. Later types of augury were even more complicated and messy. "Extispicy" was the attempt to divine the future from the entrails (*exta*) of sacrificed animals. The priests and people seem to have believed that these entrails contained the "written" messages of their gods.

> In other words, whoever invented the *I Ching* was convinced that the hexagram worked out in a certain moment coincided with the latter in quality no less than in time. To him the hexagram was the exponent of the moment in which it was cast—even more so than the hours of the clock or the divisions of the calendar could be—inasmuch as the hexagram was understood to be an indicator of the essential situation prevailing in the moment of its origin.
>
> This assumption involves a certain curious principle that I have termed synchronicity, a concept that formulates a point of view diametrically opposed to that of causality. Since the latter is merely a statistical truth and not absolute, it is a sort of working hypothesis of how events evolve one out of another, whereas synchronicity takes the coincidence of events in space and time as meaning something more than mere chance, namely, a peculiar interdependence of objective events among themselves as well as with the subjective (psychic) states of the observer or observers. (Preface to the *I Ching*, in Jung, xxiv)

What to Believe?

We begin by believing what we are taught, and by striving to see what we are told is there. Eventually we realize that not all our information is accurate, and that we need to revise some of our beliefs. When a child learns the truth about Santa Claus, many other beliefs have to be modified. Beliefs are not isolated atoms in a memory bank, subject to inspection and removal one by one. They interact and hang together in such complex ways that to change one is to redraft countless related details of our picture of the world.

We begin by assimilating the beliefs of those around us from beliefs about what food is safe to beliefs about how the world came into being. We can satisfy ourselves that some of these beliefs are correct, but not the religious ones. And this is awkward because, given our natural and normal standards for belief-acceptance, religious beliefs seem prime candidates for rejection. But many believers are not prepared to evaluate religious beliefs according to these standards. They simply take the existence of their favorite supernatural being as an axiom and then make their other beliefs square with this questionable but unquestioned assumption.

If we suggest to these believers that the existence of evil is a reason not to believe in God, they will reply that since God exists and is omnipotent, omniscient, and omnibenevolent, it follows that evil is an illusion. When the archaeologist points to ocean fossils on the tops of mountains to establish the antiquity of the earth, believers will defend the notion of a four-thousand-year-old earth by arguing that fossils were put here by God to test our faith. But the goal, if we happen to have forgotten, is to find out what is true, not to establish some specific dogma against reasonable criticisms. We know we are going astray when we find ourselves exercising all our ingenuity trying to preserve the thing we refuse to question. That is not what sensible beings trying to get along in a difficult world do.

We face the question of whether supernatural beings exist and communicate with humans even if (especially if!) we hear a voice from the sky assigning us some great work. When God told Gideon he had been chosen to deliver Israel, Gideon, even after being granted one miracle, was not satisfied and put God to an interesting and astute test. He put down a fleece and told God that if he was serious, he should let the dew fall only on the fleece and not on the surrounding ground. The next morning the ground was dry but Gideon got a bowl of dew from the fleece. Then he said to God:

> Do not be angry with me, but give me leave to speak once again. Let me, I pray thee, make one more test with the fleece. This time let the fleece alone be dry, and all the ground be covered with dew. (Judges 6:39–40)

And that is what happened, so Gideon finally believed God had chosen him for the task. Like Gideon, we have plenty of ways to check things out and to verify what people (or gods) tell us, and unless the people (or gods) are prideful and perverse, they will not mind. After all, God cooperated with Gideon rather than blasting him on the spot for his caution.

But *we* should remember that we are not Gideon holding a wet fleece, we are humans holding a book and reading stories that were written thousands of years ago. Our question is not whether to accept the evidence Gideon elicited from God but how to understand, and perhaps whether to accept, the story. Sometimes stories of Biblical miracles alone are taken as evidence for the existence of God, but they are really only evidence for the existence of the storytellers.

The healthiest diet for our natural belief-forming process is information, alternative hypotheses, and, when possible, firsthand experience. When we hear a report of a present-day supernatural phenomenon—a haunted house, a message from Jesus or the devil, a miracle of healing—the natural question is "What really happened?"

It is surprisingly easy to respond to a report of some supernatural phenomenon by generating a competing naturalistic explanation. We are likely to think that a photograph of someone levitating is really a photograph of someone falling, and we can all think of ways that a video of poltergeist activity might have been faked. Voices in the sound of the stream are quickly explained by auditory fatigue, cures by the inner strength false belief can inspire, and pictures of the Holy Family on water towers by rust and projection. Our first and very natural impulse is to explain the unknown in terms of the known, the unfamiliar in terms of the familiar. We are familiar with fraud and the effects of rust, and necessarily puzzled about levitation, poltergeists, and miracles. It takes considerable "education" to make the puzzle appear to be the solution.

Julian Jaynes's account of the origin of religious belief is a good example of the tendency to provide a naturalistic explanation for belief in gods and in the supernatural. It is only to be expected that believers will find his conclusions threatening. But how can anyone fault his approach? In trying to explain what was going on when ancient people heard voices, tried divination, felt guilt, and sacrificed animals, he brings in material from Homer to brain physiology. The religious fundamentalist, by way of contrast, has no *explanation*, only the dogmatic assurance that everything stated in some scripture is true. If what the scripture relates clashes with science, history, or common sense, then (unless we can "reinterpret" the scripture) so much the worse for science, history, or common sense.

Right or wrong, Jaynes and other "revisionists" offer interesting alternatives to what we have always heard. Because their explanations conflict with what we have been taught and with what is generally believed, our internal conservative censor of new ideas tells us to ignore them. But even when we break our conservative habits and give some unfamiliar belief a chance, we may not know how to proceed. How do we evaluate the claim that the origin of religious guilt is the breakdown of the bicameral mind and the retreat of voices that we ourselves create and then attribute to gods? How do we determine what to believe about spirits, gods, and ghosts when we know that humans have always believed in them and that reports of miracles, visitations, and revelations never stop?

Most of us would be willing to attribute the majority of the visitations and voices to a combination of drugs, deception, and delusion, but only "most." People invariably make exception for the miracles, visitations, and revelations of their own religion. From the perspective of a believer, this is appropriate, but from an objective standpoint, it is puzzling. If the hypothesis of auditory hallucinations explains Babylonian, Assyrian, Egyptian, Indian, Chinese, Greek, Islamic, and Mormon religious phenomena and texts, why should it not be used to account for Hebrew religious phenomena and texts as well?

It is easy enough to talk about "an objective standpoint" and to say that we must base our beliefs on the evidence, but it is misleading. We never look at *all* the evidence but always at some presorted and biased selection. We develop a version of reality *before* we acquire the skill to examine and weigh evidence. The features of our initial conceptions of reality conspire to defend themselves against undermining and corrosive data. Even when we try to eliminate bias and let the evidence speak for itself, deciding whether to believe in spirits or divination is not like putting two quantities on a balance to see which is heavier. No matter how objective we are trying to be, we cannot escape our subjectivity—which is to say that in the end *we* evaluate and somehow assign meaning and weight to the data we have. Is a relic, say a bone fragment, evidence of the bodily existence of a god, or of the gullibility of human beings? Is my broken arm the "problem" the fortune-teller mentioned?

Accepting a belief forces an unconscious correlation of what we have learned with what we already believe—a subtle reinterpretation of the world to make room for new information, and a subtle interpretation of the information to make it fit the picture. As we move about in the world, we pick up information that our brain automatically processes and merges with what we already know. When we discover hard data—letters, tapes, information about secret bank accounts, fingerprints on the knife—we alter our theories and beliefs, if we are healthy, to incorporate what we have learned.

Our interpretation of experience, our understanding of what is going on, is too deep and detailed to have been arrived at by conscious rational deliberation. Fortunately, nature has not assigned this important task to such a fragile instrument. We usually take in new information, and make it fit with the old, as naturally as breathing, and as automatically as we digest our food. Jaynes calls this activity "conciliation" and characterizes it as the process of "making excerpts or narratizations compatible with each other" (Jaynes, 65). Because so much of this activity takes place "offstage" we are occasionally surprised by the beliefs we develop and the changes we go through. One day it may simply occur to us that we no longer believe in the resurrection, the creation account in Genesis, the existence of Marduk, the truth of astrology, or the fidelity of a mate. Another time, like a Zen monk experiencing a *satori*, or like Saul/Paul falling from his ass, we may be struck or jolted by some insight or conversion experience we had been unconsciously nursing for years.

So again, what *are* we supposed to do when we meet something as unorthodox as Jaynes's claim that before 1000 B.C. nearly everyone was unconscious and guided by hallucinated voices, or Stone's account of the origins of paternal religion, or Ryle's relocation of Socrates' trial? We should begin by reminding ourselves that a claim is not disqualified because it goes against our ordinary beliefs. We are constantly being forced to revise our versions of reality, so we can expect to lose some of our favorite beliefs over time. If we want to see things as clearly as we can, and arrive at the most accurate version of reality we can get, we will have to keep our minds open to new information.

Of course at any given time there are many things that we do not and cannot keep an open mind about. Some elements of our world-pictures may stand firm no matter what happens. It is not that we have carefully and rationally decided that these are the fundamental elements of our belief systems. Rather, by whatever process, they have evolved into the assumptions we are unable to doubt. As Ludwig Wittgenstein pointed out in *On Certainty*, the very fact that we can doubt and raise questions depends on "the fact that some propositions are exempt from doubt, are as it were like hinges on which those turn" (Wittgenstein [5], 341). But he is talking about the mundane beliefs that make life on the planet possible, not philosophers' propositions like "I think I am experiencing a red sensation," or "I exist," or theological or metaphysical propositions like "God exists," or "All is one."

> The child learns to believe a host of things. I.e. it learns to act according to these beliefs. Bit by bit there forms a system of what is believed, and in that system some things stand unshakeably fast and some are more or less liable to shift. What stands fast does so, not because it is intrinsically obvious or convincing; it is rather held fast by what lies around it. (Wittgenstein [5], §144)

If we allow ourselves to be exposed to new information, if we take a full and friendly look at what counts *against* our beliefs, then the modifications in our belief systems that result will help us find our way. But they will neither be worked out by reason nor decided by free choice—*they will just happen*. Instead of saying, "Don't confuse me with the facts," we would be better off to review as many alleged facts as we can, and then just relax and wait to see which beliefs develop. As we pile up data, beliefs crystallize out of the confusion. This will not take forever, but it may take some time. Fortunately, time is not usually an issue when it is a matter of determining what to believe about bicameral breakdowns, consciousness, or the existence of gods.

The Genetic Fallacy Fallacy

Logic books contain a discussion of a mistake in reasoning called the *genetic fallacy*. For example:

> [The genetic fallacy is] a type of argument in which an attempt is made to prove a conclusion false by condemning its source or genesis. Such arguments are fallacious because how an idea originated is irrelevant to its viability. Thus it would be fallacious to argue that . . . since the early forms of religion were matters of magic, religion is nothing but magic. (Engel, 194)

Any argument of this form is about as bad as an argument can be:

Bill is a jerk.
Bill believes *p*.
Therefore *p* is false.

The Nazis, for example, used to argue that what Einstein said about the Universe was false on the grounds that he was Jewish. The fact that we think badly of someone should never automatically lead us to dismiss his or her opinions.

Another way to commit the genetic fallacy is to reject a person's belief on the grounds that it was formed in some improper way.

> In attacking another person's claim or assertion, it is a logical fallacy to try to refute it by somehow assailing or discrediting the *cause* of that person's belief rather than its *justification*. Reasoning making this mistake is said to commit "the *genetic fallacy*." . . . For example, some people have talked as if it were relevant to the question of the existence of God to claim that belief in God is basically motivated by a desire to have a heavenly father to replace the earthly parents we all lose. But even if this psychological claim about motivation were true, it would be logically irrelevant to the truth or falsity of the claim that God exists. (Thomas, 200)

We must agree with Stephen Thomas's claim that we cannot show that a belief is false by pointing to a psychological (neurotic) cause. But when a belief is controversial, and when the ordinary methods of deciding matters are unavailable, we must do what we can. Sometimes it will only be good sense to "consider the source" of a belief we are trying to evaluate.

Most people will admit that no proof of the existence of God is airtight and invincible. They will then add that proofs that God does not exist are no better off. With arguments out of the way, believers turn to "faith," as if that were a responsible and even unavoidable option. On the other side, non-believers are impressed by the fact that believers rarely embrace their religion as a result of rational deliberation or ordinary reasoning. According to those who warn us against the *genetic fallacy*, this does not count against the truth of their belief in God; but according to those who might want to warn us against what we can call the *genetic fallacy fallacy*, it should not be ruled irrelevant to what we think about their belief.

If early religions were forms of magic, it would be a mistake to conclude that religion now is also "nothing but magic." But it would be appropriate to wonder whether this might be so. If religion *now* is not magic but *early* religion was magic, what is the difference?

If we can offer a coherent and plausible social, political, or psychological explanation of early religions, then those religions, and their contemporary versions, lose some of their plausibility. Those who warn us against the genetic fallacy tell us that even if we prove that the founders of the major religions were certifiably psychotic, this would not prove that their claims and beliefs were mistaken. And technically they are right—it is possible that madmen have true beliefs. But if we take this too seriously, if we give eccentric views the benefit of too small a doubt, we will be committing the *genetic fallacy fallacy*. Surely the undeniable fact that a view was foisted on ignorant, superstitious, near-savages by self-interested and cynical con men does not prove that the view is mistaken, but it ought to make us wonder more than it usually does.

To think that information about the source of a belief is irrelevant, and should in fact be ignored, is to commit the genetic fallacy fallacy, the mistake of thinking that considerations about the origin of a belief ought to have no bearing on whether we accept it. When we are trying to decide what to believe, we need all the help we can get. If belief in gods originated in voices heard in dreams and hallucinations, coupled with ignorance of the laws of nature and a need for social stability—we need to take this into consideration. The truth and probability of a statement remain what they are no matter whose statement it is, but when we do not have much in the way of hard evidence, it only makes sense to ask about the reliability of those who have put the statement forward. If we learn that their ability to collect information and to interpret it was impaired (by drugs, madness, fear, or ignorance) how reasonable is it to say that this information should have no bearing on what we finally believe?

> Then the LORD God planted a garden in Eden away to the east, and there he put the man whom he had formed. The LORD God made trees spring from the ground, all trees pleasant to look at and good for food; and in the middle of the garden he set the tree of life and the tree of the knowledge of good and evil. (Genesis 2:8–9)
>
> The LORD God took the man and put him in the garden of Eden to till it and care for it. He told the man, 'you may eat from every tree in the garden, but not from the tree of the knowledge of good and evil; for on the day that you eat from it you will certainly die.' (Genesis 2:15–17)

God-based Moralism

Crime may or may not pay, but nearly everyone would say that it *ought* not pay and that deities, if they exist, have the *right* and the *authority* (if not the obligation) to punish the wicked. A common belief among religious moralists is that we deserve to be punished for stealing, adultery, (some) killing, and so forth because these things are morally wrong, and that they are morally wrong because a deity has forbidden them. This account of the source of moral obligation is sometimes referred to as the *divine command theory*.

A divine *command* theory should be understood as an attempt to answer a question about obligation or duty, but a related theory that involves no commands can be put forward as an account not of obligation but of value. Someone may say that what *makes* kindness, mercy, and generosity good is the fact that they are liked, admired, cherished, or desired by God. These things remain good even if no one has received any divine commands, indeed, even if no one has managed to discover what God prefers. Divine command theories tell us that our *obligation* is to do whatever God commands, whereas a god-based account of value tells us that the *value* of a thing is a function of God's attitude toward it.

The best known (if not the clearest) discussion of the divine command theory appears in Plato's dialogue *Euthyphro*. The dialogue opens as Socrates meets Euthyphro on his way to prosecute his own father for the murder of a slave. Because the case itself was ambiguous and because the prevailing morality emphasized family loyalties and did not mandate justice for slaves, Euthyphro's action was unusual. It surprised Socrates, who uses it as the occasion to ask Euthyphro if he understands piety so well that he can go ahead with the case without fear of being impious. When Euthyphro says that he does, Socrates' predictable response is to ask him to explain what piety is. If we interpret 'piety' as thinking and behaving properly in matters having to do with the gods (ceremonies, oaths, and duties), then we can understand Euthyphro's first answer, which is:

> What is pleasing to the gods is pious, and what is not pleasing to them is impious. (Plato [2], 7)

An action is pious—that is, proper—if it pleases the gods, otherwise it is impious—that is, improper. This makes the entire value of the action flow from the attitudes and feelings of the gods. Their attitude makes something valuable in the way that heat makes an object change color, though in the case of value no molecular change takes place.

Socrates criticizes this way of looking at things by pointing out that when something pleases some of the gods and displeases others, "the same thing will be pious and impious" (Plato [2], 9). This threatened contradiction leads Euthyphro to reverse his position, and to say that a thing

> is loved by the gods because it is pious; it is not pious because it is loved by them. (Plato [2], 12)

According to Euthyphro's new answer, the gods love some actions (ceremonies, rituals, behaviors) because they are pious—that is, proper—and dislike others because they are impious—that is, improper. This propriety or rightness is completely independent of, and prior to, what the gods want and feel. It is why they feel as they do.

But this answer does not hold up either, and Socrates manages to lead poor Euthyphro back to his former view that "piety means what is loved by the gods." Socrates is undaunted and suggests starting all over again. Euthyphro, who is considerably deflated by this time, replies: "Another time, then, Socrates. I am in a hurry now, and it is time for me to be off" (Plato [2], 20). Nobody who has read the entire dialogue, short as it is, can blame him.

One thing that undermines Euthyphro is his willingness to allow that the gods do contradict themselves or each other. Someone who did not believe in a plurality of discordant and squabbling gods would not be impressed by that part of Socrates' refutation. What, then, can be said to a religious moralist who is a monotheist, or whose gods all agree?

One way to attack god-based morality is to attack the theism on which it is based but, as we are about to see, "divine command" morality is in trouble even if we assume that some deity does exist and does issue commands. Not all purported commands are real commands, and not all real commands generate moral obligations. So even if some commands are pronounced by a god, we can ask if he or she is really in a position to issue commands that bind us. How many people today would acknowledge Marduk's authority to command them to sacrifice a goat? The key point is that it is always possible to ask what it is about divine commanders that explains how and why their commands create moral obligations.

God's Power

If there are gods who issue commands, punish the disobedient, and reward those who submit, then we all have good prudential reasons to obey them. Yet we would probably all agree that might, even infinite might, does not make right. The power to punish those who cross him and to reward those who follow his orders does not make Yahweh a moral authority any more than immense power made Adolf Hitler one. After Abraham demonstrated his complete obedience by being willing to kill his son Isaac, God said: "Your descendants shall possess the cities of their enemies. All nations on earth shall pray to be blessed as your descendants are blessed, and this because you have obeyed me" (Genesis 22:18). This is quite a reward for murdering just one child, but most of us would reject the idea that when the price is right it becomes a moral obligation to kill our children. We would all be horrified (and moralists would feel moral outrage) if someone sacrificed a child to escape some difficulty, or to win the favor of some powerful being. This shows that we do not think something is right just because it is commanded by someone with the power to destroy or hurt us if we disobey.

There is only one way to get the obligation to obey God from God's power, but it is a short and uninteresting one. Simply include within God's omnipotence the power to make it the case that we ought to obey God's commands. There are two ways a critic of religious morality might reply to this move. The first is to resort to the strategy used by John Mackie in *The Miracle of Theism*, where he argues that there is no such god. The second is to bypass the question of the existence of a god and to argue that this mechanism of creating obligations ex nihilo is too mysterious to be taken seriously.

Possession and Creation

In the story in Genesis we may feel that God had a right to order Adam not to eat the fruit because it was God's tree and God's garden. He used his power to make the tree spring up from the ground. But he also used that power to form Adam from the dust, and Eve from Adam's rib (or whatever). Does this mean that Adam, Eve, and all their descendants belong to God in the same sense in which the tree belongs to God? Is this why the divine command theorist thinks we are morally obliged to obey God's every command?

John Locke thought so. He claimed that we ought not harm one another in any way since we are all "the workmanship of one omnipotent, and infinitely wise maker; all the servants of one sovereign master, sent into the world by his order, and about his business." We are God's property, "made to last during his, not one another's pleasure" (Locke [2], 9).

Property is a human concept, and a social one. It may have its roots in a territorial instinct, but as we now understand the concept, it is tied up with labor, occupancy and use, deeds, contracts, signatures, wills, rights, exchange, and transfers. When we talk about God's tree we are relying on our human understanding of the human institution of ownership, and on the natural belief that if we have produced something, we own it. But the idea that a single being "owns" everything does not fit with the concept of property as we understand it. God's ownership of everything may be too different from my ownership of anything to allow me to use the latter to make sense of the former.

But even if it made sense to talk about a transcendent being owning the world and its denizens, it still does not follow that such a being has absolute authority over the persons who occupy its real estate. We consider our children *our* children, and while we usually take ourselves to be responsible for their well-being, we do not feel that we own them as we own our furniture or our pets. As they grow older they remain ours, but any claim we make to ownership, and with it jurisdiction, becomes ludicrous.

The Mesopotamians looked on themselves and their cities as the property of their gods, just as they looked on their slaves as their own property. They were both masters and slaves, owners of other humans, and owned by their gods. The first duty of a slave is obedience, and as a slave-owner sees it, it is morally permissible to demand obedience from slaves, and to do what is necessary to secure it.

Job, who was said to be a "righteous man," had five hundred slaves, and God, who considered Job his "servant," treated the old man like a laboratory hamster. This slave mentality is no longer acceptable in most parts of the world, but even when the institution of slavery was flourishing, it was, like the ownership of land, organized around certain procedures and rules by which some people became the property of others. There may have been a purchase or proceeding, and often there were documents. By what procedure and according to what rules, then, did we all become the property of God?

As we have seen, the usual answer is that God's ownership is based not on conventional contracts or laws but on the fact of creation. He created the world out of nothing, Adam out of mud, and the natural laws that lead from Adam and Eve to us. That is why we are his possessions, his property. That is why we are morally obliged to obey him.

But suppose that billions of years ago scientists from a distant galaxy performed certain experiments that resulted in the formation of our galaxy, our sun, the planets, and finally, life as we know it. Suppose that their life spans are as great as their power, and that they return and insist that since they created us, we are obliged to obey their commands, to participate in their circuses, and to serve as laser fodder in their imperialistic adventures. We might be forced to obey these aliens, but few of us would accept the argument that it is our moral duty to obey their commands simply because they created us. Why, then, do we think that we owe obedience to some god, just because he, she, or it, set going the process that resulted in our short and often miserable existence? If there is anything about Yahweh that makes us morally obligated to obey his commandments, it must be something other than his claim to be the Creator.

God as Parent

Sometimes the analogy between a god and a parent is used to support the claim that we are obligated to "do the will" of our creator. But there are very few respects in which God "the Father" is like anyone's parent. He does not speak to us, and if one of us were about to fall off a cliff, he would not lift a finger to save our life. When you think about it, it makes more sense to call the earth our mother. At least we are grown out of her substance. But the earth does not issue commands or demand obedience.

Even if there were several similarities between God "the Father" and a father, we must remember that a parent's order would rarely be thought to create more than a prima facie obligation—that is, an obligation that is overturned if the order is crazy, or even in conflict with the prevailing moral standards. A child is not obliged to steal television sets because her father orders her to do it, nor is her obligation *not* to steal television sets a function of her parent's will. The analogy between God and a father, therefore, is of very little value to the divine command theorist, who appears to believe that if God wants us to steal a television set (or to wipe out a rival tribe or a city) then we have a moral obligation to do just that.

Baruch Brody, in a discussion of the moral relevance of the fact that God is our creator, mentions "our special obligation to obey the wishes of our parents." He notes that the strongest objection to this analogy is the claim that these obligations to our parents "are due to something that they do other than merely creating us, something that God does not do" (Brody [1], 144). Brody thinks the divine command theorist can reply to this by saying that just as our parents nourish and sustain us, so does God.

We can reject Brody's defense in either of two ways. We can, as we have seen, criticize the analogy by denying that God nourishes and sustains us the way our parents did. Or, if we accept the claim that God sustains us in a metaphysical sense—perhaps by keeping the universe running, we can simply point out that this seems no more likely to generate the right to be obeyed than does creating the world once and for all at the start. It simply means that God can destroy us by omissions as well as by acts.

For the Love of God

Love is a difficult matter at best. It is not clear whether we are supposed to be obligated to obey God because we love him, or because he loves us, or both. If we love each other though, why aren't we obligated to obey each other?

It is very hard to see what there is about love that creates an obligation to obey. If we love an ordinary person (not a god or a goddess) nobody thinks our love obligates us to obey his or her commands. Indeed, the idea that love requires obedience is a pathological understanding of love. It is true that love often inclines us to act in ways those we love want us to act. It is therefore often effective to appeal to another person's love when we want them to do something for us. So if we love a god or goddess, we may be inclined to do what we think he or she wants us to do. But inclination to obey a "divine" being is one thing and obligation to obey one is something else (or nothing at all).

In a recent attempt to revive the divine command theory, Robert Adams has introduced the idea that what it is for something to be wrong is for that thing to be contrary to the commands of a loving God. A *loving* god is introduced to avoid the problems caused by the possibility that a god might command cruelty for its own sake, with the unfortunate result that cruelty would then become a moral duty. Any old god might command any old thing, but a loving god would not, could not, command cruelty for its own sake. This stipulation evades one problem, but it has no bearing on the real problem, which is to explain why we have a moral obligation to obey divine commands, even when the content of those commands is morally impeccable.

Goodness and Perfection

There is obviously something odd about any attempt to base God's ability to create value on his alleged goodness or perfection. If something *becomes* good when and only when God loves it, then the claim that God is good is made true by the fact that God loves himself. But the fact that a being loves itself can hardly be counted as a reason why it should be obeyed or why its likes and dislikes should be normative for the rest of us. If God's goodness, on the other hand, flows from some *other* source, then not all value depends on God after all, and god-based moralism crumbles.

In "Morality and the Will of God," Kai Nielsen discusses the claim that "the only truly adequate foundation for moral belief is a religion that acknowledges that absolute sovereignty of the Lord, found in the prophetic religions" (Nielsen [1], 242–43). Nielsen claims that God (the God of the "Prophets") is "by definition" perfectly good, and he argues that this means that *religion depends on morality* because we cannot even speak of God unless we are already stocked with an independent idea of goodness. Hence, he concludes, "a moral understanding must be logically prior to any religious assent" (Nielsen [1], 256). Only if we try to find something other than God's goodness on which to base his moral authority can we escape from the field of paradoxes looming here.

We are no better off if we attempt to defend religious morality by insisting that God is, by definition, a perfect being. We have no conception of what a perfect being is, and even if we did, and one of them existed, we still have not been told why its perfection obliges us to obey its orders or satisfy its desires. One might think, rather, that its perfection would make it unnecessary for it to issue any orders, and impossible for it to have any desires.

Intelligible and Unintelligible Beings

Imagine a line along which divinities are arranged in the following way. At one end are gods with very human qualities: They have human form, consort with other humans, lie, disregard private property, and suffer from human emotions like anger, fear, jealousy, love, and impatience. They see, smell, feel, remember, communicate, and rest. The more any particular divinity resembles a human, the more we humans can relate to it. Unfortunately, the more it resembles a human, the less plausible it is to suppose that its bare preference creates value or that its mere word morally obligates us to do something.

A BEING WHO IS______________________

human-like	like a decent human	like an enlightened human	like a wise and advanced alien	like a wildly different and vastly superior alien	like a mysterious consciousness	a total mystery

ZONE OF UNINTELLIGIBILITY

As we move along the line we subtract human qualities like lust, pride, jealousy, brutality, and a bad temper. At the same time, we intensify qualities we find desirable in humans. The divinities thus constructed are quite a bit nicer than the other ones, but not really much nicer than enlightened humans. While we respect enlightened humans, and if we know what is good for us, listen to them when we have a chance, we do not allow their mere words to determine our moral duties.

We have obviously not moved far enough along the line. Perhaps it is time to bring in other standard attributes of gods—attributes like omniscience, omnipotence, perfection, atemporality, eternality, and infinite love, patience, and mercy. About qualities like this there are two things to be said. First, they throw the beings who are alleged to possess them into what can be called the "Zone of Unintelligibility." Second, even if we could understand the idea of a being with qualities that are inconceivable to us, we have no reason to think that the possession of these inconceivable qualities would turn that being into a source of value or obligation.

At one end of our line we find human-like divinities, at the other end stranger and stranger beings. The less they are like us, the harder they will be to understand. As they take on strange and new qualities, we will no longer be able to attribute their behavior to human-like beliefs and motives. But this puts us in a bind, for what other kinds of beliefs and motives do we understand? What sense can we time-bound humans make of a being who, like Kurt Vonnegut's Tralfamadorian, sees all time spread out before it like a mountain range? What is it like to be an omniscient being? Does it even make sense to speak of an omniscient being as conscious? Doesn't consciousness require a focusing of attention and a suppression of information? An omniscient being would have to be immediately aware of what everyone is thinking (consciously and subconsciously), and where all the plants, animals, and rocks are. How can this mean anything to us when we cannot even listen to two simultaneous conversations without getting confused, or keep track of our keys?

As long as we think only of divinities that make sense to us, divinities capable of having preferences, issuing commands, and really minding when we disobey, there is no obvious connection between the moral law and the all too human preferences of these beings. But if we start to add extraordinary super-qualities, they enter the Zone of Unintelligibility, to reside with disembodied aliens, beings from other dimensions, stars that think, and Brahman. These "entities" are so remote from anything with which we have had experience that it is ridiculous to speak of them as if they engage in human-like ratiocination, suffer human-like emotions, give away real estate, and issue commands. Their spectacular qualities make them inaccessible and unintelligible to us. We dare not speculate about their motives. How can they be the source of our moral laws? They are all mysteries, and the less said about them the better.

Finally, even if we were able to understand what such beings were like, *and* able to make sense of their ability to issue commands and have preferences, there is still no reason to think their super qualities make them the source of value and moral obligation. We have already noted that even infinite might (omnipotence) does not make right. Omniscience does not help either, though it would have a bearing on the quality of a (well-meaning) being's advice. Perfection is not a quality, and eternality, atemporality, and infinity, to the limited extent we understand them, seem not to bear on moral authority at all. Why should unending existence or the ability to experience things timelessly make one's word morally binding?

Conclusion

Unless a god is given some rather special (and superhuman) characteristics, he, she, or it is no more qualified to be the source of obligation and value than an advanced or enlightened human. When we do attribute these special characteristics to a being, we push it into the Zone of Unintelligibility, with the result that we no longer know what we are talking about, no longer understand what such a being would be like, and no longer understand how it could be enough like a human to have preferences and issue commands. Finally, even if we could understand what such beings were like and could make sense of their issuing commands and having preferences, there is still no reason to suppose that these super qualities qualify a being to serve as the source of value and moral obligation. Why did we ever think they did?

In *The Future of an Illusion,* Freud gave a psychological explanation of the persistence of religious belief in the face of embarrassingly minimal evidence. Religious beliefs, he said, are held because they are "fulfillments of the oldest, strongest and most urgent wishes of mankind" (Freud [2], 30). For the believer they provide answers to questions about the meaning of life, they guarantee protection against the terrors of the unknown and the known, they offer hope for a life after death, and they can be used to motivate the sociable behavior societies must ask from their citizens. According to Freud, gods offer those who believe in them the moral authority and the protection from danger that real fathers offer to frightened but willful children.

Freud was, you may recall, a "hard-liner" regarding human nature. He saw us as instinctively selfish, aggressive, and inconsiderate. These "unserviceable" instincts "have to be tamed by acts of repression, behind which, as a rule, lies the motive of anxiety" (Freud [2], 43). This anxiety produces childhood neuroses, most of which are outgrown "spontaneously in the course of growing up." Freud thought that the development of society as a whole parallels the development of each of its members. Just as young children need (or at least often get) a stern father to drive them crazy with repression, young societies pass through a similar stage and develop analogous forms of neuroses. In society at large the role of the father is played by God ("our father in Heaven"). Freud's claim, then, is that religion is "the obsessional neurosis of humanity" (Freud [2], 43). It is not necessary to agree with everything that Freud said to be impressed by the similarity between the roles Gods and fathers are supposed to play. In any case, what we have seen here is that neither gods nor fathers, nor even mothers, in spite of their previous behavior, their love, and their power, can, by their attitudes and words, bring value and moral obligation into being.

9

Experience and Reason: Secular Morality

> Belief in God, or in many gods, prevented the free development of moral reasoning. Disbelief in God, openly admitted by a majority, is a very recent event, not yet completed. Because this event is so recent, Non-Religious Ethics is at a very early stage. We cannot yet predict whether, as in Mathematics, we will all reach agreement. Since we cannot know how Ethics will develop, it is not irrational to have high hopes.
>
> —*Derek Parfit,* Reasons and Persons

IN CHAPTERS 5, 6, and 7 we trace the emergence and early development of morality in India, China, and Greece. The moralists in those countries were the priests, the bureaucrats, the scholars, and the plain people who educated their children and influenced their neighbors. A Confucian describing some action as *ren* or as required by the *li*, a *brāhmin* insisting on the duty of non-*brāhmins* to support *brāhmins*, and Plato characterizing his vision of a just society are all functioning as moralists, all promoting what they present as non-conventional, binding, and objective values, obligations, or virtues.

Given the distinction between ethics and morality introduced in Chapter 1, it is fair to say that no society could exist without an ethics—that is, without its own collection of rules, requirements, and recommendations. It is less clear that societies also need morality, which not only promotes the rules about how members should act and be, but offers them as "objectively prescriptive," as binding even those who do not accept them. Moralists will be asked (even by other moralists) to explain the nature of the objectivity and the source of the bondage. In Chapter 8 we learn that the attempt to trace this objective bondage to divine commands and preferences is natural and inevitable, but that it is open to serious objections. If the conclusion of that chapter is correct, moralists will have to provide morality with a secular foundation or none at all.

Rationalist Attempts to Make a Secular Morality

The story of a large part of Western philosophy is one of two movements—rationalism and empiricism. Although there are empiricist elements in rationalism and vice versa, we can see a real difference between two distinct approaches to similar problems. While the empiricists found the source of ideas and of knowledge in sense experience, the rationalists believed in innate ideas and in truths that could be known only by reason.

Early Rationalists

Plato, who did not trust the senses and who compared the passions to an unruly mob, can be called a rationalist. He thought that reason alone is capable of grasping the true nature of things, but his description of the philosopher's attainment of wisdom goes well beyond what we might expect from acts of deliberation. The final grasping of the Form of the Good sounds more like an ecstatic experience at a mystery ceremony than anything a philosopher is likely to *think* his way to. So we *can* call Plato a rationalist, but only if rationalism is allowed to encompass an intuitive, non-conceptual "vision."

The classical rationalists of the modern West, René Descartes, Gottfried Wilhelm Leibniz, and Baruch Spinoza, made no serious attempt to construct a reason-based secular morality. Descartes and Leibniz spoke of a God who designed and created the world and who made the rules. Spinoza was a determinist and a pantheist who held that the highest good is the intellectual love of God, who (or which) he identified with Nature.

British Rationalists

Moralists in England wanted to reject Thomas Hobbes's belief that we are motivated solely by self-interest and his claim that in a state of nature, where there is no one to legislate and to enforce laws, nothing can be unjust and "the notions of right and wrong, justice and injustice, have there no place" (Hobbes, 108). Half the problem was solved when Bishop Joseph Butler (1692–1752) convinced nearly everyone that there is a good argument against psychological egoism. All that remained was to establish the legitimacy or authority of morality, and to do this without appealing to a divine command.

Henry More (1614–1687) and Ralph Cudworth (1617–1688) belonged to a group of Anglican moralists known as the Cambridge Platonists. They were serious moralists but unwilling to base their morality on their religion. More argued that there are twenty-three fundamental self-evident moral truths, and Cudworth argued that "it is not meer Will that Obligeth, but the Natures of Good and Evil, Just and Unjust, really existing in the World" (Cudworth, 250).

Samuel Clarke (1675–1729), another moral rationalist, agreed with Cudworth that morality is independent of God's will. His idea was that what is right and wrong is a function of a natural relation of *fitness*. Some things, he says "are in their own nature Good and Reasonable and Fit to be done, such as keeping Faith, and performing equitable Compacts, and the like." Other things "are in their own nature absolutely Evil" (Clarke, 9).

> 'Tis evidently more Fit, even before all positive Bargains and Compacts, that Men should deal one with another according to the known Rules of Justice and Equity, than that every Man for his own present Advantage, should without scruple disappoint the most reasonable and equitable Expectations of his Neighbours, and cheat and defraud, or spoil by violence, all others without restraint. (Clarke, 5)

To someone not impressed by the credentials of this moral relation of fitness, it may appear that Clarke simply declares the things he likes "evidently more fit" than their opposites. It would be hard to show that this impression is mistaken.

Clarke opposes Hobbes's doctrine, which he characterizes as the view that "there is no such thing as just and unjust, right and wrong originally in the nature of things," and that "men in their natural state are not obliged to universal benevolence, nor to any moral duty whatever." But when he begins to devise arguments to counter this amoralism, the best he can do is to twist some of Hobbes's words around to make him appear to hold a form of moralism. He says, for example, that Hobbes thinks the destruction of humanity would be a "great and unsufferable Evil" and that it is "reasonable, that, to prevent this Evil, Men should enter into certain Compacts to preserve one another." Then he adds:

> Now if the destruction of Mankind by each other's Hands, be such an Evil, that, to prevent it, it was fit and reasonable that Men should enter into Compacts to preserve each other, then, before any such Compacts, it was manifestly a thing unfit and unreasonable in itself, that Mankind should destroy one another. . . . Which is directly contradictory to Mr. Hobbes's first Supposition, of there being no natural and absolute difference between Good and Evil, Just and Unjust, antecedent to positive Compact. (Clarke, 7–8)

This bad argument is popular even among moralists of today. The trick is to find something an amoralist does not like, and then insist that this is enough to show that the amoralist believes that something is bad and that it ought to be avoided. But a preference cannot so easily be blown up into a value that generates an obligation.

John Locke is usually identified as the father of empiricism, but he was a rationalist when it came to morality. Hobbes holds that in a state of nature nothing is right or wrong, and that morality in civil society is purely conventional. Locke disagrees, claiming that "The *state of nature* has a law of nature to govern it, which obliges everyone." Reason, he says, "teaches all mankind, who will but consult it, that being all *equal and independent*, no one ought to harm another in his life, health, liberty, or possessions" (Locke [2], 9).

Locke defends these moralist claims by appealing to the total ownership of the universe by God. Since we are all the property of God, he argues, if we hurt someone else (or even commit suicide) we will be damaging God's property.

Empiricist Attempts to Make a Secular Morality

The empiricist philosophers who wrote in England, Ireland, and Scotland in the eighteenth century—Locke, George Berkeley, and David Hume—were committed (in varying degrees) to what their senses told them, and suspicious (in varying degrees) of everything else. Empiricist purism has led many to cast suspicious glances at the concepts basic to moralism, and both non-cognitivism and the error theory have their roots in empiricism.

But not all empiricists are amoralists or non-cognitivists; some are moralists. There are (at least) three ways to embrace both empiricism and moralism. First, we can insist that we do experience moral properties like fitness and intrinsic value. Those who fail to do so are simply defective moral perceivers who do not know how (or where) to look. This is the way of the intuitionist.

The second way to combine empiricism and moralism is to say that while we do not actually perceive the properties of goodness or badness, we have a moral sense that is activated by those qualities. When exposed to badness, we feel moral indignation; when exposed to goodness, we feel moral approval. The moral emotions can be taken as signs of the presence, in the world, of the moral properties. Here we have what has been called an *objective interpretation of the moral sense*—the moral sense reacts to objectively real moral properties.

Many empiricists favor what can be called a *subjective interpretation of the moral sense*, according to which our feelings of moral approval, disapproval, guilt, and responsibility are not triggered by objective evaluative properties, but are elicited when we encounter certain natural properties. This "anti-realist projectivism" is embraced by John Mackie and probably by Hume, and it undergirds C. L. Stevenson's non-cognitivism as well.

But here we are seeking a third way to be an empiricist *moralist*. It is clear how a subjective interpretation of moral sense can project us out of a belief in moralism, but can we accept projectivism and, at the same time, retain an intelligible form of moralism? We can if we are willing to say that moral properties exist, only not as the peculiar "non-natural" items moralists sometimes suppose them to be. Rather, we can say, they are identical with perfectly unobjectionable and empirically respectable "natural" properties. If goodness and rightness are (disguised) natural properties, says the *naturalist*, there is nothing problematic about them, and no need to fear arguments from queerness. We shall soon look more closely at intuitionism and naturalism, but we must begin by thinking about the idea of a moral sense.

Against Hobbes, Francis Hutcheson (1694–1746) asserts that we sometimes desire the happiness of others as an end, and not merely as a means to our own happiness. He also believes that in addition to *being* benevolent, we have a moral sense that *approves of* ("attaches approbation to") benevolence. "This approbation," he says, "cannot be supposed an image of any thing external, more than the pleasures of harmony, of taste, of smell" (Mackie [2], 33). So Hutcheson clearly gives us a subjective interpretation of the moral sense.

One objection regularly made to Hutcheson's and other forms of subjectivism is that they are not faithful to our experience. Moral approbation and disapprobation seem to be more than mere emotional responses. As Mackie says:

> We have some tendency to feel that the moral wrongness of a proposed act is an externally authoritative feature which tells us not to do this—which is part of what Clarke was getting at with his talk about necessary relations of fitness and unfitness. (Mackie [2], 34)

The question, of course, is what to make of this tendency? Moral realists will use it as prima facie evidence for objectivism, a way to put the burden of proof on the critic of morality. There is no way to deny that people do hold and propagate objectivist beliefs about morality. But if this objectivist inclination can be explained by instinct and moral education, then the fact that one feels objectively bound need not be seen as evidence for the claim that one *is* objectively bound. Hume offers just such a subjectivist explanation of the moral feelings.

David Hume

David Hume (1711–1776) found himself in opposition to the moral rationalists and to those empiricists with objectivist interpretations of the moral sense. While moralists before him sought to establish the reality of an independent and objectively binding morality, Hume saw morality as conventional, and wrote to explain its origin and character.

In the *Enquiry concerning the Principles of Morals*, Hume presents a catalog of the virtues of his day—everything from benevolence and justice to cleanliness and chastity. His aim is not to justify his high regard for these qualities but to explain why we praise some traits as virtues and condemn others as vices. He asks whether moral distinctions are

> derived from Reason, or from Sentiment; whether we attain the knowledge of them by a chain of argument and induction, or by an immediate feeling and finer internal sense; whether, like all sound judgment of truth and falsehood, they should be the same to every rational intelligent being; or whether, like the perception of beauty and deformity, they be founded entirely on the particular fabric and constitution of the human species. (Hume [2], 170)

With some qualifications, we can say that Hume choses the second of each of the above alternatives.

The message of both the *Treatise of Human Nature* (1739–1740) and the *Enquiry concerning the Principles of Morals* (1751) is that while the "reality" of moral distinctions cannot be denied, they are not discovered by reason but born from within us. For Hume, the "reality of moral distinctions" consists in the fact that we (*his* "we") feel approval for such qualities as benevolence, justice, honesty, chastity, and cleanliness, and call them "virtues," and the fact that we feel "disapprobation" for other qualities, and call them "vices." To know which is which, one need only ask whether he "should desire to have this or that quality ascribed to him" (Hume [2], 174). The distinction between virtue and vice, Hume observes, is built into language itself.

> The very nature of language guides us almost infallibly in forming a judgment of this nature; and as every tongue possesses one set of words which are taken in a good sense, and another in the opposite, the least acquaintance with the idiom suffices, without any reasoning, to direct us in collecting and arranging the estimable or blameable qualities of men. (Hume [2], 174)

When he says that morality cannot be derived from reason alone, Hume is using the word 'reason' broadly enough to make this claim into a denial of both rationalist and empiricist forms of moral objectivism. He sees his task as twofold. First he has to show that reason (broadly construed) does not give us moral distinctions. Second, he has to offer his own explanation of the origin of moral distinctions and of the power morality has to move us.

The famous and fertile argument (or arguments) Hume uses to show that reason does not give moral distinctions is presented in the *Treatise* and recapitulated in the *Enquiry*:

> Premise 1: Reason alone can never have any influence on our actions and affections.
> Premise 2: Morality has (moral beliefs, judgments, and pronouncements have) an influence on our actions and affections.
> Conclusion: The rules of morality, therefore, are not conclusions of our reason. (Hume [1], 457)

Hume believes that reason alone is incapable of moving us to any action. "Reason," he says, "is, and ought only to be the slave of the passions, and can never pretend to any other office than to serve and obey them" (Hume [1], 415). Reason draws conclusions, assigns causes, and predicts effects, it tells us what is the case. In moral deliberation, reason lays the "circumstances and relations" before us, but then its work is done.

> The approbation or blame which then ensues, cannot be the work of the judgment, but of the heart; and is not a speculative proposition or affirmation, but an active feeling or sentiment. In the disquisitions of the understanding, from known circumstances and relations, we infer some new and unknown. In moral decisions, all the circumstances and relations must be previously known; and the mind, from the contemplation of the whole, feels some new impression of affection or disgust, esteem or contempt, approbation or blame." (Hume [2], 290)

Critics of Hume argue that reason plays a greater role in determining the will than Hume's early rhetoric suggests, but Hume never backs down. In the *Enquiry*, which he implores us to take as his final word on the subject, he says that "it is probable that" the

> final sentence . . . which pronounces characters and actions amiable or odious, praise-worthy or blameable; that which stamps on them the mark of honour or infamy, approbation or censure; that which renders morality an active principle and constitutes virtue our happiness, and vice our misery . . . depends on some internal sense or feeling, which nature has made universal in the whole species. (Hume [2], 172–73)

So we know where Hume stands.

It is, of course, possible to disagree with Hume. Perhaps he is right when he says that deductive and causal reasoning do not yield moral distinctions, but what about plain old perception (which he sometimes includes under the heading of reason)? The first premise would be false if the objective goodness of some virtue were a matter of observable fact, and, moralists are quick to mention, Hume does not show that this is not so. As we are about to see, a procession of moral intuitionists have sought a path to objective morality through this gap in Hume's argument.

Hume holds that "the chief spring or actuating principle of the human mind is pleasure or pain," without which "we are, in a great measure, incapable of passion or action, of desire or volition" (Hume [1], 574). Moral utterances move us, when they do, precisely because of their connection with pleasure and pain. Hearing or contemplating the names of the virtues and vices, we imagine their various effects in terms of happiness and unhappiness, and by sympathy we then feel actual happiness or unhappiness, and in some circumstances this is enough to move us to action.

Hume's argument for his claim that moral distinctions are not derived from reason is complex, it is not deductively valid as it stands, and there are serious problems buried in the premises. Hume is safe when he says that propositions of formal logic and statements of causal relation neither express nor yield moral distinctions. But since 'reason' also includes perceptual knowledge, he needs a way to rule out the possibility that objective moral qualities are perceived by and only by those who know where or how to look.

Hume tried to eliminate this possibility by adapting an argument already deployed in his discussions of causality and the self. He had sought, but failed to find, a source in experience for the ideas of a substantial self and a necessary connection between events. In the case of moral qualities, virtues and vices, he found the same lack.

> Take any action allow'd to be vicious: Wilful murder, for instance. Examine it in all lights, and see if you can find that matter of fact, or real existence, which you call *vice*. In which-ever way you take it, you find only certain passions, motives, volitions and thoughts. There is no other matter of fact in the case. The vice entirely escapes you, as long as you consider the object. (Hume [1], 468)

Since the vice is not in the act or the actor, you "never can find it, till you turn your reflexion into your own breast, and find a sentiment of disapprobation, which arises in you, toward the action" (Hume [1], 468–69).

Hume invites us to look for objective moral facts, sure that we will replicate his failure to find them. But not everyone ends up with this result, and it is not clear what Hume could say to someone who claimed to discern binding moral properties, except to ask, as we all must, for an explanation of their nature and of the nature of the apprehending.

After showing that the distinction between virtue and vice is not discovered by reason, Hume's next project is to explain the true origin of the distinction. Why do we approve of virtues and disapprove of vices? His answer is that we approve of virtues because of their usefulness and "agreeableness" to ourselves and others. We need not ask why we approve of things useful or agreeable to ourselves, but the question of why we approve of things that are useful and agreeable to *others* is more difficult. Hume answers it by appealing to a natural tendency to be happy at the thought of the happiness of others. Everything that contributes to the happiness of society, he says, "recommends itself directly to our approbation and good-will" (Hume [2], 219). In the *Treatise*, he explains that when a quality or character of a person "has a tendency to the good of mankind, we are pleas'd with it, and approve of it; because it presents a lively idea of pleasure; which idea affects us by sympathy, and is itself a kind of pleasure" (Hume [1], 580).

> As in strings equally wound up, the motion of one communicates itself to the rest; so all the affections readily pass from one person to another, and beget correspondent movements in every human creature. When I see the *effects* of passion in the voice and gesture of any person, my mind immediately passes from these effects to their causes, and forms such a lively idea of the passion, as is presently converted into the passion itself. In like manner, when I perceive the *causes* of any emotion, my mind is convey'd to the effects, and is actuated with a like emotion. (Hume [1], 576)

Hume does not allow his insight about the sentimental origin of morality to lead him into radical subjectivism. While we do feel greater sympathy for those near us, we are aware that this is unjustifiable partiality. Indeed, we realize that since we each have a unique vantage point, we could not even carry on a conversation "were each of us to consider characters and persons, only as they appear from his peculiar point of view" (Hume [1], 581). What we do, then, is "fix on some *steady* and *general* points of view," and place ourselves there in thought. Thus, beauty at a distance does not give as much pleasure as beauty up close, but we know what effect it does have up close, "and by that reflexion we correct its momentary appearance" (582).

Hume is not as clear as he could be about the change reflexion brings about. His remarks suggest either a change in the way a thing appears, a change in the kind of pleasure we feel, the addition of a new disinterested kind of pleasure, (which he calls "esteem"), or at least a change in the judgment that, upon reflexion, we would finally make.

Our first tendency is to praise and blame people according to their nearness and the effect of their actions on us. But we learn to praise and blame from a less egocentric, more objective, point of view. "Experience soon teaches us," Hume says, "this method of correcting our sentiments, or at least, of correcting our language, where the sentiments are more stubborn and inalterable" (Hume [1], 582). While we never expand our concern to the point where we feel equal affection for all, "reflexion" tells us that of two instances of a vice, one that is remote and unrelated to us "wou'd excite as strong sentiments of disapprobation" as one that touched us directly, "were it plac'd in the same position" (584).

In the *Enquiry*, Hume is less specific about this process, but he says that seeing or thinking about human happiness or misery "excites in our breast a sympathetic movement of pleasure or uneasiness." He calls this sentiment that we feel from an impartial point of view "humanity," and describes it as "some benevolence, however small, infused into our bosom; some spark of friendship for humankind; some particle of the dove kneaded into our frame, along with the elements of the wolf and serpent" (Hume [2], 271).

> The notion of morals implies some sentiment common to all mankind, which recommends the same object to general approbation, and makes every man, or most men, agree in the same opinion or decision concerning it. It also implies some sentiment, so universal and comprehensive as to extend to all mankind, and render the actions and conduct, even of the persons the most remote, an object of applause or censure, according as they agree or disagree with that rule of right which is established. (Hume [2], 272)

Hume observes that the objectivity of morality comes from the nearly universal presence of benevolent feelings, and that this impartial "rule of right" flows from this universal and comprehensive sentiment. This rule, however, is clearly a rule we give the world, and not one that exists there to be discovered. The objectivity of morality is a projection resulting from reflexion. This is probably not enough objectivity for serious moralists, who refuse to believe that the strong ought-to-be-ness they discover in their moral rules has such a subjective source. It was not enough for two British moral philosophers writing in Hume's wake, both of whom tried to develop a kind of realistic moralist empiricism.

Richard Price and Thomas Reid

Richard Price (1723–1791) criticized the subjectivism in Hutcheson's account of moral sense by pointing out that anyone who accepts this view must believe that "moral right and wrong signify nothing *in the objects themselves* to which they are applied, any more than agreeable and harsh; sweet and bitter; pleasant and painful; but only *certain effects in us*" (Mackie [2], 133). This was, of course, exactly what Hutcheson believed, but Price was a moral objectivist who thought that "right and wrong are real characters of actions." He was one of the first after Hume to suggest that we have a "moral faculty" capable of discerning objective moral properties.

> It is scarcely conceivable that anyone can impartially attend to the nature of his own perceptions, and determine that, when he thinks gratitude or beneficence to be *right*, he perceives nothing *true* of them, and *understands* nothing, but only receives an impression from a sense. (Mackie [2], 135)

We have just seen Hume acknowledge that we can, and even must, develop an impartial and general set of moral beliefs. We may support a policy of gratitude or beneficence because we have moved to a neutral standpoint and corrected our feelings and language, both of which tend to be partial. But this impartial point of view does not itself take us all the way to an objective moral property. Objectivity as impartiality is too weak a form of objectivity to satisfy Price. Nor would it have satisfied Thomas Reid (1710–1796), who says that "all moral reasonings rest upon one or more first principles of morals, whose truth is immediately perceived without reasoning, by all men come to years of understanding" (Mackie [2], 19). Long before G. E. Moore claimed that we can intuit the presence of the non-natural property of goodness, Price and Reid were taking this intuitionist path, and claiming that we "immediately perceive" right and wrong.

When Reid confronts subjectivism, he relies heavily on the way morality presents itself as objective: "That I ought not to steal, or to kill, or to bear false witness, are propositions, of the truth of which I am as well convinced as of any proposition in Euclid" (Mackie [2], 142). Mackie thinks that Reid is right about this, and that this "rules out" the non-cognitivist account of moral thinking. But, as we have already seen, there are explanations for this moral conviction, and for the feeling of moral bondage, that make no use of moral properties. The fervent conviction and the sense of objectivity and bondage can be understood to result from the socialization process and the human needs that dictate the form morality must assume to be effective.

> Where a passion is neither founded on false suppositions, nor chuses means insufficient for the end, the understanding can neither justify nor condemn it. 'Tis not contrary to reason to prefer the destruction of the whole world to the scratching of my finger. 'Tis not contrary to reason for me to chuse my total ruin, to prevent the least uneasiness of an *Indian* or person wholly unknown to me. 'Tis as little contrary to reason to prefer even my own acknowledg'd lesser good to my greater, and have a more ardent affection for the former than the latter. (Hume [1], 416)

> For the pure thought of duty and of the moral law generally, unmixed with any extraneous addition of empirical inducements, has by the way of reason alone (which first becomes aware hereby that it can of itself be practical) an influence on the human heart so much more powerful than all other incentives which may be derived from the empirical field that reason in the consciousness of its dignity despises such incentives and is able gradually to become their master. (Kant [3], 22)

> Afterwards a sentiment of morals concurs with interest and becomes a new obligation upon mankind. This sentiment of morality, in the performance of promises, arises from the same principles as that in the abstinence from the property of others. *Public interest, education,* and *the artifices of politicians,* have the same effect in both cases. The difficulties, that occur to us, in supposing a moral obligation to attend promises, we either surmount or elude. For instance; the expression of a resolution is not commonly suppos'd to be obligatory; and we cannot readily conceive how the making use of a certain form of words shou'd be able to cause any material difference. Here, therefore, we *feign* a new act of the mind, which we call the *willing* an obligation; and on this we suppose the morality to depend. But we have prov'd already, that there is no such act of the mind, and consequently that promises impose no natural obligation. (Hume [1], 523)

Immanuel Kant

Immanuel Kant (1724–1804) was satisfied neither with Hume's idea that objectivity is projected nor with the intuitionist's belief that it is there to be discovered by some moral sense; and he saw no role in morality for emotions and feelings of approval or disapproval. He was convinced that the empiricists must always fail to provide morality with the universality and necessity he believed it to require.

Hume was satisfied to take his own list of eighteenth-century virtues as given, and so was Kant, who said that "neither science nor philosophy is needed in order to know what one must do to be honest and good, and even wise and virtuous" (Kant [3], 16). They did not quibble with their societies, and neither need we. We can glance through the ethical writings of the world and assemble a list of twenty or so virtues that nearly everyone would agree upon. This core of what common sense tells us will help with our social existence includes truthfulness, sincerity, compassion, courage, fidelity, respect, industry, among others. Many of them are found on Confucius's list of virtues, and are recommended by Jesus and the Buddha. They turn up as the "conventional virtues" mentioned in Plato's *Republic,* and they appear in Hobbes's Laws of Nature. Hume wants to explain the feelings we have and the claims we make about some of these qualities, and he thinks this can be done by citing our natural tendency to approve of things that are useful or pleasing to others or to ourselves, and our ability to reflect on what it is to take a point of view.

Kant wants more. The moral feelings of humans play no role in his theorizing, since he is looking not for the origin of our approval but for the foundation of the moral law that commands all rational beings so far as they are rational. His announced goal in the *Grounding for the Metaphysics of Morals* is to arrive at "pure rational knowledge separated from everything empirical," knowledge that would yield "the principles of morality." He insists that

> unless we want to deny to the concept of morality all truth and all reference to a possible object, we cannot but admit that the moral law is of such widespread significance that it must hold not merely for men but for all rational beings generally, and that it must be valid not merely under contingent conditions and with exceptions but must be absolutely necessary. Clearly, therefore, no experience can give occasion for inferring even the possibility of such apodeictic [necessary] laws. (Kant [3], 20)

This moral law, like the law of causality, is not given by experience, but is a feature of the form of experience. The law of causality guarantees that our experience will uniformly exhibit causality, and the moral law guarantees that morality will meet the formal condition of the Categorical Imperative: "I should never act except in such a way that I can also will that my maxim should become a universal law" (Kant [3], 14).

But there is a real question about what this moral law gives us. If it is a test other maxims have to pass, then it only rules out maxims that do not satisfy it. Since this is less than we usually want from morality, Kant sometimes gives the impression that the Categorical Imperative generates more specific commands. He says that reason commands "pure sincerity in friendship" (Kant [3], 20), and he tries to generate (by arguments that are widely acknowledged to be less than cogent) prohibitions against suicide and lying promises, and injunctions to develop our talents and give aid to others (31).

"When it is said that you should not make a false promise," he claims, "the assumption is that the necessity of this avoidance is no mere advice for escaping some other evil, so that it might be said that you should not make a false promise lest you ruin your credit when the falsity comes to light" (Kant [3], 28). The command not to make a false promise does not depend on any bad effects, and holds even if the effects of doing so would be very good. The command is categorical, binding, and objectively obligatory; and if we were to follow only reason, we would automatically acknowledge its universality and necessity. Unfortunately, no one really believes Kant was able to show that reason has access to universally binding moral principles, or authority to command. What we may take away from Kant, even after far more attention than we have given him here, is an understanding of what a serious secular moralist might really have to say, and of how difficult it would be for anyone to defend, or even explain, categorically binding moral imperatives.

Intuitionism

A modern version of intuitionism, similar to the one offered by Price but focusing on 'good' rather than on 'right', is found in the writings of G. E. Moore, who believes that goodness, like yellowness, is a simple property, that it is indefinable, and that it is presented directly to the knower. The difference is that yellowness is a *natural* property, open to visual inspection (and the instruments of science), while goodness is a *non-natural* property, and is therefore not to be discerned in the way colors or sounds are. Other modern intuitionists contend that we intuit duties and obligations rather than values.

G. E. Moore's Secular Morality

Moore's philosophy is a reaction to a British version of German Idealism that grew out of the philosophy of Georg Wilhelm Friedrich Hegel, and to "naturalistic" ethics, which was, in its turn, a secular reaction to the religious morality that flourished in the first half of the nineteenth century. This idealism resembled the monism embraced by the thinkers of the *Upaniṣads*—reality is one, everything is connected, and nothing is independent of consciousness. The thought and language of these idealists was subtle, abstract, and vague, and they were alienated from both science and common sense. Moore, on the other hand, had a passion for clarity and simplicity that astonished even his friends and made him constitutionally unable to carry on the argument in the idealist's terms.

While Moore respects science, he believes that philosophy, and in particular "Ethics," must be carried on along quite different principles. The attempt to extract obligations or permissions from the laws of evolution was a popular move in Moore's day, and it was one of his favorite targets. *Principia Ethica* (1903), Moore's major ethical work, is written in deceptively clear and simple prose. Without adopting all of commonsense morality, Moore embraces many of the assumptions lying behind it. The simple, dogged belief that some things just *are* good is nowhere more clearly embraced than in this work.

The fact that Moore's beliefs about language are primitive helps explain his understanding of morality. He believes that predicate terms (terms like 'yellow', 'large', 'happy', 'good', 'right', and 'triangular') are meaningful because they denote either simple or complex properties, and he believes that words denoting complex properties can be defined by words denoting the simple ones. Speaking of the word 'good', Moore says:

> In fact, if it is not the case that 'good' denotes something simple and indefinable, only two alternatives are possible; either it is a complex, a given whole, about the correct analysis of which there may be disagreement; or else it means nothing at all, and there is no such subject as Ethics. (Moore, 15)

Moore's "theory of meaning" requires meaningful terms to denote properties, so the possibility that words like 'good' may fail to denote a property and yet still be meaningful was not a possibility for him. Since his common sense tells him of a vast difference between sentences like 'X is good' and meaningless strings of sound, he is eager to reject the idea that value judgments are meaningless. This leaves him with the conclusion that 'good' denotes a property, and his only real question is whether it denotes a simple property or a complex one. He firmly believes that it denotes a simple property—not a simple natural property (as it would if 'good' meant 'pleasant' and pleasure were simple), but a simple non-natural property.

Because he believes 'good' denotes a simple non-natural property, Moore directs his arguments against those who hold that the word denotes a complex property or a simple natural one. He calls "the supposition that 'good' can be defined by reference to a natural quality" *naturalism,* and devises "the open question argument" to demolish all forms of naturalism, and more generally, every attempt to define 'good'.

This open question argument depends on assumptions about language, meaning, and definitions that are far more controversial than Moore realized. There is no good reason to suppose that every predicate term that fails to denote a property is meaningless but, more basically, there is so much unclarity about what properties and denoting are that it is impossible to discuss these matters without stumbling into a swamp of confusing and outdated philosophical terms and assumptions. Still, it is worth asking how the open question argument goes (or went), because it encapsulates a thought about definitions of ethical terms that is both natural and healthy to entertain, and because it has been exploited and attacked for a century.

If you tell me that 'to procrastinate' means the same thing as 'to put things off', part of what it is for me to understand and to accept your definition is for me to come to use and understand the two expressions in the same way. If I accept the definition, I will freely substitute one phrase for the other, and I will be no more inclined to say

(a) I know Bill is procrastinating, but is he putting things off?

than I am to say

(b) I know Bill is putting things off, but is he putting things off?

Question (b) is obviously not an open question, and anyone who accepts the definition of 'to procrastinate' has to admit that question (a) has the same status, superficial appearances to the contrary.

Moore argues against those who said that 'good' means 'pleasant' by insisting that if they were right then the question:

(c) Is pleasure good?

should be no more open than the questions:

(d) Is pleasure pleasant?

But, Moore insists, question (c) is open in a way that question (d) is not:

> Whoever will attentively consider with himself what is actually before his mind when he asks the question 'Is pleasure (or whatever it may be) after

> all good?' can easily satisfy himself that he is not merely wondering whether pleasure is pleasant. (Moore, 16)

While the answer to question (d) is given as soon as the question is asked, this is not the case with question (c). That is what it is for question (c) to be *open*. Now, since question (c) *is* open, Moore concludes, 'pleasant' does not mean the same thing as 'good' and the naturalist's definition is mistaken.

Moore wants to say that the question "Is this N thing good?" where 'N' stands for any "natural property," is always open. He believes that this shows that any naturalistic definition of 'good' will always be incorrect. He says that any philosopher who uses definitions to identify goodness with any natural property is committing the "Naturalistic Fallacy."

The reviews this argument received were mixed in a predictable way. Naturalists found it unconvincing and "non-naturalists," those who did not want to identify ethical properties with natural properties, found the argument congenial, and used it themselves, even when they disagreed with Moore about almost everything else. Eventually the torch of the struggle against naturalism passed to the non-cognitivist, who adapted Moore's argument by translating it from an argument about meaning into an argument about use. According to the non-cognitivist, no naturalistic definition can be given because evaluative language has an expressive or imperative function that the naturalist's pure statements of fact do not have. "Reason," here understood as the domain of "factual language," does not move us to action.

Moore does not reject all definitions, only those aimed at giving the meaning of the word 'good'. In *Principia Ethica* he claims that it is true by definition that it is right (or even obligatory) to produce goodness. He puts it this way:

> What I wish first to point out is that 'right' does and can mean nothing but 'cause of a good result,' and is thus identical with 'useful'; whence it follows that the end always will justify the means, and that no action which is not justified by its results can be right. (Moore, 147)

This has the strange consequence of making utilitarianism true by definition, a procedure to which there are plenty of objections. Moore was not the first moralist to try to make it true by definition that the end justifies the means, but perhaps he should have asked himself his own open question. "That is useful, but is it right?" seems to be the kind of question a sensible moralist would want to be open, but if we accept Moore's definition, it is not.

Moore says that the word 'good' denotes a simple, indefinable, "non-natural" property. This property cannot be discovered by the ordinary senses, nor can its presence be established by argument. It can only be noticed by a special kind of apprehension that he fails to explain, but calls intuition. Moore thinks this is not so strange, and says that when we say we know something by "intuition" we are saying no more than that we know it without being able to prove it.

We would all admit that there are things we know but cannot prove—but in every case we suppose that something in the world makes what we know the way we know it to be. Moore says that what makes something good is the property of goodness, and perhaps this would seem more helpful if he had been able to say *anything* informative about goodness, or about our ability to discern its presence. Goodness is supposed to be a property, but it is quite different from properties like yellowness with which it is compared. If someone is not able to see that a yellow fire engine is yellow, then we know there is a problem with the light or with his eyes or brain. But if someone is not able to "see" that certain things are good, the intuitionist does not have the faintest idea what to say.

Color has a scientific explanation and color blindness a physical basis, but intuitionists never even pretended that "moral blindness" has a physical basis. We learned our basic property words in connection with ordinary properties we can observe, check, and measure with instruments. Properties like yellow exist in a network of beliefs about the relation of color to light, prisms, paint, physiology, and photography. Non-natural properties do not fit into any system like this—that is what is meant by calling them *non-natural.*

If goodness were a property it would be a very strange and unusual property, utterly different from the standard properties we grew up with, all of which connect with the world of science and experience we all share. As we have seen, John Mackie calls this objection "the argument from queerness." G. J. Warnock expresses it in the following summary of his own objections to intuitionism: "Now we have . . . seen that the theory [intuitionism] leaves it, at best, unclear how pieces of moral information are related to any other features of the world, and rather more than unclear how their truth can be established or confirmed" (Warnock, 15). Criticism of this sort may have failed to undermine the belief that goodness and badness are objective qualities because that assumption is built into our language and our conventional ways of talking and thinking about morality. As Mackie says, "intuitionism merely makes unpalatably plain what other forms of objectivism wrap up" (Mackie [1], 38).

If objectivity is implied by the use of evaluative language, then we will not be able to question objectivity on the basis of an analysis of moral language. This may be why some who take ordinary language as a guide are inclined to agree with Moore, and why the intuitionists were not impressed by the argument from queerness. What did impress them was widespread agreement about basic moral principles and the sheer strength, clarity, and obviousness of many of our important moral beliefs. But we have already seen that even universal agreement would not show that a moral principle is objectively true, justifiable, or rational to believe; and while moral reactions to certain kinds of cruelty can be spontaneous and clear, both the universal agreement and the spontaneous reactions can be explained by the hypothesis that we are taught by our peers, and even by our language, to presuppose our local form of moral objectivity.

This point is made by Peter Singer, who argues that our ethical beliefs, rules, and principles have a complex biological and cultural explanation. Without such an explanation, he says, we might be led to think that our confidence in our most deeply held beliefs flows from a clear apprehension of some objectively existing moral truth. Biological and cultural explanations of our moral beliefs and intuitions, however, should "make us skeptical about thinking of them as self-evident moral axioms" (Singer [3], 70–71).

H. A. Prichard and W. D. Ross

In 1668 Henry More argued that his twenty-three moral principles were "self-evident moral truths." Over 250 years later we find W. D. Ross characterizing propositions about "prima facie" duties in the same terms and H. A. Prichard maintaining that we are capable of perceiving some course of action to be our duty.

Prichard wrote a famous article called "Does Moral Philosophy Rest on a Mistake?" His answer is that it does, and that the mistake it rests on is "the mistake of supposing the possibility of proving what can only be apprehended directly by an act of moral thinking" (Prichard, 16). He holds the objectivist moralist belief that some actions are right but, in opposition to Moore, he is certain that we do not come to appreciate our obligations by hearing an argument. "Our sense of the rightness of an act," he says, "is not a conclusion from our appreciation of the goodness either of it or of anything else." (9).

The problems with Prichard's intuitionism are similar to those facing Moore. If *goodness* is a "queer property," can rightness or obligatoriness be less peculiar? Prichard says that we "appreciate" our obligations, but how is this done? He says that if we make ourselves aware of the pattern of circumstances surrounding some action—the consequences, relevant previous behavior of those involved, intentions, contracts and agreements in force, and so forth—then at some point we will just *see* what we ought to do. We do not deduce our duty from the fact that the consequences are such and such, we "appreciate the obligation immediately or directly." In that case what is *apprehended* is a moral truth that Prichard insists is, like an axiom of geometry, self-evident.

While Prichard says that in given cases we can "appreciate the obligation immediately," Ross says that it is not the rightness of *particular* acts that we "apprehend," but rather the rightness of *kinds* of acts, for example promise keeping or paying debts. He further differs from Prichard by introducing the concept of a "prima facie duty." To say that an action is a prima facie duty is to say that it is the kind of act that would be the right thing to do unless other morally relevant factors intervene.

Ross lists several kinds of prima facie duties. *Duties of fidelity* are ones that rest "on a promise or what may fairly be called an implicit promise, such as the implicit undertaking not to tell lies which seems to be implied in the act of entering into conversation" (Ross, 21). *Duties of reparation* arise when someone has done a "wrongful act." *Duties of gratitude* rest on previous acts of others. Other duties, he says, rest on the "fact or possibility of a distribution of pleasure or happiness . . . which is not in accordance with the merit of the persons concerned" (21). Surprisingly, Ross says that in such a case we have *duties of justice* "to upset or prevent such a distribution." However, the radical teeth of this prima facie duty are pulled because it is *only* a prima facie duty, and because it is not clear what is meant by 'merit'.

Some duties rest on the fact that we can "improve our own condition in terms of virtue or intelligence," and some on the fact that we can improve the virtue, the intelligence, or even the pleasure of others. The former duties are *duties of self-improvement*, the latter are *duties of beneficence*. Somewhat less demanding than the duty to do good for others is the duty not to do harm, the *duty of non-maleficence*.

Ross deviates from Prichard's position in another way. He rejects

Prichard's idea that the "property" of rightness is sui generis (totally unrelated to and uncompounded of other things). According to Ross, "whether an act is a duty proper or actual duty depends on all the morally significant kinds it is an instance of." Is it a case of promise keeping and truth telling that at the same time damages someone? Then what must be done depends, in some way that Ross never specifies, on these three morally relevant factors. He is only able to say that when there is a conflict,

> what I have to do is to study the situation as fully as I can until I form the considered opinion (it is never more) that in the circumstances one of them is more incumbent than any other; then I am bound to think that to do this *prima facie* duty is my duty *sans phrase* in the situation. (Ross, 19)

Neither Ross nor Prichard avoids the problems confronting Moore's theory. All three fall victim to the argument from queerness, and while the intuitions of Ross and Prichard may correspond more closely to our actual moral beliefs and attitudes than the conclusions of the utilitarians, this may be because those intuitions are objectifications of those moral beliefs and attitudes. After all, if our moral beliefs and attitudes are placed in us early, if some of them are even a function of our biology, then how could they seem other than obvious to us? The intuitionist takes this appearance of obviousness as a sign of objective truth, but, as we now know, there are other ways to explain it.

Neointuitionism

Moore, Prichard, and Ross developed their forms of intuitionism in the early years of this century. By the middle of the century, intuitionism was suffering from terminal neglect, a victim of the success of philosophy influenced by science, and of non-cognitivism. In recent years, however, moral philosophers have sought ways to say the things intuitionists said, but without buying into the objectionable metaphysical and epistemological assumptions. These "neointuitionists" *say* that we can have direct moral knowledge, or that we can know or even see that some act is right or wrong, or that some thing is good or bad, but they reject peculiar evaluative properties and the fantastic epistemology that went with them. They *say* that there are values, but they may think this is made so by our entrenched ways of using evaluative language and our habit of seeing certain configurations as possessing value.

In Chapter 3 we see how Sabina Lovibond tries to develop a "metaphysically inoffensive account of moral intuition in terms of seeing as" (Lovibond, 49–50). Because of our training in the language and traditions of our culture, we see some things as good, others as bad, and we see some ways of acting as right and others as wrong. These evaluations are not perceptions of unique properties, but spontaneous "observations" that present themselves with force and seeming objectivity. This phenomenon may have supported the classical intuitionists in their crazy objectivity, but neointuitionists know better than to suppose or to claim that they are directly aware of genuine mind-independent moral properties. They want to embrace moral realism without falling into crazy objectivity, and they believe that this can be done by constructing a kind of intersubjective objectivity out of consensus. They then argue that while this is not the sort of objectivity we would get with independently real moral properties, it is all the objectivity we can expect in ethics, and all the objectivity we need for moral realism.

Contrary to Mackie's claim that intersubjectivity is not objectivity, Lovibond holds that when intersubjective agreement exists, "the particular discourse grounded in it can properly be called 'objective', regardless of its subject-matter" (Lovibond, 42). This may encourage the moral realist, who is seeking a more relaxed interpretation of objectivity, but it is a dangerous principle. It is as if we are being told that any broadly held belief, however peculiar, gives rise to entities of the sort believed in. But there must be a limit to what we can say exists, a limit that has nothing to do with what people believe in or agree about. Further, if intersubjectivity is objectivity, then objectivity (at least in ethics) is nothing more than intersubjectivity, and that is a hard pill to swallow. The intuitionist gains the right to call morality objective by dropping the very feature that makes it useful and gives it power. Lovibond's "modest form of intuitionism" is too modest to satisfy a serious moralist, since it is only a construction out of subjective attitudes.

> Intuitionism seems, in retrospect, so strange a phenomenon—a body of writing so acute and at the same time so totally unilluminating—that one may wonder how to explain it, what its genesis was. The idea that there is a vast corpus of moral facts about the world—known, but we cannot say how: related to other features

> of the world, but we cannot explain in what way: overwhelmingly important for our conduct, but we cannot say why—what does this really astonishing idea reflect? One may be tempted to say: the absence of curiosity. And what the absence of curiosity reflects may be the absence of doubt. (Warnock, 16)

Making Moralism True by Definition

Jeremy Bentham identified goodness with pleasure in order to give a quantifiable substitute for what would otherwise, he said, be a meaningless notion. In Chapter 2 we see that this strategy lies behind subjective forms of moral relativism and Gilbert Harman's definition of the moral 'ought'. "Naturalists" say that there are moral facts because moral facts are identical with natural facts, and naturalists who are definists make the identification a matter of definition. Even divine command theorists can try to make it true by definition (of 'ought' or of 'God') that we ought to do as God commands, thus generating a kind of "supernaturalist" definism.

Subjective Definitions

The divine command theory is a special case of what can be called "subjectivism." Subjectivists base value and/or obligation on "subjective" mental states and actions. They hold that nothing would have any value if there were no beings with desires, attitudes, and preferences. We get different forms of subjectivism depending on which being or beings we set up as the one or ones whose desires and preferences count. Richard Taylor, for example, claims that while words like 'good' and 'bad' designate nothing "in the world," when humans desire things, or when they take a positive interest in things, then those things "become" good. He says that we could not even draw the distinction between good and evil "in a world that we imagined to be devoid of all life," that "if we suppose the world to be exactly as it is, except that it contains not one living thing, it seems clear that nothing in it would be good and nothing bad" (Taylor, 123).

The idea that values can be brought into being by desires and attitudes is not easy to defend. How can the mere fact that someone likes or wants something *make* that thing, whatever it may be, good? Surely the object does not change because of what we think about it. But if there is no change in the object, but only in the mind of the being with the attitude, what warrants our saying that the *object* has become good? A subjectivist who is sensitive to this problem may try to *identify* the goodness of a thing with the feelings some being has about it, or the wrongness of an action with the fact that it has been forbidden by an authority, a law, or a god. A subjectivist who is also a definist will say that this identity is a matter of definition.

But subjectivists who want to be moralists are like drunks who search for their keys next to the streetlight because that is where the light is. They understand desires and feelings (or think they do), so they try to change the subject from what we *ought* to do to what we *want* to do, or to what we *like*. At the same time, they keep on using the old language of morality, complete with its assumption of objectivity. No wonder Moore made the motto of his book "Everything is what it is, and not another thing." If "being good" *is* really being desired or favored by the appropriate party, then there is nothing more to being good than *that*, and that is not enough.

Non-Subjective Definitions

Definitions of moral terms may make use of subjective notions like interest and desire, but there are other possibilities. Some have said that 'right' can be defined in terms of a tendency to promote survival, or that 'good' means *natural*. Moore aimed his open question argument at all such definitions, and it still reminds us that it makes sense to ask if it is always right to seek survival, or if the best behavior is really the behavior that comes most naturally.

Neonaturalism

Some definists offer such complicated definitions that the open question argument, which is grounded in our intuitions about our everyday words, cannot be used against them. Others, who can be called "neonaturalists," identify evaluative properties with factual properties but make no effort to secure the identification by a definition. They say that the identity between evaluative and natural properties is not a matter of meaning but something we might learn, as we learned that water is H_2O, that clouds are masses of water droplets, and that genes are segments of DNA molecules.

William Lycan, one of many who have recently defended neonaturalism, argues that Moore, his naturalist targets, and his emotivist critics who attack him with their own version of the open question argument, are all caught in a network of superstition about meaning, properties, and identity. As a result, they neglect the possibility that moral properties are *in fact* identical with complex natural properties involving "utility, harm, degradation or the like" (Lycan, 86). Another avowed neonaturalist, Nicholas Sturgeon, says that it is a mistake "to require of ethical naturalism that it even promise reductive definitions for moral terms" (Sturgeon, 59).

The picture Lycan offers us is this: a term like 'bad' has come to designate a complex of properties "involving (dis)utility, harm, degradation or the like" (A-properties); and a capacity to detect A-properties has evolved in humans, whose chances for survival were improved by an ability to identify, and a disposition to avoid, things with A-properties. Though we were taught to avoid such things, and to call them *bad,* we were not taught that these things have A-properties. What we discover is that we have all been using 'bad' to apply to things with A-properties—just as we discover that we have all been using 'water' to speak of stuff that is H_2O.

A neonaturalist will say that the B-property, badness, is not different from a complex of A-properties. But part of what it is to take certain things to be *bad* is to believe that these things ought to be avoided, that they have a crucial blot or defect, that they rank low when judged by some objective standard. We have been conditioned to think that things with A-properties (things we have been programmed to avoid) posses the B-property itself, with all the evaluative trimmings (an implied duty to avoid, low status, justified disdain, and objective ought-not-to-be-ness).

According to Lycan, without "any special reason for thinking that B- and A-properties are distinct, Occam's Razor at least strongly encourages the identification" (Lycan, 86). But there is a special reason for thinking that moral properties and natural properties are distinct. Moral properties make demands on us, they require things from us, they bind us. The B-property comes with the evaluative trimmings just mentioned, and these trimmings are what make evaluative language so useful. The value of value is that when (and if) we are able to establish that a thing has positive value, we have provided ourselves with a warrant, and others with a reason, for seeking it. This is how goodness differs from redness—a thing that is good is, for that very reason, worthy of being pursued. Whatever redness turns out to be, it will not emerge that we are obliged to own more red objects, or to maximize the redness in the world.

The trouble with both naturalism and neonaturalism is that natural properties (pleasure, pain, survival, even being desired) do not automatically provide this sort of warrant or reason, and values do. It is a matter of the law of identity. If two things are different, they can not be identical. Water, being H_2O, has no feature H_2O lacks. If moral properties bind us and require things from us, then they can not be identical with any constellation of properties that lacks this feature. And if they are identical with a constellation of natural properties, then either the natural properties bind us, which makes no sense, or the moral and evaluative properties do not, which is a violation of their essence.

The problem with naturalistic identifications (whether they are definitions or not) is that they backfire. If 'good' and 'pleasant' are really synonyms, as the naturalist definists thought, then our talk about goodness and pleasantness is really talk about only one thing—and that thing is most easily identified as pleasure. We do not reduce the familiar to the strange. By trying to define value into existence, the classical naturalists actually defined it *out* of existence. Rather than giving values a boost by identifying them with facts, naturalist definists paved the way for a value-free conception of the world.

Neonaturalists do no better. Even if Mother Nature has fitted us with tendencies to avoid things that are harmful and that lead to pain, this does not warrant realism about value. It is natural that our innate dislike should be expressed in language, and perhaps even natural that it should be projected onto the object of the dislike. But why, given the plausibility of Humean projectivism, should we not ascribe spontaneous moral beliefs to training, indoctrination, evolution, and language-fostered habits? Why go beyond this perfectly reasonable explanation to embrace realism about moral properties? Is there any reason for thinking the realist explanation is closer to the way things are than the projectivist explanation? Lycan knows that this question is a serious one, and he admits that if it eventually turns out that there is "simply no evidence of any brain detection of morally charged properties, then so much the worse for moral facts; we would have little reason to believe in them" (Lycan, 87–88).

There is currently little or no evidence that we do detect moral or evaluative characteristics, so we may wonder why anyone would want to hold to the idea of intrinsic value, or speculate so imaginatively about what moral properties are. The answer Lycan gives is that, difficult as it may be to discover the real character of value and to deal with all the objections of skeptics and nihilists, spontaneous moral judgments are too insistent to be relegated to the realm of invention (Lycan, 88). There is no doubt that some spontaneous moral judgments are insistent, but insistency proves nothing, and is easily explained by our style of moral education. Our moral feelings are almost certainly the result of evolution and social conditioning, and our moral beliefs a linguistic manifestation of this indoctrination. The feeling that we are presented with moral facts and objective values is simply a sign of how thorough our education has been.

Conclusion

Divine command theorists, of course, are moralists. Plato, Aristotle, Kant, and the British rationalists also fall in the moralist camp. So do those empiricists of the moral sentiment school who hold that moral properties in objects give rise to special feelings, which then alert us to the objective properties. But it is more difficult to know what to say about definists who think that 'good' means 'pleasant'. When they say that something is "good," should we charge them with believing in the existence of objective moral properties, or (perhaps more plausibly) with adopting a misleading way of saying that something is pleasant?

To the amoralist, pleasure is pleasure and pain is pain. We seek pleasure, we enjoy it, and it is *good for* us. We avoid pain when we can. Amoralists know that pleasure is *desired*—they even desire it; but the moralist adds that it is *desirable*. Few are aware how great that step from the 'ed' to the 'able' is. Something that is "desirable" *deserves* to be desired. It has certain features that demand a positive evaluation from those who see clearly. Other phrases that express the same idea are 'intrinsically good', 'good as an end', 'good in itself', 'valuable', and 'worthwhile'. Moralists trade in these notions, but the amoralist will insist that while there are many sensible uses of 'good' and 'desirable', the categorical, non-conventional, non-hypothetical uses adopted by moralists are devices we can and, given that we want to avoid deception, *ought* to do without.

10

A Survey of Moral Theories

> *Intense, long, certain, speedy, fruitful, pure*—Such marks in *pleasures* and in *pains* endure. Such pleasures seek, if *private* be thy end: If it be *public*, wide let them *extend*. Such *pains* avoid, whichever be thy view: If pains *must* come, let them *extend* to few.
>
> —*Jeremy Bentham*, An Introduction to the Principles of Morals and Legislation

IT IS ARGUED in Chapter 8 that we are unlikely to find an unproblematic source for moral bondage in the commands or attitudes of a God, and in Chapter 9 that the natural world offers no more support for objective prescriptivity than does the supernatural one. When we ask what the claims and concepts of religious and secular moralists mean, and whether they are to be accepted, we are asking *metaethical* questions. And when we ask what entities, acts, and attributes religious and secular moralists take to be good, bad, right, and wrong, we are asking about their *normative* ethical claims. A survey of metaethics is a survey of answers to questions *about* normative ethics; and a survey of normative ethics is a survey of answers to questions about what we ought to seek, and do, and be.

In this chapter we chart the philosophical space moralists occupy, occasionally slowing down to take a more detailed look at some particular normative or metaethical position. Any amoralist will think that all normative positions are defective, but a critical look at some types of moralism is only part of the case for amoralism. No matter how many specific forms of egoism or utilitarianism one has managed to find reasons for rejecting, there will always be new forms that, like mutant viruses, have become immune to medicine developed for simpler strains. Still, every time a normative position is shown to have some fatal flaw, the amoralist's position becomes just a little stronger.

Metaethics

According to Gilbert Harman, it should have been obvious to philosophers sooner than it was that "the whole distinction between meta-ethics and normative ethics had to be abandoned" (Harman [2], viii). It would, he thinks, be better to investigate the philosophical problems of morality "without the meta-ethical baggage" (viii). Two things are wrong with metaethics: it is based on "highly controversial and possibly even incoherent assumptions about meaning," and it is not interesting. Yet Harman himself asks and answers metaethical questions. We have already seen how he explicates the moral 'ought', and throughout *The Nature of Morality* and recent writings he attacks competing metaethical theories and defends his own form of ethical naturalism.

Another philosopher who takes a dim view of metaethics is Richard Taylor, who opens the preface to his book *Good and Evil* with these words:

> One would search in vain in these pages for any discussion of the naturalistic fallacy . . . or the other fastidious puzzles that have somehow come to be thought of in some circles as important to ethics. Also missing are appraisals of utilitarianism, deontologism, intuitionism, cognitivism, and the rest of the baggage of what has pretentiously come to be known as *metaethics*. (Taylor, xi)

Like Harman, Taylor fails to avoid all involvement with metaethics. His claim that "the moral rightness or wrongness of anything is entirely relative to accepted rules of behavior, and without meaning except in relation to such rules" is pure metaethics, as is his claim that moral right and wrong "can be defined in terms of rules" (Taylor, 139–40).

Both Taylor and Harman speak about metaethical *baggage*, a metaphor that suggests unnecessary supplies and superfluous equipment. As they see it, just when we get excited about some question about what is good or right, the "metaethicist" snaps open his bag and drags out endless distinctions, demands for justification, and quibbles about meaning. We may never get back to the real questions unless we can manage to keep that Pandora's bag of metaethical diversions closed.

We will only be in a position to determine the fairness of this complaint if we invite the metaethicist to lay some of the contents of the bag before us. What are these "boring" questions and "fastidious" puzzles but questions and puzzles about meaning and justification? When we ask what words like 'good', 'right', 'justice', 'rights', or 'duty' mean (or what some person means by them), or how they are being used in a moral judgment, or even what a moral judgment is, we are asking a metaethical question. When we learn that G. E. Moore believes that "the enjoyment of beautiful objects" is intrinsically good, we learn something about his normative theory of value. When we ask what he means by 'good', we have asked a metaethical question, and when he claims that there is no way to answer this question, that 'good' is an indefinable term, he is taking a metaethical position.

Taylor does not want to waste time with "utilitarianism, deontologism, intuitionism, cognitivism, and the rest of the baggage," but responsible moralists cannot ignore (or adopt) these theories just because it pleases them to do so. Moore was an intuitionist who believed that goodness is a "property," and a utilitarian who thought that the principle of utility is true by definition. Would Taylor encourage us not to ask whether these ideas are to be accepted or rejected?

Moore's main metaethical targets were those who thought that 'good' *can* be defined. We have seen that the controversy between Moore and his opponents was flawed by a primitive concept of meaning, but even when we let primitive concepts of meaning go, we cannot safely ignore the question, "What do you mean by 'good'?" Those who use words like 'good' and 'right' in moralist ways are caught by the conventions of the system we all share, and one of those conventions is that people who make moral judgments and declarations of value may be asked to explain their words and support their claims.

When questions about meaning were considered more important than they are now, one way to classify metaethical positions was by looking at what they claimed about the meanings of words like 'good' and 'right'. The available positions regarding this are displayed in Figure 10-1.

Anyone who believes that some term like 'right' or 'good' can be defined is a definist *relative to that term*. Anyone who believes that a term cannot be defined is a non-definist *relative to that term*. One may

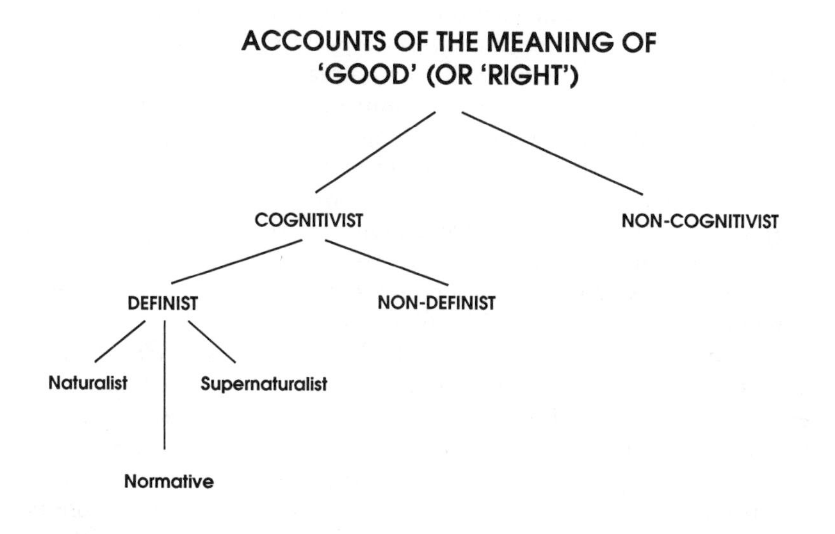

Figure 10-1

be a definist relative to some terms and a non-definist relative to others. In the context of morality, "*the* definist" is someone who believes that all moral and evaluative terms can be defined using only naturalist or supernaturalist definitions. "*The* non-definist," on the other hand, holds that at least one moral or evaluative term cannot be defined. Moore once thought that 'right' could be defined as "the cause of a good result," but that 'good' could not be defined at all. This made him a definist relative to 'right', but ultimately a non-definist.

The emotivists rejected both definism and non-definism. A. J. Ayer said that evaluative terms have neither a definable meaning nor an indefinable one, because they have no meaning at all—they are "mere" verbalizations of emotions and attempts to influence attitudes and behavior. Eventually, cognitivists and non-cognitivists agreed that most evaluative judgments have both descriptive and emotive meaning, though they disagreed over what follows from that. Other (and probably wiser) philosophers dropped the question of meaning.

However bizarre and irrelevant these controversies may appear to those lucky enough to have seen through their mistaken presuppositions, it is still in order to ask people what they mean when we do not understand them, and to ask them why they believe what they do. No one who wants to be taken seriously can just issue moral pronouncements and refuse all requests for interpretation, clarification, and defense. What, then, is the point of complaining about metaethics? What could be clearer than the contrast between making moral judgments and discussing their meaning, use, and support?

We must admit that our metaethical baggage does contain, in addition to our necessities, superfluous distinctions and fastidious puzzles. No matter what the topic, some of the philosophers who discuss it will end up light-years away from the heart of the issue. But a topic is not disqualified as a legitimate candidate for investigation by the fact that it can lead philosophers astray.

Even if we ban philosophical talk about meaning, there remain many legitimate and sometimes answerable questions about how people are *using* moral and evaluative language. If these questions made no sense, then those who argue about rights, duties, goodness, badness, and obligation could never discover that their disagreement is (or is not) merely verbal. When contemporary moral philosophers talk about bypassing or ignoring metaethics (that is, doing without the baggage) we must hope that they do not intend to forbid us to ask them what they mean by their words and why we should believe what they say.

> In fact, we shall take ethics to be primarily concerned with providing the general outlines of a normative theory to help us in answering problems about what is right or ought to be done, and as being interested in meta-ethical questions mainly because it seems necessary to answer such questions before one can be entirely satisfied with one's normative theory (although ethics is also interested in meta-ethical questions for their own sakes). (Frankena [1], 5)

> Third, there is a branch of ethics that *surveys* normative ethics with the intent of clarifying its problems and its terminology, and with the intent, in particular, of examining the sorts of reasons by which its conclusions can be supported. It is called "analytical" ethics, though it also goes under alternative names such as "meta-ethics" and "critical" ethics. Socrates was engaged in analytical ethics when he asked, for instance, whether virtue is knowledge, or whether virtue, like knowledge, can be taught. It is accordingly an old branch of the subject; and writers on normative ethics have rarely been content to ignore it, simply because normative ethics has been thought to need the near-logical discipline that analytical ethics has sought to provide. (Stevenson [4], vi)

Normative Ethics

Some *normative* judgments tell us how we ought to act, some tell us what we ought to be, and others express evaluations. Moral judgments, aesthetic judgments, even judgments of etiquette, are normative judgments. General normative judgments offer and promote norms—standards of value and behavior—and specific normative judgments express particular obligations or evaluations.

Normative *ethics* is traditionally divided into the *theory of value* and the *theory of obligation*. The question "What things are goods or ends in themselves?" says Moore, is the "fundamental question of Ethics" (Moore, 184). It is, at least, the fundamental question of the theory of value. But the theory of value is not everything. When we are concerned with what is right we have moved to the theory of obligation, to questions about moral duties, principles, and prohibitions. Do we have a duty to increase the happiness in the world or to treat others as we would like to be treated? When, if ever, is killing, or lying, or stealing morally permissible?

Two further areas of normative ethics require pigeonholes of their own. The belief that we have moral rights, and the set of associated beliefs about what bearing this has on what we must and may do, are now inalienable components of many moral theories. If you have a moral or a natural right to free speech, then anyone who stops you from speaking is doing something morally wrong. If you have a moral right, others have a moral obligation to behave in ways that respect that right. Even normative theories that do not make rights basic must explain where rights come from and why they appear to be so important.

A fourth and final form of moralism takes us back to Aristotle. Rather than talk of values, obligations, or rights, we might concentrate on virtues. The claim that honesty is a virtue is more than praise for honesty and more than a recommendation to be honest. When we call something a virtue, we are saying or suggesting that it is a way of being (a habit, perhaps) that is not quite optional. When we say sloth is a vice, we are not saying that no one ought to take it easy, but we are saying that something is wrong with someone who refuses to get off the couch. A virtue is a good quality, a desirable quality, a quality we would have if we managed to be all we could (and should) be. A vice is something "to be avoided."

It is natural to have preferences, to make demands, and to promote behavior we prefer. Everyone who lives with others has what

Bernard Williams calls an "ethics," but moralists think that some "ethics" are objectively correct, and that our bondage by moral requirements is more than just conventional. These are the beliefs that encourage moralists to demand that others live "morally." We can find this demand in the ancient world and in the modern world, in the East and in the West, and we will probably find it on other planets if we ever get there.

To say that a knife is a good one, or that someone is a good burglar or a good friend, is to make a value judgment, but not a judgment of intrinsic value. These value judgments depend on interests, purposes, and standards that even amoralists may find useful to adopt, or impossible to do without. Sharpness in knives, stealth in burglars, and loyalty in friends are qualities sought by everyone looking for "good" knives, burglars, or friends.

The words '–ought', 'right', 'must', 'obligation', and 'duty' are used in making judgments of obligation. To have an obligation is to be bound to do something. If it is a moral obligation then we are "morally bound," but not all judgments of obligation are judgments of moral obligation. When we say that someone who wants to avoid colds ought to take Vitamin C, our 'ought' is not a moral 'ought'. It is the 'ought' we use to make recommendations. When we just assume that someone wants to avoid getting a cold, and say "You ought to take some Vitamin C," we are still speaking hypothetically: "If you want to avoid a cold, you ought to take Vitamin C." This is not the moral 'ought' because moral 'oughts' are *categorical,* which is to say that they are put forward as statements of what people ought to do, no matter what they want.

There are non-moral uses of other key terms of the theory of obligation. When we say it is the *duty* of a letter carrier to deliver the mail, we are talking about a "postal duty," an "assigned duty," not a moral one. Letter carriers acquire this "postal obligation" by virtue of their job. Other professions generate other professional (but not yet moral) obligations. Teachers *ought* to meet classes, keep appointments, and give grades related to the students' performance; bus drivers *ought* to stop at bus stops, and plumbers *ought* to make house calls.

The concept of a right also has both innocent and moralist uses. Not everyone who speaks of "a right" is automatically talking about a moral right. Many times when we speak of our rights, we are thinking of legal or constitutional rights, or perhaps of conventional ones we grant to each other. There is no cause for skepticism about these rights—if the constitution or the laws say we have them, we have then—even if we are not allowed to exercise them. We do not have to be moralists or believe in abstract moral rights to acknowledge the right to make a right turn on a red light, or to remain silent when arrested.

Value

Moore makes the metaethical claim that 'good' is the name of a simple nonnatural property, but when he begins to enumerate the things with that property, he is answering a normative question about value. His answer is a *pluralist* one: many kinds of things have the property named by the word 'good'. He says that while the "mere existence of what is beautiful does appear to have *some* intrinsic value," that value is negligible beside "that which attaches to the *consciousness* of beauty" (Moore, 189).

Monists about value say that only one kind of thing is good in itself, and that if anything else is good, it is because it is related in the right way to what is good in itself. *Hedonism* is the best known monistic theory of value. A hedonist says that *all* pleasure is intrinsically good, and that while other things may be (derivatively) good, *only* pleasure is good in itself. Other value monists identify *the* good as power, or friendship, or life, or naturalness, or virtue, or happiness.

There are other, *variable*, accounts of value that are initially undecided about monism, but have monist or pluralist outcomes depending on what the facts turn out to be. Moralists who maintains that something is good if and only if it is loved by God are monists if God loves just one kind of thing, but if God loves different kinds of things, they are pluralists. Similarly, those who think that everything *desired* is also *desirable* will subscribe to monism if they think only one kind of thing is actually desired, and pluralism if they think our desires are many.

For as long as there have been hedonists, there have been questions about the nature of happiness and about its relationship to pleasure. Happiness is usually said to be deeper and longer lasting than pleasure. In Aristotle's famous words, "One swallow does not make a summer, nor does one day; and so too one day, or a short time, does not make a man blessed and happy" (Aristotle [2], 1098 a 18–20). But not all hedonists distinguish between pleasure and happiness. Jeremy Bentham (1748–1832), who tells us that the standard of right and wrong is "fixed to the throne" of pleasure and pain, uses 'pleasure' and 'happiness' as synonyms and says that "benefit, advantage, pleasure, good, or happiness" all amount to the same thing (Bentham, 2).

John Stuart Mill (1806–1873), who also holds that pleasure and the freedom from pain are the only things desirable as ends, stipulates that "by happiness is intended pleasure and the absence of pain; by unhappiness, pain and the privation of pleasure" (Mill [2], 7).

Even though Bentham and Mill claim to be using 'happiness' and 'pleasure' synonymously, there are important differences between their interpretations of these concepts. Bentham throws a barrier in front of our understanding with his list of synonyms for the word 'pleasure', but he appears to think of pleasure and pain as feelings, definite comparable sensations with quantitatively comparable intensities and durations—equal quantities of pleasure are equally good, but greater quantities are better. "Quantity of pleasure being equal," he said, pushpin (a child's game) is "as good as poetry." If we get twenty units of pleasure—philosophers jokingly call them "hedons"—playing some stupid game, then that is exactly as good as if we get twenty hedons listening to Bach, discussing philosophy, or solving chess problems.

Mill cannot bring himself to believe in this quantitative approach and insists that "some *kinds* of pleasure are more desirable and more valuable than others" (Mill [2], 8). It is better to be "a human being dissatisfied than a pig satisfied, better to be Socrates dissatisfied than a fool satisfied," he says. The *quality* of the happiness available in a human life or Socrates's life must be capable of outweighing the immense quantity of pig's or fool's pleasure felt by the most favored pig or fool.

When Mill asks himself "What makes one pleasure more valuable than another?", which is the right question, his answer is that the better of two pleasures is the one that would be preferred by those acquainted with both. But this only gives us a way to *tell* which pleasures are better. It is silent about what *makes* these pleasures better. It cannot be that they are made better by the fact that they would be chosen by the people who prefer them.

Kant also subscribes to a belief in intrinsic value. He says that a "good will" is not good because of its effects, it is good in itself. "When it is considered in itself, then it is to be esteemed very much higher than anything which it might ever bring about merely in order to favor some inclination, or even the sum total of all inclinations." Even if a good will is powerless to attain its end, it would "like a jewel, still shine by its own light as something which has its full value in itself" (Kant [3], 7–8).

Three fundamental phrases of the theory of value are 'intrinsically valuable', 'good in itself', and 'good as an end'. It is only to be expected that amoralists and nihilists will have questions to ask about these notions. It cannot be considered impolite to ask someone who thinks that things have intrinsic value what is meant by 'intrinsically valuable'. One who makes the claim opens the door to the question. We need not be turned aside here by ritualistic scorn for "metaethical baggage."

Each of these phrases can be given a similar initial explanation. *Intrinsic goodness* is a kind of goodness a thing has apart from its relation to other things. A thing is intrinsically good if it is good no matter what else is true and no matter how people feel about it. A thing is *good in itself* when it is good just because of the kind of thing it is—its goodness is, presumably, part of its nature. Finally, a thing is *good as an end* when it is worth choosing apart from any consequences that might flow from choosing it, or use to which it might be put. But while this might "explain" the intrinsic part, it does not explain the goodness.

We learn to apply words like 'good' and 'bad' on the basis of experience and example. At the same time we also pick up the standards and the attitudes of those we hear using the words. Amoralists can feel comfortable with many of the standard uses of 'good' and 'bad'. Since we all want to live and to be healthy and happy, we can say that good food and good habits are those that promote health and happiness. But what do we say when someone asks us what makes health and happiness good? It is not easy to say what happiness is good *for*, and if we do think of something, call it *X*, we will soon find ourselves facing the further question of what *X* is good for, and so on till we run out of answers or time. The claim that something is *intrinsically good* is designed to stop this game by heading off further questions. If a thing is intrinsically good, it is good, period, and nobody gets to ask "What makes it good?" or "What is it good for?"

Even if that is how it is supposed to work, how are we to understand this question stopper? Since we learn to use 'good' to evaluate actual items according to familiar (if implicit) standards and purposes, why should we think we can extend it to encompass such an abstract notion as intrinsic goodness? When there are established standards it is natural to rank things on the basis of those standards. Something is a good apple if it is tart, large, unmarked, and wormless. A car that does not break down and is fast (or easy on gas, or impressive) is a good car. Bill is a good plumber and Bob is a good friend. But what is it for a thing not to be a good *X*, and not to be "good-for *Y*" or "good as *Z*," but just good, period—good-in-itself? If someone were to speak up for the "intrinsically useful," that which is useful in itself, useful as an end, we would see the joke. The amoralist in his incarnation as a "value nihilist" wants to say that the notion of intrinsic goodness is just as empty as the notion of intrinsic usefulness.

Aristotle reasoned that if *X* is good because it brings about *Y*, and *Y* is good because it brings about *Z*, eventually we will find something that is good in itself and anchors the chain. But there is absolutely no reason to accept this conclusion. The chain will stop when we get tired of asking questions, or when we run out of answers. It will not stop because we have come to a place where no question can be asked. There may be things we desire and accept for their own sakes, and about which we ask no questions, but this does not mean that these things are intrinsically valuable. Even if everything anyone desired turned out to be desired for the sake of happiness, this would not make happiness intrinsically good—it would just mean that it alone was desired for its own sake.

The claim that something is intrinsically good, good as an end, or good in itself defies both explanation and understanding. And yet the idea is as widespread as moralism itself. Most moralists would say that unless some things are good in this special way, we are doomed to arbitrary meaninglessness. Depending on how 'arbitrary meaninglessness' is defined, the amoralist can either reject that conclusion or point out that since nothing is intrinsically bad, neither is arbitrary meaninglessness. The worst thing about not having intrinsic value or obligation to anchor our choices is the frustration of our desire for security—but that desire itself can be overcome, and the lack of intrinsic value can eventually be seen as liberating. In any case, we gain no stability by dropping our anchor into a perfect vacuum.

Obligation

If we say a thing has intrinsic value, nothing follows about what we or anyone ought to do. We can believe that pleasure is good in itself without believing we are morally obliged to experience or to cause as much of it as possible. The idea that the value of something requires action from us takes us beyond the theory of value to the theory of

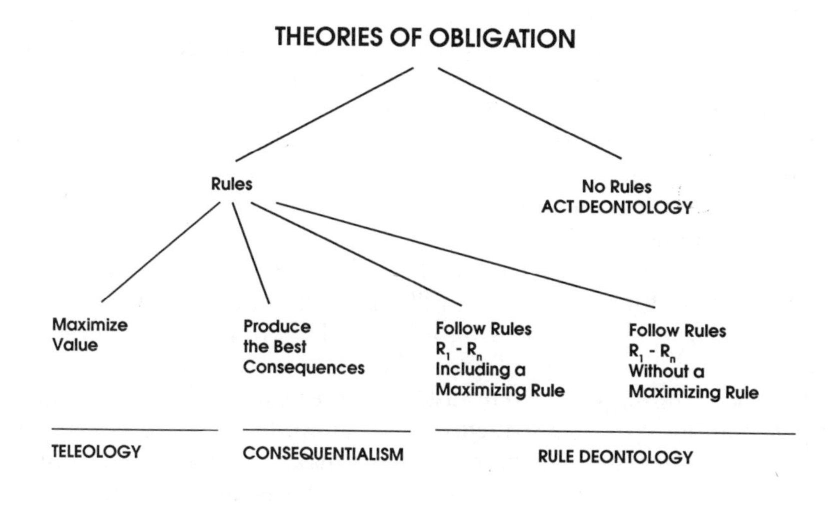

Figure 10-2

obligation, where we encounter the idea that we are bound, in the moral way, to do, or to refrain from doing, something.

Since most moralists think obligations are expressed by rules and principles, we can classify most theories of obligation on the basis of the kinds of rules they contain. Those who believe that our obligation is to maximize the good in the world are called *teleologists*, and those who want us to choose actions with the best consequences are called *consequentialists*. By contrast, *rule deontologists* reject this exclusive focus on value, and make moral obligation depend on something *other than* or *in addition to* the value produced. Some rule deontologists say the duty to produce good is only one of a number of duties we have; others say that the value we produce by acting is irrelevant to whether we have done what is right.

Consequentialism

Consequentialism is the view that we ought to do what produces the best consequences. A consequence of some action is something that *results* from the action, something the action brings about. Suppose that a consequence of doing A is that ten hedons come to each of nine people, but none to Sarah. One might say, so far so good, we are ahead ninety hedons. But the consequentialist will remind us that there were alternative actions that might have been performed and will want us to compare what *was done* with what *might have been done*. A second act, B, might have produced nine hedons for each of the original nine, and nine for Sarah. The total in both cases is the same, but many would insist that the second outcome is morally superior. And more would insist that both A and B ought to be chosen over C, which gives all ninety hedons to Sarah. One objection to consequentialism is that it is incapable of choosing among A, B, and C. Ninety hedons is ninety hedons.

The first line of defense for the consequentialist is to affirm the hedonism and insist that there will always be future effects and side effects that will justify choosing B over either A or C, and A over C. But it would also be possible for the consequentialist to abandon the hedonism and move to a pluralist account of value. The hedons may be equal, but other consequences that cannot be measured in terms of pleasure may have intrinsic value that makes a difference. A third way to deal with the case is to abandon the consequentialism for some form of teleology that brings the value of things other than consequences into the deliberation.

Consequentialists say we ought to do what results in the best consequences, but they do not urge us to evaluate and compare all our options before we make our choice. The consequentialist presents an account of moral obligation, a standard of rightness, not a decision-making procedure. Most consequentialists will encourage us to make our actual decisions by consulting secondary principles rather than by trying to calculate the values of consequences—they wisely think this will be for the best.

We can distinguish objective and subjective versions of consequentialism. The objective version says that we ought to do what will lead to the best consequences; the subjective version says that we ought to do what *we believe* will lead to the best consequences. Both type of consequentialism have their problems. Consider the objective variety. Unless we can restrict what can be counted as a consequence, it is no easier to find out what we should have done after the fact than it was before the fact. If we allow that the consequences of our actions continue even after our deaths, we will go to our graves without knowing whether any action of ours was right or wrong. Worse, there may not even be such a thing as *the* (total set of) consequences of an action. Even at judgment day there may be no way to sort out some set of items (events, things, people) that could be called the total set of the consequences of one of my actions. But even if we could make sense of the idea of the consequences of what we did, we will still never know which of our many possible choices *would have* produced the best consequences overall, because there is no way for even the most vivid imagination to enumerate or lend much color to the many roads we did not take.

When we move to the subjective form of consequentialism, we will no longer be required to compare actual with alternative possible consequences but we will have departed further from consequentialism than the description of our position may suggest. If our obligation is only to do what we think will produce good consequences, we are not morally bound to produce good consequences at all. In fact, we can produce very bad consequences without doing anything wrong because on this view what makes an act right has nothing to do with consequences, but depends on what someone believes. Whatever we call this account of obligation, there is little reason to think we *are* morally obliged to do what we think will lead to the best consequences, since sometimes our beliefs are the results of carelessness, prejudice, manipulation, or avoidable ignorance.

Consequentialists try to remedy the situation by moving to a form of consequentialism according to which we ought to do what, after adequate investigation and deliberation, we believe will lead to the best consequences. This might solve the problem that bothered the purely subjective version, but it is still a rather demanding requirement, and the notions of "adequate" and "sufficient" have never been explained. How much investigation is enough, and how is that determined?

Since the consequentialist says that our obligation is to do what leads to the *best* consequences, we still need a theory of value to tell us which consequences are the best. "Hedonistic utilitarianism," the claim that we ought to do what maximizes pleasure and minimizes pain, is the simplest and best known version of consequentialism. Other accounts of value produce other versions.

There is one question we must put to all prospective consequentialists. When they urge us to base morality on consequences, we need to know who they want us to take into consideration. Consequentialist accounts of obligation can be classified on the basis of who falls within the sphere of considerability—that is, whose happiness (or whatever) is taken into account in judging the action. As we can see by glancing at Figure 10-3, at one end of the spectrum we find the *ethical egoist*, who holds that our duty is only to consider how the consequences affect us. At the opposite end we find those who want us to take into consideration the happiness or interests of all sentient beings—all beings capable of feeling or having interests. These people are frequently identified as *utilitarians*, but so are those less universal-minded moralists who count only the humans.

Utilitarians need not agree on the extent of their spheres of considerability, but if a sphere excludes any humans from consideration it is probably inaccurate to call the associated view "utilitarianism." Those concerned only about the good of the citizens of their own country (state, county, or city), or those who include within their sphere of considerability only blood relatives, or people of the same race, religion, or sex, cannot be called utilitarians. But even those utilitarians who include all sentient beings within their sphere of considerability can be asked whether they also include future as well as present sentient beings, and whether they are willing to compare the value that has come to actual beings with the value that alternative beings might have enjoyed, had different choices been made. In deliberating about an abortion, for example, are we to compare the value of State of Affairs I, a state that includes everyone but the aborted child, with the value of State of Affairs II, a (hypothetical) state that differs from the previous case by including that child? There are no good answers to these questions.

Since ethical egoism is sometimes used to rationalize selfishness, we can understand why someone may embrace it. But it is hard to imagine that anyone could believe that our only moral duty is to maximize the good for ourselves. How could anyone defend *that* duty, or take seriously a moral theory that made self-sacrifice immoral, and exploitation of others an obligation? Where would the duty to be selfish come from? It is clearly not a feature of our conventional morality, which points in the opposite direction.

While there is little call for a morality that limits the sphere of moral considerability to the person performing the action, there is an almost irresistible drift toward a kind of universalism. One reason for this is that we prefer generosity to selfishness in others. Another is that it is difficult to provide a moral justification for limiting our concern to any subset of the whole. If we consider only *some* of the creatures that suffer, how is the suffering we have ignored irrelevant? Bentham was clear about this and explicitly included "the rest of the animal creation" within his sphere of moral considerability. That makes sense because when we recognize a duty to increase happiness or diminish suffering we must either include all beings capable of happiness and suffering within our sphere, justify excluding some, or admit that our discrimination is arbitrary.

A PERSON OUGHT TO DO WHAT LEADS TO THE GREATEST GOOD FOR

himself/ herself	the members of his/her family or tribe	the people in his/her state (country)	all humans with some special feature	all human beings	all rational beings	all sentient beings
ETHICAL EGOISM	TRIBAL MORALITY	NATIONALISM	RACISM SEXISM	SPECIES-ISM		
				UTILITARIANISM		

Figure 10-3

Objections to Utilitarianism

The moral advice of the utilitarian may turn out to be as bizarre as that of the egoist, but for the opposite reason. The idea that we have an obligation to act so as to maximize the good of others is revolutionary and demanding. The hedonistic utilitarian, for example, says it is our duty to neglect our own happiness and that of our families and friends when doing so will increase the general happiness, which it almost always will. It is no wonder that those who understand what these utilitarians are saying want to know why they think we have a moral obligation to engage in perpetual self-sacrifice, neglect our families and those to whom we have conventional duties, and engage in unrelenting altruism.

The fact that it is so out of harmony with conventional morality allows philosophers to generate counterexamples to utilitarianism at will. The method is simple: find a conflict between what a utilitarian must say about our duty and what our conventional morality says about our duty, and then count this against the utilitarian. The counterexamples come in four traditional styles.

1. There is some M (act which maximizes the total good) that we are obligated not to do. Suppose you can maximize the total happiness in the world by publicly torturing a universally hated villain. According to the utilitarian, this is what you ought to do, but in fact, says the critic of utilitarianism, it is something that you ought not do.
2. There is some M that we are not obligated to do. If you can relieve much suffering by selling your expensive audio-visual home entertain-

ment center and distributing the proceeds to help feed hungry orphans, the utilitarian may have to say that, unless there is some alternative that will produce even more good, you ought to do so. But, the critic of utilitarianism will say, this is not something that you ought to do.

3. There is some non-M (act that does not maximize the total good) that we ought to do. Suppose you have made a deathbed promise to bury someone with his unfinished manuscript. According to the utilitarian you ought to break your promise if publishing the manuscript will produce more happiness than not publishing it; but, a critic may insist, you ought to keep your deathbed promise even if doing so subtracts from the world's happiness.
4. There is some non-M that we may do. Just about anything we do that has no moral significance can be offered here. We are not maximizing the total good when we are taking a walk or a nap, watching television, eating fudge, or reading books about ethics. If there are alternatives to these actions that will produce more good (and there are), then the utilitarian will say that we ought to choose these alternatives. But if anything is clear, says the critic, it is that these innocent pleasures are morally permissible.

Counterexamples of these types can be (and have been) offered by the hundreds. The consistent hedonistic utilitarian appears to be committed to the belief that we ought to give up our own happiness, disregard agreements, lie, steal, kill, cheat, and even use torture when doing so increases the total amount of happiness. The plain fact is that next to nobody believes this is what we ought to do.

W. D. Ross says that the "essential defect" of utilitarianism is that "it ignores, or at least does not do full justice to, the highly personal character of duty" (Ross, 22). The utilitarian insists on producing the maximum good without taking into consideration the nature of (and the relationships among) those who get it; these additional factors are usually considered to be morally relevant. John Rawls is objecting to the same narrowness when he counts as one of its defects the fact that utilitarianism "does not take seriously the distinction between persons" (Rawls, 27).

It is open to the utilitarian with a hedonistic account of value to say that when lying to everyone or betraying our family or country leads to a net increase of happiness, then we ought to lie and betray. When philosophers call taking this position "biting the bullet," they intend to emphasize the willingness of these utilitarians to embrace a theory with consequences most people would find difficult to accept. What most people would see as a counterexample, the radical utilitarian sees as a mere consequence of a defensible theory. "Yes," the radical utilitarian replies, "my account goes against conventional morality, but that does not mean I am wrong; indeed, it is by neglecting utility that conventional morality goes wrong." With tenacity, even a hedonistic utilitarian can ward off many, if not all, counterexamples.

We have, as it happens, a clear example of someone who was impervious to the conflict between his utilitarianism and conventional morality. William Godwin (1756–1836) emphasizes rational persuasion over physical force, thinks the best social system is anarchism, and is a dedicated utilitarian who concludes that resources ought to go where they will do the most good. He argues, in a chapter on justice, that gratitude is improper because if it will do the most good for you to give me something, you have an obligation to give it and I to take it. He also accepts the punishment of the innocent and a number of other bitter pills philosophers try to force upon the utilitarians, who are usually too conventional to swallow them (Godwin, 168–77).

There are a number of moves open to hedonistic utilitarians. They can bite the bullet and insist that a conflict with conventional morality does not refute their view, or they can say that when we do our calculations carefully we find less conflict with conventional morality than critics suppose. Utilitarians can also abandon hedonism for a more complex theory of value. The "personal character of duty," for example, can be accounted for by adopting a theory of value that places justice and family ties among the valuable items. If "the keeping of promises" is declared intrinsically good, it may turn out to be wrong to break promises even if some other good like happiness is thereby increased.

Bentham said that the value of an action is determined by its consequences, but utilitarians now realize that it is impossible to calculate the consequences of each contemplated action, and crazy to try. This is why they sometimes urge us to follow general rules, even if these rules lead us to do what is, by utilitarian computation, wrong.

The *act* utilitarian classifies moral rules like "It is wrong to steal" or "Everyone ought to tell the truth" as rules of thumb only—our actual moral obligation in each case is still a function of the consequences. By contrast, the *rule* utilitarian says that what is *actually* right or wrong in a given case is determined not by the consequences flowing from the act, but by whether or not the act is in conformity with a "justified rule." If "Do not lie" is a justified rule, then even when lying leads to better consequences than telling the truth, it is still wrong to lie. What makes a rule justified is the fact that following it promotes the greatest good. The rule utilitarian asks not which *action* has the greatest utility but which *rules* do.

If it is hard to determine the consequences of any particular action, it is far more difficult to determine the consequences of general adherence to a rule or practice. If you doubt this, consider the differences between trying to find out what might happen if you tell the truth on a particular occasion and trying to find out what would happen if everyone always told the truth. Rule utilitarianism, apparently, involves even more fantasy than does act utilitarianism. But it has the advantage of being more nebulous, and hence more difficult to criticize.

Has the rectitude of this principle [the Principle of Utility] been ever formally contested? It should seem that it had, by those who have not known what they have been meaning. Is it susceptible of any direct proof? It should seem not, for that which is used to prove everything else, cannot itself be proved; a chain of proofs must have their commencement somewhere. To give such proof is as impossible as it is needless. (Bentham, 4)

Utilitarianism is the belief that we ought to do what leads to the greatest good for the greatest number, no matter what the consequences. (From an exam in Introduction to Ethics)

In the same manner as my property, I hold my person as a trust in behalf of mankind. I am bound to employ my talents, my understanding, my strength and my time, for the production of the greatest quantity of general good. Such are the declarations of justice, so great is the extent of my duty. (Godwin, 175)

Deontology

Consequentialists and teleologists adopt a single standard for right action—our obligation is to produce the best consequences or the most value. *Act deontologists* think there are no general rules about what is right and wrong, and *rule deontologists* accept rules *other than* or *in addition to* the maximizing rules of teleologists and consequentialists (see Fig. 10-2). Rule deontologists and rule utilitarians both appeal to rules, but rule utilitarians say the rules are justified by the good that would result from everyone following them. This justification is not available to rule deontologists, who often give no defense of their preferred moral rules—but then neither do utilitarians defend the principle of utility.

Most forms of consequentialism are out of touch with our moral feelings and beliefs. Deontologists bring us back to earth by acknowledging the demands of conventional morality. The deontologist accepts rules against torture, duplicity, unfairness, and property violations as if they were the most natural things in the world, which they are. The conventional moral notions these rules reflect are easy to identify because they are *our* conventional moral notions.

H. A. Prichard, in his article "Does Moral Philosophy Rest on a Mistake?" argues that all forms of consequentialism fail "to correspond to our actual moral convictions", and he takes this to support his own claim that we can directly know what we ought to do (Prichard, 4). His view can be called "act deontology" because it looks at rules like "It is wrong to steal" as no more than guidelines, generalizations made on the basis of intuitions about particular cases. Our basic intuitions are about particular cases, and we get them by examining closely and imaginatively each particular case in some detail. We "apprehend" the rightness or wrongness of an individual action (*this* theft or *this* lie) not of a class of actions (stealing or lying).

Prichard is right when he says that consequentialist theories of obligation have their problems, but the failure of consequentialism, or even the failure of *all* rule theories, does not automatically establish the truth of act deontology. There is always amoralism, the rejection of both teleological and deontological theories of obligation. But amoralism was probably never seriously considered by intuitionists like Prichard, who reckoned that if we cannot prove that some actions are right, we must know it without proof.

Another modern intuitionist who is a deontologist, but a rule deontologist rather than an act deontologist, is W. D. Ross. At the end of Chapter 9 we see how Ross claims that we apprehend moral rules, or what he calls *prima-facie duties.* Of the duties he mentions (fidelity, reparation, gratitude, justice, beneficence, self-improvement, and non-maleficence), only the duties of beneficence and non-maleficence would be recognized by consequentialists, who take truth, justice, and fidelity to be justified in terms of their consequences. Here rule deontology manifests our ordinary morality better than act consequentialism. The rule deontologist will say that the duty of self-improvement tempers the duty of beneficence, so that we are probably not morally required to drop out of college to help the sick and hungry. The duty of justice would require or permit us to choose B (distributing nine units to each of ten equally deserving people) rather than A (distributing ten units to each of nine of them). The duty of fidelity would often require the keeping of promises and paying of debts, even if we could produce more value in some other way.

Ross's rule deontology is intuitively plausible because it is derived from the sort of morality we have given ourselves. The lesson is taught so thoroughly that the duties seem to be dictated by nature itself, self-evidently true, deniable only by a maniac. But why should we believe that this appearance of self-evidence is any more than a function of our training? Why should we believe with Ross that duties are intuited rather than absorbed and then projected back onto the world?

Because the demand to maximize the good remains both counter-intuitive and forbiddingly demanding, moralists have adopted deontological constraints—competing prima facie duties that put the moral brakes on reform-prone utilitarian "do-gooders." These deontological constraints work by tapping into our tendency to objectify our desires. We want truthfulness and respect for life, and so we are willing to set up other duties that compete with the utilitarian duty of beneficence. We want to be left alone to pursue projects that would be difficult to justify from the point of view of eternity, so we claim to have a duty of self-improvement, or a right to pursue harmless activities of our own choosing.

Rights

Critics of consequentialism and teleology point out that people have always been robbed, enslaved, tortured, silenced, and killed in the name of "the good." Deontological rules like Ross's duty of self-improvement manage to shield us from the demands of unbridled consequentialism, but critics of rule theories say that we will never find a rule that applies in all cases, and that no one has the slightest idea how to extract an actual duty from a competing host of prima facie ones. These and other difficulties and defects of rule theories sometimes turn rule theorists into rights theorists, for rights seem even more useful than rules when we want to protect our interests against the demands of consequentialists and teleologists.

If we have any moral intuitions at all, they tell us that it is wrong to harvest the organs of one healthy but unwilling individual to save the lives of five who need various organ transplants. Most moralists would even say that it is wrong to kidnap some vagrant and take one of his kidneys in order to save the life of a scientist on the verge of discovering a cure for cancer. It is wrong, many would say, because it violates that vagrant's rights.

Rights are useful because we can appeal to them without making fantastic and unbelievable calculations and projections. Forbidding some people to speak may or may not have good consequences, but we do not need to know the truth about this (if there is a truth) to claim that someone's right to freedom of speech has been violated. We do not violate fundamental rights for slight gains in utility.

But what is this idea of a right? There are, of course, legal and constitutional rights, and these notions are not difficult to explain. We have a legal or constitutional right if the law or constitution says that we do. If we belong to some organization with rules, then we have the rights given us by the rules. These notions have their complications and difficulties, but compared to the idea of a *moral* right, they are straightforward and simple.

It is entirely possible that the concept of a moral right gets what meaning it has by borrowing it from legal, political, and institutional contexts. We naturally think of rights in terms of being granted them. If an earthly sovereign grants us our legal rights, then perhaps a superhuman sovereign grants us our moral rights—as the Declaration of Independence says. This divine gift theory of moral rights, like the divine command theory of moral obligation, is open to criticism. But so is the alternative, which is that we have rights simply because we are human. This idea is vague, and unless we are content with blatant speciesism, we will have to allow that the same argument gives dogs, cats, and snails rights as well—just because they are dogs, cats, and snails.

We might rule out the animals by saying that we get our rights by entering into agreements with others like ourselves, but then we are left with a watered-down idea of rights, one that makes it hard to see how they can be binding or inalienable, as they are often thought to be. If we agree to grant each other certain rights, then we can agree, or at least decide, to stop doing so.

Thomas Hobbes says that in a state of nature each person has a right to all things. He calls this the *Right of Nature*, and his idea is that people in a state of nature are "permitted," in the sense that they are not forbidden, to do as they choose. This is a right in the "weak sense" because it is really no more than the complete absence of restrictions.

No one is required to do anything to respond to the fact that we have such a right.

The rights that matter are rights in the "strong sense." If a person has a right in the strong sense, then others are restricted from acting, or required to act, in certain ways. Rights in the strong sense may be either *negative rights*, which require others not to interfere with the right-holder, or *positive rights*, which require others to aid the right-holder. Someone who "takes rights seriously" will concentrate on negative and positive rights in the strong sense.

John Locke gives us a stronger concept of a 'right' than the bare liberty acknowledged by Hobbes, though the rights he has in mind seem to be negative rather than positive ones. He says that even in a state of nature each person has a right to life, liberty, and private property, with the result that it is wrong, even in a state of nature, to kill or hurt others or to deprive them of property that is theirs. Your right to life and liberty makes it is wrong for me to kill or confine you, but Locke does not say that it is wrong for me to fail to supply you with what you need to stay alive, as someone would who believed the right to life was a strong positive right.

The idea that we all have individual, inalienable, God-given rights was deployed against those who insisted that an absolute sovereign rules by divine right, and should never be deposed. If God gave us our rights, it was argued, then there are times when it is proper to depose an earthly sovereign who threatens our life, property, liberty, or freedom.

In 1789 the French National Assembly proclaimed the "Declaration of the Rights of Man and the Citizen." Among our "imprescriptable" rights they included rights to liberty, property, and security, and the right to resist oppression. From then on, there have been strong and vocal defenders and critics of such rights. In *Nonsense upon Stilts*, Jeremy Waldron collects three major attacks on this natural rights tradition: one by Jeremy Bentham, one by Edmund Burke, and one by Karl Marx (liberal, conservative, and socialist critiques of rights). Bentham thought so little of the idea of rights that he wrote something he called "No French Nonsense: or A Cross Buttock for the first Declaration of Rights: together with a kick of the A—for the Second . . . by a practitioner of the Old English Art of Self Defense" (Waldron, 32). He thought that the many rights claims made during the French Revolution were arbitrary and groundless expressions of selfish personal preferences, and he described the claim that people have rights ungrounded by consequences as "nonsense upon stilts."

John Stuart Mill, who does not follow Bentham on all points, follows him on this one. He declares himself willing to "forego any advantage which could be derived to my argument from the idea of abstract right as a thing independent of utility" (Mill [1], 14). "To have a right," he says, is "to have something which society ought to defend me in the possession of. If the objector goes on to ask why it ought, I can give him no other reason than general utility" (Mill [2], 52). To this consequentialist derivation of rights Mill adds an explanation of the "peculiar energy" of the feeling of obligation that goes with the concept of a right. Our passion for rights is inflamed by our need for security, something "no human being can possibly do without" (53). Since it is a matter of "making safe for us the very groundwork of our existence," the emotions that gather around our rights tend to be the strongest, and our claim to a right "assumes that character of absoluteness, that apparent infinity and incommensurability with all other considerations which constitute the distinction between the feeling of right and wrong and that of ordinary expediency and inexpediency" (53).

Every identifiable group speaks of and for its rights, and everyone who wants something tends to claim it as a right. This was perhaps the thing about rights that bothered Bentham so much.

> When a man has a political caprice to gratify, and is determined to gratify it, if possible, at any price, when he feels an ardent desire to see it gratified but can give no reason why it should be gratified, when he finds it necessary to get the multitude to join with him, but either stoops not to enquire whether they would be the better or the happier for doing so, or feels himself at a loss to prove it, he sets up a cry for rights. (Bentham, 36)

It is clear, at least to the amoralist, what is going on here. It is no more likely that we will be able to make intelligible our claim to have fundamental moral rights than it is that we will be able to support this claim on consequentialist grounds. As usual, our intuitions about what rights we have, and even about what rights are, depend on our needs, desires, interests, and education.

> Individuals have rights, and there are things no person or group may do to them (without violating their rights). So strong and far-reaching are these rights that they raise the question of what, if anything, the state and its officials may do. (Nozick, ix)

> To say that someone has a right, of whatever sort, is to speak

either of or within some legal or moral system: our rejection of objective values carries with it the denial that there are any self-subsistent rights. To say that someone has a certain liberty, then, may be to say that the system in question, whatever it is, does not forbid him to act in the way indicated—or (speaking within the system) it may be to give him permission so to act, or explicitly refrain from forbidding him to do so. (Mackie [1], 173)

Virtue

Consequentialism, deontology, and rights-based theories offer information about how we should or should not act; and theories of value tell us what is good and bad. Virtue theorists, sensitive to the problems endemic to these other theories, speak instead of virtues and vices, and they do not (at least in any obvious way) base their accounts of virtue on moral obligations, duties, or rights.

When we reflect on the unsatisfactoriness of the other normative theories, we can appreciate the resurgence of interest in the virtues. Many see it as a return to a tradition that began even before Plato and Aristotle wrote, one that promises to offer something better than an indefinite list of ambiguous commands and prohibitions. Rules will never cover all situations, and principles almost always have exceptions; but since a virtue is a habit, its application is automatic and uncalculating. We will never come up with a list of the cases in which it is morally permissible to steal, but if we come up with an honest person, we need no such list, or so the virtue-theorist argues.

In the days of Homer, courage, honor, loyalty, physical strength, and cunning counted as virtues. Plato stressed temperance, courage, wisdom, and justice. Aristotle complicated things by distinguishing between intellectual virtues, which come by teaching, and moral virtues, which are habits (dispositions) acquired by practice. His list of moral virtues included courage, temperance, liberality, magnificence (spending the right amount), magnanimity, and other qualities prized by Greek aristocrats.

To a subset of these pagan virtues, the Christians added faith, obedience, piety, chastity, love, mercy, and humility. The Greeks, of course, saw neither faith nor chastity as virtues, and Aristotle even characterized humility as a vice. Christians, on the other hand, would have found Aristotle's virtuous man short on love and sinfully proud.

David Hume thought that some of the Christian virtues like

humility were actually vices, and he added other eighteenth-century virtues and vices to his list. Jane Austin supplemented the list by advancing the claims of constancy, a virtue she thought necessary for the possession of any of the others, and amiability, which she contrasted with the more superficial agreeableness. Benjamin Franklin added cleanliness, silence, and new definitions for some of the familiar virtues like chastity (MacIntyre, 170–71). Today, different people would construct different lists, and we can hardly avoid concluding that the virtues are culturally dependent and subject to cultural change; they are relative to roles, classes, professions, castes, and gender within any given society at any given time.

In the face of such variety, a virtue theorist who does not want to subscribe to a subjectivist form of moral relativism will have to ask which alleged virtues are really virtues and which are not. After we arrive at a satisfying list of virtues, the next task will be to discover how our virtues are related to one another and to other moral aspects of situations. Are some virtues fundamental, primary, or at least more important than others? Are some separate from, related to, reducible to, derivable from, or identical with, others? If we find ourselves torn between the opportunity to manifest or acquire two different virtues, how do we decide which one to manifest or acquire? And what do we do when virtue demands one thing and other moral considerations demand another?

A theory about the virtues is no more immune to questions about justification than are theories that resort to value or obligation. It is always possible to ask what makes *this* a virtue and *that* a vice. Why is cleanliness a virtue and dirtiness a vice? Perhaps both are extremes and the virtue is a compromise—a disposition to be slightly soiled. Virtue theorists will have to find some way to deal with the questions of skeptics, relativists, and amoralists.

Talk about virtue is widespread, but we should not think that everyone who discusses the virtues is a "virtue theorist." Hume writes about virtues, but he treats them as characteristics to be explained rather than justified. He discusses a long list of "natural virtues" (including benevolence, generosity, industry, patience, temperance, and resolution) and a shorter list of "artificial virtues" (including justice, honesty, respect for property, fidelity, and chastity), and offers an explanation of why we approve of them. We approve of the natural ones, he claims, because we anticipate some good from each case, and perhaps also out of a natural inclination to approve of such qualities. We approve of artificial virtues like honesty and chastity, by contrast, because of their value to society.

Fans of specific normative theories will be anxious to "define" virtue in their own terms, thereby "reducing" virtue theory to whatever theory they take to be primary. They might, for example, try to explain virtue in terms of obligation by defining a virtue as a disposition to do the *right* thing, or a characteristic that we *ought* to have. It is even easier to see virtue theory as a branch of the theory of value. A virtue, it can be said, is nothing more than a disposition that is *good*, or a disposition to make a *good* choice. If Hume, who set himself only to *explain* why some characteristics are approved as virtues and condemned as vices, should not be called a virtue theorist, neither should the egoist or the utilitarian, who defend virtue on the grounds of its usefulness to the agent or to society. A real virtue theorist is a moralist who places virtue first, and refuses to explain its "value" in terms taken from some alternative normative theory.

Now the way is open to ask the real virtue theorist the usual questions. Which traits are virtues, how are the virtues related, and what makes something a virtue or a vice? The standard way to deal with these questions has been to appeal to *human nature*, and here virtue theory looks back to Aristotle. If we (humans) do have a fundamental nature, we might want to say that a virtue is a quality we have when we develop what we naturally are: We become virtuous when we become what we could be if we realized our nature.

But of course issues about human nature are controversial, and those who favor virtues like strength or courage will be disposed to see human nature as including a large component of innate aggressiveness. Those who prefer the pacific virtues will find human nature stocked with innate tendencies to cooperate. The fact is that humans are flexible—there are countless things they could become, and countless directions in which they might develop. Anyone who is determined to distinguish good habits from bad ones will have to make some judgments about ends, and so will almost certainly be committed, at some fundamental level, to a theory of value.

Conclusion

Uncountable are the ways to moralize and the disagreements among moralists. Those who agree to treat the theory of obligation as basic will still be convinced that proponents of other theories of obligation have failed to see the truth. Utilitarians hardly ever agree among themselves about how to state utilitarianism, and rights-theorists usually disagree about which purported rights are actual. Only amoralists are united in their total and universal rejection of the normative claims of all moralists.

11

Amoralists, Critics, Pseudo-Amoralists, and Backsliders

"The amoralist" is the name of somebody.

—*Bernard Williams,* Ethics and the Limits of Philosophy

MORALISTS HAVE internal opponents, external opponents, and some ambivalent associates. Their internal opponents are other moralists who advance alternative moral systems. Their external opponents are nihilists, emotivists, and anti-realists, who might also be called amoralists. Two ambivalent associates are relativists and skeptics, who alarm some moralists, but need assert nothing incompatible with moralism. Another ambivalent associate is the subjectivist, who identifies moral judgments with descriptions of human (or divine) attitudes, desires, or commands. Skeptics, relativists, and subjectivists may not agree with moralists about the objectivity of morality, but they all agree that the amoralist's position is too extreme.

Bernard Williams opens his book *Morality* with an attempt to answer "the amoralist," who is "supposedly immune to moral considerations" (Williams [1], xii). Gilbert Harman's *The Nature of Morality* contains an argument against "extreme nihilism," which he characterizes as the belief that "nothing is ever right or wrong, just or unjust, good or bad," coupled with the belief that "we should abandon morality" (Harman [2], 11). In *Moral Thinking*, R. M. Hare identifies the amoralist as someone who is "unwilling to think morally" and who "refrains from making moral judgments at all." He says that such a view is consistent but searches for "non-logical reasons for not being an amoralist" (Hare, 169, 183, 186).

Recently the term 'amoralist' has been adopted to refer to a different position. David Wong, David O. Brink, and Wm. David Solomon, among others, have characterized the "amoralist" as someone who recognizes, acknowledges, and even believes in "moral considerations," but who remains unmoved by them (Wong, 15; Brink [2], 27; Solomon, 382). As Brink says, "an amoralist makes moral judgments with no intention of expressing his attitudes or of influencing the conduct of others" (Brink [2], 27). Brink and Solomon are interested in the question of whether a being like this is possible because if such a being is "conceivable," they think, an argument against moral realism, Mackie's argument from queerness in fact, may be weakened.

One way to be an amoralist is to be a non-cognitivist. The non-cognitivists have always built prescriptivity, in one form or another, into moral judgments. This is what they believed set moral judgments apart from factual ones. They then concluded that if moral judgments are reports of facts, those facts will have to be "prescriptive facts," and, of course, a prescriptive fact would be a very "queer thing." Now, if the amoralist in the Wong-Brink-Solomon sense is conceivable, then moral judgments can be motivationally inert. They can be reports of moral facts that no longer have to be both objective and prescriptive. The Wong-Brink-Solomon amoralist can detect the presence of a moral fact and be utterly unmotivated, or at least inadequately motivated. Moral judgments can be plain statements, and any prescriptive or motivational punch they may have can come from external sources—from education, threats, indoctrination, or whatever. With the impossible burden of supporting both objectivity and prescriptivity removed from moral properties, the argument from queerness cannot be used against those who believe in them.

There are three reasons why we need not respond to this argument. First, the genuine queerness of moral properties and facts lies not in their alleged power to motivate but in their alleged authority to command—whether or not they motivate. The normal way of understanding moral requirements is to think that they "apply" to us whether we are motivated or not. The usual way of thinking about intrinsic value is to suppose that something that has it possesses it no matter what anyone thinks or wants, and that things that do have it, like human beings, deserve our respect just because they have it. The issue is about intrinsic value and objective obligation, not motivation (See Garner [1]).

The second reason we need not pursue the argument in which

this "amoralist" has been called upon to star is that it involves non-cognitivist forms of amoralism, and the form of amoralism developed here is an anti-realist error theory that is quite comfortable with a cognitivist account of moral judgments (and an externalist account of motivation, if motivation were the issue).

The third reason for moving on is that the question about the use of 'amoralism' is a minor terminological one. One problem with the Wong-Brink-Solomon use, also minor, is that if we do call this being an "amoralist," then we have an "amoralist" who accepts as true the propositions of morality. According to the terminology adopted in *this* book, anyone who accepts the propositions of morality as true and binding is a moralist. The word 'amoralist' is used to stand for someone who does *not* believe in the truth of the propositions of morality, and this may be because they are believed to have no truth value, or because they are believed to be all false. Our "amoralist," then, will not be a moralist without willpower, but someone who rejects those claims we have found to constitute moralism, and particularly the claim, implicit in all moralism, that moral facts are both objective and prescriptive.

As we have seen, non-cognitivism is one kind of amoralism, but the problem with non-cognitivism is its account of moral language. People who say that killing, or lying, or kicking dogs is wrong usually see themselves as expressing objective truth. They think that kicking dogs is "really wrong." Mackie's error theory is preferable to non-cognitivism because it is more faithful to what people intend to claim when they moralize. And it does not require us to believe that people are doing things they would honestly claim not to be doing.

We can hardly expect philosophers under the influence of moralism to wear themselves out constructing a coherent external challenge to their own presuppositions. But their responses to their imagined external opponents are typically directed against weak versions of foolish positions, against those who violate (or promote the violation of) conventional moral standards, and against selfishness and heartless misanthropy. Nihilists and amoralists are imagined to be inconsiderate monsters, sociopaths, and predators. Williams suggests that they may not even be "recognizably human" (Williams [1], 8). Amoralists, in the sense of that word adopted here, will not be moved by the alleged morality of moral considerations, but, as we shall see, they might be moved by the very factors the moralist cites to justify a moral demand.

> Let us use the term *amoralist* to name one who has no moral system. . . . It may seem unclear whether any general terms are applicable to describe the behavior of the amoralist. Does he possess motivations? By definition he is at least indifferent to moral considerations. That would suggest that he cannot care about other people's interests, nor can he be relied upon to keep promises, honor contracts, or return favors. . . . It would seem that a person without any morality at all could only be parasitic upon a society, trying by whatever means to get whatever he wants from others, but acknowledging no obligations to accept responsibilities, share benefits, or permit reciprocal treatment. (Ashmore, 4)

The Amoralist Need Not Be an Immoral, Heartless, Selfish Jerk Who Denies the Obvious

Amoralism has been criticized for contributing to immoral behavior—behavior that violates conventional morality. Maybe it does and maybe it does not. There are moralists who lie, cheat, steal, and despise humanity; and there are amoralists who tell the truth, play fair, and treat others with respect. Given that one can always concoct a moral rationalization for violating conventional morality, it is not easy to judge how much positive effect a belief in objectively binding moral principles will have on a person's behavior.

Some critics confuse the amoralist with the pathological egoist. They say that amoralists are necessarily selfish and either lack compassion or feel it arbitrarily and sporadically. But what we believe about morality is independent of how much we care about others; it is also independent of how many of them we care about. When Williams says that the amoralist "in his pure form" is "immune to moral considerations," he means that the amoralist is unmoved by the suffering of others. This amoralist has no "inclination to tell the truth or keep promises if it does not suit him to do so" (Williams [1], 3). But compassionate amoralists can also be said to be "immune to moral considerations." It is just that when they promote the welfare of others, they are not led to do so by any moral beliefs. These amoralists are moved by the suffering of others, but not by being told that suffering is intrinsically bad, or that others have a moral right to help.

We are right to worry about people who are unmoved by the pain of others. We understand Williams when he calls them psychopaths and monsters. But they are not psychopaths and monsters because they "reject morality," they are psychopaths and monsters because they do not care about the suffering of others. Someone bound only by the dictates of some morality and utterly without affection, sympathy, or kindness would be a monster too—a moral monster.

Sometimes amoralists are presented as denying some obvious truth, or asserting something too horrible to be accepted. Harman says that extreme nihilism (the belief that "nothing is ever right or wrong, just or unjust, good or bad") implies "that there are no moral constraints—that everything is permitted. As Dostoevsky observes, it implies that there is nothing wrong with murdering your father. It also implies that slavery is not unjust and that Hitler's extermination camps were not immoral. These are not easy conclusions to accept" (Harman [2], 11). Whatever extreme nihilists might mean by saying that nothing is right or wrong, just or unjust, good or bad, they will not want to deny that there are conventional moral constraints, and that law, custom, other people, and our own rules forbid many things.

Similarly, the amoralist is not denying that we have a conventional morality, and the moralist is saying more than that we have created sets of conventional rules and rights. The moralist insists that the immorality of death camps and slavery does not depend on what people happen to think, want, believe, buy into, or choose. The amoralist can join with the moralist in this rejection of subjectivism, but must demur when the moralist adds that death camps and slavery are *really* wrong, not just unacceptable by conventions we adopt from our society or inherit from our genes.

Amoralists who do not want to misrepresent themselves will not say that the extermination camps were immoral, however much they may detest them. If we do not want to be mistaken for moralists, we must avoid moralist ways of expressing ourselves. We can be sure that plenty of amoralists give in to the temptation to exploit the power of moral language. Those who do are fair game for anyone who wants to score a point for moralism by exposing an amoralist committing morality. But when this happens, the problem is with the amoralist, not with amoralism.

Some Responses to the Amoralist

Those who believe that amoralists are disposed by their beliefs to exhibit anti-social behavior may try to think up techniques to make them change those amoralist beliefs, or, on the supposition that the amoralism is truly incorrigible, they may work to contain its behavioral effects.

Argument

In *Morality*, Bernard Williams looks for an answer to the "amoralist" who cares about no one—the amoralist psychopath. He knows that *this* amoralist will not be moved by arguments, and that "the idea of arguing him into morality is surely idiotic" (Williams [1], 8). Accordingly, he supplies us with a less extreme amoralist—one it is, presumably, not idiotic to try to argue into morality. His example is the stereotype from a gangster movie (the mobster), "who cares about his mother, his child, even his mistress" (9). He helps people, but only when he feels like it; he considers the interests of others, but not consistently. Williams says that if "morality can be got off the ground rationally," we ought to be able to get it off the ground in an argument with him.

The mobster cares about his close associates, but there is a wide gap between this feeling and the belief that he *ought* to care about people he does not even know, and yet another gap between that belief and any actual caring behavior. The only thing the moralist can do is catch the mobster making some moral judgment of his own, and then try to convince him that unless he makes similar judgments about relevantly similar cases, he will have to add inconsistency to his list of crimes. If, however, the mobster knows how to argue, he knows enough to deny that the cases are relevantly similar, to withdraw his moral judgment, or to tell the moralist to get lost.

If the amoralist is right, arguments will never get their hooks into someone, however rational, who wishes to resist them. Even if one has been forced to admit in public that justice is the greatest of all goods, that has no necessary connection with what one subsequently believes or does.

Persuasion

It is not hard to persuade attentive, open-minded, non-defensive people to treat others with more consideration. We can describe suffering in detail and paint in unattractive colors the life of the person who profits from the misery of others. We can document the complex reality of homelessness and give it a human face. We can say a variety things to people, hoping that something we say will set off a sympathetic reaction.

"Realizing" that there are such things as death squads is very different from merely being aware of the fact that there are. To "realize" that there are death squads is to confront what death squads do. This is to go beyond assent to the words "There are death squads," and to allow our imaginations to supply some horrible details—orphans, widows, grieving mothers, ruined lives, broken hearts, agony, despair, unbearable loss.

We eat veal, pork, beef, and chickens without a thought of what happened to the animal on the way to our plates. Because we are so insulated from the effects of what we do and cause to be done, Peter Singer's few pictures of animals in factory farms in his book *Animal Liberation* may have done more for animal welfare than all his arguments. But just as arguments do not take hold unless the victim has the right principles, this less logical form of persuasion works only when we can show someone something that will interact with desires or attitudes they already have—some compassion, malice, pity, love, or fear.

There are, of course, people who will be completely unruffled by a picture of thousands of chickens packed into a hot, smelly, cement-block building, or by a picture of an iron-starved veal calf in a cramped wooden stall. But more will be moved, and, as a general rule, the more we *realize* what we are seeing, the more moved we will be. Fortunately for all living things, few humans lack a capacity to be moved by suffering and joy. Unfortunately for all living things, humans have managed not to pay much attention to the things that would move them if they ever came to realize they were going on.

Coercion

When argument and persuasion fail, we can give up, or we can turn to force or fraud. Moralists who identify the amoralist as a sociopath with whom arguments and pleas are useless may decide that we need to threaten amoralists, to isolate them, or even to hunt them down and put them into prison. Needless to say, these remedies are not necessary to cope with the average amoralist, who has as many decent impulses as the next person, or with the informed and compassionate amoralist, who has more. These remedies might, however, be required for the sociopath—especially if that sociopath is also a moralist!

There is a place in life for coercion, and while amoralists will not believe that laws can be given a moral justification, they are not likely to want to live without them. Coercion by law falls equally on the heads of moralists and amoralists, and both can be glad there are penalties for murder and for dumping toxic waste in the river.

Denial

One way to combat amoralism is to show that some form of moralism is true, another is to show that some form of amoralism is false, and a third is to deny that amoralism is possible. Some argue for the third option by saying that to desire something is to value it, and that to value it is to think it valuable. Therefore, no one who acknowledges the existence of desires can deny the reality of value.

Or, someone might say that the mere fact that we choose one course of action over another shows that we have moral principles. When "amoralists" behave as if they subscribe to moral principles, we can conclude that they do subscribe to moral principles, perhaps without realizing it. Amoralists who are fair can be accused of believing in justice, and amoralists who tell the truth and help others can be charged with holding moral principles of truthfulness and beneficence.

But really, only sophistical tricks can help the moralist here. Just as there is no non-fallacious path from the desired to the desirable, there is none from my desiring something to my believing that it is desirable, or from my choosing something to my believing that I ought to have chosen it. The non-duplicitous amoralist has a policy of telling the truth, and a *moralist* might call this policy a moral principle and accuse the amoralist of moralism. But amoralists will not think about that policy of honesty as moralists would: They will not see it as objectively binding, they will not feel that truthfulness is imposed upon them by Reality itself. Amoralists who allow their principles of action to be called "moral principles" run the risk of giving the impression that they subscribe to the moralist assumptions that usually accompany the moralist way of talking.

If we have adopted some policy like truthfulness as a non-binding guideline, then we may be prepared to explain how we understand it, why we have adopted it, and why we recommend it to others, when we do. But if we are amoralists, we will not even try to give it a moral justification. Friendly amoralists can be as helpful and truthful as they want to be without once thinking their actions are required by anything other than their own policies.

Moralists, who would rather have obligations and values dictated from a more objective source, may complain that the choice of these friendly policies is arbitrary and that there is nothing to stop the amoralist from selecting some harsher alternative. But this is misleading. It is not as if amoralists arrive at their ways of coping with others carelessly or at random—our ways of interacting result from a lifetime of experience, reflection, and indoctrination. We do not adopt a way of dealing with others as we might adopt a dog from the pound. Our "way of interacting" is part of who we are, formed over the decades, warped and straightened by our successes and failures. So the charge of being arbitrary does not amount to much. It is true that the amoralist has no unquestionable moral principles on which to base choices, but as it turns out, neither does the moralist. The difference is that the amoralist neither thinks nor pretends to think that someday such principles might emerge from hiding.

Pseudo-Amoralists and Backsliders

We now look at three characters (one fictional and two real ones) who may be *mistaken* for amoralists. Callicles and Friedrich Nietzsche attack conventional morality but turn out to be moralists with a conventionally immoral morality, and Ludwig Wittgenstein, despite some striking amoralist pronouncements, regularly lapses back into moralistic ways of talking and thinking.

Callicles

In Plato's dialogue *Gorgias*, Callicles defends the view that conventional morality is a system devised by the weak to keep the strong from getting everything they can. Conventions and laws are made

> by the weaklings who form the majority of mankind. They establish them and apportion praise and blame with an eye to themselves and their own interests, and in an endeavour to frighten those who are stronger and capable of getting the upper hand they say that ambition is base and wrong, and that wrong-doing consists in trying to gain an advantage over others; being inferior themselves, they are content, no doubt, if they can stand on an equal footing with their betters. (Plato [5], 78)

We should not allow this attack on conventional morality to trick us into calling Callicles an amoralist. He rejects conventional morality only to claim that nature "demonstrates that it is right that the better man should prevail over the worse and the stronger over the weaker" (Plato [5], 78). He holds that strength and political power are good, and that the powerful and strong, being superior to the weak, deserve whatever their strength enables them to take. Callicles looks back to the old pirate morality that rejects equality, opposes measures to protect the weak, and finds the existence of a class system proof that some people are better than others.

Callicles is right when he says that this is the kind of view most of us want to discourage. If only a few practice it, they may prosper, but if many do, society will be shattered. But whether we can refute extremely immoral forms of moralism or not, the point is that they are forms of *moralism*. Take away the moralism of Callicles and you take away his ability to defend his selfish behavior. What Callicles needs to be told is that strength is one property among many, *none* of which is special enough to justify preferential treatment for anyone. Without moralism, nobody starts off deserving more than anyone else. Without moralism, there can be no moral defense of inequality and exploitation.

Nietzsche

In Chapter 2 we were introduced to Nietzsche's desire to take a stand "beyond good and evil," and his claim that "there are altogether no moral facts." It is now time to ask what these amoralist-sounding utterances amount to, and whether Nietzsche deserves to be called an amoralist. He probably does not, but it is hard to know what to make of some of his remarks.

> One knows my demand of philosophers that they place themselves *beyond* good and evil—that they have the illusion of moral judgments *beneath* them. This demand follows from an insight first formulated by me: that *there are no moral facts whatever*. Moral judgment has this in common with religious judgment that it believes in realities which do not exist. (Nietzsche [3], 65)

This certainly seems to be a denial of moralism—at least it does until we realize that when Nietzsche talks about going beyond good and evil he does not mean going beyond good and bad.

Nietzsche is known for having distinguished between "master

morality" and "slave morality." Slave morality is, as Callicles said, introduced by the many and the weak to keep the strong and the few from taking advantage of their strength. Master morality, on the other hand, is Nietzsche's name for the morality of the strong, the noble, the aristocrat, the *agathos*.

> Here is the place for the origin of that famous opposition of "good" and "evil": into evil one's feelings project power and dangerousness, a certain terribleness, subtlety, and strength that does not permit contempt to develop. According to slave morality, those who are "evil" thus inspire fear; according to master morality it is precisely those who are "good" that inspire, and wish to inspire, fear, while the "bad" are felt to be contemptible. (Nietzsche [2], 207)

'Evil' is the name the weak use to refer to the strong. 'Bad' is the name the strong use to refer to the weak and the "base." 'Good' is, naturally, used by the strong to refer to the strong and by the weak to refer to the weak.

As Nietzsche sees things, in a healthy society the nobility (the strong, those at the top) consider themselves *good* and their subjects (their slaves, their inferiors) *bad*. This is the distinction between good and bad, and Nietzsche does not want to throw it away. The weak, the slaves, and the poor resent their lowly status and envy the privileges of their masters. They band together to promote and praise the altruistic virtues and the virtues of acceptance, passivity, and temperance. They call themselves and these virtues (which they would discard in a moment if they had the strength) *good*, and they call their "masters," those strong and fear-inspiring aristocrats, *evil*.

Nietzsche thinks that conventional morality, compassion, pity, and aversion to suffering (one's own or another's) are all born of weakness, fear, and resentment. They provide security and comfort for the herd, but lead in the end to stolid mediocrity.

> Let us articulate that new claim: we need a critique of all moral values; the intrinsic worth of these values must, first of all, be called in question. . . . Nobody, up till now, has doubted that the "good" [Nietzsche is here using the word as the weak and the base would use it] man represents a higher value than the "evil," [namely, the strong] in terms of promoting and benefiting mankind generally, even taking the long view. But suppose the exact opposite were true. What if the "good" [the weak] man represents not merely a retrogression but even a danger, a temptation, a narcotic drug enabling the present to live at the expense of the future? More comfortable, less hazardous, perhaps, but also baser,

> more petty—so that morality itself would be responsible for man, as a species, failing to reach the peak of magnificence of which he is capable? What if morality should turn out to be the danger of dangers? (Nietzsche [1], 155)

Amoralists could agree with much of this. Morality may indeed hold us back from something higher, or at least from something different and more satisfying. Yet what Nietzsche sees as higher is not what most people see as higher, and the state of affairs Nietzsche would bring about is not necessarily the one that would be chosen by an amoralist. Nietzsche opposes conventional morality not because it is morality, but because it is too kind, and he urges us to replace it not with any form of amoralism, but with an unconventional morality that promotes strength, competition, aggression, and the elimination of compassion, which he identifies with weakness.

> You want, if possible—and there is no more insane "if possible"—*to abolish suffering*. And we? It really seems that *we* would rather have it higher and worse than ever. Well-being, as you understand it—that is no goal, that seems to us an *end*, a state that soon makes man ridiculous and contemptible—that makes his destruction *desirable*. The discipline of suffering, of *great* suffering—do you not know that only *this* discipline has created all the enhancements of man so far? (Nietzsche [2], 153–54)

There is nothing obviously wrong with "well-being," and when Nietzsche calls a contented person ridiculous and contemptible, and then desires his destruction, one is led to wonder not about the contented person but about Nietzsche. Nevertheless, his point deserves to be taken seriously. We must struggle in order to survive and grow, and a serious pursuit of excellence in any field demands dedication and a certain amount of competition, struggle, and suffering. But this is not what Nietzsche is talking about when he says that only "great suffering" brings about the "enhancements of man." For *those* enhancements we need the suffering of martyrs and heroes, and that of the masses unable to get out of the way of these heroes. What are these "enhancements" if not the political and financial empires built on the suffering and early deaths of millions of soldiers, slaves, and workers?

From what has been said, it is clear that Nietzsche, like Callicles, utterly fails to qualify as an amoralist. Both hold a theory of value that makes strength a good, and a theory of obligation that gives the strong person a right to do anything that he wants to. Nietzsche asks "What is good?" and answers "All that heightens the feeling of power, the will to power, power itself in man." Then he asks "What is bad?" and answers "All that proceeds from weakness" (Nietzsche [3], 125).

These values deviate from those of the conventionally moral person, but they are still values. Nietzsche is not just expressing affection for power and distaste for weakness. If we say that an *immoralist* is a moralist with a morality that most people would consider immoral, we can call Callicles and Nietzsche *immoralists*—what we cannot, without confusion, say is that they are *amoralists*.

Wittgenstein

One theory about the world that Indian and Greek thinkers developed was atomism, the belief that everything is made of minute indivisible elements. In a world of atoms swimming in the void there is no room for value, no way to give sense to the claim that one event is preferable to another. Whatever happens, from self-sacrifice to acid rain, is simply a neutral fact of nature—just one of those (combinations of) things.

Atomists believe that "reality" consists of combinations of simple and indivisible elements, but not all atomists think that these elements are physical particles or esoteric theoretical entities like quarks and glueons. Some say the ultimate units are *sensations* (which makes reality mental), and others refuse to speculate about their nature.

Logical atomists claimed that language can be analyzed into absolutely simple statements by the means of logic, and that reality divides into correspondingly simple facts. This led them to hold that there could be a perfect match or fit between an *adequate* language (which ours is not) and reality. Reality consists of complex facts that can be analyzed into simple facts, and an adequate language consists of complex propositions that can be analyzed into simple propositions. A simple proposition states the simple fact that a simple object has a simple property. For each and every simple fact there is a simple proposition that expresses it.

Logical atomism was the remarkable enterprise of trying to glean the true structure of reality by deciding what a perfectly orderly and completely logical language would be like. When Wittgenstein wrote *Tractatus Logico-Philosophicus*, he was a logical atomist. He wrote that the world consists of facts and that facts are combinations of simple and indescribable "objects." Whatever "objects" are, all facts are natural facts about how objects are combined. The only meaningful statements are simple "atomic" statements saying how objects are combined or related (like '*a* is to the left of *b*') and complex "molecular" statements formed by combining, disjoining, and otherwise operating logically with atomic statements. The philosopher, after making all of this clear, plays the watchdog that barks at people who try to say things that cannot be said.

> The correct method in philosophy would really be the following: to say nothing except what can be said, i.e. propositions of natural science—i.e. something that has nothing to do with philosophy—and then, whenever someone else wanted to say something metaphysical, to demonstrate to him that he had failed to give a meaning to certain signs in his propositions. (Wittgenstein [3], 6.53)

Words are meaningful only when used to state facts. If it is a fact that *a* is to the left of *b*, it is not a further fact that it is good that *a* is to the left of *b*. In the world, says Wittgenstein, "everything is as it is, and everything happens as it does happen: *in* it no value exists—and if it did, it would have no value" (Wittgenstein [3], 6.41). So, "it is impossible for there to be propositions of ethics" (6.42).

Wittgenstein once tried to make his idea of the Ethical clear by contrasting it with the Factual.

> Suppose one of you were an omniscient person and therefore knew all the movements of all the bodies in the world dead or alive and that he also knew all the states of mind of all the human beings that ever lived, and suppose this man wrote all he knew in a big book, then this book would contain the whole description of the world; and what I want to say is, that this book would contain nothing that we would call an *ethical* judgment or anything that would logically imply such a judgment. (Wittgenstein [4], 6)

According to Wittgenstein, there are no propositions of ethics and those who use evaluative language are producing nonsense. But Wittgenstein was more subtle than those who followed him, and more guarded about what he said about what can and cannot be said. Remarks at the end of the *Tractatus* have convinced some that he believed in a "realm of value," quite "real" but beyond the power of language to express.

The Logical Positivists, who took the watchdog role of philosophy more seriously than Wittgenstein seems to have done, were perplexed and annoyed by his remarks about "the Mystical" and the inexpressible. They called themselves "radical empiricists," and rambunctiously declared *all* moral, aesthetic, religious, mystical, and metaphysical utterances "nonsense." As his friend and critic Frank Ramsey said: "What you can't say, you can't say; and you can't whistle it either."

Post-positivist philosophers often find Wittgenstein's remarks about the inexpressible to be the most important, or at least the most interesting, sentences in the *Tractatus*. They claim that it was because the positivists and logicians failed to take account of these ideas that Wittgenstein rejected their interest in his work. There is some evidence that Wittgenstein was unwilling to dismiss these things that cannot be said. He says that "the sense of the world must lie outside the world" (Wittgenstein [3], 6.41). He also claims, "There are, indeed, things that cannot be put into words. They *make themselves manifest*. They are what is mystical" (Wittgenstein [3], 6.522).

In *Wittgenstein's Vienna*, Stephen Toulmin and Allan Janik put this aspect of Wittgenstein's thought into its historical and philosophical setting. They quote from a letter to Ludwig Ficker in which Wittgenstein writes that "the book's point is an ethical one," and that he once meant to write the following sentence in the preface:

> My work consists of two parts: the one presented here plus all I have *not* written. And *it is precisely this second part that is the important one*. My book draws a limit to the sphere of the ethical from inside as it were, and I am convinced that this is the ONLY rigorous way of drawing those limits. (Toulmin and Janik, 192)

All this seems to mean that there *is* a "sphere of the ethical" and a sense of the world. This interpretation is supported by Wittgenstein's friend Paul Engelmann.

> Positivism holds—and this is its essence—that what we can speak about is all that matters in life. *Whereas Wittgenstein passionately believes that all that really matters in human life is precisely what, in his view, we must be silent about.* (Toulmin and Janik, 191)

Wittgenstein's remarks in the letter to Ficker indicate that he may indeed have thought that "the ethical" is a *something* about which nothing could be said. Even so, it is not clear that we should take this as a reason for calling him a moralist; nor is it clear what it would mean for the disagreement between the moralist and the amoralist if there were a "sphere of the ethical" beyond the limits of language. Would it mean that the moralist is right after all, but unable to think or say anything moral?

When we examine the entries Wittgenstein made in his notebook while working on the *Tractatus*, we can find passages that sound like amoralism: "I am either happy or unhappy, that is all. It can be said: good or evil do not exist" (Wittgenstein [2], 74). In other passages, he seems to veer into a form of voluntarism. After stating that "the world in itself is neither good nor evil," he adds that "good and evil only enter through the *subject*" (Wittgenstein [2], 79). He mentions Arthur Schopenhauer, another voluntarist, and uses his two key concepts (*will* and *idea*) to express some ideas about ethics and the will: "But can we conceive a being that isn't capable of Will at all, but only of Idea (of seeing for example)? In some sense this seems impossible. But if it were possible then there could also be a world without ethics" (77).

If Wittgenstein does hold some form of voluntarism, then he may be a moralist in spite of having said that in the world there is no good and evil. Since he did not work out this theory, we cannot know what form his voluntarism would have taken. He might have emerged as a moralist with a theory of language that would not allow him to make moral judgments. That would not have been a comfortable position to occupy, but it may be one he shared with Søren Kierkegaard and Leo Tolstoy. What is left for such moralists is to demonstrate (to "show") the ethical in their lives.

It is also possible that Wittgenstein held the clearly moralist position that while there is no good or evil in the world, the willing subject, which is not *in* the world, can be said to be good or evil. "What is good and evil is essentially the I, not the world" (Wittgenstein [2], 80).

None of this is clear, but it is clear that Wittgenstein was unable to stop with the declaration that value is totally devoid of reality of any sort. This inability, however, seems to have been a psychological or perhaps a cultural inability, not one dictated by logic or experience. In any case, being devoid of features, if not of reality, nothing in "the sphere of the Ethical" could have any possible bearing on our conduct—so what good would it be?

The temptation facing the amoralist at this point is to insist that anyone who places morality beyond language and beyond thought has, for all practical purposes, adopted amoralism. How much difference is there between *a something about which nothing can be thought or said* and *a nothing*? It is difficult to say.

The Amoralist

In Chapter 1 we observe that the amoralist need not, perhaps even cannot, do without an *ethics*, which is merely a set of conventions, practices, rules, and habits. What the amoralist rejects are the distinctive beliefs of moralism about what we ought and ought not do, and about what is good and bad. Moralists claim to believe in natural rights, moral duties, intrinsic value, or the power of reason to discover what we ought to do and avoid. Amoralists, by contrast, see rights as conventional and duties as a product of optional roles. To the amoralist, the idea that guidelines are set for us by Reality or by God is a fiction—some say a necessary one, but others reject even that.

A person's amoralism will take shape against a background of moralism. We assimilate moralist assumptions as we learn to use moral language, and it takes a concentrated effort to see what is actually going on. Amoralists inevitably develop their amoralism in reaction to the kinds of moralism they have experienced or formerly embraced. What they have in common is not a positive dogma about the absence of something clearly defined, but a disposition to reject the central assumptions of moralism, and an immunity, in the sense we have already discussed, to "moral considerations." When the moralist asks the amoralist "What exactly are you denying?" the amoralist must reply "What exactly are you asserting?"

We know that the amoralist's opposition to morality need not be self-interested or mean-spirited. It is not a dogma or a set of beliefs, but a stance that emerges from an all-encompassing version of reality. The amoralist looks at moral arguments, disagreements, and theories, and sees morality as nothing more (and nothing less) than an "institution" aimed at regulating interpersonal relationships. Amoralists do not reject the beliefs of moralists because they want to be free from control, or because they want to see people act without considering others; they reject them because they think they are incorrect and because they think we get a more accurate version of our world by calling a convention a convention, by learning to see things and people without the distortions imposed by evaluative concepts, and by not pretending to be bound when we are free.

Amoralism is not one specific belief so much as a way of looking at the world that *finds* valuing but no value, and reasons for action but no moral obligation. It is a perspective that can be found among scientists, mystics, and very ordinary people. It also pervades the thought of the Classical Daoists. Zhuang Zi asks "How can speech be so obscured that there should be a distinction between right and wrong?" (Chan [1], 182; see also 185) and Lao Zi offers the following recommendation and rhetorical questions:

> Abandon learning and there will be no sorrow.
> How much difference is there between "Yes, sir," and "Of course not"?
> How much difference is there between "good" and "evil"?
>
> (Chan [1], 149)

In a footnote to this passage, Chan remarks that a Confucian would never say "Abandon learning," and would "sharply distinguish between good and evil." He adds that the scholar Wang Yang-ming was "widely attacked for teaching that 'in the original substance of the mind there is no distinction between good and evil' " (Chan [1], 150).

In India, the Cārvākins offer the clearest example of amoralism, but it is not difficult to find expressions of amoralism in much Hindu and Buddhist thought. Franklin Edgerton, in his commentary on the *Bhagavad Gītā*, says that while most

> Hindu systems teach a practical morality, they also teach that no degree of morality, however perfect, can lead to the final salvation. In this, too, they are anticipated by the Upaniṣads. The perfect soul is "beyond good and evil." Neither good nor evil can affect him. At times the Upaniṣads seem even to say or imply that when a man has attained enlightenment, he can do what he likes without fear of results. This somewhat dangerous doctrine is, however, not typical, and is probably to be regarded only as a strained and exaggerated manner of saying that the truly enlightened soul cannot, in the very nature of things, do an evil deed. If he could, he would not be truly enlightened. (Edgerton, 126)

Note that when Edgerton explains what the "Hindu systems" mean by the claim that the perfect soul is "beyond good and evil," he does not himself question the "reality" of good and evil. His point is that the perfect soul will not be affected by them—whatever that means.

Edgerton also contemplates the more radical and "somewhat dangerous" doctrine that an enlightened person can live a life without constraints and "do what he likes without fear of results." Yet as soon as he mentions this, he draws back from it; or better, he trades it for the persuasive definition we find at the end of the passage, according to which a "truly enlightened" person cannot do an evil deed. This way of putting things also acknowledges evil, and by implication good, as objective qualities of deeds.

Edgerton observes that the *Bhagavad Gītā* says that the possessor of perfect knowledge passes beyond virtue and vice "and rises to a plane on which moral terms simply have no meaning. Morality applies only in the world of karma, the world of ordinary empiric existence, which the enlightened man has left behind him" (Edgerton, 127). This leaves the rest of us, who happen to inhabit "the world of ordinary empiric existence," stuck with the morality we have inherited. Should we think of this morality as relative, then, or subjective, or as *merely* conventional? It depends on how we decide to interpret the claim that it "applies" in our world, the world of karma. If that means we are objectively bound by it, then we cannot say it is merely conventional.

My amoralists, who have also left good and evil behind, are not lost beyond words and language, but are walking around the ordinary empirical world and interacting with moralists. For them, moral terms do have meaning and it is because they understand this meaning that they are encouraged to try to leave morality behind. Amoralists who are informed, attentive, and compassionate pose no danger to anyone. Their lives have plenty of constraints. Why should we think that the only, or even the most effective, constraints are moral ones? As we have seen, moralists who lack the constraints of affection, interest, sociability, and compassion are likely to be the real danger of dangers.

> The knowledge of the ancients was perfect. In what way was it perfect? There were those who believed that nothing existed. Such knowledge is indeed perfect and ultimate and cannot be improved. The next were those who believed there were things but there was no distinction between them. Still the next were those who believed there was distinction but there was neither right nor wrong. When the distinction between right and wrong became prominent, Tao was thereby reduced. Because Tao was reduced, individual bias was formed. (Zhuang Zi [Chuang Tzu], in Chan [1], 185)

What Is Wrong with Morality?

The conventions of morality are based on the widely held but mistaken assumption that the demands of morality are objectively authoritative, categorical, rational, justifiable, and sometimes universal. People are taught and encouraged to think of moral judgments as expressing such demands, and this teaching is reinforced by the presuppositions underlying the use of moral language. Nearly everyone assumes it would be dangerous not to have an objective morality. Even John Mackie, who sees through the pretenses of the moral realists, spends the second half of his book trying to "invent right and wrong." G. J. Warnock and Philippa Foot, who also reject objective prescriptivity, want to know what sort of a morality we need.

My suggestion is that we do not need any. If morality requires objective prescriptivity and there is no such thing, then when we realize this we either have to abandon morality or agree to participate in a conspiracy to promote it as something we know it is not. It is risky, unnecessary, and more difficult than we think to control others by misleading them about the true character of the world; but this is exactly what we do when we continue to use moral language in a way that implies things we do not accept. Hence, as we have seen, the honest amoralist who despises Nazi atrocities will not even say that the Nazis were evil, or that they were morally wrong to do what they did.

The questions of morality are so controversial, so related to even more controversial questions in philosophy, and so interwoven with personal interest and self-esteem, that it would be naive to think that even the simplest of them is going to be resolved by philosophers engaging in cool, rational deliberation and discussion. If the devil can quote scripture, more-human monsters can construct (or hire moral philosophers to construct) a moral defense for anything they want to do.

Moralists claim that morality is superior to compassion and kindness, since these feelings come and go. But morality only defeats compassion and kindness if it does its job better than compassion and kindness do its job. What may be true, however, is that morality is not as reliable as those feelings when it comes to influencing behavior and moderating the force of selfishness. Compassion, after all, is a direct motivator, and it needs no justification. It is a way of looking, and a disposition to help. If you care about somebody, if you want them to be happy, there is nothing to prove and no problem about motivation. If you merely think it is your duty to help them, then it will always be possible to dig up some excuse for not doing anything.

So what is wrong with morality? Well, it is not what people think it is, and if they saw it for what it is, it would not work. It encourages deception and even self-deception. Anything can be given a moral defense by a clever sophist, but no moral judgment can be conclusively established, no moral debate resolved once and for all. Morality can be (and has been) used to defend cruelty, selfishness, exploitation, and neglect. By itself morality is insufficient for motivation, and its actual contribution to any decision is far from clear.

Morality is not necessary for the kind of behavior it is thought to be a device to promote. People can be conventionally good without believing in the objectivity of morality, so it makes sense to consider some alternatives that might lead to this result. *The* alternative is, and always has been, expanded information and sympathy—the ability to realize the plight of others and the disposition to care. If we could establish habits of curiosity (a strong disposition to take in information), calmness (a quiet mind capable of taking in clean information), and compassion, we would quickly be in a position to leave morality, with its lies and its guilt, its rationalizations, its bogus heteronomy, its capacity to be exploited, its unresolvable arguments, and its perpetual flirtation with religion, behind us. Sigmund Freud was probably right when he called religion a childhood neurosis; but what he did not say (because he did not believe it) was that morality is an adolescent one.

12

Desires and Emotions

You can't always get what you want.

THERE ARE AMORALISTS who would agree with Friedrich Nietzsche's remark that morality may be "responsible for man, as a species, failing to reach that peak of magnificence of which he is capable," but they would disagree about what is to be found at the peak. Nietzsche hated morality because it kept the "good" (that is, the strong) down; but it is also possible to be dissatisfied with morality because it does *not* keep them down enough. Morality may be the "danger of dangers" because it gives the strong a way to rationalize their aggression. It allows egoism and self-interest to parade in the respectable moralist garments of rights, duties, and claims. It may be the danger of dangers because it can be used to defend the status quo and to hold us back from a world in which there is concern for life and compassion for suffering.

Moralists try to help by offering moral reasons for doing things, and by exposing the goodness of things they want us to choose and the badness of things they want us to avoid. Some say, for example, that many of our natural desires and emotions are evil. By teaching this, they may hope to encourage us to overcome temptations they fear will destroy us. But the amoralist has no use for the claim that desires are evil, and no need to call obviously harmful emotions "bad." Those who have left moralism behind are able to deal with their desires and emotions without being burdened by the need to defend or explain the claim that any of them is evil (or good).

What to Do about Desires and Emotions

Since our resources are finite and our desires numberless, many of them are not going to be satisfied. Emotions, too, can be relentless and painful. So, if we are smart we will look for some way to keep from being incapacitated by unbounded desires and intense emotions. If we can not find a way, we are in for some hard times and regrets.

How do we deal with our desires? Do we satisfy them, eliminate them, or choose only some to satisfy? Do we give our emotions free reign, or squelch them? Do we try to distinguish between desirable and undesirable emotions? In India, the Cārvākins urged people to "eat, drink, and be merry," and in Greece the Cyrenaics recommended satisfying as many desires as possible. But Greece also produced the Cynics, and India the Jains, who urged the elimination of *all* desires, even the desire to live and the desire to eliminate all desires. Between these extremes we find two frequently recommended "middle ways." One urges us to make distinctions among desires and emotions and to eliminate some; the other advises reducing not their number, but the influence they exert on us.

One Extreme: Eliminate Desires and Emotions

Antisthenes is often named as the founder of the Greek school of Cynics. Another well-known Cynic was Diogenes of Sinope. The name of the Cynics happened to be the same as the word for 'doglike': this name mirrored and reinforced the general opinion that the Cynics lived like dogs, caring nothing about where they slept or what they ate. "I would rather go mad than feel pleasure," said Antisthenes (Wheelwright, 148). They wanted to be independent of circumstance, and it seemed to them that the way to achieve this was to reject the artificial and the conventional, and to "follow nature."

The Jains adopt an Indian version of this position. They also promote the elimination of all desires, and by 'all' they mean *all.* Everything we think or do results in karma, which leads to future rebirths—a bad thing in their opinion. The Jain sees himself as a pure "life-monad" encrusted by karma resulting from deeds. To return to purity, one must stop accumulating karma and somehow scrape off what has already been acquired. The sources of future karma can be eliminated by the complete cessation not only of desires but of all action.

> By the time Alexander had ascended to the throne of Macedon the fame of Diogenes, then some seventy years old, had spread throughout Greece. One day, as the old philosopher lay sunning himself in his tub, Alexander came riding up with a great retinue, and drawing rein in front of the tub: "I," he announced, "am Alexander the great King." "And I," replied the other with composure, "am Diogenes the Dog." "Are you not then afraid of me?" Alexander asked. "Why, what are you, something good or something evil?" "Something good, of course." "Well," retorted Diogenes, "who would be so foolish as to fear anything good?" Struck with admiration of this answer, Alexander exclaimed, "Ask anything you wish of me, and I will grant it." "Then be so kind," said Diogenes, "as to get out of my sunlight." (Wheelwright, 149)
>
> A basic fact generally disregarded by those who "go in" for Indian wisdom is this one of the total rejection of every last value of humanity by the Indian teachers and winners of redemption from the bondages of the world. . . . For perfect non-activity, in thought, speech, and deed, is possible only when one has become dead to *every* concern of life: dead to pain and enjoyment as well as to every impulse to power, dead to the interests of intellectual pursuit, dead to all social and political affairs—deeply, absolutely, and immovably uninterested in one's character as a human being. (Zimmer, 231–32)

The Other Extreme: Indulge Desires and Emotions

Extreme indulgence is recommended in India by the Cārvāka school, and in Greece by the Cyrenaics. The Cārvākins were atheistic materialists who thought the soul was physical and death the end of consciousness. Look at the list of pronouncements attributed to them in the section on their philosophy in Chapter 5, concluding with the claim that "chastity and such ordinances" are rules created by "clever weaklings." Their materialism may have led the Cārvākins into amoralism, but their preference for young women, fine clothes, perfumes, garlands, and sandal paste does not flow from their amoralism. After all, an amoralist can be an ascetic.

The Greek Cyrenaic school was founded by Aristippus of Cyrene over a hundred years after the death of Socrates in 399 B.C. The Cyrenaics set their views against those of the Cynics and recommended living for the immediate enjoyment of the moment. Aristippus says that we do not control pleasure by staying away from it, but by learning how to enjoy it without being carried away by our desires. That sounds reasonable, but some Cyrenaics, not content to seek their pleasure in moderation, reasoned that if some pleasure is good, more pleasure is better. The typical Cyrenaic is represented as recommending the unrestrained and relentless pursuit of physical enjoyment, in all its forms.

These extreme positions leave one with a sense of unreality. It is hard to believe that anyone ever seriously recommended either that we give up every single desire we have or that we yield to every desire the moment it arises. It is not even clear what would count as following either of these recommendations.

It makes more sense to talk about reducing our desires and about satisfying only those we take to be most important. These are goals for humans, not ideals for iron-willed ascetics or abandoned orgiasts. But even here we could go wrong by adopting an oversimplified conception of desires. We should not think of them as discrete, reidentifiable mental atoms; they are not psychic items we can inventory and then set about satisfying or eliminating, one by one. The mind is much more fluid than that. We can change its direction, modify its tendencies, but we can not snip off and discard the desire for a vacation or a larger paycheck as if it was an overgrown fingernail. The changes in our desire systems are gradual and global, and if we want to stop desiring a certain thing, there may be many preliminary things we must accomplish.

A Middle Way

If we agree that we *can* eliminate or modify *some* of our desires, we can turn to a set of considerations that support reducing their number: (1) Desires cause pain when they are not satisfied, and since no one can satisfy all the ones that arise, the more we have, the more we will leave unsatisfied and the more pain we will feel; (2) Even when we do succeed in satisfying some of our desires, many of them have been imposed on us by other people for *their* benefit and profit; (3) Often we satisfy a desire only to end up dissatisfied with what we got and disinterested in the fruits of our success; (4) Desires distort our perception because when we desire something we pay attention primarily, if not solely, to what seems likely to help us get it. Consequently the more we have, the more difficult it is to find our way around in our already complex world; (5) And finally, no matter how many desires we manage to satisfy, everything is sooner or later lost to time, change, disaster, or, finally, to death.

For all these reasons, then, it may be in our interest to eliminate some, possibly even many, desires. Perhaps Lao Zi was right when he said, "The sage desires to have no desires" (verse 64 quoted in Chan [1], 170); and perhaps he was just playing with us. In another passage he is perfectly clear and straightforward: "Reduce selfishness; have few desires" (verse 19 quoted in Chan [1], 149). We now turn our attention to several versions of that suggestion.

The Epicureans

It is ironic that the word 'epicurean' connotes feasts, fine wine, rich sauces, and fancy plates. As we are about to see, this was not the original Epicureans' idea of a good time. Epicurus (*b.* 341 B.C.) and his friends spent their time discussing philosophy and cultivating a life of simplicity and moderation. His secret to happiness was a distinction he made among desires. "We must consider that of desires some are natural, others vain, and of the natural some are necessary and others merely natural; and of the necessary some are necessary for happiness, others for the repose of the body, and others for very life" (Epicurus [2], 31). Desires for food, water, and shelter are natural and necessary, but the desire for sex appears to be natural but not necessary. "Sexual intercourse," he says, "has never done a man good, and he is lucky if it has not harmed him" (Epicurus [1], 45). Desires for wealth, power, and fame are neither natural nor necessary. Epicurus suggests that we satisfy the necessary desires, and eliminate as many of the others as we can. "In so far as you are in difficulties, it is because you forget nature; for you create for yourself unlimited fear and desires" (Epicurus [1], 49). He was content with bread, cheese, cheap wine, and good conversation. "All that is natural," he says, "is easy to be obtained, but that which is superfluous is hard" (Epicurus [2], 32).

Epicurus mentions *both* fear and desires as causes of our difficulties. Those who follow this first middle way will want to work on emotions as well as desires, a practice that can be supported by adapting the considerations already given for reducing desires. For example, emotions (fear, hatred, anger, jealousy [love?]) distort our perception by blinding us to the complexity of the actual situation and leading us to expend energy reacting to our projections rather than attempting to understand the situation as it is. Consequently, the more emotions we have, the more difficult it is to find our way around in an already complex world.

The Stoics

Cynics deliberately flouted the customs and conventions of their society. They called themselves citizens of the world and refused to give allegiance to any conventional organization like the state. Stoicism is a socialized development of Cynicism—it is Cynicism with religion and a social conscience. Like the Cynics, the Stoics adopted the maxim "Live according to Nature." But when the Cynics talked about living according to nature they were talking about sitting nude in the dirt, cohabitation without marriage, and deferring to nobody. Stoics, on the other hand, understood "Nature" to be the universal order of things, the natural and moral laws of the universe, and sometimes, because of their pantheism, a God.

Like the Epicureans, the Stoics advise us to reduce desires, and thereby be independent of external circumstances. The Roman Stoic Epictetus (A.D. 50–138) was born a slave, sent to Rome, given his freedom, and ended his days teaching philosophy. He lived in a simple house with a mat, a bed, and a lamp. His attitude about desires will not surprise us.

> Remember that desire demands the attainment of that of which you are desirous; and aversion demands the avoidance of that to which you are averse; that he who fails of the object of his desires is disappointed; and he who incurs the object of his aversion is wretched. If, then, you shun only those undesirable things which you can control, you will never incur anything which you shun; but if you shun sickness, or death, or poverty, you will run the risk of wretchedness. Remove [the habit of] aversion, then, from all things that are not within our power, and apply it to things undesirable, which are in our power. (Epictetus, 2:216–17)

Epictetus was a slave. Marcus Aurelius, another Roman Stoic, was an emperor, a sincere, modest, and gentle man who did his best to keep the Empire together and the barbarians at bay. His diary contains reflections on his feelings, expressions of his Stoicism, self-criticism, and reminders to himself. The Latin title of his book translates "To Myself," but the title by which it is known in English is *Meditations*.

Marcus acknowledges the orderly yet ceaseless change that occurs in Nature. Things come and go, but sooner or later all things pass away. While change pervades the universe, there is a pattern and a plan. He has many names for this plan (or possibly for its author)—Reason, Nature, Mind, Zeus, God, and Fire. The belief that the world is the result of a deliberate plan distinguished the Stoics from the Epicureans, who saw the universe as an accidental grouping of atoms. The Stoics thought that our own individual minds are little fragments of this Mind, and our reason is "that portion of Zeus that is in us all." Everything is a necessary element in a plan that is incomprehensible to us. Given the vastness of the plan and the evident superiority of the Mind that designed it, Marcus concludes that grumbling about how things are is foolish, even a kind of illness, and a sure sign that one is out of tune with the divine harmony.

> For a human soul, the greatest of self-inflicted wrongs is to make itself . . . a kind of tumour or abscess on the universe; for the quarrel with circumstances is always a rebellion against Nature—and Nature includes the nature of each individual part. (Marcus Aurelius, 50)

> O world, I am in tune with every note of thy great harmony. For me nothing is early, nothing late, if it be timely for thee. O Nature, all that thy seasons yield is fruit for me. (Marcus Aurelius, 68)

> Your part [recall that Marcus is talking to himself] is to be serene, to be simple. Is someone doing wrong? The wrong lies with himself. Has something befallen you? Good; then it was your portion of the universal lot, assigned to you when time began; a strand woven into your particular web, like all else that happens. (Marcus Aurelius, 69)

If this is right, discontent is out of place, and we would be much better off if we could eliminate our grumbling and negative emotional reactions.

Think of people who allow themselves to be angered or disturbed by the weather. The Stoic feels the cold and the heat but he does not let it bother him. People annoyed by the cold or the heat suffer twice—first from the cold or heat, and then from their reaction. Stoics prefer to suffer only once—so they welcome what comes and refuse to assess it as evil.

> For you, evil comes not from the mind of another; nor yet from any of the phases and changes of your own bodily frame. Then whence? From

> that part of yourself which acts as your assessor of what is evil. Refuse its assessment, and all is well. Though the poor body, so closely neighbouring it, be gashed or burned, fester or mortify, let the voice of this assessor remain silent. (Marcus Aurelius, 72)

The Stoics were not the only ones aware of this technique. We can hear the same suggestion from the other side of the world in the words of the Zen master, Hui Hai, who recommends that we learn "to behold men, women and all the various sorts of appearances while remaining as free from love or aversion as if they were actually not seen at all" (Blofeld [2], 48). He urges his students not to think in terms of good and evil, and denies that "our own nature" contains either good or evil (50, 119). When he is asked, "Then what should we do to be right?" he answers, "There is nothing to do and nothing which can be called right" (119).

People criticize the Stoic (and the Buddhist) for this passive attitude of acceptance. They say this attitude makes social reform impossible. If someone is not disturbed about injustice, poverty, war, inequality, political oppression, and crime, then nothing will be done. The engine of reform is driven by the energy of anger. Accepting one's "portion of the universal lot" has meant accepting slavery, corruption, oppression, exploitation, illness, and early death for the majority of humans.

The Stoic can say two things in response to this criticism. The first is that it is not clear that emotional hotheads bring about more social reform than people who work calmly and steadily toward a goal. After all, the Stoic is only recommending that we accept the actual situation without pointless emotion and useless resentment. If our perceptions are distorted by resentment and anger, many of the actions we take in an effort to remedy things will be based on incomplete understanding and emotional distortions.

The second thing the Stoic can say is that the critic fails to distinguish between Stoicism and Cynicism. Perhaps it would have been fair to complain that the Cynicism of Diogenes would, if widely practiced, rule out social progress. But the Stoics grafted a sense of duty (and even propriety) onto this nihilistic Cynic position. They did this by treating Nature as purposive and by accepting and even welcoming their role in the working out of the Great Plan.

Those who think a "great mind" designed the universe often express the belief that what happens is not only inevitable, it is for the "best." Marcus does this, and in doing so he loses points for consistency. If he had really been serious about silencing his assessor, he would have refrained from saying that everything that happens is for the best.

Greek Techniques

The gulf between theory and practice is often wide. It is one thing see what is troubling you as part of a great plan, but that information does not automatically make you feel better about things. Marcus tells himself to consider the "rational part" of the mind to be that "particle of himself, which Zeus has given to every man for ruler and guide" (Marcus Aurelius, 87). To agree with Fate is simply to agree with that larger Reason of which your little mind is simply an isolated bit. To kick and squeal against fate, to feel annoyance or resentment, is to act in weakness and ignorance. The only freedom a person has is the mental freedom to conform graciously with the plan: "Is your cucumber bitter? Throw it away. Are there briars in your path? Turn aside. That is enough. Do not go on to say, 'Why were things of this sort ever brought into the world?' " (Marcus Aurelius, 132).

The Epicureans and the Stoics offer their suggestions and maxims to help people find happiness, but in their conception, happiness is a minimal (though not negligible) thing: freedom from pain and mental suffering. Epicurus is completely clear about this:

> When, therefore, we maintain that pleasure is the end, we do not mean the pleasures of profligates and those that consist in sensuality, as is supposed by some who are either ignorant or disagree with us or do not understand, but freedom from pain in the body and from trouble in the mind. (Epicurus [2], 32)

While the Epicureans are content with friendship, knowledge, and simple pleasures, the Stoics are less relaxed. While some of them value friendship, others recommend doing away with the emotion of love on the grounds that the loss of loved ones is inevitable and bound to lead to suffering. The Epicureans remind us of the Daoists, while the Stoics resemble the more earnest and down-to-earth Confucians. Epicurus, for example, says: "We must release ourselves from the prison of affairs and politics" (Epicurus [1], 43).

It is clear to Epicurus that some of our fear and consequent suffering comes from false beliefs about the supernatural. His way of relieving that suffering is to encourage a naturalistic understanding of nature. He insists, for example, that the happenings attributed to ghosts are all natural occurrences. "A man cannot dispel his fear about the most important matters if he does not know what is the nature of the universe but suspects the truth of some mythical story. So that without natural science it is not possible to attain our pleasures unalloyed" (Epicurus [3], 36). Epicurus did not rely exclusively on natural science and helpful maxims, but he created the material conditions for peace by dropping out of ordinary society and joining a community of like-minded friends. The Stoics did not take this option and they did not resort to atomism to allay their worries about an afterlife. They were comforted in their belief that events are not random jostlings of atoms, but products of intelligence. This served as the basis for helpful sayings and slogans they recalled to themselves as circumstances put a strain on their Stoicism. Marcus mentions meditation and says that "nowhere can man find a quieter or more untroubled retreat than in his own soul." This seems to involve little more than calming down and remembering his maxims and rules of life: "Recurrence to them will then suffice to remove all vexation, and send you back without fretting to the duties to which you must return" (Marcus Aurelius, 63).

Buddhism

By the time Marcus was emperor, Buddhists had spent over five hundred years developing meditation. They had learned that it takes more than recalling maxims to escape the vexation and fretting that comes when our desires are frustrated. Buddhism began when Siddhartha Gautama discovered what he characterized as the origin of suffering and the way to its elimination. His teaching originally was a psychological one about mental discipline, and this is how his early disciples understood it.

As Buddhism traveled far and wide, it took many forms, and most of them were religious. But however mired in superstition Buddhism became, Buddhists never lost sight of the basic insights announced in the Four Noble Truths: Birth, decay, sickness, death, failure, success—in fact everything—is suffering; this suffering is brought about by desire and can be eliminated by eliminating the desire.

If we ask the Buddhist how to reduce desires and useless emotions like fear, pride, and envy, the first answer will involve meditation. Buddhist meditation is not an unstructured withdrawal into oneself, but a unique discipline designed to strengthen the mind. There is as much reason to think this works as there is to think that physical exercise strengthens the body. Meditation is, for the Buddhists, the *main thing*, and many things that do not look like meditation turn out to be meditation in disguise. For example, repeating the name of a *bodhisattva* over and over is recommended as a way of calling upon that *bodhisattva* for help, but in fact doing this teaches one to concentrate on one thing, which is a form of meditation that not only strengthens the mind, but leaves no room for stressful doubts and worries.

Buddhists, Epicureans, and Stoics offer similar advice, but its strong emphasis on meditation makes Buddhism more complete. Unlike the Epicureans and Stoics, many Buddhists retreated to monasteries to practice full-time meditation with like-minded friends. The Epicureans also withdrew from the world, but they relaxed and participated in gentle conversations over wine and cheese, while the Buddhists congregated together to impose severe discipline and much silence on each other. The two approaches are as different as a vacation on Maui and Olympic training camp. What links them is the attempt to find a "middle way" between the ascetic and the libertine, but, as it happens, it is not the only middle way there is.

Nothing is sufficient for him to whom what is sufficient seems little. (Epicurus [1], 44)

47 There is no calamity greater than lavish desires.
There is no greater guilt than discontentment,
And there is no greater disaster than greed.
He who is contented with contentment is always contented.
(Lao Zi, in Chan [1], 162)

All desires should be abandoned.
But if you are unable to do so,
Let your desire be for salvation.
Thus will be found the cure.

(Nāgārjuna, 44)

Another Middle Way

Desires and emotions can not be uprooted one by one and discarded like weeds. Many "unnecessary" ones are still very natural and very insistent and even when we think we have eliminated one, we may merely have forced it underground from whence "it" will later emerge in another form. Some Buddhists tried to eliminate sexual desires by meditating on how gross, ugly, and disgusting the human body is. They sat in cemeteries and thought about rotting corpses. This probably worked for some of them, but it involves more negative thinking than a sensible Buddhist would be likely to put up with.

Another way to deal with sexual (and other) desires is to forget about trying to eliminate them, and instead work on reducing their effect. There is no sure way to eliminate a desire, but there may be a way to neutralize it. The idea is not to stop wanting things, only to stop taking our wants so seriously. Our desires are only one kind of item in a vast network of circumstances that determines our choices. Looked at objectively, which is one way to look at things, our desires are no more important than any of the desires others hold with equal warmth. This realization affects different people differently, but it opens the door to the second middle way. In the next two sections we peer through that door at two versions of this approach to desires and emotions.

Karma Yoga

In chapter 2 of the *Bhagavad Gītā*, Kṛṣṇa gives Arjuna the secret of action that allows him to leave the *Vedas* behind:

> On action alone be thy interest,
> Never on its fruits;
> Let not the fruits of action be thy motive,
> Nor be thy attachment to inaction.
>
> (Edgerton, 14)

The world has always known of ascetics who pursue their path by renouncing the world. Both Mahāvīra and Buddha left their families, and Jesus recommended it to those who would follow him. According to the social customs of Hinduism, the last two quarters of a *man's* life are to be spent in seclusion, travel, meditation, and a search for liberation. There is little doubt that detachment from public business and personal affairs, quiet meditation in mountain gardens, a vegetarian diet, and some hard work will produce a rich harvest of tranquillity. But the hard fact was (and is) that not everyone can renounce the world and move to the mountains or the monasteries. Karma yoga is the yoga or discipline of *work*, and it is designed for those who do not, will not, or cannot withdraw from the world. It does not tell us to renounce actions, but to perform actions *without a concern for the consequences.* This is presumably what it means not to allow the fruits of action be your motive.

There is little doubt that we can and do act without considering the consequences. Sometimes this is described as spontaneous action and sometimes as rashness, but given that it happens, the obvious question is, "If we are not motivated by a concern for consequences, how are we motivated?" One answer of the *Bhagavad Gītā* is that if we can abandon our ego, our will, our conscious decision-making mechanism, our desires, ends, purposes, and goals, then we can invite God into our lives and allow him to work through us. This is how Kṛṣṇa explains it to Arjuna in chapter 18:

> Dwelling in solitude, eating but little, controlling speech, body and mind, and ever engaged in meditation and concentration and taking refuge in dispassion.
>
> And casting aside self-sense, force, arrogance, desire, anger, possession, egoless and tranquil in mind, he becomes worthy of becoming one with Brahman.
>
> Having become one with Brahman, and being tranquil in spirit, he neither grieves nor desires. Regarding all beings as alike he attains supreme devotion to Me.
>
> Through devotion he comes to know Me, what My measure is and who I am in truth; then, having known Me in truth, he forthwith enters into Me.
>
> Doing continually all actions whatsoever, taking refuge in Me, he reaches by My grace the eternal, undying abode.
>
> Surrendering in thought all actions to Me, regarding Me as the Supreme and resorting to steadfastness in understanding, do thou fix thy thought constantly on Me.
>
> Fixing thy thought on Me, thou shalt, by My grace, cross over all difficulties; but if, from self-conceit, thou wilt not listen (to Me), thou shalt perish. (Radhakrishnan, 370–72)

Note the sequence. First one purifies oneself by becoming worthy of being one with Brahman, then one attains supreme devotion to Kṛṣṇa, then one "enters into" Kṛṣṇa. Only then is one helped to cross over all difficulties.

Some followers of Kṛṣṇa say that one need only chant his name, sing his praises, and love him. When one reaches the proper state of love or egolessness, Kṛṣṇa takes over. If Kṛṣṇa operates through you, it is impossible for you to make a mistake or to store up bad karma—even if you wipe out a city or slaughter all your cousins in a bloody battle.

When one fixes one's thought on Kṛṣṇa, utters his name repeatedly with devotion, one's conscious mind is filled with that name, and there is no room for ratiocination, deliberation, calculation, worry, or regret. Desires, interests, hopes, likes, dislikes, and plans are disengaged. They float by, alongside the other aspects of the situation—objects of contemplation, but no longer the determiners of action they once were. This is detachment, and is described in Book 2 of the *Bhagavad Gītā*:

> He unto whom all desires enter as waters into the sea, which, though ever being filled is ever motionless, attains to peace and not he who hugs his desires. (Radhakrishnan, 128)

When one adopts the method of karma yoga the desires may be there, but their influence is taken away. One is not moved by them. But what is this motionlessness? It is not literal lack of activity because one is supposed to be "motionless" even in the midst of action. What is motionless is the will, the ego, the self, the conscious planning mind. One is calm and attentive, no matter how tumultuous one's surroundings. One cannot be like this if one takes one's desires too seriously (hugs them).

This method is familiar to Christians who believe in possession, and it can be found wherever trances are used to make contact with "another world," or meditation is used to calm the mind. It is very likely that possession by Kṛṣṇa, or by any alleged divine or not so divine being, can be understood with the help of what we now know about the operation of the brain. As the left hemisphere carries out the make-work task of repeating Kṛṣṇa's name, the intuitive right hemisphere gains more access to the springs of action. However it is explained, people who believe themselves in touch with a god often do gain in power and in powers.

There is no doubt that in peace as well as war it is helpful to be able to call on our hidden sources of strength; but it would be nice if we could unlock power and inspiration without falsehoods, myths, terrifying rituals, and radically altered states of consciousness. Will we ever learn to act with strength and grace without attributing our best moves to a fictional being? Why is it more difficult to take credit for our achievements than accept blame for our failures?

Wu Wei

Some things Kṛṣṇa says about non-action remind us of the Daoist idea of *wu wei*, and of Lao Zi's claim that by doing nothing the sage manages to do everything. But of course doing nothing does not mean doing *nothing*. *Wu wei* is not simple inaction or unmoving passivity. Some say that *wu wei* is acting without straining, or never applying more force than you have to. But while it is true that Daoists will not apply "too much" force, something deeper and more complicated is meant by this notion.

Wu wei involves various elements, the most important of which is inner stillness. This suggests that we may be able to achieve a quiet mind without resorting to the noisy expedient of chanting our verbalization into silence. Some say the Daoists practice a form of breathing meditation similar to that of the Buddhists, but however they achieve their inner stillness, that is what enabled them to know and "realize" what is going on. And it is that connectedness with things that guarantees that when the time to act comes, the response will be intuitive, natural, spontaneous, and appropriate. Decisions will then emerge as naturally and spontaneously as beliefs.

The Daoist's identification with the Dao, Marcus's attempt to harmonize his will with Reason, the *Bhagavad Gītā*'s advice to yield to Kṛṣṇa, and the Christian's talk of possession by the Spirit are birds of a feather. In each case we relinquish control to something (or Someone). In some versions, this Something, unlike the finite and confused ego, knows (or wrote) the Master Plan and can make no mistakes. This is a blessing to those who worry, a path out of guilt, and an invitation to act without trying to figure out all the angles, which is, in any case, impossible.

The difference is in the accompanying stories. Christianity and karma yoga require a conscious divinity with the power and ability it takes to inhabit our bodies, and the willingness to do so. Stoicism requires only that Nature be intelligent and purposive. Daoism needs no theistic dogma or false belief, only the freedom from false beliefs and confused categories, an appreciation of the vastness of nature and the wonder of change, and the willingness to move attentively and harmoniously.

The similarity between *wu wei* and karma yoga has been noted by Victor H. Mair in his new translation of the *Dao De Jing*. Mair suggests that Daoism may have been influenced by the teaching of the *Bhagavad Gītā*, and that there is "convincing evidence that the obvious resemblances between the two traditions are not merely happenstance" (Mair, 141). This is an intriguing possibility, but even if influence can never be established, similarity of method is undeniable. Both movements developed a technique to unlock powerful physical, mental, and creative energy, and to unleash our spontaneous practical wisdom.

Conclusion

We are not slaves of our desires. If we are slaves of anything it is of a too simple picture of what desires are. Desires exist only as abstractions from the total mental flow that is our ongoing consciousness. Talking about them helps us understand our own behavior, but only in an oversimplified and linguistically bound way. If we adopt the suggestion that we weaken their influence, then we will develop a more relaxed and accepting approach to people and events. But moving in this direction is not easy, and many people need the help of religion or companions or both in order to go any significant distance. This is why the Sangha, the order of monks who live and work together, is considered one of the Three Treasures of Buddhism.

But what is going on when we change our minds, when we lose our desires, or control our thoughts? How does meditation help Buddhists attain quietude or reduce their desires? How do we empty or purify our minds so that we can begin to take advantage of the method of *wu wei*? In chapter 13 we turn once again to some ideas about the two hemispheres of the brain as we think about decision and choice. We survey some of the ways we are shaped and controlled, and look for a way to harmonize our active and passive modes of operation. The chapter concludes with some directions for those who seek to take what can be called "The Path of Harmony."

13

Decisions, Control, and Harmony

But we could say: The happy life seems to be in some sense more *harmonious* than the unhappy. But in what sense?

—*Ludwig Wittgenstein,* Notebooks: 1914–1916

EPICUREANS, STOICS, and Buddhists recommend eliminating desires and emotions, but they do not advise us to eliminate them *all*, or blame us for satisfying the necessary and modest ones. The Daoist practice of *wu wei* and the Hindu path of karma yoga also seek to avoid the extremes of self-indulgence and self-denial, but they do this by working to reduce the power rather than the number of desires and emotions. The two approaches are compatible and complementary, and anyone who thinks desires and emotions cause suffering will want to use both.

Making Decisions

Whether we see ourselves as monomaniacal pleasure-seekers or as having more complex motivations, we face questions about the roles deliberation and self-interest play in our choices. Four pictures of decision making can be distinguished on the basis of the importance attributed to these two factors.

1. Someone with unlimited self-interested desires and a policy of evaluating each action on the basis of how many of those desires it is likely

to satisfy can be called a deliberate egoist. Such beings appear in philosophy books and philosophical discussions, but no actual human could operate in this way. Bishop Joseph Butler, who usually gets credit for providing the classical argument against the belief that we are always and only motivated by self-interest, says that our problem is not that we think too much of our own welfare, but that we do not think of it more often. Whether that is right, we certainly do not think of it *all of the time*. Of course we have desires and try to satisfy them, but even if we were clear about our ends, we would not have enough time or information to determine which of our available options would best serve them. Our conscious ability to calculate all the variables relating to the outcome of an action, and to estimate the relative importance to us of the many factors involved, is about as reliable as a sundial made of butter. Introspection tells us that we do not always try to maximize the good for ourselves, and common sense tells us that if we ever tried to operate according to a policy of deliberate egoism, we would find it impossible to act.

2. We might get a more plausible picture of decision making by giving up the belief in all-out conscious deliberation and keeping the egoism. Perhaps an *unconscious* mechanism, programmed to maximize our interests, controls our choices and overrides altruistic impulses for the promise of even slight personal gain. This would make the pursuit of selfish ends automatic and inevitable, and our belief that we act non-selfishly the result of self-deception and rationalization. The idea that we are unaware of some of the factors that influence our behavior is familiar and credible. If we do not assume that unnoticed reckoning is going on, we have no way to explain spontaneous moves of athletes, musicians, artists, and Nintendo experts. The problem is not with the claim that unconscious processing, correlation, integration, and deduction influence our behavior, it is with the claim that we only choose what we unconsciously calculate will bring us the most of what we want. This does not seem to be the way we work, and most of the evidence we have suggests that our unconscious springs of action are as varied as our conscious ones seem to be. We have more on our unconscious minds than our own welfare.
3. One problem with the idea that we are deliberate egoists is the egoism, but another is the belief in the supremacy of deliberation. The more factors we discover influencing our decisions, the more difficult it becomes to give priority to the conscious, the rational, and the deliberate. A third picture of decision making abandons the egoism but keeps the deliberation, pretending that each choice is the result of deliberate and thoughtful reflection. We do deliberate, of course. We

parade a variety of factors before our consciousness, we construct chains of thought around them, we worry a little or a lot, and we try to imagine consequences and alternatives. But we do not consciously determine which alternatives to present and which to ignore, or the order in which they are presented, or the importance each is to be given in the final resolution. Far more is involved in our decisions than we imagine, and it is only when we understand this that we are ready to appreciate the next picture of decision making, which is the only one that makes sense.

4. The fourth picture of decision making is little more than an acknowledgment of the unfathomable complexity of the human organism. An open channel to our "decision-making mechanism" receives our ongoing verbalizations, but these are blended with elements of radically different kinds—things we know but have never stated even to ourselves, chemical and hormonal pressures, the genetic contribution, and habits of all sorts. We are equipped with principles and slogans that guide our actions and buttress our prejudices, and we are lodged in a one-sided narratization, structured by concepts and metaphors that organize our experience and guide our behavior. When we decide, we mobilize all of these elements and more. We puzzle over dozens of considerations, spend hours reviewing the pros and cons, and then suddenly, in a flash, we decide: "I will quit my job and go back to school." "I will tell the truth at the hearing tomorrow." We may congratulate ourselves for having thought things through and made a rational decision, but if we review the whole process, we may come to feel that our conscious deliberation was not the only thing at work, and that the best thing to say is that conscious and unconscious factors of many types mix together to produce the decisions we take credit and blame for making.

The Bicameral Brain Again

Buddhists, Daoists, and mystics have urged us to silence our rational consciousness, to quiet the voice in our heads, to embrace the emptiness, and to eliminate our egos. This advice may be interpreted as a suggestion to silence the hyperactive left brain—the rational, verbal, conceptual consciousness—so that "the other side of the brain" can participate more fully.

No one thought much of the fact that the brain is divided into symmetrical hemispheres until about a hundred years ago. In 1861 Paul Broca noticed a connection between the inability to construct grammatical sentences and damage in a specific area of the brain. Thirteen years later, Carl Wernicke related damage in a different area of the brain to problems with the interpretation of sentences. Since both "Broca's Area" and "Wernicke's Area" are in the *left* hemisphere, people came to believe that linguistic abilities (and other abilities depending on language) are located there.

In the first half of this century, brain researchers uniformly underestimated the role and importance of the right hemisphere; they called it the "minor" hemisphere, and thought of it as an inactive back-up unit. We have only recently learned of the different but crucial contribution it makes to our success as individuals and as a species. Some researchers now go so far as to say that different types of thought correspond to left and right hemispheric activity. This opinion is expressed by Robert E. Ornstein who, in his introduction to a collection of papers on human consciousness, writes of two modes of thinking that together "form the basis of complete human consciousness." One mode, he says, "involves reason, language, analysis, and sequence." The other "is tacit, 'sensuous,' and spatial, and operates in a holistic, relational manner" (Ornstein, 63).

Joseph E. Bogen, whose article "The Other Side of the Brain: An Appositional Mind" appears in Ornstein's anthology, thinks it is too simple to say that the left hemisphere is verbal and the right hemisphere spatial. He notes that the right hemisphere uses words, though not in the way the left hemisphere uses them. Thought in the left hemisphere is propositional, logical, and often grammatical. We know much less about "thought" in the right hemisphere, and Bogen introduces the word 'appositional' (in contrast to 'propositional') to characterize it (Bogen, 111).

In "Bimodal Consciousness," Arthur J. Deikman may be making the same distinction as Bogen when he distinguishes between the *action mode* and the *receptive mode*. "The action mode is a state organized to manipulate the environment." It involves "focal attention, object-based logic, heightened boundary perception, and the dominance of formal characteristics over the sensory." It is a "state of striving, oriented toward achieving personal goals that range from nutrition to defense to obtaining social rewards, plus a variety of symbolic and sensual pleasures, as well as the avoidance of a comparable variety of pain" (Deikman, 68). By contrast, the receptive mode is "organized around intake of the environment rather than manipulation." Language is essential to the action mode because with language "we discriminate, analyze, and divide up the world into pieces or objects which can then be grasped (psychologically and biologically) and acted upon" (70).

If we really function by combining a rational, linguistic consciousness with a non-rational, non-linguistic, unconscious mode of thought or processing, then we might as well acknowledge the contribution of both parts, even if we are unlikely to come to a conscious understanding of the unconscious element. Otherwise we will take our descriptions of events to be the *whole story* and settle for a narratization filled with misleading and half-baked explanations like these:

> We went to war over oil.
> I am angry with him because he insulted me.
> She sacrificed her future because she loved him.
> He became a skinhead because he hated strangers.

Sometimes these remarks are true "as far as they go," but that is usually not very far. Real life is complicated, and there is a danger that these one-liners will stand between us and an adequate understanding of events. Wars have complicated causes and people get insulted without becoming angry, love without sacrificing, and hate strangers but keep their hair.

Verbal descriptions and explanations belong to the more-or-less coherent story that constitutes our verbally encoded version of reality. It is with and within this structure that we reason, but our decisions are not the pure output of this reasoning, since our right hemisphere (or our unconscious processing, wherever it may be located) is normally working quietly behind the scenes. There are many forces working within and on us, and our choices emerge from this welter of impulses, habits, feelings, beliefs, fears, thoughts, resolutions, and stored verbal commands from ourselves and others. What we end up doing is the resultant vector of these incalculable and often invisible forces.

Socialization

Things are complicated, and the antecedents of our actions are everywhere. Our left hemisphere, the linguistic analytical part of our brain, categorizes and simplifies, reasons and argues. These verbalizations affect our choices, but innumerable factors combine to produce the final result: deliberate behavior. If we ignore the complexity and subscribe to inadequate conceptualizations of what we are—selfish computers, altruistic hominids, rational paragons, or lumbering gene machines—we will overlook features that do not fit those conceptualizations. It would be better to say that we are all four, and other things as well, if only to indicate that selfish desires, altruism, reasoning, genetic factors, and more, make a contribution to what we are and what we do.

If we want to understand why we do what we do, we must look at as many of the factors that exert pressure on us as we can find. We may never learn the exact recipe of any given decision, but we can develop an inventory of the larder of available ingredients. What follows is a brief discussion of some of the factors we ourselves introduce into the causal stew—ways we have of giving one another (and ourselves) reasons for doing things.

Force and Threat

Physical force and the threat of it are used by parents, friends, enemies, bullies, nations, and the legal systems of all societies. We do many things and refrain from doing many others because we believe or fear that someone will respond to our action or inaction with force. If you think "human nature" is evil, or even selfish, you will be inclined to use and threaten force.

Actual physical punishment is one kind of force, but there are others. We can take property or liberty away from people (if they have it) or eject them from our house, tribe, or country. These are not direct applications of force, but they cannot be carried through unless they are backed by enough power to enforce compliance. When people fail to conform to our requirements we can also withdraw attention, support, or affection. Many would rather be punished physically, and only those who have transcended the need for attention, support, and affection will be unmoved by this type of pressure.

Positive Reinforcement

When Han Fei Zi told the emperor to grasp the two handles of control, he was speaking of punishment and reward. Controllers debate over which is the more powerful motivator, and over which is more costly to employ. It certainly appears more expensive to reward those who conform to our requirements than to punish those who do not; but when we calculate expenses we must remember that not all rewards are material. Non-material rewards can range from smiles and kind words to medals, trophies, and other inexpensive symbols.

When calculating the relative costs of rewards and punishments, we should not forget to take into account the damage punishment does to the person punished and to the punisher.

Alleged Natural Consequences

Everyone can make predictions about the future, dire or rosy, as the situation demands. Our decisions depend on beliefs about the future, so an inexpensive way to influence people is to convince them that if they do things your way the result will be something they want. The trouble with this is that the future is highly *unpredictable* because what finally happens depends on much that is unknowable at the time of the prediction—on new discoveries, wars, revolutions, fads, and "acts of God." We never learn the whole truth about the consequences (if it even makes sense to talk about this) until it is too late, and even then we never learn what would have happened had we made different choices.

This is not to deny that rough predictions can be made, and issues decided on the basis of those predictions. It is only common sense not to build a nuclear reactor on a live volcano, but what about nuclear power itself? There, when we come to weigh the advantages and the disadvantages, the proponents and the opponents seem to be living in two different worlds. Whenever there is legitimate doubt and uncertainty, those who want things to go one way invariably find themselves believing just those predictions that happen to support their preferred alternative. The invention of fabricated threats was a milestone in the history of behavior modification. If I give you a physical threat, I have to be able to supply the force. If I give you an emotional threat, it will fail if you do not care. But if I tell you that certain actions will kill you, make you impotent, or make your hair fall out, then, if you believe me, you have a strong reason to avoid those actions.

Mythical Creatures and Gods

We must admire contemporary "doomsayers" who sit up with their flocks waiting for God to put an end to the world at the moment they have predicted. So far, they have all been disappointed, but at least they were not afraid to go out on a limb. If we threaten people with the end of the world or fire from the sky, we had better have some trick up our sleeve, or we will be discredited when nothing happens at the appointed time. It makes more sense to promise the rewards and punishments at unexpected times or, better yet, after death.

It is clear why divine punishment, karma, and other forms of postmortem justice are popular, but it is hard to say how much credit these threats and promises get for the peace and order we have enjoyed. Is it really only a fear of divine justice that keeps my fundamentalist friend from stealing my spare change? Finally, even if the threat of divine retribution does keep some people under control, we must balance any security that results from this method of control against the paranoia, ignorance, superstition, and fear its use requires and promotes.

Morality

Morality must be counted as another of the devices used to influence our behavior. A moralist who says that something is a duty is not saying that unless we do it we are going to get our neck broken, be reborn as a leech, or spend eternity in a bath of molten lead. When moralists say that something is a duty, or that a way of acting is morally right, they are telling us that it is something that, no matter what rewards or punishments gods and people promise, we ought to do, something we deserve to be blamed for not doing, something anyone in similar circumstances ought to do.

These ways of stating the matter, and others we have already considered, imply things we have no good reason to accept. Without a commitment to objectivity, morality amounts to little more than a request, and without prescriptivity, it makes no claim on our behavior. It is an open question how much effect morality actually has had on conduct, but it is clear (and disturbing) that moral rules and principles work better if they are accepted "mindlessly." Otherwise one simply learns how to rationalize disobedience as justifiable exception.

World-Views

It is one thing to control people by informing (or misinforming) them about some fact, and it is something else altogether to do so by giving them a complex and all-encompassing world-view. When Marcus Aurelius told himself that the world was designed, or when he thought of himself as a scattered fragment of a great mind that is everywhere, he was pushing himself into a fundamental gestalt that promotes cooperation, acceptance, and self-effacing responsibility. ("O world, I am in tune with every note of thy great harmony!") Stoic and Hindu pantheists, Christians who believe in innumerable souls, and atomists who believe only in matter and the void, see things as differently as if they inhabited different worlds. Even when their actions are similar, their justifications, rationalizations, and explanations differ predictably.

Mo Zi wanted to replace family and clan loyalties, which he correctly saw as a cause of civil strife in Zhou China, with what he called "universal love." He urged people to love each other as if they were of the same family, but he had no effective suggestions for bringing about this radical change. He told people that gods and ghosts would punish them if they failed to feel universal love, but since it is impossible to intimidate people into love, Mo failed.

The Buddhists, thanks to a world-view that included the doctrine of reincarnation, were able to generate reasons for loving strangers. In his introduction to Tsong-ka-pa's *Illumination of the Thought,* itself a commentary on Chandrakirti's *Supplement to the Middle Way,* Kensur Lekden (1900–1971), a Tantric abbot from Tibet, concludes that given infinite time, a finite number of souls, and reincarnation, it follows that in some former existence every present enemy was a friend, a loved one, perhaps even a mother. Consequently, he reasons, it is appropriate to love everyone as if they were our closest relative because in some former existence they were (Hopkins, 77–78).

Ideals and Slogans

It takes a considerable investment of time and energy to promote a general picture or conception of reality. It is far easier, and sometimes just as effective, to produce a memorable slogan. Great changes have been brought about, and countless people have been influenced, by powerful maxims, directives, principles, and slogans such as: "Never take anything not freely given," "A promise made is a debt unpaid," "No man is an island," and "Just do it!"

If the ideals are taken seriously and if the maxims and slogans are repeated often enough, they become part of our public and personal dogma and affect the way we act. They float about in our semi-consciousness, rising at appropriate and inappropriate times, almost like the voices of Jaynes's bicameral mind: "You deserve a break today," "It's a dog eat dog world," "All's fair in love and war."

A political advisor in India once formulated "the law of the fishes," which says: "The big ones eat the little ones." If people repeat and applaud this saying they will become more aggressive, and they will be more successful whenever ruthlessness brings success. More recently we have been told that "God helps those who help themselves," we have been advised to "Look out for Number One," and we have heard the judgment that no amoralist could make, "Greed is good." Such sayings erase guilt and can be flung at scruples and critics to rationalize conquest and exploitation.

Language

Language is powerful. Even those who reject emotivism allow that words are often charged positively or negatively. There are words we do, and words we do not, want applied to us—words that make us angry, proud, and ashamed. There are words that move us to action and words that freeze us in our tracks. Our ways of categorizing things are based on our words, and our version of reality is formed around the categories we develop and the metaphors and explanations we devise to make sense of experience. Most of us are pleased that we have learned to form linguistic representations, but there are those who think it has brought us trouble and cut us off from a more direct relationship to reality. When we turn to the topic of language in Chapter 14, we discuss some aspects of this dispute.

Guilt and Shame

One kind of guilt is legal. To be guilty is to be judged guilty after a prescribed hearing. But more often guilt is personal, a discomfort we feel when we believe we have hurt someone, an internalization of the anger we believe others would feel when we realize that we have failed to meet their requirements. *Moral* guilt, as it would be characterized by the moralist, is discomfort we ought to feel when we have done what we ought not to have done, or when we have neglected to do what we ought to have done.

Guilt, and the desire to avoid it, is a very powerful motivation. If I get tired enough of the way I feel when I look at my stack of unanswered letters, I may be moved to answer them. One way to avoid feeling bad for letting someone down is not to let them down. In its milder forms, guilt is not necessarily harmful, and when used with awareness it may have some motivational value. There is nothing wrong with refraining from saying something cruel because you know you would feel bad about hurting the victim of your remark—it is just that there are other motivations for the same restraint that might be more efficient and more reliable. For example, we may refrain from a cruel remark because we do not want to hurt the other person or, best of all, because such remarks never even occur to us.

So while there is a use for guilt, when parents, spouses, friends, and enemies use it as a technique of control, they capitalize on the desires of their victims not to cause suffering. If this form of compassion is called upon too often, it goes away or becomes distorted. Guilt used relentlessly as a form of control can become a parasite that feeds on and kills healthier reasons for acting.

Guilt is usually contrasted with shame, and sometimes much is made of the difference, which is fundamentally this: you feel guilt for letting someone else down and shame for letting yourself down. Both shame and guilt are used as forms of control, and both cause harm if used to excess. If we take our principles, standards, and goals seriously, then we do not have to be moralists to feel shame when we do not live up to them. But if we take them too seriously, we are capable of driving ourselves insane with shame for setbacks and lapses that others would consider insignificant.

Ritual

When Confucius urged those in authority to deal with people as if they were officiating at a great ritual, he was promoting a ceremonial adherence to established ways of doing things. Since almost all relationships in his world involved some kind of authority (ruler/subject, husband/wife, father/son), this advice was far-reaching. He thought that much trouble could be avoided if everyone would follow rules of propriety in their daily interactions.

We probably underestimate the extent of the rituals in our own lives. We indulge in them when we shake hands, bow, or do any of a thousand things that have become so automatic we rarely notice doing them. Whether it is a high mass or a high five, rituals bind individuals to groups and to one another. But there are costs when we push the ritualization of life to extremes. First, there is the ever-present danger that repressed feelings will explode with cataclysmic fury. And second, as behavior becomes ritualized there is a loss of spontaneity, and with it a loss of creativity and innovation. Rituals help us feel comfortable because they tell us exactly what to do. Like many other helpful devices, they are useful in their place, but dangerous when used mindlessly and without attention to the specifics of the situation.

Lies and Deception

A simple and cost-effective way to control people is to lie to them. Often the lie will not be discovered, and even when it is, it can be justified by appealing to the good it was expected to do. Deception may be involved in any of the forms of control we have already mentioned, but it need not be. We may intend to carry out our threats, believe in the power of gods to punish, and accept the moral bondage we promote—or we may not. When we do not, we join the propagandists who propose to control people with noble lies and convenient fictions.

Controlling others by manipulating their picture of the world is not uniquely human—non-human animals have their own forms of camouflage and deception—but we have raised the practice to an art, and to consciousness. Our human systems of linguistic and non-linguistic conventions give us an almost unlimited capacity to deceive and offer us countless ways to improve our situation by controlling the beliefs of others. Since we are aware how vulnerable we are to deception by those we trust, truthfulness and non-duplicity are very important to us. Trust is so vital for our cooperative enterprises that without it, no project will succeed. This topic too is taken up in more detail in Chapter 14.

Moral Fiction

'Moral fiction' is fiction that is deliberately created to teach a moral message, to provide moving examples of virtues and vices, to show us how to live. It includes fables, novels, television productions, films, and plays. Children's books have always been crafted to this end—urging children to save their souls, their pennies, their neighbors, their newspapers, or their planet. On television we cannot find a drama or sitcom without some moral message for the audience. It is unthinkable for the bad guy or the cause of the trouble not to receive his or her just deserts. Life should be so fair.

Summary

The previous discussion is not intended to be a handbook for manipulating other people, but everything that has been mentioned can be exploited to influence (educate, control, shape, direct, or guide) others. Not all of the practices and techniques of socialization and control we discuss are harmful, but some are, especially the ones that require deception or rely on physical or psychological violence. Compassionate moralists and amoralists alike will hesitate to use them. Much more needs to be said about each of the devices discussed, and about other devices not even mentioned. The better we understand them, the better we will understand why we act as we do.

It is the nature of the people to be orderly, but it is circumstances that cause disorder. Therefore, in the application of punishments, light offences should be regarded as serious; if light offences do not occur, serious ones have no chance of coming. This is said to be "ruling the people while in a state of law and order." . . . If the people are brave, they should be rewarded with what they desire; if they are timorous, they should be put to death in a manner they hate. (Shang Yang, in Duyvendak, 209)

The gods . . . favor the just and hate the unjust. And the favorite of Heaven may expect, in the fullest measure, all the blessings that heaven can give, save perhaps for some suffering entailed by offences in a former life. (Plato [4], 347)

"Calamity has come on you, my brethren, and, my brethren, you deserved it. . . . If today the plague is in your midst, that is because the hour has struck for taking thought. The just man need have no fear, but the evildoer has good cause to tremble. For plague is the flail of God and the world his threshing floor, and implacably he will thresh out his harvest until the wheat is separated from the chaff." (Camus [1], 81–82)

The great masses of the people . . . more easily fall a victim to a big lie than to a little one, since they themselves lie in little things, but would be ashamed of lies that were too big. Such a falsehood will never enter their heads, and they will not be able to believe in the possibility of such monstrous effrontery and infamous representation in others. (Hitler, 231)

The purpose of our meeting today is precisely to ensure that literature and art fit well into the whole revolutionary machine as a component part, that they operate as powerful weapons for uniting and educating the people and for attacking and destroying the enemy, and that they help the people fight the enemy with one heart and one mind. (Mao, 70)

If the principles of Yang and Mo are not stopped, and if the principles of Confucius are not brought to light, perverse doctrines will delude the people and obstruct the path of humanity and righteousness. When humanity and righteousness are obstructed, beasts will be led on to devour men, and men will devour one another. (Mencius, in Chan [1], 72)

Faced with the sheer quantity of suffering in the world, it is tempting to believe that the plight of the sick and hungry will only be relieved when society and morality are transformed and to take refuge in a utopian philosophy. But if we wish to grapple with the problem, we must make use of the tools we possess to construct persuasive arguments for social change, and among the most powerful of these implements is our existing morality. . . . A convincing argument will therefore have to be parasitic on the beliefs we already hold; and to argue in a constructive spirit for a more extensive duty to relieve harm, we will be well-advised to begin by asking what well-entrenched aspects of our current morality lend themselves to this task. (Susan James, 15–16)

Force and Control

To interact is to influence. By talking to, working with, and just being around other people we affect them and they us. Sometimes the influence is planned and sometimes it is inadvertent, but unless we live alone on an island, our concepts and our words, our actions and our inactions, play a causal role in the lives of those they touch. Strategies for dealing with other people, who seem never to do or be exactly what we would have them do or be, range from non-coercive to dictatorial. Those attracted to a more passive style of interaction are reluctant to apply force and prefer to cooperate and to compromise. Those on the active side prefer to do things their way; they want others to harmonize with them.

The Legalists

Hard-liners emphasize control, as do those whose approach to life is primarily in what Deikman calls the action mode, and describes as "a state organized to manipulate the environment." The Legalists were strong advocates of force. It was Han Fei Zi who insisted that "awe-inspiring power can prohibit violence" and that "virtue and kindness are insufficient to end disorder." What one wants to say about this is: "Well, yes and no." The unification of China was accomplished by Qin Shi Huangdi, a very strong leader who, by following the advice of the Legalists, ended the civil war, established order, standardized writing and axle sizes, and smashed feudalism. That is why we feel like saying "yes". On the other hand, the empire lasted fifteen years, and when the First Emperor died, his heir was murdered and the members of his "household" were at each others' throats. They could have used a little "virtue and kindness."

Confucius and the Confucians

Confucians were less deeply involved with force than were the Legalists, but they were still very interested in controlling the lives of the citizens. Confucius did not think humans were evil, and many Confucians believed in education and example. Compared with those of the Legalists, their methods were non-coercive and flexible, but when we compare them with the Daoists, we have to say that the Confucians were still very much advocates of control and were as concerned as the Legalists to shape humans to fit a pattern they saw as ideal.

Plato

Xun Zi and his Legalist students thought humans were fundamentally evil, and hence they were more interested in taking control of their development than was Mencius, who thought that if we just stand back, everyone's intrinsically good heart will lead them to choose the right path without any coercion. Plato, who is neither as cold-blooded as the Legalists, nor as optimistic as Mencius, is notorious for the amount of control he would give to his rulers. He devises a plan to educate a class of philosopher-kings who are wise enough be trusted to employ "the medicine of the lie" when they judge it is needed for the good of the country. For example, when it comes to marriage and child-bearing, the Rulers are to be called upon to "administer a large dose of that medicine we spoke of earlier" (Plato [4], 158). Plato has Socrates prescribe a mating festival with a lottery rigged to guarantee that "there should be as many unions of the best of both sexes, and as few of the inferior, as possible." Only the rulers are to know of this ruse; "otherwise," he says, "our herd of Guardians [the Auxiliaries] may become rebellious" (159). Socrates adds that while both true and fictitious stories are to be used in education, "we shall begin our education with the fictitious kind" (68). Other deceptive practices occur in the testing of young Guardians, and wherever the Rulers think their use is indicated.

Someone who hopes to regulate the behavior of people by manipulating their information is just as surely a proponent of control as is someone who uses awe-inspiring power, indoctrination, or automatic weapons. Their tools are different, but not their aim of causing others to do things they would not choose to do if they were free and informed.

Control and Harmony

Control has its place. But just as we can never satisfy all of our desires, so we can never get the world to proceed exactly according to our script. No matter how hard we try, we never get our way more than some of the time. But if it is foolish to try to control everything, it is also a mistake to drift like a cloud. Daoists who speak of getting things done by *wu wei* are not talking about mindless, unstructured drifting. The advice that we deal with problems before they arise, or while they are still small, tells us how to control things with a minimum of effort. A proponent of what can be called "The Way of Harmony" knows that there are times to take control and times to yield, and that we can only find out which is which by understanding the situation. This includes understanding how others understand it. Such understanding is almost impossible when we are bewitched by desires, emotions, language, prejudice, propaganda, or power.

> The greatest principle of all is that nobody, whether male or female, should be without a leader. Nor should the mind of anybody be habituated to letting him do anything at all on his own initiative; neither out of zeal, nor even playfully. But in war and in the midst of peace—to his leader he shall direct his eye and follow him faithfully. And even in the smallest matter he should stand under leadership. For example, he should get up, or move, or wash, or take his meals . . . only if he has been told to do so. In a word, he should teach his soul, by long habit, never to dream of acting independently, and to become utterly incapable of it. (Plato, quoted in Popper, 7)

> From this a dispute arises whether it is better to be loved than feared, or the reverse. The answer is that one would want to be both the one and the other; but because it is difficult to put them

> together, it is much safer to be feared than loved, if one has to lack one of the two. . . . And men have less hesitation to offend one who makes himself loved than one who makes himself feared; for love is held by a chain of obligation, which, because men are wicked, is broken at every opportunity for their own utility, but fear is held by a dread of punishment that never forsakes you. (Machiavelli, 66–67)

The Way of Harmony

D. T. Suzuki illustrates one of the differences between Eastern and Western approaches to nature by comparing a poem by the seventeenth-century Japanese poet Basho with some verses by the nineteenth-century British poet Alfred Tennyson (Suzuki, 1–3). Basho's poem is a seventeen-syllable *haiku*:

> When I look carefully
> I see the *nazuna* blooming
> By the hedge!

Tennyson's verses also deal with a flower:

> Flower in the crannied wall,
> I pluck you out of the crannies;—
> Hold you here, root and all, in my hand,
> Little flower—but if I could understand
> What you are, root and all, and all in all,
> I should know what God and man is.

Basho looks, Tennyson plucks. Tennyson tries to understand, Basho experiences. Tennyson kills the flower, Basho does not touch it. Suzuki says that Basho "lets an exclamation point say everything he wishes to say" (Suzuki, 3). Tennyson not only wants to understand the flower, he wants to use it to satisfy his epistemological lust to understand everything else, even God and man.

Suzuki says that Tennyson exemplifies the Western mind, which is analytical, discriminating, objective, scientific, conceptual, organizing, individualistic, power wielding, and disposed to impose its will on others. Basho, on the other hand, represents the Eastern mind, which, according to Suzuki, is synthetic, non-discriminating, subjective, non-systematic, intuitive, non-discursive, and interested in harmonious solutions to problems. But while Suzuki's generalizations are accurate about some Westerners and some Easterners, and certainly well-illustrated by the two poems, they may mislead us. It is not East or West that determines whether people respond from the action or the reception mode but the habits and traits they acquire as they are socialized.

Hemispheric Specialization, Dominance, and Imperialism

The hypothesis of hemispheric *specialization* assigns different tasks to the hemispheres of the brain. The left hemisphere is said to be logical, linear, and linguistic, the home of verbalized thought; and the right hemisphere is characterized as intuitive, holistic, and good at solving spatial and relational problems. When researchers believed that all the important work was done by the left hemisphere, they spoke of left hemisphere *dominance*. Since the left hemisphere controls the right side of the body, a physical manifestation of left-hemisphere dominance is right-handedness (and one of right-hemisphere dominance is left-handedness).

Left-hemisphere dominance may be the price we pay for our linguistic and logical abilities, and as a strategy for coping it has not fared so badly. But when discussions turn into arguments, and arguments into debates; when we insist on explicit definitions rather than overall clarity; when we become compulsive talkers, planners, and categorizers, left-hemisphere dominance has metamorphosed into left-hemisphere *imperialism*.

The very fact that we find the first efforts to control excessive verbalization and conceptualization in India and China should warn us against saying that Indians or Chinese are less dependent on words and concepts than Westerners. If they did not also have "monkey-minds" filled with random thoughts and needless verbalizations, there would have been no need for them to have developed yoga and meditation, or to have attacked conceptualization and verbalization. Many of the practices developed by the Hindus, Buddhists, and Daoists—the various forms of meditation, the mantras, the monotonous chanting—were designed to silence our verbalized thoughts, to quiet our calculating consciousness, to "pacify our minds," to smash what we have now identified as imperialism of the left hemisphere.

Smashing Hemispheric Imperialism

In Zen Buddhism and Daoism we find a preference for the relatively pure receptive approach expressed in Basho's poem; but even someone who takes this approach will supplement the wordless appreciation with a careful use of language. Note that Basho calls a nazuna a "*nazuna*" and a hedge a "*hedge*." The Zen Buddhist mistrusts arguments and avoids nebulous concepts but is comfortable with words when they are used, as Ludwig Wittgenstein says, in the language games that are their original homes.

Because words are important, it makes absolutely no sense to escape domination by the left hemisphere only to be taken over by the right, which is what would happen if we were to replace our oververbalization with silence. The hours of meditation recommended by the Buddhists are designed to quiet the nervous activity of *both* hemispheres. Only when we have learned to be still, to observe, and to wait is the way cleared for us to act and speak spontaneously and appropriately.

Imperialism of the left hemisphere can lock us into rigid and confining social structures, and it is particularly hard on personal relationships, which require flexibility and much non-verbal understanding. It is implicated in bad ideas like slavery, the subjugation of women, and political imperialism. But, harmful as it may have been, imperialism of the left hemisphere is well protected and deeply rooted. It is not easy to argue against arguments, or to find words to criticize language. Nevertheless, some have found their way through the verbal and conceptual maze by which language protects its power and have learned to attend to things other than the words in their heads and the stories they have been told (and tell themselves) about who they are and what is going on.

If rigid concepts and simple explanations keep us from seeing clearly, then we will have to loosen up our concepts and deepen our explanations. When we have broken the grip of left-hemisphere imperialism, we will be in a position to develop a receptive and informed mind that uses, but is not used by, language. Fortunately, there are techniques available to help us do this. Yoga, meditation, the martial arts, and chanting praise to Kṛṣṇa quiet our inner verbalization, displace disturbing emotions, restrict our rational operations, and open the way for intuitive insights and creative processing.

Yoga and meditation can also be used to oppose imperialism of the *right* hemisphere, the home of emotional responses and intuitions. If our choices are guided by irrational fears or by intuitions that scorn our hard-won linguistic knowledge, then we will end up hurting ourselves and our friends. The strength we acquire through various forms of inner conditioning steadies us in the wake of sudden onslaughts of emotion and intuition. Only if we are stable enough to *attend* to these events without leaping to a response can we begin to distinguish between those that deserve our attention and those that do not.

When we smash imperialism of either hemisphere, we give the other hemisphere its job back, and, at the same time, we free the perpetrator of the imperialism from self-designated but excessive responsibilities. We are after balance. We want our hemispheres to work together—harmoniously. When it is time for logic we want logic, and when it is time for intuition we want intuition. If a fear is groundless, we want that to matter, but if it is the result of some correct insight, we want to be open enough to realize it. The techniques of mind control developed in the East were designed to help us achieve this sort of balance by teaching us how to restrain both the noisy verbal chatter of the left hemisphere and the relating and emoting of the right. Just as the distinct images presented by our two eyes are resolved into a three-dimensional representation, something analogous happens when we harmonize our linguistic and our nonlinguistic understanding into a comprehensive vision beyond, but not without, words. Hemispheric imperialists of both sorts are trying to get a clear view by closing one eye.

Reprogramming for Harmony

We would be wise to reflect on our ways of interacting with the world and its inhabitants. How are we controlled by others and how do we control them? What devices do we use to get our way and to shape the character and actions of others, and do these devices have dangerous side effects? There is a natural tendency for us, being users of language, to overdo the emphasis on categorization and control, which is why so many of our serious problems can be traced to excessive left-brain activity. We conceptualize to the point of stereotype. We apply our local standards and superficial explanations, distorting the past, oversimplifying the present, and trying to shape the future. We construct a reality in which events and people are in many ways imaginary—the products of our needs, our ignorance, and our conceptualizations. We buy into systems of belief and discovery that make us deny the evidence of our senses and that remove us from the world we inhabit.

Most forms of meditation and concentration are designed to teach us ways out of the conceptual prisons and torture chambers we have constructed for ourselves. They help us still our minds, neutralize our linguistically nourished stereotypes, and see things with fresh eyes. Even a little progress in this direction will enable us to assimilate more information and to construct an improved version of events. Clean and copious information will improve our decision making, trigger our natural compassion, and make it relatively safe for us to trust our spontaneous impulses. We all stand to gain if we can diminish conflict by seeking internal harmony among our various impulses, and external harmony with others. The question is, "How do we do this?"

When the *Bhagavad Gītā* told people that by repeating the name of Kṛṣṇa they could secure his presence and his help, it offered those who believe in Kṛṣṇa a powerful technique that will produce results whether Kṛṣṇa actually exists or not. Not everyone can sit in meditation for seven years, or even for twenty minutes, but anyone can repeat a name, or some short verse over and over again. The surprising and wonderful thing is that many immediate beneficial effects can flow from this minimal effort. Whoever focuses on and repeats Kṛṣṇa's name (or any sound at all) will, at the very least, be distracted from problems and worries. Those who think Kṛṣṇa possesses and then works through them will feel no fear of making a mistake, no guilt, and at the same time will be open to their intuition. Chanting, praying, and whistling in the dark calm us down by distracting us from nagging worries and fears. Even the device of counting to ten when angry is an elementary application of this method. For those who do not feel comfortable appealing to a divine being or taking up meditation or Yoga, there are other paths that lead to a more harmonious style of life. Anyone suffering from symptoms of left-hemisphere imperialism can follow a simple, four-step, totally secular program to achieve a more harmonious balance of active and passive tendencies.

The first step in reprogramming for harmony is to admit in clear and unequivocal words that this is our intention. We have to admit, if only to ourselves, that we are out of balance; that we think or talk too much; that we pay insufficient attention to what others are doing, saying, or feeling; and that we are victims of our prejudices, desires, emotions, and concepts.

The second step, which may involve considerable struggle, is to learn to "look carefully." We can never harmonize with reality if our version of it is distorted by defensive reactions and rigid categories. We do not have to look to the East to hear this suggestion. Actually it is just common sense, and yet it is the cornerstone of the receptive mode and the Way of Harmony. Marcus Aurelius reminds himself to work on it in his *Meditations*.

> Do away with all fancies. Cease to be passion's puppet. Limit time to the present. Learn to recognize every experience for what it is, whether it be your own or another's. (Marcus Aurelius, 110)

> Fix your thought closely on what is being said, and let your mind enter fully into what is being done, and into what is doing it. (Marcus Aurelius, 110)

> Never go beyond the sense of your original impressions. These tell you that such-and-such a person is speaking ill of you; that was their message; they did not go on to say it has done you any harm. I see my child is ill; my eyes tell me that, but they do not suggest that his life is in danger. Always, then, keep to the original impressions; supply no additions of your own, and you are safe. Or at least, add only a recognition of the great world-order by which all things are brought to pass. (Marcus Aurelius, 132)

The Chinese Chan Master Huangbo (Huang Po) offers a Buddhist version of the same advice when he uses a vivid image to encourage us not to go beyond our original impression.

> Observe things as they are and don't pay attention to other people. There are some people just like mad dogs barking at everything that moves, even barking when the wind stirs among the grass and leaves. (Blofeld [1], 54)

The third step in reprogramming for harmony is to bring ourselves to accept the workings of the "great world-order by which all things are brought to pass." Suppose we have prepared for a picnic and it rains. We can either accept the storm and without grumbling adapt to the new situation, or we can come to think that not only our plans but our *day* has been spoiled. One who understands the Way of Harmony does not worry about spoiled plans and does not have spoiled days. Nobody can take the third step without taking the second. If we are incapable of appreciating the interesting quality and variety of the alternatives, we will never be flexible enough to enjoy them.

So far we have been talking only about learning to comprehend and accept situations as they are. Nothing yet has been said about deciding or doing. But the amazing thing is that when we have taken care of the first three steps, the fourth takes care of itself. Comprehending and accepting are the very things that make it possible for us to trust our spontaneous actions and decisions. If we have not been purified by a dose of relatively accurate and unbiased information, our program is filled with glitches; if we have, we are ready to decide without calculation and to act without action.

Here the analogy between life and certain of the arts practiced in the East is informative. One of the best popular books about Zen Buddhism is Eugen Herrigel's *Zen in the Art of Archery*. It is no secret that the desire to do well can interfere with our performance. So can idle thoughts, worries, fears, and excessive deliberation and planning. Before students of archery were even allowed to pick up a bow they were taught to be calm and to empty their minds—to breathe, to wait, and to pay attention. When Herrigel's teacher finally allows him to work with a bow, he tells him that

> the shot will only go smoothly when it takes the archer himself by surprise. It must be as if the bowstring suddenly cut through the thumb that held it. You mustn't open the right hand on purpose. (Herrigel, 29)

On another occasion, the Master admonishes the stubborn and intellectualizing Westerner with the following words:

> "The right art," cried the Master, "is purposeless, aimless! The more obstinately you try to learn how to shoot the arrow for the sake of hitting the goal, the less you will succeed in the one and the further the other will recede. What stands in your way is that you have a much too willful will. You think that what you do not do yourself does not happen." (Herrigel, 31)

With a "too willful will" we fail for trying too much, too hard, or too soon.

One of the main causes of failure is a misapprehension of the situation. We may try too hard because we think success matters more than it does, or try too much because we overestimate our resources, support, or strategy. If we "look carefully" we are less likely to make these mistakes, and less likely to make inflexible or unrealistic demands on ourselves and others. When we understand our situation in the way promoted by the second and third steps, decisions come when it is time for them to come. Our job is to prepare ourselves with unbiased information and deep understanding. The better we do this, the more pleased we are going to be with the results of the decisions that spontaneously emerge from "who knows where?"

Examples and Exercises

The best way to examine the Way of Harmony is to try it. Even someone addicted to control can learn to let go briefly, just to see how it feels. Here you will find a few easy exercises anyone can perform to experience a taste of the fruits of harmony. They have to do with "looking carefully" and appreciating the contribution of the remainder of the universe.

Weather. We cannot control the weather at all, so this is a good case with which to illustrate the advantages of the Way of Harmony. The first exercise is to accept the weather, whatever it is, without grumbling. For a day, or for as long as you can, stop complaining about the cold, the heat, the rain, or the snow. Achieving meteorological harmony does not mean going without a coat in the winter, or taking no measures to keep cool in the summer. On the contrary, the exercise is designed to encourage an appropriate response to weather; that response will be one that does not include annoyance or anger. If we simply go about our business and treat the cold or the heat as a neutral, if uncomfortable, aspect of the situation, we will nor suffer twice—we will just be cold or hot.

It goes without saying that it is not a good idea to try this exercise for the first time in a hurricane, or when the temperature exceeds one hundred degrees. But if we can learn to accept average bad weather without complaint, we can go further and reinforce this newfound harmony by doing something pleasant that is made possible by the unexpected or undesired weather. If our picnic was washed out by the rain, then we can read, listen to music, walk in the rain, take a nap, go to a movie, or visit our favorite mall—thanks to the rain.

Bees and Other Dangerous Animals. People say that if you do not threaten bees they will not sting you. Perhaps bees can sense or smell fear, and perhaps not, but they can certainly sense hostility behind frantic attempts to swat them. Who is more likely to get stung, someone who lashes out at every bee that comes within swinging distance, or someone who routinely ignores, normal non-hostile bee behavior?

The first exercise set us the task of finding harmony with an aspect of inanimate nature. Now we can turn to animate nature. To make the exercise interesting forget about loveable animals like pandas, baby seals, whales, and dolphins, and even domestic favorites like dogs, cats, and birds. These animals are too hard to dislike, so let us turn to the more difficult cases. If you dislike snakes, spiders, bats, or rats, take the trouble to learn more about them. Watch them as they go about their business. Throw away stereotypes, loathing, and fear. There are so many kinds of snakes and spiders, with so many different behavior patterns, it may not even be possible to hate them all. The payoff comes when we learn to admire rather than loathe some creature, and when our first impulse is no longer to kill.

Some of the most dangerous and disagreeable animals alive turn out to be members of our own species, so there is no need to limit this exercise to non-humans. We have stereotypes about humans too—racial, cultural, social, and gender stereotypes. When we have learned to like, or at least to respect, bats or beetles, we can move on to human beings.

Driving a Car. On a freeway, fast-moving cars change lanes, merge, adjust to each other, and usually stay out of accidents. When things are going well the process is fascinating to observe, and a delight to participate in. We can, in this potentially dangerous situation, find trust, care, attention, compromise, and real rewards in striving for harmony. The exercise is to drive your car for a day (or even an hour) more harmoniously than usual. Look for opportunities to yield to pedestrians and to other drivers, stop for someone who wants to pull out of a parking space. Experience the gratitude and friendly feelings of those to whom you have shown a small courtesy and then drive on, searching for another victim on which to inflict your consideration.

Once again a warning is in order. Just as it is not wise to present a swarm of enraged killer bees with Buddhist tranquillity, it may be equally unwise to try to drive courteously on some New York streets or Los Angeles freeways. The point of mentioning these exercises is to suggest simple ways to sample the flavor of harmony. Someone who tries them under circumstances that guarantee their failure probably does not want to sample harmony.

Looking at Things from a Different Point of View. In Chapter 3 a distinction is made between *taking* a point of view and *looking at something* from a point of view. Even atheists can *look at* things from the religious point of view by imagining (or remembering) themselves as believers, and then asking how they would (or did) understand and respond to events. When we look at things from the point of view of self-interest or of morality, we determine what the self-interested or the moral solution to a problem is. When we look at things from the point of view of our child, our partner, our neighbor, or our opponent, we try to imagine how they see and interpret things and how they feel.

While there is a difference between defending a position and looking at things from the point of view that contains that position, the easiest way to begin to appreciate a different point of view may be to try to support the claims typically made by those who occupy that point of view. When we try to argue for an alternative opinion, we are forced to find out something about how people who hold that position actually think. So, as an exercise, practice arguing the case of someone with whom you do not agree. If you do this well, you may even develop some sympathy for that opinion and respect for the person who holds it.

Listening and Silence. There are times when it is hard to be silent, but listening (like oratory) is a skill that can be learned. There is much to recommend listening as a habit, but for now just consider it as an exercise. Warm up by giving your full attention to a report on National Public Radio. Do not drift off or argue with what you hear—just listen. To do this we have to know how to be quiet, how to focus on what is happening, and how to allow our thoughts (what we are thinking) to be controlled by someone else. We will know we have succeeded at this when the words coming from the radio determine the structure and the content of the experience. Do not think this is easy—being able to focus on one thing lies at the heart of all meditation.

When we can listen to a voice on the radio without wandering off into our private thoughts, it is time to try our skill on real people. The advantage of our warm-up exercise is that the inclination to answer the radio is reduced to a minimum, if not extinguished. We cannot listen if we are busy preparing an answer to what is being said, or to what we imagine is being said. To listen carefully, we must achieve a kind of emptiness, we must become like the clear mirror that reflects with a minimum of distortion. But the exercise is to listen carefully, not to become a conversational zombie. A careful and skillful listener will know when to listen, when to encourage the speaker with questions, and when to talk.

Yielding and Compromising. In Chapter 6 we encounter the Confucian virtue of *rang*, which involves deference, or yielding precedence. We do not achieve harmony unless we yield, for we cannot expect reality, in its animate or inanimate form, to follow our lead.

This exercise is simple: Give in on some matter. Against your desire, or even your better judgment, let someone do something their way, and do this with grace and appropriate enthusiasm, not with sullen and grudging cooperation. More than half the time you will be pleasantly surprised at how well things go. (If it happens that you are a person who always yields, then perhaps your exercise should be to hold firm on some matter, or to take control.)

Resolving Conflicts

As long as society is composed of people, there will be conflicts of interest. We all have our beliefs, hopes, claims, aims, and desires, and they often clash. There are many ways to deal with these conflicts, but nearly everyone admits that there is a sense in which we all start off equal. Many moralists and all amoralists would say that the poorest, dirtiest, most ordinary person in the world is worth no less than any king, queen, president, pope, or media star. This is our moral equivalence as rational beings, children of God, or receptacles of pleasure and pain. For the moralist this is because humans are equally valuable, but for the amoralist it is because all ideas of value have been left behind.

When we are prepared to recognize other people as moral (or amoral) equals and willing to try to look at things from their point of view, which requires that we shut up and listen to what they are saying about their priorities and their lives, then hard problems become easy. When this sort of consideration is mutual, hard problems disappear.

Imagine now that you have made substantial progress along the path of harmony. Your assessor has been, if not silenced, at least quieted; your mind is steadier and calmer; you have developed an openness to the details and circumstances of situations; and you have a greater awareness of your own motivations. Because of these changes, you will probably get along better with others, have fewer conflicts, and get into less trouble. You will also be likely to cause others less unhappiness and to perform tasks better, and you may even have better health and a longer life. This is not to say that anyone who moves any distance in the direction of harmony will inevitably be happier. Sometimes, in difficult environments or unfortunate circumstances, the result will be unhappiness, pain, or even death. Everything is a risk. But in the majority of cases we can say with certainty that harmony pays.

14

Language, Truth, and Non-Duplicity

> Then away with all malice and deceit, away with all pretence and jealousy and recrimination of every kind!
>
> —*1 Peter 2:1*

Language

LANGUAGE IS CUSTOM-MADE for the task of promoting the traits and behavior we want to see. Even in its rudimentary forms, language conveys behavior-relevant information and expresses commands, demands, and reprimands. Our threats are intensified by our ability to describe undesirable situations, and no consequence, dire or desired, can be predicted unless it can first be described. Words make possible our belief in gods and in morality, and without them we have no coherent version of our place in the social and natural world.

From linguistic philosophers and philosophers of language we learn how important and powerful language is, and how easy it is to mislead ourselves and others when we abuse the power of words. Ludwig Wittgenstein goes so far as to say that philosophy is "a battle against the bewitchment of our intelligence by means of language" (Wittgenstein [1], I §109).

The imagined simplicity of the relation between a "name" and its object may have led some philosophers to hold that all meaningful words refer to things. G. E. Moore was operating under the influence of this error when he reasoned that if 'good' does not denote something simple, it either denotes something complex, or else "means nothing at all, and there is no such subject as Ethics" (Moore, 15).

Other philosophers, also misled by simplistic accounts of meaning, set out to discover what meanings are. Strange kinds of things—ideas, concepts, classes, relations, thoughts, propositions—were identified as meanings. The word 'dog', for example, was said to have the concept, idea, or image of a dog as its meaning. Wittgenstein, who had helped philosophers get into this trouble, pointed the way out. He advised us to turn our attention from meaning to *use*. "A main source of our failure to understand," he said, "is that we do not *command a clear view* of the use of our words" (Wittgenstein [1], I §122). He saw philosophy at its best as a kind of therapy that helps us see how the philosophical problems that befuddle us arise when we use ordinary words like 'refer', 'meaning', or 'know' in extraordinary ways.

We now take a brief look at some ideas about the origin of language and its place in our world; we then ask how conceptualization and speech help us, and how they harm us. Finally, we investigate the suggestion that we can avoid the harm by "eliminating" some of our concepts.

If we create "an intelligible and manageable world" by constructing a version of events, then one efficient way to control others is to manipulate their versions. While there is no such thing as "the whole truth," and while we need not expect "total honesty" from anyone, we hope and even expect that we will not be deceived by those with whom we interact. We want non-duplicitous associates, but, as we shall see, what counts as duplicity varies from situation to situation, depending on the conventions and expectations we develop. In the final sections of this chapter we consider the nature of non-duplicity and its place in a world without morality.

The Origin of Language

Richard E. Leakey and Roger Lewin argue that we gained our ability to speak as we developed ever more complex social organizations. They say this process began as long as three million years ago, and that we may have had rich language skills for a million years (Leakey and Lewin [2], chap. 10). But there are other opinions. Julian Jaynes claims that we did not even start developing language until around forty thousand years ago; and Jacob Bronowski splits the difference when he says that "it is unlikely that human speech as we know it is even as old as half a million years" (Bronowski, 23). More recently, Roger Lewin observes that by the time *homo sapiens* evolved (perhaps two hundred thousand years ago), language was clearly a possibility. He adds that since "the creation of paintings, carvings, and engravings is surely unthinkable in the absence of language," we can conclude that language has been in use for at least thirty thousand years, and he suggests that it may have been in use long before that (Lewin, 186).

The Nature and Use of Language

What does language do for us? Bronowski says that because we have language "we have built a world of outside objects, a world which does not exist for animals" (Bronowski, 38). According to Jaynes, each new stage of words "*literally created new perceptions and attentions*" (Jaynes, 132). Leakey and Lewin agree with Jaynes and Bronowski, and add that "it makes good biological sense to see language as a rather useful by-product of an ever sharpening pressure to understand and manipulate the components of the environment." Because we use names and form concepts, they say, we create "a more sharply delineated world" inside our heads (Leakey and Lewin [1], 204). This improves our ability to imagine, to look back into the past, and to project into the future.

The effect of language on the social world may be even more profound than its effect on our relation to the physical world. The problems of finding food and shelter are simple compared to the difficulties we encounter trying to deal with other people, and with their attempts to deal with us. We needed a keener consciousness, a linguistic consciousness, Lewin suggests, "so that we could understand—and perhaps manipulate—others better" (Lewin, 174).

Words are important, but a full account of why we do what we do would include more than information about the words we and others say to and about ourselves. We respond to clues that cannot be put into words, and employ skills that transcend our conscious awareness. We process and collate information without knowing we are doing so, and we have intuitive, non-linguistic, and non-rational ways of dealing with situations.

John Searle has written about the complex and often unconscious assumptions, presuppositions, capacities, and practices on which our lives are built. An intention to do something can only exist in a "network" of beliefs and desires, and "most of this Network," he claims, "is submerged in the unconscious and we don't quite know how to dredge it up" (Searle, 142). Even deeper than these unconscious assumptions is "the Background," which is "a set of skills, stances, preintentional assumptions and presuppositions, practices, and habits" that underlie our ability to think or speak about things (Searle, 146–47, 154).

Our use of language in structuring reality and in communicating relies to a surprising extent on metaphor and other non-literal devices. The linguist George Lakoff and the philosopher Mark Johnson emphasize the role of metaphors in our perception of, interaction with, and thought about the world. Metaphors are not mere matters of style and decoration because "our ordinary conceptual system, in terms of which we both think and act, is fundamentally metaphorical in nature" (Lakoff and Johnson [1], 3). Metaphors form systems that enable us to comprehend one thing in terms of another. In this way we emphasize some features of a thing and obscure others. If we "live by" the metaphor ARGUMENT IS WAR, we will argue differently from someone who favors ARGUMENT IS CONVERSATION, or ARGUMENT IS DANCE. The ARGUMENT IS WAR metaphor gives rise to countless ordinary expressions:

> Your claims are *indefensible*.
> He *attacked every weak point* in my argument.
> His criticisms were *right on target*.
> I *demolished* his argument.
> I've never *won* an argument with him.
> You disagree? Okay, *shoot*!
> If you use that *strategy*, he'll *wipe you out*.
> He *shot down* all of my arguments.
>
> (Lakoff and Johnson [1], 4)

After considering a variety of metaphorical systems, Lakoff and Johnson argue that "in all aspects of life, not just in politics or in love, we define our reality in terms of metaphor, and then proceed to act on the basis of the metaphor" (Lakoff and Johnson [2], 322).

Consider, for example, the metaphor of bondage so popular with moralists, who seem to believe that moral principles exert a kind of objective but surmountable force, a "moral gravity" pulling everyone in the right direction. Many metaphors serve the moralist cause—morality as a guide, a quest, a set of laws; or a "good will" as something that "like a jewel, shines by its own light." Thinking of value as a "substance" or a "property" leads us to think of it as present in things, as quantifiable, objective, and comparable.

The Good News

Language makes a real difference to what a being can do. Learning a language is like acquiring a new sense, or like learning to read minds. Language lets us tell others things that could be conveyed in no other way. With language we preserve complex lessons from the past, make plans about the future, and fix past, present, and future in a comprehensible story. With language we clarify, transmit, and promote rules. When we learn the words for things we gain power over them—the power that comes from being able to generalize.

Words bring order to a reality that would otherwise be overwhelming. If you look up from this page, your entire visual field will be filled with objects you can either name or describe—the wall, a chair, a computer, a paper clip on the rug. Nothing is nameless. Now that we live in a sea of named things, it may be impossible to imagine what the experience of beings without language might be like. It is certainly not like what happens when we experience a wordless moment or forget a name.

The Bad News

Words and concepts help us make sense of what is happening, but they also lead us to ignore features of the objects and events we use them to describe. We call a person friendly, honest, sneaky, or brave—and from then on, we deal with this person as with a person of that kind, and we interpret his or her behavior as the behavior of a person of that kind. Our projections create new evidence for our categorizations, and our categorizations govern our projections. As a result, we overlook change, and then respond in inappropriate ways.

The first bit of bad news, then, is that we can become the victims of our own categories, creating a world that bears little relation to everyday reality, and one that calls forth incongruous and potentially disastrous behavior. But there is more to worry about. Words and concepts make explanation possible, but at the same time they make it easy to offer simplistic explanations for complex events and states:

We went to war over oil.
I am angry with him because he insulted me.
She sacrificed her future because she loved him.
He became a skinhead because he hated strangers.

While these familiar types of explanations may point to relevant factors or illuminate events, they are often wrong and always absurdly simple. In Chapter 13 we see that even when such explanations are not completely mistaken, they tempt us to stop asking questions much too early.

The more closely we look at our simple explanations, and at the vague and loaded concepts we use in constructing them, the clearer it becomes that language is not an infallible instrument for making sense of the world. It may create "a more sharply delineated world inside our heads," but it also allows us to be lazy, dull, and literal.

A bad experience with a co-worker might lead us to decide that he is giving us a hard time because he hates us. This explanation simplifies the situation, and it locates the source of the trouble in an irrational feeling on the part of the *other* person. But the truth is that all behavior has multiple and complex causes, and people who do things we do not like are sometimes responding to things we have done. We are better off if we know this, as the Buddha indicated when he said that whoever sees causality sees the *Dharma*.

So, while our words help us construct a story of the universe, without which we would be lost, they tempt us to neglect important details, and to be satisfied with generalizations, easy answers, stereotypes, and slogans. If we are not careful, we will become victims of this "useful tool," befuddled and manipulated by words and by those who use them to control what we feel, think, and do.

Does this mean that we should stop verbalizing our reality—abandon words and explanations? This seems to be the advice of the Chan master Huangbo.

> Let there be a silent understanding and no more. Away with all thinking and explaining. (Blofeld [1], 34)

> Do not deceive yourselves with conceptual thinking, and do not look anywhere for the truth, for all that is needed is to refrain from allowing concepts to arise. (Blofeld [1], 75)

It is also the advice of his student Hui Hai, who tells us that "right thinking" is refraining from thinking in terms of good and evil, sorrow and joy, beginning and end, acceptance and rejection, likes and dislikes, aversion and love. More positively, he says:

> You should know that setting forth the principle of deliverance in its entirety amounts only to this—WHEN THINGS HAPPEN, MAKE NO RESPONSE: KEEP YOUR MINDS FROM DWELLING ON ANYTHING WHATSOEVER: KEEP THEM FOR EVER STILL AS THE VOID AND UTTERLY PURE (WITHOUT STAIN): AND THEREBY SPONTANEOUSLY ATTAIN DELIVERANCE. (Blofeld [2], 78)

When we are urged to work for a silent understanding it is because words can blind us to what is before our eyes, or bind us to our habitual roles and responses. But any "silent understanding" a fluent speaker manages to attain will flow from a comprehensive wordless appreciation *and* a language-structured representation. It may be a silent understanding, but it will not be one developed in ignorance of what can be said.

"When things happen, make no response." We now know that this is not advice to stand around like a statue or a camcorder. Remember that *wu wei* is not about immobility, it is about spontaneous action unmediated by conscious and word-bound deliberation. When we are urged to make no response we are being told to keep a steady mind not just in the face of events, but also in the face of the verbal barrage from the left hemisphere and the emotional one from the right. To "make no response" is to refrain from jumping to conclusions, applying rigid and misleading concepts, and acting from confused emotions. We may hear what we say to ourselves, but we need not take that as the last word, or even as the truth.

Eliminating Concepts

If a concept is a capacity to use and understand a word, then we will not want to "destroy" or "forget" our concepts because we need them to understand what others are saying. What needs to be eliminated is not our ability to understand certain concepts, it is our careless and thoughtless use of the words that express them. We can all use words like 'nigger' and 'queer', but most of us do not want to do so because of what they and their use imply. Even if we manage to eliminate such words from our *active* vocabulary, we still understand them and know how to use them. So in that sense at least, we will not have eliminated any concepts. But when we stop using words like these in our own descriptions and reflections, when we stop thinking in these terms, we will have neutralized these concepts, and protected ourselves from the misleading and false assumptions that underlie their use. A moratorium on the public and private use of these and other pernicious terms will force us to think more about concrete individuals, and to base our choices more squarely on how things are.

Hui Hai said that when someone who "has not yet perceived his own nature," that is, someone who has not attained understanding, "speaks of green bamboos, he forms a rigid concept of green bamboos as such; and, when he speaks of yellow flowers, he forms the same sort of rigid concept" (Blofeld [2], 105). Now, what is this disease? With a rigid concept of green bamboos or yellow flowers (or of Christians, Chinese, lesbians, or engineers) we lose the ability to appreciate and react to differences.

What now of the concepts of morality? They are respected and protected by those who depend on them—but they are also questionable. The idea of dumping them can horrify serious moralists, but that is one of our options if morality is no more than a collection of conventional restraints treated as more than conventional, subjective values treated as objective, and conditional demands treated as categorical. When we understand that there are no unquestionable starting points, and that we do not discover but inherit and invent values, the central concepts of value become intelligible (we understand their use), optional (we can use them or not), and potentially duplicitous (we can manipulate others who take them more seriously than we do).

"Away with All Jealousy"

If we develop a clear view of the use of our words, we come to understand something about the ways we are influenced by our concepts and metaphors, and manipulated by those who use them. When we get a clear view of some particularly dangerous or confused notion, we can begin to build up an immunity to its influence. Sometimes we are changed by an understanding of how some habitual way of thinking sets off feelings and behavior we find undesirable. A full and painful awareness of the actual effects of our envy, hatred, meanness, or jealousy might be enough to start us on the path of reform.

Consider jealousy. Daniel Farrell has characterized it as an emotion of anger or "bother" arising in "a three-party context" (Farrell, 529, 539). When one person is jealous of a second person, it is because some third person seems to be voluntarily favoring the object of the jealousy (the second person) in some respect, and because the jealous person wants to be the one favored in that way and believes or suspects that he or she is not.

If this is jealousy, then there is a natural path to its conquest. We simply eliminate the desire to be favored, or break the connection between it and the emotions of anger and bother at its frustration. This takes us into familiar territory. If we decide that our feelings of jealousy must go, we know we can get help from those who espouse the elimination and neutralization of desires.

Because no emotion is unloved by everyone, there will be those who defend jealousy. It is easy to see the evolutionary value of a tendency to become angry or even violent at the idea that a favorite person is choosing to bestow affection and attention on a third person rather than on us. But do we still need this response, or have we come to the point in our evolution where the emotion does us more harm than good? It may no longer make sense to buy into concepts and metaphors of possession and revenge that make it easy to rationalize domination, anger, and violence.

If we do not like to feel anger or "bother" (and who does?), how do we manage to eliminate, neutralize, or at least diminish the intensity of the desire to be favored or the desire that the object of our jealousy not be favored? One way is to make an effort to understand the situation from other points of view. Since this is the general strategy of many informed and compassionate amoralists, they will have a head start at "eliminating" this dangerous concept, or neutralizing its power to make us feel bad and do strange things. As amoralists they have abandoned the idea that anyone has a duty to favor them, so they will be unlikely to feel moral outrage when someone rejects them. Being informed and compassionate, they will be willing (some more, some less) to take the beliefs and desires of other people seriously and wish them well. A vivid appreciation of the world from different points of view, and an average dose of compassion should be sufficient to neutralize many of the feelings of anger and bother that constitute jealousy and make it so ugly.

Another way to overcome the power of jealousy is to contemplate the fact that it involves a desire for something not easily achieved—a jealous person wants someone to have different preferences. Since we are usually clumsy at making other people prefer us to those they now prefer, jealousy can lead to counterproductive acts of desperate and obvious manipulation. When these fail, the result is often violence, misery, and death. Jealousy destroys the jealous person's ability to assess the situation, and when anger, resentment, possessiveness, insecurity, and other related forms of craziness take their toll, no one needs to ask whether it is a good idea to follow Saint Peter's advice.

Linguistic Therapy

Wittgenstein, Sextus Empiricus, Buddhists, Daoists, and plenty of others have warned us that words can lead us astray, and have offered us ways to avoid the danger. Sextus recommends the habit of "nonassertion" regarding controversial matters, and a simple yielding to what is obvious. By ruling some questions unworthy of an answer, he found quietude "in matters of opinion" and tranquillity. Philosophical questions like "Is untasted honey really sweet?" which apparently had caused him some problems, could be abandoned.

Sextus also thought that moralistic assumptions about value compound our difficulties. The "ordinary man," he said, is troubled both "by the feelings themselves [his examples are coldness and thirst] and not less by the fact that he believes these conditions to be evil by nature." Since the skeptic rejects the notion that things are evil by nature, he "gets off more easily" (Sextus Empiricus, 42).

This same freedom from dogmas and from metaphysics was encouraged by the Buddha, who is notorious for dismissing philosophical questions. When asked where an enlightened person is reborn, he once answered that it "would not fit the case" to say that he is reborn, or that he is not reborn, or that he is both reborn and not reborn, or that he is neither reborn nor not reborn. He also refused to discuss whether the world is eternal, or the mind identical with the body. "The theory that the world is eternal is a jungle, a wilderness, a puppet-show, a writhing, and a fetter, and is coupled with misery, ruin, despair, and agony, and does not tend to aversion, absence of passion, cessation, quiescence, knowledge, supreme wisdom, and *nirvāṇa*" (Radhakrishnan and Moore, 290).

Wittgenstein sees us as bewitched by problems that will only be dissolved when we "*command a clear view* of the use of our words." (Wittgenstein [1], I §122) Like the Buddha, he is aiming at "*complete* clarity," but, he adds, "this simply means that the philosophical problems should *completely* disappear. The real discovery is the one that makes me capable of stopping doing philosophy when I want to" (Wittgenstein [1], I §133).

There are two metaphors at work here: PHILOSOPHY IS THERAPY and PHILOSOPHY IS DISEASE. The philosopher (as therapist) cures the philosopher (as patient) from philosophy (the disease). We suffer from the disease when we are consumed by some stupid question that exists only because of some quirk of language. To be cured is to see through the trick in a way that enables us to abandon the question.

Sextus was a physician and he saw his "skeptical sayings" ("I determine nothing" or "I suspend judgment") as remedies to use when confronted with one of the dogmatic positions of the day. They are to be resorted to on the first symptoms of an attack of dogmatism, and they work like purgative medicines, which "not only remove the humors from the body but expel themselves together with the humors" (Sextus Empiricus, 86). The Buddha is often called "the great physician" and is presented as having found a cure for the only serious ill, suffering. Finally, Wittgenstein is well known for having said, and operated as if, "the philosopher's treatment of a question is like the treatment of an illness" (Wittgenstein [1], I §255).

There is the disease (dogmatism, ignorance, or conceptual confusion), the therapy (skeptical detachment, meditation, or a clear view of language), and the state of the cured person (quietude, enlightenment, freedom from confusion). When we are cured, questions no longer cry out for answers, problems disappear, and so does the needless suffering generated by the mistaken belief that the questions need answers. We do not answer the questions, we become immune to them.

But immunity comes only with exposure, and so unless one has thought about gods, freedom, goodness, or the meaning of life, these problems will remain dormant, ready to strike at any time. Only someone who has struggled with a problem, and seen where reflection can lead, can leave that problem behind once and for all. The state of a person before becoming infected by an unanswerable question and the state of that same person after being cured will be no different on the surface, but the mind that has been healed will have built up an immunity, not only to that question, but to others like it.

> Here it is difficult as it were to keep our heads up,—to see that we must stick to the subjects of our everyday thinking, and not go astray and imagine that we have to describe extreme subtleties, which in turn we are after all quite unable to describe with the means at our disposal. We feel as if we had to repair a torn spider's web with our fingers. (Wittgenstein [1], I §106)

> The more narrowly we examine actual language, the sharper becomes the conflict between it and our requirement. . . . The conflict becomes intolerable; the requirement is now in danger of becoming empty.—We have got on to slippery ice where there is no friction and so in a certain sense the conditions are ideal, but also, just because of that, we are unable to walk. We want to walk; so we need *friction*. Back to the rough ground! (Wittgenstein [1], I §107)

> First, words are our tools, and, as a minimum, we should use clean tools: we should know what we mean and what we do not,

> and we must forearm ourselves against the traps language sets us. Secondly, words are not (except in their own little corner) facts or things: we need therefore to prise them off the world, to hold them apart from and against it, so that we can realize their inadequacies and arbitrariness, and can re-look at the world without blinkers. (Austin, 181–82)

Truth

Language plays an enormous role in the way we understand and deal with the world. It gives us clues about how to interpret experience and it lets us communicate our beliefs, desires, and instructions; it influences our own version of reality and is used to affect the versions constructed by others. This is where truth comes in. When we use words to inform, the presumption is that we are speaking truly. We expect and want the truth from others, who expect and want the truth from us. We so value not being deceived that we can promote truthfulness in any of the styles of moralism—we can speak of the value of truth, the duty to tell the truth, the right to be told the truth, or the virtue of veracity.

Truth is important because information is important. We need to know what is going on because we cannot even begin to cooperate with others unless they are willing and able to share information. We know that people are neither perfectly honest nor perfectly informed, and we take that into account, but life is much easier when we can assume that our associates are usually trying to tell us the truth.

The Whole Truth

Truth is important, but it is also difficult to pin down, and there is no shortage of theories about what it is, or of skeptical philosophers who doubt it is ever attainable. Some of the skeptics stay skeptical, but others mutate into dogmatists after discovering non-conventional or even mystical means to apprehend extraordinary truths about Reality, Being, God, or some other elusive entity.

Skeptical doubts and mystical certainties flourish when, in Wittgenstein's words, "language goes on holiday." Our ordinary standards for truth and knowledge tell us when to say that a statement is true and when to say that we know something. We are not after, or even interested in, perfection. The amount of accuracy or completeness we require depends on our project, so when we say that we can *never* know anything, or that truth is unattainable, we are using 'know' and 'truth' with radically inappropriate rigor. Just as we do not use the word 'flat' to mean 'appears perfectly flat through a good microscope', we do not use the word 'true' to mean 'unblemished by any inaccuracy'. When what we say is accurate enough, given the circumstances and the understanding we share with our audience, then what we say is true.

In most cases that matter, it will be clear enough what is true, or at least clear enough what it would take for us to find out. People want the truth, and moralists praise it, because the more of it we have, the more appropriate our behavior is likely to be. We do not need, and can never get, "the whole truth" if that means some verbal characterization that would convey as much as (or even more than) we would learn if we were observing for ourselves. What we need is the "simple truth," something that can often be delivered in a few straightforward words or sentences: Did you eat the last of the strawberries? Did you break my stereo? Where is my car? What did Klaus have to gain from the death of his wife? Situations are complicated, but it is usually clear what information we need. When we want the truth, we do not want just any old truth, but the relevant or salient one, the one that bears on our concerns.

Truth from the Moral Point of View

We are so clear about our need for correct information that it would be hard to find or imagine a moral code with no prohibitions against lying and deception. It is widely believed that there is something wrong with lying, but that under some circumstances we ought, or at least we have a right, to lie. Only rarely does anyone take the extreme position that it is always wrong to lie.

But 'rarely' does not mean 'never'. Augustine and Immanuel Kant differed in many ways about the question of truthfulness, but they agreed that we should never lie. Augustine based his belief on a verse in the Bible that says that while God hates iniquity, he will "destroy all who speak a lie." This convinced him that lying is worse than mere iniquity, and that since "eternal life is lost by lying, a lie may never be told for the preservation of the temporal life of another" (Augustine, 235).

Kant also thought that duty forbids us to lie even to save a life. In a note called "On a Supposed Right to Tell Lies from Benevolent

Motives," he makes his absolutism clear and explicit: "Truth in utterances that cannot be avoided is the formal duty of a man to everyone, however great the disadvantage that may arise from it to him or any other" (Kant [1], 362).

In contrast to Augustine and Kant, the utilitarian, who sees expediency as everything, has no objections to a lie simply because it is false and deceptive. Jeremy Bentham says that as long as the falsehood is not accompanied by any "material effects" it "can never, upon the principle of utility, constitute any offense at all" (Bentham, 223).

Most of us will reject both Kant's absolutism and the utilitarian idea that there is nothing wrong with lying unless the consequences turn out to be bad. The most common view is that there is an initial presumption against lies, a prima facie duty not to lie. The intuitionist W. D. Ross argues that this duty can be derived from the more fundamental prima facie duty of fidelity. We have, he claims, by the mere act of entering into conversation, made an "implicit promise" not to tell lies (Ross, 21). He believes that we also have prima facie duties to bring about good and prevent harm, but because of our prima facie duty not to lie, when equal amounts of good result from a lie and the truth, our actual all-things-considered duty is to tell the truth. This way of thinking about lying has the merit of reflecting the judgments and decisions many of us do make, but Ross was never able to say anything to support, or even to explain, the claim that we apprehend objective duties—even if they are only prima facie.

> Let us define lying as making a false statement in order to lead someone to have some related false belief. It thus becomes clear that if it is rationally required to want others not to lie to one, this is not because a false statement is being made, but because one is being led to have a false belief. A rational person would want to avoid being led to have a false belief by silence, by gestures, even by a true statement made in a certain tone of voice; it is being led to have a false belief that is important, not that it is done by making a false statement. Thus the rule should be concerned with prohibiting acting so as to lead someone to have a false belief. I shall formulate this rule as "Don't deceive." (Gert, 126)

> I believe that we must at the very least accept as an initial premise Aristotle's view that lying is "mean and culpable" and that truthful statements are preferable to lies in the absence of

> special considerations. The premise gives an initial negative weight to lies. It holds that they are not neutral from the point of view of our choices; that lying requires explanation, whereas truth ordinarily does not. (Bok, 32)

Non-Duplicity

It is worth noting the reason Ross gave to support the prima facie duty to tell the truth. By the mere act of entering into a conversation, he said, we tacitly agree to speak truthfully. To lie is to break that agreement. This argument had already been advanced by both Kant and Hugo Grotius, and it led both of them to stress the wrongness of lying but to tolerate substantial *non-verbal* deception.

Verbal and Non-Verbal Deception

In *The Law of War and Peace* (published in 1625), Grotius begins a discussion of lying by distinguishing between verbal and non-verbal forms of deceit, explaining that the "unpermissible" form, falsehood, violates an agreement we have with others. His idea is that when we speak with others, our use of the common language signifies a willingness—"as if by some tacit agreement"—to allow others the freedom to form their opinions without encumbering them with false data. Thus we each have, and grant to other speakers, the right to "the liberty of judgment" to determine what is true, a right that is violated when someone tells us a lie. Here the idea of the social contract is extended to the institution of language use, and an agreement among speakers is seen as the source of the right to the truth and the duty not to lie.

Like Grotius, Kant claims that there is a "right of mankind" to be told the truth. Grotius bases this right on a tacit agreement we make merely by speaking, and Kant seems to agree when he says that "every lie is objectionable and contemptible in that we purposely let people think that we are telling them our thoughts and do not do so. We have broken our pact and violated the right of mankind" (Kant [2], 228).

Both Grotius and Kant distinguish between verbal and non-verbal deception, and both assume that only verbal deception is covered by the tacit linguistic contract we undertake when we speak. Since we have made no agreement to refrain from what Grotius calls "pretense," he concludes that all such devices "are of such a sort that they may be employed by anyone at his discretion." He mentions the "Romans who threw bread from the Capitol into the posts of the enemy that they might not be believed to be distressed by famine" (Grotius, 609). Following the "Medievals," he calls this "management."

Kant develops his distinction between verbal and non-verbal deception by noting that "it is possible to deceive without making any statement whatever." He says that an act of deception of this sort, such as packing his luggage to make people think he is going on a journey, is no lie. In such a case, another person has "no right to expect that my action will express my real mind" (Kant [2], 226).

A Duplicitous Person

The fact that there are so many ways to mislead others without actually lying suggests that the question of when we lie, and of when we do wrong by lying, are elements of a larger and more important set of questions about non-duplicity, information, and virtue. A duplicitous person regularly and deliberately causes, or profits from, the false beliefs of others. By contrast, a non-duplicitous person strives to transmit and sustain an appropriate quantity of accurate and relevant information. Non-duplicity is the "virtue" we exhibit (the amoralist would call it a habit or a policy) when we come close to hitting the mean between giving too much and giving too little information.

The distinction between lying and other verbal and non-verbal forms of deception is not as relevant as Grotius and Kant think because our "contract" with others is neither the simple agreement to refrain from saying what is false, nor the impossibly strong commitment never to allow our words or deeds to mislead. We do share with all other speakers a general convention that our remarks will not be deceptively false or deliberately misleading, but beyond this we can find complex, vague, and changing understandings about how careful we are required to be to promote and preserve correct belief in the minds of those with whom we interact.

It is not duplicitous to withhold information from casual acquaintances, unless we stand to reap a direct advantage by doing so—as when we neglect to mention the intermittent noise in the transmission of the car we are trying to sell. But it is duplicitous to lie, even to strangers, or to contrive to cause them to believe what is false. Our interactions with people we do not know are based on this minimal general presumption of non-duplicity, but when we turn from strangers and temporary associates to those we know well, the general conventions about truth and non-duplicity are complicated by additional explicit and tacit understandings.

Two people who interact on a regular basis can develop extensive rapport—each knows what to expect and what is expected, and each knows the other knows this. In many "exclusive" relationships, each party allows or encourages the other to believe the following declaration: "I am not 'interested in' or 'involved with' anyone else, and if this situation changes I will let you know." In this situation, not saying anything will imply that nothing remarkable happened. When something remarkable does happen and nothing is said, no lies are told, but the agreement (tacit or explicit) is violated and the private linguistic contract broken. The silent partner has been duplicitous. If, however, there had been no understanding, or the understanding had been different ("Do what you must, but I don't want to hear about it"), the silence would not have been duplicitous.

The habit of non-duplicity is not limited to what we say and how we say it. Someone who is non-duplicitous will see no important difference between producing a false belief by an elaborate charade and producing that same belief by telling a lie, and will be disinclined to do either. Non-duplicity may even lead us to correct mistaken impressions that arise from what we innocently do. This is not to say that a non-duplicitous person will feel compelled to make sure that every stranger who jumps to a conclusion is set straight, but not everyone is a stranger. If something leads you, my closest friend, to think something false about me, perhaps to give me more credit or honor than I deserve, then it is duplicitous of me not to correct your mistaken impression.

Others form their beliefs in response to what we say and do, but also on the basis of how we look. We may feel tired, miserable, or ecstatic, but since we know that the manifestation of these traits can be unwelcome and disruptive, we present ourselves not as we are but as we want to be seen, or as we think circumstances require us to be. Much of this is harmless and probably even socially necessary; but some of it is harmful, and unless we attend to the complex conventions and assumptions at play, and to their actual effect in and on our lives, we will be unable to tell which is which. It is not duplicitous to conceal our troubles and pains from those who neither expect nor want to hear about them, but when some cooperative activity depends on my mental, emotional, or physical contribution, it is duplicitous for me to conceal a state that would disqualify me or, if known, would change the actions or decisions of my partners. Whether "Fine" is a duplicitous answer to a question about how we feel depends on how we feel *and* on who asked the question and why.

Presenting ourselves to others as we want them to see us certainly cannot be called lying, and much of it does not even deserve to be called deception. Nevertheless, when we "tint" our hair, or put on wigs, girdles, elevator shoes, or shoulder pads, we generate an image that is not in accord with the way things are, and this does lead others to hold false beliefs about us. When we consciously intend for someone to make some decision on the basis of a false belief our false appearance has produced, a charge of duplicity can be sustained.

A duplicitous person gives out incorrect, insufficient, or irrelevant information, and in other ways produces, nourishes, and exploits mistaken beliefs. A non-duplicitous person is inclined to avoid producing or permitting *too many* false beliefs, but how many are too many depends on the topic, the participants, the "communicative contract" in force, and the type and level of cooperation being undertaken. Normally we know what to expect from others and what they expect from us because we have, by interacting, hammered out the tacit rules of mutual disclosure and thereby set the boundaries of duplicity for that relationship. Just as we internalize rules about how to say things, we also internalize relationship-sensitive rules that help us determine what to say and show. Grotius and Kant are inaccurate about our "pact" with others because neither of them sees, that we ask more from one another than mere abstinence from lies. If I indulge in some elaborate charade to get you to do something for me, it is a flimsy defense for me to point out that I did not once lie to you. Such an attempt at controlling you (by controlling what you believe) is probably no less of a violation of our mutual understanding about how we are to deal with each other than an outright lie would have been.

Amoralism, Lies, and Non-Duplicity

Outright lies, deceptive truths, premeditated management, and other forms of duplicity are all attempts to gain something by creating or exploiting error or ignorance. Informed compassionate amoralists are likely to be disposed toward non-duplicity. Being informed, they are aware of the harm duplicity can do, and being compassionate they have a tendency to want others to fare well. This would lead them to want others to have an accurate version of the world. Moralists (unless they, too, are compassionate and informed) have only a highly qualified rule against lying and very little to say, from the moral point of view, about non-verbal forms of deception.

But one does not have to be compassionate to have reasons to refrain from duplicity. All the familiar practical reasons for avoiding lies also support wider forms of non-duplicity because the damage done by deception is rarely a function of the method used. When we are deceived, we are harmed because our version of reality—our basis for choice—is distorted. This is why the standard reasons for refraining from lies can be offered as reasons for avoiding other forms of deception.

1. Lies and other forms of duplicity tend to multiply. Even clever people who manage to deceive without lying may be forced to maintain their deception with a lie when asked the right question. This is the tangled web we weave when we practice, not just to lie, but to deceive. If the Romans throw bread out one day, they will have to throw it out every day or the effect of the first day's activity will be lost.
2. Furthermore, both the lie and any clever bit of non-verbal deception endanger our relationships, which are based on trust. If you find out that I have lied to you, I will lose credibility, but the loss may be even greater if you catch me in an act of non-verbal trickery. That will give you cause to doubt not only my words but also to be suspicious of my actions. When you learn that I have failed to reveal something you had the right to expect I would reveal, you will have cause to suspect me even when I am saying and doing nothing. What, you might wonder, am I covering up with my silence?
3. Our lies and acts of duplicity complicate our own version of reality by adding the alternatives they create. When we transmit or sustain some false belief, we need to act (and speak) as if that belief were true. If we do this often enough, we can lose track of what we have told others and, perhaps, even of what is really going on. If we must act as if something is true or false when we know it is not, our behavior fails to reflect who we are, and so we might lose track of that as well.
4. No one can doubt that the necessity to maintain expanding fictions is stressful. The constant danger of discovery eats away at our peace of mind and sours the fruits of our deception. When we decide to conceal some event or trait, everything that might give us away will have to be suppressed. Spontaneity becomes impossible. If we have nothing to hide, then we can simply respond to events as they occur, answer questions without fear or caution, and say what seems appropriate. The freedom that comes with non-duplicity generates a sense of ease

and well-being. Duplicity makes us slaves to our deception, perpetually servicing the false realities we have created.

5. Lies and other forms of duplicity are calculated to create or nourish a false version of some aspect of reality. But the false beliefs our acts of duplicity generate and support do not sit harmlessly inert in our victims' memory banks, but must fit with their other beliefs. Long after my aim in deceiving you has been achieved, false beliefs left by my duplicity can linger, like toxic waste, to pollute your information supply and distort your version of reality. Compassion will incline us not to endanger others by infecting their data with false beliefs. Once again, the practical question is not whether to lie, but whether to create false beliefs by whatever method.
6. All forms of duplicity deprive the deceived of autonomy by subverting the "right to liberty of judgment" that Grotius mentions. We are autonomous when we make our own decisions, but if our information is managed, then the decisions we make are not ours. For autonomy we need both freedom and information, and duplicity strips us of the first by withholding the second. If we do better when we are free to make our own decisions, then once again, the compassionate amoralist who understands this will be disinclined to restrict the freedom of other people by deceiving them in any way.

A Clear View

We are good at dealing with novel circumstances because we can understand causal connections, imagine alternatives, describe solutions, and resolve clusters of considerations into a decision. But everything depends on knowing what the situation is. Without a clear view of what is going on, our explanations are fantasies, our alternatives are restricted, and our solutions and decisions inappropriate.

Language helps us construct a version of the world, but, like any tool, it can be used skillfully or clumsily. We cannot command a clear view of the world without commanding a clear view of the use of our words. With a clear view of language, we understand both the value and the limitations of our descriptions and explanations. Just as we gain perspective by focusing the different images given by the two eyes, something similar is achieved when we focus our linguistic and our non-linguistic outlooks, and blend our verbal and our silent understanding.

When we understand language so well that words no longer confuse or inflame us, we are in a position to get a clear view of the events that surround us and their connections, a clear view of causality (as the Buddhist urges), or of the Way of things (as the Daoist recommends). This will include a clear view of many of the needs, aspirations, motives, and ideas of others, and while this is not guaranteed to trigger compassionate impulses, it usually does. Other things being equal, the better we know and understand someone, the more difficult it is to cause or allow him or her to suffer. This is why we foster superficial stereotypes of our enemies and our victims.

When we are able to clear our minds of fictions, illusions, prejudices, and fears, and to break free of conceptual traps and conventional lies, we are ready to consider trusting our spontaneous decisions. If we have not purified our system of the major sources of false belief and error, we will never get a clear view of what is going on, and our spontaneity will flow from ignorance, fear, or some other powerful emotion, and the outcome will be a matter of luck—usually bad luck.

If an accurate version of reality is important, then we should trust our natural information processing devices when we can, and stop trying to force beliefs on ourselves and others. We do not need noble fictions and inspired myths to make sense of the world, which they never really do, or to guide us in our choices, which they usually do with unfortunate effect. Skeptics say that nothing is knowable, metaphysicians that everything is unreal, priests that magic works, and moralists that morality is objectively prescriptive; but when we "command a clear view" of our words and the world, we can begin to see these pronouncements for what they are, and to see beyond them to the ordinary world that words were designed in and for, a world of trees and truths, of conventions and useful standards, and of explanations that make sense.

In these last four chapters we ask whether and how it is possible to live "beyond morality," and whether it is a good idea to do so. If it turns out that morality has all the drawbacks and hidden blemishes I enumerate, then living without it will be easier than living with it, especially if we can get each other to practice non-duplicity, and if we can pay attention to the truths that are being revealed.

15

Applied Amoralism

A man is truly ethical only when he obeys the compulsion to help all life which he is able to assist, and shrinks from injuring anything that lives. He does not ask how far this or that life deserves one's sympathy as being valuable, nor, beyond that, whether and to what degree it is capable of feeling. Life as such is sacred to him.

—*Albert Schweitzer,* The Philosophy of Civilization

Applied Ethics

THANKS TO the conventions that guide our discussions, questions about meaning and justification are always just around the corner when we take a moral stand; and thanks to the complexity of the problems and their interconnections, attempts to answer those questions can quickly strand us in areas of philosophy remote from ethics. Recent attention to metaethics was an honest attempt to confront natural questions about meaning and justification, but the linkage and the inherent difficulty of the related problems made every controversy indefinitely expandable. When this finally became clear, moral philosophers moved to avoid the "interminable metaethical squabbles" by putting questions about meaning and justification to one side, and turning directly to "applied ethics," to questions about life and death, peace and war, crime and punishment.

A question from applied ethics is a question about the morality of some act or practice. When, if ever, is abortion morally permissible?

Is suicide wrong? Is the death penalty justifiable? What moral duties do we have to the poor, to relatives, to future generations, to non-humans, to species, to the ecosystem? Applied ethics brings these questions to the center of the stage—sometimes by "applying" theories like utilitarianism to generate answers, and sometimes by plunging in without a determinate starting point in normative ethical theory.

When we take a moral stand on some issue, we must be ready to defend that stand. The usual way to do this is to anchor our argument in the shifting sands of normative ethics. We might take some set of duties as fundamental, or we might resort to the Categorical Imperative, the Golden Rule, the Principle of Utility, or the "Rights of Man." But, as we now know, when we participate in this practice we make assumptions that have never been, and never will be, defended against all reasonable and natural objections and misgivings.

What does it take to "apply" a normative theory like utilitarianism to a specific practical question? First, we would have to formulate and adopt a specific interpretation of the principle of utility, and we would have to assume, since we surely will not be able to establish, that this version of the principle is true or warranted in a way that competing versions and competing principles are not. Before drawing *any* conclusions, we would need to determine the limits of our "sphere of considerability" and our theory of value. Further, the entire process is built on the assumption that some kind of quantitative or qualitative comparison is a possibility and not a philosopher's fantasy, and that our knowledge of the present and the future is more extensive than it could possibly be. Of course every other normative theory faces problems at least this difficult, which is why *amoralists* might be in a better position to deal with the questions of applied ethics than moralists. At least the amoralists are not encumbered by a system of belief that can not survive critical scrutiny, and that works only when we believe something false, or cause others to do so.

The Interest in Applied Ethics

Despite the daunting theoretical difficulties confronting them, moral philosophers remain bullish on applied ethics. This is partly explained by the fact that they now realize how easy it is to become lost in the "interminable squabbles." It was a serious error to think that a brief interlude of metaethics would clear things up and allow one to return, fortified with metaethical wisdom, to solve the problems of normative and applied ethics. Questions about the meaning of 'good' lead to questions about the meaning of 'meaning'—and beyond. So, if the bog of metaethics can be avoided, we can advance to the high ground of applied ethics with clean feet.

Another part of the explanation of widespread interest in applied ethics is commercial. By the early 1970s, those who teach and write about moral philosophy and their publishers were moving to meet the demand for relevance so urgently expressed in the late 1960s. Countless anthologies were produced, and quickly revised as public attention flitted from one hero, villain, or event to another. Few ethics courses taught in colleges and universities neglect applied ethics, and few new anthologies of writings about morality contain anything else.

A third factor that helps account for the current attention to applied ethics is the increased public interest in specific ethical issues. Since no serious problem can be solved without some people being placed at risk, dislocated, regulated, and in other ways inconvenienced, arguments that appeal to justice and rights are a permanent feature of our social and intellectual environment. When the media spot interestingly wicked or virtuous behavior, the questions of applied ethics fly like gossip. Computer networks and communications satellites facilitate the process by binding us together in a global community that has the capacity to learn about *and* discuss events as they happen.

Unfortunately, most of those who participate in these arguments have serious personal interests at stake, and they come to the argument with unquestioned moral dogmas, and with a tendency to employ crude versions of tricks philosophers have refined to an art—tricks like equivocating, dismissing important questions and challenges, and giving persuasive definitions. Caught by the metaphor ARGUMENT IS WAR, they argue for victory and rarely think of doing what a curious and compassionate amoralist might start by doing—dropping the moral and evaluative concepts and trying to find out what is really going on, which includes finding out what other people think is going on.

Applying Ethics

In *Ethics and Its Applications*, Baruch Brody "applies" one form of utilitarianism and one form of deontology to some of the problems of applied ethics: suicide, euthanasia, abortion, crime and punishment, the justification of law, and the distribution of wealth. His deontologist has intuitions about rights and the need for retribution, and his utilitarian thinks punishment is justified only when it deters. The utilitarian calls an act a crime if the gains from stopping it outweigh the losses, while the deontologist says that crimes are acts that harm people by violating their rights. The utilitarian wants to lower the standard of evidence in order to convict more criminals, and supports plea bargaining. The deontologist wants to retain the requirement of proof beyond a reasonable doubt, and thinks that plea bargaining is unfair.

In most of these cases the moral result does follow from the selected normative theory (and from an interpretation of the facts—which is another problem). But Brody acknowledges that the version of utilitarianism and the version of deontology he develops are not the only possible ones, and, as we observe in Chapter 1, he is aware that both theories face horrendous problems that moral philosophers have always known about but never overcome. He agrees that the challenges of nihilists, skeptics, subjectivists, and amoralists are serious, but says that he need not concern himself with them because they are problems for theoretical ethics, and his book "is not about theoretical ethics" (Brody [2], 6).

It is a weakness, not only of Brody's book but of applied ethics in general, that so many of these "theoretical" questions are put to one side and so much is taken for granted. We must feel sympathy for the applied ethicist who, wanting to avoid getting mired in foundational, metaphysical, epistemological, and linguistic questions, yields to the temptation to treat "theoretical" questions as annoying distractions. But when we ignore these questions, or dismiss them in short paragraphs as Brody does, we run the risk of being seen as constructing theories of sand on a foundation of thin air.

A different approach to applied ethics can be found in Peter Singer's *Practical Ethics*. While Brody prefers a form of deontological intuitionism, Singer is a preference utilitarian—that is, a utilitarian with a theory of value according to which the good is not happiness but the satisfaction of preferences. From the basic principles of his utilitarianism, Singer generates answers to questions about taking life and about the distribution of resources. It follows from his view that we ought to maximize preference-satisfaction, that it is wrong to kill most of the animals we now kill, that abortions are not morally wrong, that sometimes infanticide is justified (Singer [2], 122), and that "those earning average or above average incomes in affluent societies, unless they have an unusually large number of dependents or other special needs, ought to give a tenth of their income to reducing absolute poverty" (181). Needless to say, neither the premises nor the conclusions of Singer's arguments have been accepted by omnivores and those with a strong belief in property rights and the right to life.

The amoralist surveying the battlefield of applied ethics will be impressed by the energy expended by competing moralists, but also by the ritualistic character of the arguments and their apparent ability to go on forever. There are so many approaches to values, duties, rights, and virtues; so many forms of egoism, utilitarianism, and deontology; and so many predictions about consequences and ways to interpret events that we can defend whatever answers we want to defend by making the right assumptions and predictions.

The Alternative—Applied Amoralism

What, if anything, does an amoralist have to say about the questions of applied ethics? Not much, because amoralism, which is a set of beliefs *about* morality, gives no answers to questions about what to do. We have seen that amoralists are not, as such, immoral, heartless, or selfish—but they might be. What allows us to cause great suffering for small personal gain is not a rejection of morality but a lack of affection, compassion, sympathy, and consideration. We are predisposed to harm others when we do not like them, when their suffering does not bother us, and when we have no tendency to think of how they are feeling.

We are natural information gatherers and problem solvers, and when our problems involve other people, it can be disastrous not to learn what we can about the circumstances—including the beliefs, interpretations, explanations, values, and feelings of the people involved. We spend our lives constructing our unique version of reality, but others have different versions. Unless we attend to the versions of others, and to their versions of our version, we will fail to understand why they do what they do.

Information about what others think and feel, about what principles they presuppose and what values they support, will become part of the developing version of reality on which our spontaneous decisions and actions are grounded. But there is more, for this "deep" information about others is the sort of information most likely to trigger our compassion, which is a built-in aversion to the suffering of others.

Without the compassion we may not be inclined to act on any other-regarding moral principles we do accept; with it, it is hard to see why we need the moral principles. If we are as short on compassion and information as some pessimists believe, then all the morality in the galaxy will not help us—our species will surely expire and the animals we have not taken with us will be able to breathe a sigh of relief.

The Questions

If applied ethics is flawed, as any amoralist will say it is, what is to be done about the difficult and urgent questions that have attracted the attention of applied ethicists? How do informed and compassionate amoralists deal with questions about abortion, euthanasia, suicide, capital punishment, discrimination, and the treatment of animals and the environment?

While amoralists are in at least as good a position as anyone else to discuss these matters and give advice, they will not feel the need to take a stand on every real and imagined moral question. Moralists, however, who assume that moral questions do have right answers, seem to think that even very unlikely and totally imaginary cases merit extended discussion.

Moral philosophers have spent thousands of philosopher-hours writing and thinking about the following situation: We are trapped in a cave because a fat man is stuck in the only exit, his head protruding into the world above. Water in the cave is rising and everyone in the group, with the exception of the fat man, will soon drown. One of the group has a stick of dynamite and argues that the only way to escape certain death is to blow the fat man out of the hole—thereby killing him. Should we do it? Kai Nielsen, working with act utilitarian assumptions, concludes that "if there really is no other way of unsticking our fat man and if plainly, without blasting him out, everyone in the cave will drown, then innocent or not, he should be blasted out" (Nielsen [2], 186). The example is underdescribed, but no amount of explication would place us, sitting in our comfortable chairs, in a position to decide what someone else should do in a case as bizarre as this, or even to know, with any confidence, what our own response might be in that situation. When we actually find ourselves in an unprecedented situation like this, where no option is attractive, the decision we ultimately make will result from any number of factors, only some of which will be present to our awareness. If we are not actually in a situation but just read about it in a book or hear about it from a moral philosopher, what we tell ourselves about what we would do, or even think, in that situation is merely an imaginative response to an abstraction.

When amoralists *are* faced with genuine hard choices, they can make decisions *at least* as efficiently and intelligently as moralists. Like everyone else, they have sensitive decision-making skills and a reservoir of information. But because the mechanism the amoralist uses to make these difficult decisions runs best on concrete details about real people, it is not available for service with whimsical examples and underdescribed thought experiments.

In real life we often must find a satisfactory ground between too much and too little. How much shall we give, help, learn, demand, support? Who, or what, is to be included within our sphere of considerability? How much deception, coercion, and exploitation is too much? Amoralists are fortunate to be in a position to think about these questions without the need to find the right answer, indeed, without the debilitating handicap of believing that there are right answers. Amoralists are not distracted from the actual details of a situation by the need to prove something or to remain within pre-established moral guidelines. The next few sections show how this helps them when they confront some of the major issues of applied ethics.

Crime and Punishment

Amoralists are not anarchists. Even informed and compassionate amoralists will want laws to protect them and others from human predators and to regulate important transactions. They will not say that the state is morally justified in enforcing these laws, but they can support the practice, given the entirely reasonable preference for living in a society that restrains thieves and killers. Amoralists will not consider themselves *morally* bound to follow the laws of their state or the conventions of their society, but there is no reason to think they will conform to those laws and conventions any less than moralists. If they lack a moral reason to obey laws, they also lack a moral excuse for breaking them.

Amoralists will not believe that punishment is morally justifiable or that it is morally wrong, but they can still take a stand on various policies of punishment. An amoralist who believes that strict laws and harsh punishment lead to happiness, and who also favors things that lead to happiness, will side with the Legalists and hard-liners. Another amoralist with different beliefs may prefer more civil ways to promote civility. Decisions about what laws and policies to support are difficult enough without bringing in normative assumptions that mask prejudice and that encourage us to pretend to know the answers to unanswerable questions about value, obligation, and rights.

Amoralists who support punishment can even say that offenders *deserve* a penalty, in the way that the winner of a race deserves the promised prize; but apart from contractual and conventional contexts, amoralists will have to do without desert. There is no natural justice, no inexorable law of karma, no demand from the universe that things be balanced equally. "Heaven and earth are not humane." Nature does not cry out for (or against) the death of a killer. Apart from the conventional desert already mentioned, nobody deserves to die—or to live.

Informed and compassionate amoralists may support legal sanctions, but their desire to understand the situation before deciding what to do about it will lead them to look carefully into the circumstances of the perpetrator, and their informed compassion will often suggest mercy. But compassionate amoralists also feel compassion for the victims of crime, and this may lead them to favor the Daoist expedient of dealing with crime before it occurs. This can be done, but not if we are ignorant of what is happening, burdened with stereotypes and moralistic illusions, preoccupied with punishment, and unwilling to invest in our society. If we really want to reduce crime, there are many things that will work: We can reduce poverty, ignorance, hunger, boredom, alienation, or the number of laws. Punishment alone is not sufficient, and may or may not be necessary, to establish order.

The Death Penalty

One way to support the death penalty is to say that some people, because of what they have done, deserve to die. It may appear that by taking a life, a killer has created an imbalance, a gap that can only be filled by his or her own death. This is a deontological and somewhat mysterious idea, based on a metaphor that probably conceals a desire for revenge. Utilitarians, however, support the death penalty (when they do) on the grounds that we are better off with it, and they oppose it (when they do) on the grounds that we are better off without it.

The deontologist can make sense of limiting the death penalty to killers, but the utilitarian has no particular reason to stop there. If the death penalty really deters murderers, perhaps it would deter drug sellers and users, thieves, white-collar criminals, and corrupt politicians. The failure to do justice to desert gets the utilitarians into as much trouble here as the dependence on desert causes the deontologists, some of whom will say that murderers deserve to die, no matter what the consequences.

What happens when we abandon moralism and look at the death penalty from the amoralist point of view? The amoralist who believes in the deterrent power of the death penalty can support the death penalty as enthusiastically as the staunchest utilitarian or deontologist. The moralist may speak of our moral duty or right to impose the death penalty and the amoralist will not, but both will vote the same way.

Other amoralists may oppose the death penalty. Being amoralists, they will not be able to say that life is sacred or that it is always wrong to kill, but they can still have plenty of reasons for opposing it. Perhaps they find it inconsistent to embrace the murderer's assumption that killing is one way to deal with a problem. Or they may feel that the death penalty is an archaic remedy that does not deter murderers nearly as well as any number of less final but more expensive alternatives would.

It is not just compassion for murderers and potential murderers that recommends the politically unpopular remedy of investing in the reduction of the causes of crime mentioned above. We can save lives, and money too, if we can prevent a substantial number of crimes; and we can prevent much crime if we are willing to overcome various forms of self-indulgent resistance. Perhaps David Hume was right when he said that an emotion like selfishness could only be overcome by another and stronger emotion. If we are lucky, compassion for potential victims of crime and their loved ones will be strong enough to overcome the built-in selfishness that prevents us from making the investment necessary to head off crime and the consequent suffering of both criminals and their victims.

Abortion

Questions about abortion are more complicated than other questions about killing because the status of the "victim" is unclear.

Though a newly fertilized ovum is genetically human, it is already contentious to call it a person or a human being. Terminology is not neutral. Whether you refer to the fetus as a "person," as "fetal tissue," as an "unborn child," or as a "living, defenseless tiny human being" will depend on what conclusion you hope to establish, what attitude you seek to elicit, or what behavior you desire to support.

If we take words as they are used, a fertilized egg is not a person, nor is a fetus. When we ask how many people were at a party, we do not count pregnant women as two, nor are they charged double admission. The usage of the founders seems to have been the same as our own. In his majority decision in *Roe v. Wade*, Justice Harry Blackmun wrote that the use of 'person' in the Constitution seems to have application only "postnatally" (*Roe v. Wade*, 410 U.S. 113 [1973]).

The egg is human before it is fertilized. From conception to the third week it is called a zygote. From four to seven weeks an embryo, and from eight weeks to birth a fetus. A zygote is human and alive, but is it a "human being" or a "human life"? Perhaps it is a human life, if this means only that it is human and alive. But then we will not mean the same thing by 'human being' and 'human life', for there are many things (like cells) that are human and alive, but are not human beings. It is also impossible to say that since there is no *specific* point at which we can draw a line between a zygote and a human being, a zygote is a human being. This would turn acorns into oak trees and giants into midgets. When we apply a term like 'person' or 'human being' in some very unusual way, say to a fertilized human egg, it is almost certainly in order to discourage abortions by linking them with murder.

Information is no more neutral than the language used to convey it. Some opponents of abortion want to force women to review information about fetal progress before they are allowed to have an abortion. Others would have them view pictures of the mutilated remains of "unborn babies." But there are other things these women could be told. They could be informed that early abortions are safer than giving birth, or they could be told stories of women whose lives were ruined by unwanted pregnancies. In practice, it appears, facts take on importance as they support one's position.

But there is clean and unbiased information available to anyone who will seek it: information about the generation process; about the social, political, and psychological ramifications of abortion policies; about the attitudes of people toward abortion; about the actual situations of people who seek abortions; and about the law.

At least for the moment, the law concerning abortion stands as established in 1973 by the Supreme Court in *Roe v. Wade*. This case was brought to the court by Roe (the appellant) against Wade (the appellee), representing the State of Texas. The lawyers for Roe argued that the Texas laws forbidding abortion were unconstitutional, and that a woman ought to be allowed to have an abortion at will, for any reason, at any time. The lawyers for the State of Texas argued that abortion is murder, and ought always to be forbidden by law.

The court rejected Texas's argument because it found that the Constitution did not support the claim that the fetus is a person. But it did not agree completely with the appellant either, and decided to place no restrictions on a woman's right to seek an abortion during the first trimester, but ruled that during the second trimester, the state has an interest in regulating abortions to protect the health of the woman, and that in the third trimester, abortions may be regulated out of concern for the fetus.

The decision was based, in part, on a recognition of a right to privacy that the court found in the Constitution. But Justices Byron White and William Rehnquist wrote dissenting opinions in which they accused the majority of inventing this right. Others, who do find a right to privacy in the Constitution, are not convinced that it is sufficient to support a woman's right to choose to have an abortion.

If it were a matter of rights, the only thing strong enough to block a woman's legal (or moral) right to choose to have an abortion is a decision that the fetus is a person with rights strong enough to overcome any rights a woman may have to control her reproductive activity. The slogan "Abortion is murder" is based on the assumption that the fetus is a person, because only persons can be murdered. The slogan "Abortion on demand" is based on the assumption that the fetus is not a person, otherwise "reproductive freedom" would amount to "homicidal freedom." Since the word 'person' is so laden with rhetoric and philosophical theory, it is likely to be more difficult to show that the fetus *is* a person than to refrain from assenting to that proposition. The fetus is what it is, and an abortion decision is a decision to kill it, whatever it is called.

Amoralists will not hold that it is always wrong to kill, or that we have a right to kill to improve the quality of our lives, or for any other reason. Nor will they, if they are clearheaded, allow themselves to get caught up in the incredible rhetorical struggle to control words like 'human' and 'person'. There will be times when they will have to make specific decisions about whether to have an abortion, to support or oppose someone who wants one, or to work for or against abortion restrictions. But amoralists are in the best position to make these decisions because they are not under the influence of charged language, moral theories, and dogmas, and they are not restricted by the belief that one of the paths they are contemplating is the right choice and the others wrong.

As usual, the most helpful thing to do when we have to make a difficult decision is to collect information and advice from a variety of sources, and to try to understand the circumstances as well as possible in the time available. If compassionate people are clear about their own circumstances, the biology and history of abortion, the legal situation, the views of others, the inconclusive nature of the moralist contribution, and if they "command a clear view" of the use of language and rhetoric, then they are in as favorable a position to make their own reproductive choices as anyone could be. Informed compassionate amoralists who believe in neither an immortal soul nor the personhood of the fetus will be inclined to adopt a pro-choice position. They lack the religious and moral assumptions that would give them reasons to say it is wrong to kill a fetus, and they are free from the spell of loaded words like 'person' or 'human'. When we "look carefully" at an actual pregnant teenager who desperately wants an abortion, and then at the fetus growing inside her, it is hard to see how *any* information about the fetus could generate more compassion than information about a real young woman with a face, a name, and a full complement of hopes, fears, and plans.

Here the Daoist could remind us that the best way to reduce abortions is to reduce unwanted pregnancies. Unfortunately, a strict and confused form of moralism often blocks the shortest path to this goal by opposing efforts to supply information about, and materials necessary for, birth control to adolescents who are *already* sexually active.

Suicide and Euthanasia

Moralists do not agree about suicide and euthanasia any more than they agree about anything else. Some think we have a right to end our lives or to have them ended, and others do not. A blanket moral prohibition of suicide and euthanasia can be supported by insisting, with Aquinas, that death is always a worse evil than life, even when that life is full of pain and suffering. Aquinas claimed Aristotle's support here, but anyone not blinded by moralism can easily describe a life so full of pain and so hopelessly doomed to suffering, that death would be preferred by anyone actually in the situation.

Another way to oppose all suicide and euthanasia is to appeal to theological considerations, as John Locke did when he argued that since we all belong to God, if we hurt or kill anyone, including ourselves, we are violating God's property rights. We have seen how the idea that people can be owned can be traced back to a time when slavery was the norm, and we have seen how peculiar it is to speak of God's "property." Few people contemplating suicide will be deterred by this argument. "If God had taken better care of his property," they might think, "suicide wouldn't look like my best option."

The amoralist does not believe in the intrinsic value of life, the inherent right to life, or the duty not to take life. But even if life is not intrinsically good and pain is not intrinsically bad, each living creature "values" its own life, and has a drive to preserve it and to avoid pain. Attentive and compassionate amoralists know this, and it matters to them. They will be saddened and awed at incurable agonizing pain, and will be inclined to support those who suffer it, whether they decide to bear the pain, or to end it by taking their own lives. Only a moralist who values life absolutely, or who thinks it is always wrong to take a life, would be so presumptuous as to try to forbid or discourage all instances of suicide and euthanasia.

People worry about where this might lead, but by now we have learned to be suspicious of arguments that rely on dramatic projections. Those who take a moral stand on some problem are quick to believe the stories they tell about the future. Opponents of voluntary euthanasia argue that it is the first step along a "slippery-slope" that leads to Nazi-like killing of undesirables. There is little reason to think this will happen, but as we have seen, the important thing is to have some argument or other to fill one's allotted share of the discussion.

The informed and compassionate amoralist will be willing to leave these difficult and painful problems to those in the actual situations—to parents, children, loved ones, and their physicians. They, at least, know the details of the situation and have to live, and die, with the results of their choices.

> If there is any opinion to which the man of uncultivated morals is attached, it is the belief in the necessary connexion of punishment and guilt. Punishment is punishment, only where it is deserved. We pay the penalty, because we owe it, and for no

> other reason; and if punishment is inflicted for any other reason whatever than because it is merited by wrong, it is a gross immorality, a crying injustice, an abominable crime, and not what it pretends to be. (Bradley, 26–27)
>
> That suicide may often be consistent with interest and with our duty to ourselves, no one can question, who allows that age, sickness, or misfortune may render life a burthen, and make it worse even than annihilation. (Hume [3], 305)
>
> I am arguing only that having a right to life does not guarantee having either a right to be given the use of or a right to be allowed continued use of another person's body—even if one needs it for life itself. So the right to life will not serve the opponents of abortion in the very simple and clear way in which they seem to have thought it would. (Thomson, 56)

Censorship

The target of the censor might be anything. Some moralists want to censor representations and descriptions of elimination, nudity, or sexual activity; others try to suppress "immoral" political, religious, or social ideas. Moralists who *oppose* censorship often do so because they believe we have a moral right to free speech and expression, or because they are utilitarians and believe we are better off if these freedoms are supported.

Amoralists will not be able to say that we have a moral right to free speech or thought, but they will also lack moral reasons for restricting either. Compassionate amoralists, as we have seen, will have a bias in favor of non-duplicity because they wish others well and know how important accurate information is when decisions have to be made. This will predispose them to resist censorship that restricts information and to oppose propaganda that distorts the facts—though there will be some few occasions when any sensible person, moralist or amoralist, will want certain things to be suppressed.

It is easy to imagine amoralists wanting laws against the creation and distribution of child pornography, not because it is immoral, but because it is, like lead paint, harmful to the children. Others may, without pretext of moral justification, want it censored because they are disgusted by it. Other amoralists, however, will be attracted to it. These people will have no moral reasons to avoid it, and if the rest of us wish to protect children, we will have to find a way to provide these people with other kinds of reasons (perhaps in the form of legal and social sanctions) to avoid their temptations. Compassionate amoralists will be able to explain why they want to do this, but they will not get into the business of defending their moral right to do so.

In our own lives we are forced to draw lines to distinguish what we will and will not read, watch, and discuss. But we are not forced to draw these lines for other people, though there is always a temptation to join the many ongoing efforts to do just that. Except when it is a matter of forbidding things that are clearly harmful, we will only be able to insist on changes in the personal behavior and private lives of others by bringing in some rather powerful and demanding form of moralism.

If it happens that we (amoralists) find ourselves in a position to decide whether to censor, suppress, or conceal some information, the standard recommendation applies: Find out as much as possible about the situation and then, when it is time to make the decision, just make it. Sometimes, but rarely, the circumstances will seem serious enough to overrule a standing policy of openness and nonduplicity.

> The object of this essay is to assert one very simple principle, as entitled to govern absolutely the dealings of society with the individual in the way of compulsion and control, whether the means used be physical force in the form of legal penalties or the moral coercion of public opinion. That principle is that the sole end for which mankind are warranted, individually or collectively, in interfering with the liberty of action of any of their number, is self-protection. That the only purpose for which power can be rightfully exercised over any member of a civilized community, against his will, is to prevent harm to others. His own good, either physical or moral, is not a sufficient warrant. (Mill [1], 13)
>
> But the peculiar evil of silencing the expression of an opinion is that it is robbing the human race, posterity as well as the existing generation—those who dissent from the opinion, still more than those who hold it. If the opinion is right, they are deprived of the opportunity of exchanging error for truth; if wrong, they lose, what is almost as great a benefit, the clearer perception and livelier impression of truth produced by its collision with error. (Mill [1], 21)

Animals

Peter Singer's *Animal Liberation*, published in 1975, reanimated the discussion about our treatment of animals. Singer, a utilitarian, argues that since it is our duty to avoid practices that cause much pain, we must condemn factory farming, many uses of animals in research, and other forms of cruelty to sentient beings. He concludes that the pain suffered by these animals is so much greater than anything we gain from their use that we ought to stop using them as we do.

Singer's approach has been criticized by those who support and those who oppose "animal liberation." Tom Regan shares many of Singer's conclusions, and, like Singer, he supports vegetarianism and condemns hunting, factory farming, and the use of animals in research. But Regan argues that utilitarianism is an inadequate basis for the moral obligation to be a vegetarian, and Singer argues that vegetarianism cannot be morally defended by appealing to the rights of animals or by other considerations that have nothing to do with consequences. Each feels his own position is strengthened by his criticism of the position of the other, but this need not be the case. If both sets of objections are indeed overwhelming, we are not condemned to stick with the theory that is less overwhelmed. We can, and the amoralist would urge it, reject them both.

Singer, the utilitarian, argues that a turn to vegetarianism would yield a considerable reduction in suffering. This would be hard to deny, but Regan insists that this initial plausibility is not enough if we are really trying to *show* that we have a moral obligation to become vegetarians, or to end factory farming. To establish this, he says, the utilitarian would have to show

> (1) what the consequences *are*, all considered, for all those affected by the outcome of the harm done to farm animals, as well as what the balance of goods . . . over evils . . . are; (2) what the consequences *would be*, all considered, for all those affected by the outcome, if we were all to become vegetarians, either all at once or gradually; and (3) whether, when everything is taken into account, these latter consequences *would be* better than the former. (Regan [1], 350)

Of course neither Singer nor any other utilitarian has ever come close to providing this kind of information.

Regan has an alternative way to defend the animals. Whereas Singer bases the obligation to be a vegetarian on utilitarian grounds, Regan roots the obligation in the rights of animals. In this way he hopes to place the burden of calculation on the omnivore. If animals have a right not to be killed or harmed, then anyone who wants to kill or harm them is obliged to provide an argument to show that this is morally permissible.

Unfortunately for the animals, nothing in philosophy is that simple. Regan, and any other moralist who depends on rights, cannot avoid a host of crippling theoretical questions about the idea of rights. Singer owes us support for the utilitarian principle and some help with our utilitarian calculation, but Regan owes us support for the claim that there are such things as rights, the claim that animals have them, and the conclusion that these rights override other considerations that might be advanced on the other side.

He attempts to discharge this obligation by saying that certain beings have what he calls "inherent value," that all beings who have inherent value have it equally, that justice requires us to give "equal respect to those individuals who have equal inherent value" whether they are humans or not, and that harming a being is a way of failing to give it the respect that is its due (Regan [1], 264). This places the burden of proof and calculation on those who want to harm nonhuman animals for profit or pleasure. Unless they are willing to admit that their actions are unjustified, they can be asked to come up with some explanation of why it is, for example, "permissible" to eat or hunt or make furniture out of animals, but "impermissible" to put humans to the same uses.

The main problem with this defense of animal rights is that this notion of "inherent value" is as problematic as Moore's property of goodness. Regan spends more time telling us what it is not than he does telling us what it is. It is a mysterious quality about which we know only that everyone has it equally and that it has something to do with the fact that we all have equal rights. He says that beings with beliefs, desires, perceptions, memories, preferences, goals, psychophysical identity over time, and "an individual welfare in the sense that their experiential life fares well or ill for them," have inherent value (Regan [1], 243). But these are also the very kinds of beings it is possible and easy to feel compassion for, and respect too, when we get to know them. The compassionate amoralist will say that the equality Regan is looking for can be achieved more easily if we begin by the rejecting all value; and that the respect he believes we are all owed will only be given when we begin to see each other in ways that go beyond the superficial.

The amoralist is not required to find some feature to distinguish between beings who deserve consideration and beings who do not. No being deserves to be considered, but an animal's pain is real, it is there, and no amount of philosophizing is going to rationalize it away. Once we know about it, the only way we can refuse to consider it is by repressing our knowledge or distracting ourselves with clever arguments. The more we know about humans or animals, and the more vivid that knowledge is, the more respectful and compassionate we are likely to be. If we seriously think about what it might be like to be a veal calf suffering from anemia, sensory depravation, and diarrhea in a stall too small to lie down in—that is, if we get the full story of the treatment and slaughter of any of the animals we use for food—many of us will change our eating habits, at least until we manage to push this uncomfortable information into the background.

Information has the power to move us, but the moral arguments can all be turned aside, met with other arguments, ignored, or ridiculed. The predictable interminability of arguments about the treatment of animals illustrates the bankruptcy of moralism in the face of one more set of difficult questions about which we all have to make decisions. As it turns out, the animals could do worse than have their fate decided by informed and compassionate amoralists, who would at least have no illusions about the moral superiority of their own species.

Bernard Rollin, another writer who supports better treatment for animals, says that "the most powerful tool in the investigation of the moral status of animals" is the idea of a *morally relevant difference*:

> If we can find no morally relevant differences between humans and animals, and if we accept the idea that moral notions apply to men, it follows that we must rationally extend the scope of moral concern to animals. (Rollin, 7)

This is the argument Singer and Regan use to win the day against their opponents. It consists of catching them making moral judgments about humans and then asking them to justify withholding similar judgments about relevantly similar non-humans. They win the day against each other because, as each points out, the position of the other lacks an adequate defense. But they do not win the day against the amoralist, who is as reluctant as Singer to depend on rights, as reluctant as Regan to rest a case on consequences, and completely unwilling to make targets of themselves by espousing "the idea that moral notions apply to men."

When compassionate amoralists confront the suffering of animals, and the flimsy moral justifications given for causing it, they may well be motivated to make some changes in their diet and behavior. The animals we use for food, clothing, research, and sport often live short miserable lives, full of pain and terror. If we allow ourselves to face this fact squarely, we will need neither moral principles nor assurances that pain is intrinsically bad to modify our behavior.

Rollin introduces the idea of a *gestalt shift* to explain how a person might change from someone who does not care about animals to someone who does:

> We all know people who have stopped hunting when they suddenly realized that they are *killing a living thing for amusement*, rather than merely innocently participating in a sport. Or people who have stopped hunting when they first hear a wounded animal's exclamation as a *cry*. It is not that they have discovered some new fact, unavailable to them before. Rather, they have suddenly seen the same data in a new way. (Rollin, 44–45)

Rollin claims that arguments (of the sort he, Singer, and Regan use) prepare the ground for this shift, but the important thing is the shift—the arguments do no more than undermine the claim that we are morally justified when we consider the humans and neglect to consider the animals.

This sort of shift can lead us to change our diet and to work to end factory farming and animal testing. For every person unmoved by vivid information about factory farms, many more will be moved. The pictures of animal abuse that Singer included in his book may have done more for animal welfare than all the utilitarian and rights-based arguments ever constructed. Information that really sinks in, whether it is verbal or visual, is capable of tapping a rich vein of compassion, setting off the gestalt shift Rollin mentions, and completely changing our lives. Moral pronouncements, on the other hand, are more likely to harden our resistance and send us scurrying for counterarguments.

> The French have already discovered that the blackness of the skin is no reason why a human being should be abandoned without redress to the caprice of a tormenter. It may come one day to be recognized, that the number of the legs, the villosity of the skin, or the termination of the *os sacrum*, are reasons equally insufficient for abandoning a sensitive being to the same fate. What else is it that should trace the insuperable line? Is it the faculty of reason, or, perhaps, the faculty of discourse? But a full-grown horse or dog is beyond comparison a more rational, as well as a more conversable animal, than an infant of a day, or a week, or even a month, old. But suppose the case were otherwise, what would it avail? The question is not, Can they *reason*? nor Can they *talk*? but, *Can they suffer*? (Bentham, 311n.)

The Environment

Someone who thinks it strange to claim that animals have moral rights, or that animal welfare deserves to be promoted as much as human welfare does, will be astonished to hear the same claim made on behalf of rocks and trees, an entire species, or the ecosystem itself. The moralist who wants to bring moral considerations to bear on the way people treat the environment is facing a real challenge. Some of us are unwilling to concede considerability even to all humans, most of us are unwilling to extend it to non-human animals, and those who are prepared to make the extension to trees and rocks, and other things with no obvious claim to sentience, are few indeed. All the properties we use to justify considering the welfare of humans and even of those animals we include, are missing from non-sentient parts of the environment. Tom Regan does suggest that we could show that inanimate objects have moral rights if we could make sense of the idea that inanimate objects have inherent value, but he emphasizes how hard it would be to show that "the attribution of inherent value to these individuals can be made intelligible and nonarbitrary" (Regan [1], 246).

If we think all sentient beings (and not just humans) ought to be given moral consideration, we may not need to include rivers and mountains within our sphere of moral considerability because to protect life we will have to protect the environment. If the planet were devoid of life, it is hard to see what difference it would make whether it resembled Central Park or the surface of Mercury.

What, if anything, will informed and compassionate amoralists have to say about the environment? Is there any reason why compassionate individuals should not extend their sympathy to plants, rivers, and ecosystems? There is if it turns out that we can only sympathize with beings we think of as feeling pain or sorrow. A tree can suffer from a lack of water, but most of us would not conclude from this that a tree is capable of suffering. Rivers become polluted, trees are injured by acid rain, and ecosystems are destroyed, but it is hard (if not exactly impossible) to imagine those rivers, trees, and ecosystems in pain.

But might there not be some form of respect or concern for the integrity of tree or a stream that in no way presupposes that the object of our respect or concern has any capacity to experience pain, or anything else? It is not necessary to see something as a human being, or even as capable of feeling, in order to have a friendly impulse to allow it to flourish unmolested. If we develop the receptive aspects of our personality, the ability to be moved, as Basho was, even by the presence of a flower, then we too might extend our compassion, or something very much like compassion, to a river, a forest, or a tree.

There is nothing rational or irrational about such a feeling. It simply involves a more radical gestalt shift than the one that leads us to care about other humans or animals. The idea is not to try to believe that mountains and rivers are capable of suffering, but simply to acknowledge and cherish their place in the web of the world. First comes the information; then, if we are lucky and attentive, we come to understand and appreciate the objects of our attention. From this point it is a simple matter to develop respect and the wish that all things, living and non-living, "fare well."

It should be added that an amoralist with this attitude of respect for inanimate nature will not necessarily turn into a crazed fanatic unwilling to eat food, wear cotton, or drink water. As we have seen, countless factors influence our actual choices, and a respect for nature, if we have it, will only be one among the many. But an amoralist with understanding of, and a respect for, the ecosystem is less likely to do harm to the environment than most moralists, who will always have trouble finding moral reasons for inconveniencing themselves to protect unthinking nature.

> All ethics so far evolved rest upon a single premise: that the individual is a member of a community of interdependent parts. His instincts prompt him to compete for his place in the community, but his ethics prompts him also to co-operate (perhaps in order that there may be a place to compete for).
>
> The land ethic simply enlarges the boundaries of the community to include soils, waters, plants, and animals, or collectively: the land. (Leopold, 239)

Last Conclusion

Morality turns out to be based on mistaken assumptions, confused concepts, self-deception, duplicity, fear, and a sometimes well-meant desire to control the way others act. No rule, principle, right, value, or virtue could be both objective and prescriptive, but moral rules, principles, rights, values, and virtues have no chance of doing their work unless they are thought to be both.

Moralists have doomed themselves to endless arguments, to idle and imaginative fantasizing about future consequences, and to conflicts of interest dressed as conflicts of principle. When people complain about the lack of values, they are usually complaining about the fact that other people fail to value the things *they* value, and they are presupposing that the things they value are the things that are *truly* valuable.

None of this is necessary, and all of it is confusing. We are not going to get peace and happiness by arguing that war is morally wrong and happiness a human right. Peace and happiness will come only when we develop the habits and institutions that generate and nourish them—habits of cooperation and consideration, habits of generosity and of yielding for the sake of harmony. These characteristics are easier to acquire when we have left the trackless jungle of morality behind us. They unfold as we attain a clear view and a deep understanding of the true character of our rules and principles, our institutions and conventions, our friends and fellow beings.

When we see that morality works only because people cling to their versions of the fiction of objective prescriptivity, we can still wonder whether to exploit widespread belief in this fiction by acting as if we think the bondage is objective, categorical, and inescapable. I have tried to show that this is neither our only nor our best alternative, and that a blend of curiosity, compassion, and non-duplicity will almost always result in behavior more "virtuous" than morality alone could ever hope to produce.

If we can give up moralist language as well as moralist beliefs, if we can learn to operate beyond morality and beyond duplicity about morality, we will find ourselves in a position to be more honest and straightforward with ourselves and others. This is bound to result in a better understanding of what is happening—all around. Then, if our wider and deeper knowledge unlocks our compassion, as I predict it will, we will have transcended any need for the illusions of morality, and we and others can be comfortable with our spontaneity *and* with the conventions that give a familiar and comfortable structure to our lives.

WORKS CITED

Adams, Robert M.

"Divine Command Metaethics Modified Again." *Journal of Religious Ethics* 7 (Spring 1979).

Adkins, A.W.H.

[1] *Merit and Responsibility*. Oxford: Clarendon Press, 1960.

[2] *Moral Values and Political Behavior in Ancient Greece*. New York: W. W. Norton and Company, 1972.

Amory, Cleveland

Man Kind? New York: Harper and Row, 1974.

Anscombe, G.E.M.

"Modern Moral Philosophy." In G.E.M. Anscombe, *Ethics, Religion and Politics*. Oxford: Basil Blackwell, 1981.

Ardrey, Robert

[1] *African Genesis*. New York: Atheneum, 1961.

[2] *The Social Contract*. New York: Atheneum, 1970.

[3] *The Hunting Hypothesis*. London: Bantam Books, 1976.

Aristotle

[1] *Nicomachean Ethics*. In McKeon.

[2] *Politics*. In McKeon.

Ashmore, Robert B.

Building a Moral System. Englewood Cliffs, N.J.: Prentice-Hall, 1987.

Augustine

"Lying." In *St. Augustine's Treatises on Various Subjects*, translated by R. J. Deferrari. The Fathers of the Church, vol. 16. Washington, D.C.: Catholic University of America Press, 1952.

Austin, J. L.

"A Plea for Excuses." In *Philosophical Papers*, edited by J. O. Urmson and G. J. Warnock. Oxford: Oxford University Press, 1961.

Ayer, Alfred Jules

Language, Truth, and Logic. New York: Dover, 1952.

Bentham, Jeremy

An Introduction to the Principles of Morals and Legislation. New York: Hafner, 1948.

Berger, Pamela

The Goddess Obscured. Boston: Beacon Press, 1985.

Blackburn, Simon
"Errors and the Phenomenology of Value." In *Morality and Objectivity*, edited by Ted Honderich. London: Routledge and Kegan Paul, 1985.
Blofeld, John (tr.)
[1] *The Zen Teaching of Huang Po*. New York: Grove Press, 1958.
[2] *The Zen Teaching of Hui Hai*. New York: Samuel Weiser, 1972.
Bogen, Joseph E.
"The Other Side of the Brain: An Appositional Mind." In Ornstein [2].
Bok, Sissela
Lying. New York: Vintage Books, 1979.
Bradley, F. H.
Ethical Studies. London: Oxford University Press, 1952.
Brink, David O.
[1] "Moral Realism and the Sceptical Arguments from Disagreement and Queerness." *Australasian Journal of Philosophy* 62 (1984).
[2] *Moral Realism and the Foundations of Ethics*. Cambridge: Cambridge University Press, 1989.
Brody, Baruch
[1] "Morality and Religion Reconsidered." In *Divine Commands and Morality*, edited by Paul Helm. Oxford: Oxford University Press, 1981.
[2] *Ethics and Its Applications*. New York: Harcourt Brace Jovanovich, 1983.
Bronowski, Jacob
The Origins of Knowledge and Imagination. New Haven, Conn.: Yale University Press, 1978.
Campbell, Joseph
The Masks of God: Oriental Mythology. Harmondsworth: Penguin Books, 1976.
Camus, Albert
[1] *The Plague*. New York: Modern Library, 1948.
[2] *Caligula and Three Other Plays*. New York: Vintage Books, 1958.
Carrithers, Michael
The Buddha. Oxford: Oxford University Press, 1983.
Chan, Wing-tsit (ed.)
[1] *A Source Book in Chinese Philosophy*. Princeton, N.J.: Princeton University Press, 1963.
[2] *The Way of Lao Tzu*. Indianapolis, Ind.: Bobbs-Merrill, 1963.
Chou, Hung-hsiang
"Chinese Oracle Bones." *Scientific American*, April 1979.
Clarke, Samuel
Discourse on Natural Religion. In Selby-Bigge, vol. 2.
Copp, David, and David Zimmerman (eds.)
Morality, Reason, and Truth. Totowa, N.J.: Rowman and Allenheld, 1985.
Cornford, Francis (tr.)
The Republic of Plato. Oxford: Oxford University Press, 1941.

Creel, Herrlee G.
Chinese Thought from Confucius to Mao Tse-tung. Chicago: University of Chicago Press, 1953.
Cudworth, Ralph
A Treatise concerning Eternal and Immutable Morality. In Selby-Bigge, vol. 2.
Dawson, Raymond
Confucius. New York: Hill and Wang, 1981.
De Bary, Wm. Theodore, A. L. Basham, R. N. Dandekar, Peter Hardy, V. Raghavan, and R. Weiler (eds.)
Sources of Indian Tradition. New York: Columbia University Press, 1958.
De Bary, Wm. Theodore, Wing-tsit Chan, and Burton Watson (eds.)
Sources of Chinese Tradition. New York: Columbia University Press, 1960.
Deikman, Arthur J.
"Bimodal Consciousness." In Ornstein [2].
Dostoyevsky, Fyodor
The Possessed. Translated by Avraham Yarmolinsky. New York: Heritage Press, 1959.
Duyvendak, J.J.L. (tr.)
The Book of Lord Shang. Chicago: University of Chicago Press, 1963.
Edgerton, Franklin (tr.)
The Bhagavad Gītā. Cambridge, Mass.: Harvard University Press, 1972.
Eichhorn, Werner
Chinese Civilization. New York: Frederick A. Praeger, 1969.
Eliade, Mircea
A History of Religious Ideas: From the Stone Age to the Eleusian Mysteries. Vol. 1. Chicago: University of Chicago Press, 1978.
Engle, S. Morris
With Good Reason. New York: St. Martin's Press, 1986.
Epictetus
The Encheiridion. In *The Works of Epictetus*, translated by Thomas Wentworth Higginson. Boston: Little, Brown, and Company, 1890.
Epicurus
[1] *Fragments*. In Oates.
[2] *Letter to Menoeceus*. In Oates.
[3] *Principle Doctrines*. In Oates.
Fann, K. T.
Wittgenstein's Conception of Philosophy. Berkeley: University of California Press, 1971.
Farrell, Daniel
"Jealousy." *The Philosophical Review* 89 (1980).
Feng, Gai-fu, and Jane English (tr.)
Chuang Tsu: Inner Chapters. New York: Vintage Books, 1974.
Fingarette, Herbert
Confucius: The Secular as Sacred. New York: Harper and Row, 1972.

Foot, Philippa

[1] *Morality and Art.* London: Oxford University Press, 1970.

[2] "Morality as a System of Hypothetical Imperatives." In Philippa Foot, *Virtues and Vices.* Berkeley: University of California Press, 1978.

Frankena, William

[1] *Ethics.* Englewood Cliffs, N.J.: Prentice-Hall, 1973.

[2] "The Carus Lectures—Reply to My Critics." *The Monist* 63 (January 1980).

[3] *Thinking about Morality.* Ann Arbor: University of Michigan Press, 1980.

Frankfort, Henri, H. A. Frankfort, John A. Wilson, and Thorkild Jacobson

Before Philosophy. Baltimore, Md.: Penguin Books, 1949.

Freud, Sigmund

[1] *Civilization and Its Discontents.* Translated by Joan Riviere. London: Hogarth Press, 1946.

[2] *The Future of an Illusion.* Translated by James Strachey. New York: W. W. Norton, 1961.

Fromm, Erich, D. T. Suzuki, and Richard De Martino (eds.)

Zen Buddhism and Psychoanalysis. New York: Harper and Row, 1960.

Fu, Charles Wei-hsun

"Morality or Beyond: The Neo-Confucian Confrontation with Mahāyāna Buddhism." *Philosophy East and West,* July 1973.

Fung, Yu-lan

History of Chinese Philosophy. Princeton, N.J.: Princeton University Press, 1952.

Gadon, Elinor W.

The Once and Future Goddess. New York: Harper and Row, 1989.

Garner, Richard

[1] "On the Genuine Queerness of Moral Properties and Facts." *Australasian Journal of Philosophy* 68 (June 1990).

[2] "Are Convenient Fictions Harmful to Your Health?" *Philosophy East and West* 43 (January 1993).

Gert, Bernard

Morality. New York: Oxford University Press, 1988.

Gilligan, Carol

In a Different Voice. Cambridge, Mass.: Harvard University Press, 1982.

Godwin, William

Enquiry concerning Political Justice. Harmondsworth: Penguin Books, 1985.

Graham, A. C.

Disputers of the Tao. La Salle, Ill.: Open Court, 1989.

Grotius, Hugo

The Law of War and Peace. Indianapolis, Ind.: Bobbs-Merrill, 1925.

Hamilton, Clarence H. (ed.)
Selections from Buddhist Literature. Indianapolis, Ind.: Bobbs-Merrill, 1952.

Hare, R. M.
Moral Thinking. New York: Oxford University Press, 1977.

Harman, Gilbert
[1] "Moral Relativism Defended." *Philosophical Review* 84 (1975).
[2] *The Nature of Morality.* New York: Oxford University Press, 1977.
[3] "Relativistic Ethics: Morality as Politics." In *Midwest Studies in Philosophy.* Vol. 3, *Studies in Ethical Theory,* edited by Peter A. French, Theodore E. Uehling, Jr., and Howard K. Wettstein. Minneapolis: University of Minnesota Press, 1973.
[4] "Is There a Single True Morality?" In Copp and Zimmerman.

Herman, Arthur
An Introduction to Indian Thought. Englewood Cliffs, N.J.: Prentice-Hall, 1976.

Herrigel, Eugen
Zen in the Art of Archery. New York: Vintage Books, 1989.

Hiriyanna, M.
Essentials of Indian Philosophy. London: George Allen and Unwin, 1978.

Hitler, Adolf
Mein Kampf. Boston: Houghton Mifflin, 1971.

Hobbes, Thomas
Leviathan. Indianapolis, Ind.: Bobbs-Merrill, 1958.

Hofstadter, Douglas, and Daniel Dennett (eds.)
The Mind's I. New York: Basic Books, 1981.

Hopkins, Jeffrey
Compassion in Tibetan Buddhism. Ithaca, N.Y.: Snow Lion Publications, 1980.

Hume, David
[1] *Treatise of Human Nature,* edited by L. A. Selby-Bigge. Oxford: Clarendon Press, 1888.
[2] *An Enquiry concerning the Principles of Morals.* In *Enquiries concerning the Human Understanding and concerning the Principles of Morals,* edited by L. A. Selby-Bigge. Oxford: Clarendon Press, 1902.
[3] "Of Suicide." In *Hume's Ethical Writings,* edited by Alasdair MacIntyre. Notre Dame, Ind.: University of Notre Dame Press, 1965.

Hunt, Morton
"Man and Beast." In Montagu.

Hutcheson, Francis
Inquiry concerning Moral Good and Evil. In Selby-Bigge, vol. 1.

James, E. O.
The Ancient Gods. London: Weidenfeld and Nicolson, 1960.

James, Susan
"The Duty to Relieve Suffering." *Ethics* 93 (October 1982).
Jaynes, Julian
The Origin of Consciousness in the Breakdown of the Bicameral Mind. Boston: Houghton Mifflin, 1990.
Jung, C. G.
Foreword to the *I Ching*. In *The I Ching*, translated into English by Cary F. Baynes from the Richard Wilhelm translation. Princeton, N.J.: Princeton University Press, 1967.
Kalupahana, David J.
[1] *Causality: The Central Philosophy of Buddism*. Honolulu: University Press of Hawaii, 1975.
[2] *Buddist Philosophy: A Historical Analysis*. Honolulu: University Press of Hawaii, 1976.
Kant, Immanuel
[1] "On a Supposed Right to Tell Lies from Benevolent Motives." In *Kant's Critique of Practical Reason and Other Works on the Theory of Ethics*, translated by T. K. Abbott. London: Longmans, 1909.
[2] "Ethical Duties towards Others: Truthfulness." In *Lectures on Ethics*, translated by Louis Infield. Indianapolis, Ind.: Hackett, 1980.
[3] *Grounding for the Metaphysics of Morals*. Translated by James Ellington. Indianapolis, Ind.: Hackett, 1981.
The Koran
Translated by N. J. Dawood. Harmondsworth: Penguin Books, 1974.
Kramer, Samuel Noah
Cradle of Civilization. New York: Time-Life Books, 1967.
Kraut, Richard
Socrates and the State. Princeton, N.J.: Princeton University Press, 1984.
Lakoff, George, and Mark Johnson
[1] *Metaphors We Live By*. Chicago: University of Chicago Press, 1980.
[2] "Conceptual Metaphor in Everyday Language." In *Philosophical Perspectives on Metaphor*, edited by Mark Johnson. Minneapolis: University of Minnesota Press, 1981.
Lattimore, Richmond (tr.)
Homer's *Iliad*. Chicago: University of Chicago Press, 1951.
Lau, D. C. (tr.)
Confucius: The Analects. Harmondsworth: Penguin Books, 1979.
Leakey, Richard E., and Roger Lewin
[1] *Origins*. New York: E. P. Dutton, 1977.
[2] *The People of the Lake*. Garden City, N.Y.: Doubleday, 1978.
Legge, James (tr.)
[1] *The Texts of Taoism*. New York: Dover, 1962.
[2] *Book of Rites*. New Hyde Park, N.Y.: University Books, 1967.
[3] *Confucius: Confucian Analects, The Great Learning, and The Doctrine of the Mean*. New York: Dover, 1971.

Leopold, Aldo
A Sand County Almanac. New York: Ballantine, 1970.
Lewin, Roger
In the Age of Mankind. Washington, D.C.: Smithsonian Books, 1988.
Locke, John
[1] *An Essay concerning Human Understanding*. New York: Dover, 1959.
[2] *Second Treatises of Government*. Indianapolis, Ind.: Hackett, 1980.
Lorenz, Konrad
On Aggression. New York: Bantam Books, 1967.
Lovibond, Sabina
Realism and Imagination in Ethics. Minneapolis: University of Minnesota Press, 1983.
Loy, David
"Wei-wu-wei: Nondual Action." *Philosophy East and West* 35 (January 1985).
Lycan, William
"Moral Facts and Moral Knowledge." In *Spindel Conference 1985: Moral Realism*, edited by Norman Gillespie. *The Southern Journal of Philosophy*, 24, supp.
Machiavelli, Niccolo
The Prince. Translated by Harvey C. Mansfield, Jr. Chicago: University of Chicage Press, 1985.
MacIntyre, Alasdair
[1] *A Short History of Ethics*. New York: Macmillan, 1966.
[2] *After Virtue*. Notre Dame, Ind.: University of Notre Dame Press, 1981.
McKeon, Richard (ed.)
The Basic Works of Aristotle. New York: Random House, 1941.
Mackie, John
[1] *Ethics*. Harmondsworth: Penguin Books, 1977.
[2] *Hume's Moral Theory*. London: Routledge and Kegan Paul, 1980.
[3] *The Miracle of Theism*. Oxford: Clarendon Press, 1982.
Mair, Victor H. (tr.)
Tao Te Ching. New York: Bantam Books, 1990.
Mandeville, Bernard de
An Enquiry into the Origin of Moral Virtue. In Selby-Bigge, vol. 2.
Mao Tse-tung (Mao Zedong)
"Talks at the Yenan Forum on Literature and Art." In *Selected Works*, vol. 3. Peking: Foreign Language Press, 1967.
Marcus Aurelius
Meditations. Translated by Maxwell Staniforth. Harmondsworth: Penguin Books, 1964.
Marinatos, Spyridon
"Thera: Key to the Riddle of Minos." *National Geographic* 141 (May 1972).
Masters, Roger D.
"Introduction." *Rousseau: The First and Second Discourses*. New York: St. Martin's Press, 1964.

Mertz, Barbara
Temples, Tombs, and Hieroglyphs. New York: Dodd, Mead, 1978.
Midgley, Mary
Wickedness. London: Routledge and Kegan Paul, 1984.
Mill, John Stuart
[1] *On Liberty*. New York: Library of Liberal Arts, 1956.
[2] *Utilitarianism*. Indianapolis, Ind.: Hackett, 1979.
Montagu, Ashley (ed.)
Man and Aggression. Oxford: Oxford University Press, 1978.
Moore, G. E.
Principia Ethica. Cambridge: Cambridge University Press, 1903.
Murray, Gilbert
Five Stages of Greek Religion. Garden City, N.Y.: Doubleday Anchor, 1955.
Nāgārjuna
The Staff of Wisdom. In *Elegant Sayings*, edited by Tarthang Tulku. Berkeley, Calif.: Dharma Publishing, 1977.
Nagel, Thomas
The View from Nowhere. Oxford: Oxford University Press, 1986.
Needham, Joseph
Science and Civilisation in China. Vol. 2. Cambridge: Rainbow-Bridge Book Co., 1956.
New English Bible.
New York: Cambridge University Press, 1972.
Nice, Richard W. (ed.)
Treasury of the Rule of Law. Totowa, N.J.: Littlefield, 1965.
Nielsen, Kai
[1] "Morality and the Will of God." In *Critiques of God*, edited by Peter Angeles. Buffalo, N.Y.: Prometheus Books, 1976.
[2] "Against Moral Conservatism." In *Ethical Theory: Classical and Contemporary Readings*, edited by Louis Pojman. Belmont, Calif.: Wadsworth, 1989.
Nietzsche, Friedrich
[1] *The Genealogy of Morals*. In *"The Birth of Tragedy" and "The Genealogy of Morals."* Translated by Francis Golffing. Garden City, N.Y.: Doubleday, 1956.
[2] *Beyond Good and Evil*. Translated by Walter Kaufmann. New York: Vintage Books, 1966.
[3] *Twilight of the Idols*. Translated by R. J. Hollingdale. London: Penguin Books, 1990.
[4] *The Anti-Christ*. Translated by R. J. Hollingdale. London: Penguin Books, 1990.
Nozick, Robert
Anarchy, State, and Utopia. New York: Basic Books, 1974.
Oates, Whitney J. (ed.)
The Stoic and Epicurean Philosophers. New York: Modern Library, 1940.

Oppenheim, A. L.
Ancient Mesopotamia. Chicago: University of Chicago Press, 1964.

Ornstein, Robert E.
[1] "Bimodal Consciousness." In Ornstein [2].
[2] *The Nature of Human Consciousness*. San Francisco: W. H. Freeman, 1973.

Pipes, Daniel
In the Path of God. New York: Basic Books, 1983.

Plato
[1] *Apology*. Translated by Benjamin Jowett. In *The Dialogues of Plato*. Vol. 1. New York: Random House, 1937.
[2] *Euthyphro*. Translated by E. J. Church. New York: Liberal Arts Press, 1956.
[3] *Protagoras*. Translated by Benjamin Jowett. Indianapolis, Ind.: Bobbs-Merrill, 1956.
[4] *Republic*. Translated by Francis Cornford. Oxford: Oxford University Press, 1971.
[5] *Gorgias*. Translated by Walter Hamilton. Harmondsworth: Penguin Books, 1981.

Popper, Karl
The Open Society and Its Enemies. London: Routledge and Kegan Paul, 1945 and 1957.

Price, A. F., and Wong Mou-Lam (trs.)
"The Diamond Sutra" and "The Sutra of Hui Neng." Boulder, Colo.: Shambhala, 1969.

Prichard, H. A.
"Does Moral Philosophy Rest on a Mistake?" In H. A. Prichard, *Moral Obligation*. London: Oxford University Press, 1957.

Radhakrishnan, Sarvepelli (tr.)
The Bhagavadgītā. New York: Harper and Row, 1948.

Radhakrishnan, Sarvepelli, and Charles A. Moore (eds.)
A Sourcebook in Indian Philosophy. Princeton, N.J.: Princeton University Press, 1957.

Rahula, Walpola
What the Buddha Taught. New York: Grove Press, 1974.

Rawls, John
A Theory of Justice. Cambridge, Mass.: Harvard University Press, 1971.

Regan, Tom
[1] *The Case for Animal Rights*. Berkeley: University of California Press, 1983.
[2] *Matters of Life and Death*. New York: Random House, 1986.

Rollin, Bernard
Animal Rights and Human Morality. Buffalo, N.Y.: Prometheus Books, 1981.

Ross, W. D.

The Right and the Good. Oxford: Clarendon Press, 1955.

Rousseau, Jean-Jacques

[1] *Second Discourse: Discourse on the Origins and Foundations of Inequality*. Translated by Roger D. Masters and Judith R. Masters. New York: St. Martin's Press, 1964.

[2] *The Social Contract*. Translated by Willmoore Kendall. Chicago: Henry Regnery, 1969.

[3] *Émile*. Translated by Barbara Foxley. London: J. M. Dent and Sons, 1911.

Ryle, Gilbert

Plato's Progress. Cambridge: Cambridge University Press, 1966.

Sachs, David

"A Fallacy in Plato's Republic." In *Plato's Republic*, edited by Alexander Sesonske. Belmont, Calif.: Wadsworth, 1966.

Saggs, H.W.E.

Civilization before Greece and Rome. New Haven, Conn.: Yale University Press, 1989.

Schwartz, Benjamin I.

The World of Thought in Ancient China. Cambridge, Mass.: Harvard University Press, 1985.

Schweitzer, Albert

The Philosophy of Civilization. New York: Macmillan, 1959.

Searle, John

Intentionality. New York: Cambridge University Press, 1984.

Selby-Bigge, L. A.

British Moralists. Vols. 1 and 2. Indianapolis, Ind.: Bobbs-Merrill, 1964.

Sextus Empiricus

Selections from the Major Writings on Scepticism, Man, and God, edited by Philip Hallie and translated by Sanford Etheridge. Indianapolis, Ind.: Hackett, 1985.

Singer, Peter

[1] *Animal Liberation*. New York: Avon, 1975.

[2] *Practical Ethics*. Cambridge: Cambridge University Press, 1979.

[3] *The Expanding Circle*. New York: Meridian, 1981.

Smith, Joseph

The Book of Mormon. Salt Lake City, Utah: Church of Jesus Christ of Latter-Day Saints, 1963.

Smullyan, Arthur

"Is God a Taoist?" In Hofstadter and Dennett.

Solomon, Wm. David

"Moral Realism and the Amoralist." In *Midwest Studies in Philosophy*. Vol. 12, *Realism and Antirealism*, edited by Peter A. French, Theodore E. Uehling, Jr., and Howard K. Wettstein. Minneapolis: University of Minnesota Press.

Stevenson, C. L.

[1] "The Emotive Meaning of Ethical Terms." *Mind* 46 (1937). In Stevenson [4].

[2] "Persuasive Definitions." *Mind* 47 (1938). In Stevenson [4].

[3] *Ethics and Language.* New Haven, Conn.: Yale University Press, 1944.

[4] *Facts and Values.* New Haven, Conn.: Yale University Press, 1963.

Stone, I. F.

The Trial of Socrates. New York: Anchor Books, 1989.

Stone, Merlin

When God Was a Woman. New York: Harcourt Brace Jovanovich, 1976.

Stout, Jeffrey

Ethics after Babel. Boston: Beacon Press, 1988.

Sturgeon, Nicholas

"Moral Explanations." In Copp and Zimmerman.

Suzuki, D. T.

"Lectures on Zen Buddhism." In Fromm, Suzuki, and De Martino.

Swinburne, Richard

Revelation. Oxford: Clarendon Press, 1992.

Taylor, Richard

Good and Evil. New York: Macmillan, 1970.

Thomas, Stephen N.

Practical Reasoning in Natural Language. Englewood Cliffs, N.J.: Prentice-Hall, 1977.

Thomson, Judith Jarvis

"A Defense of Abortion." *Philosophy and Public Affairs* 1 (Fall 1971).

Tolstoy, Leo.

"Religion and Morality." In *Leo Tolstoy: Selected Essays.* New York: Random House, 1964.

Toulmin, Stephen, and Allan Janik

Wittgenstein's Vienna. New York: Simon and Schuster, 1973.

Waldron, Jeremy (ed.)

Nonsense upon Stilts. New York: Methuen, 1987.

Waley, Arthur

Three Ways of Thought in Ancient China. Garden City, N.Y.: Doubleday Anchor, 1939.

Warnock, G. J.

Contemporary Moral Philosophy. London: Macmillan, 1967.

Wasson, R. Gordon

Soma, Divine Mushroom of Immortality. New York: Harcourt Brace Jovanovich, 1971.

Wasson, R. Gordon, Carl A. P. Ruck, and Albert Hofmann

The Road to Eleusis. New York: Harcourt Brace Jovanovich, 1978.

Watson, Burton

The Complete Works of Chuang Tzu. New York: Columbia University Press, 1968.

Watt, W. Montgomery
Islamic Political Thought. Edinburgh: Edinburgh University Press, 1968.
Wender, Dorothea (tr.)
Hesiod and Theognis. Harmondsworth: Penguin Books, 1973.
Westermark, Edward
The Origin and Development of Moral Ideas. London: Macmillan, 1912.
Wheelwright, Philip
A Critical Introduction to Ethics. New York: Odyssey Press, 1949.
Williams, Bernard
[1] *Morality*. New York: Harper and Row, 1972.
[2] *Ethics and the Limits of Philosophy*. Cambridge, Mass.: Harvard University Press, 1985.
Wilson, John A.
"Egypt." In Frankfort, Frankfort, Wilson, and Jacobson.
Wittgenstein, Ludwig
[1] *Philosophical Investigations*. Translated by G.E.M. Anscombe. New York: Macmillan, 1958.
[2] *Notebooks: 1914–1916*. Translated by G.E.M. Anscombe. Oxford: Basil Blackwell, 1961.
[3] *Tractatus Logico-Philosophicus*. Translated by D. F. Pears and B. F. McGuinness. London: Routledge and Kegan Paul, 1961.
[4] "Wittgenstein's Lecture on Ethics." *Philosophical Review* 74 (1965).
[5] *On Certainty*. Translated by Denis Paul and G.E.M. Anscombe. New York: Harper and Row, 1969.
Wong, David
Moral Relativity. Berkeley: University of California Press, 1984.
Wood, Ellen Meiksins, and Neal Wood
Class Ideology and Ancient Political Theory. New York: Oxford University Press, 1978.
Wright, Arthur F.
Buddhism in Chinese History. Stanford, Calif.: Stanford University Press, 1959.
Zimmer, Heinrich
Philosophies of India. Princeton, N.J.: Princeton University Press, 1981.
Zimmerman, David
"Moral Realism and Explanatory Necessity." In Copp and Zimmerman.

INDEX

Abraham and Isaac, 212
Adam and Eve, 212
Adams, Robert M., on divine command theory, 215
Adkins, A.W.H., 163–66, 189
Aeschylus (the *Oresteia*), 189
Ahiṁsā (non-injury), 108
Alexander the Great, in India, 119
Amoralism (amoralist), 42, 43, 223, 267, 292–96, 297, 382–83; and applied ethics, 366; and Aristotle, 187; in *Bhagavad Gītā*, 293; and Buddhism, 129; of Cārvākins, 293; of Daoists, 292–93; of Daoists and Legalists, 159–60; and democracy, 182; Hare on, 276; of Hobbes, 72–73; and immoralism, 288; on lies and non-duplicity, 358–60; and Nietzsche, 285–88; on rights, 271; and standards, 254, 257–58; as value-nihilism, 258; Williams on, 276, 278, 279–80, 281; Wittgenstein and, 290–91; in the Wong-Brink-Solomon sense, 277–78. *See also* Applied amoralism; Moralism and amoralism
Anscombe, Elizabeth, on moral obligation, 56
Anti-realism, 37–41, 224, 276–78
Antisthenes, 298
Applied amoralism, 366–82; abortion, 370–73; animals, 376–80; censorship, 375–76; crime and punishment, 368–69; the death penalty, 369–70; the environment, 381–82; suicide and euthanasia, 373–74
Applied ethics, 13–14, 362–66
Aquinas, Thomas, on suicide, 373
Ardrey, Robert, 77, 80–81
Argument from queerness, 39–41, 239, 241, 277; Singer and, 68; Warnock and, 238
Argument from relativity (disagreement), 39–40
Aristippus, 299–300
Aristotle, 166, 186–88, 258, 274; on the good, 187; on happiness, 187, 255; list of virtues by, 272; on the mean, 186–87
Āryans (Indo-Europeans), 82, 95, 197; gods of, 100; in Greece, 162–63; in India, 99–101; in Mesopotamia, 83–85
Ashmore, Robert B., 279
Ashoka, 119
Asia Minor (Ionia), 163, 167, 168
Assyria, 84–85
Athens, 166–68
Ātman, 103–4, 110
Atomism: Greek, 169–70, 288; logical, 288–89
Augustine, on lies, 353
Austin, J. L., 351–52
Ayer, Alfred Jules, 30–31, 251

Babylon, 83–84
Basho, 329, 331
Belief formation, 202–7
Bentham, Jeremy, 255–56, 262, 265, 266, 380; on lies, 354; on proof, 64; on rights, 270–71
Bhagavad Gītā, 19, 101, 103, 293, 308–10, 333
The Bible: Deuteronomy, 193; Exodus, 126, 193; Ezekiel, 87, 193–94; Genesis, 100, 209, 212; Isaiah, 84, 193; Jeremiah, 83, 87, 193; Job, 197, 213; Judges, 203; Leviticus, 126, 192; Matthew, 126; Numbers, 193; Psalms, 197; 1 Samuel, 88

Bicamerality. *See* Jaynes
Blackburn, Simon, 59
Bodhisattvas, 120–22, 155–56; Amitābha (Amida), 121, 155; Avalokiteśvara, 122; Maitreya, 122; Mañjuśrī, 120, 122; Vimalakīrtī, 120
Bogen, Joseph E., 316
Bok, Sissela, 354–55
The Book of Mormon, 88
Bradley, F. H., 374–75
Brahman, 104
Brāhmin, 99–100, 101–2, 109, 122–25
Brain, the: hemispheres of, 90–94, 315–17; and hemispheric imperialism, 330–32
Brink, David O., 51, 277–78
Broca, Paul, 315–16; and Broca's Area, 316
Brody, Baruch, 6, 13–14; on applied ethics, 364–65; on divine command theory, 214–15
Bronowski, Jacob, on language, 342–43
Buddha (Siddhārtha Gautama), 109–12; and philosophical questions, 117–18, 350
Buddhism, 106, 108–22, 306–7, 308; *Abhidharma,* 119; Āḷāra-Kālāma and Udakka Rāmaputta, 109–10; *anātman* (not-self), 115–16; *anitya* (impermanence), 115; *arhat,* 119–20; in China, 154–56; criticism by Confucianism and Daoism, 155; *Dhammapada,* 125, 127, 128–29, 195–96; *dharma* (teachings), 112–18; *duḥka* (suffering), 112–14, 116; Eightfold Path, 114; Four Noble Truths, 112–14; insight meditation, 111–12, 115, 306–7; in Japan, 156; *jiriki* and *tariki,* 156; *nirvāṇa,* 113–14, 118, 120–21; *pratītya-samutpāda* (dependent origination, causality), 116–17; *Saṅgha* (order of monks), 118–22; *śūnyatā* (emptiness), 121, 122; *taṇhā* (desire), 113–14. See also *Bodhisattvas*
Buddhist Councils, 118–19
Buddhist schools and types, 118–22; Chan (Zen), 121, 155–56, 331, 335; Hinayāna, 120; Mādhyamika (Three Treatise School), 122, 155–56; Mahāsāṅghika, 119–20; Mahāyāna, 120–22, 155–56; Pure Land, 155, 156; Sarvāstivādin, 119; Theravāda, 119–20, 122, 125, 156; Tibetan, 122, 156; Yogācarā (Consciousness-Only), 122, 155
Buddhist *Sūtras: Diamond,* 19, 121, 129, 156; *Foundations of Mindfulness,* 111; *Hua Yen,* 155; *Laṅkāvatāra,* 121; *Lotus,* 121, 155, 156; *Prajñapāramita,* 121; *Pure Land,* 121; *Sutta Nipāta,* 125; *Tien Tai,* 155; *Vimalakīrti Nirdeśa,* 120
Buddhist teachers and figures: Bodhidharma, 121, 156; Huangbo (Huang Po), 334, 346; Hui Hai, 147, 304, 346, 347–48; Hui Neng, 121, 156; Kumārajīva, 121, 155; Nāgārjuna, 121, 155, 307; Nichiren, 156; Xuan Zang, 154
Burden of proof, 14–16, 51–52, 225
Butler, Joseph, 222, 314

Callicles, 284
Campbell, Joseph, 99, 102
Camus, Albert, 19, 325
Caṇḍāla, 99
Carrithers, Michael, 112
Cārvāka (Cārvākins), 106–7, 127, 299
Chan, Wing-tsit, 133, 138, 159; on Needham, 145
Chinese dynasties: Han, 151, 153–54; Qin, 153; Shang, 131, 202; Tang, 122; Xia, 131; Zhou, 131, 141, 148
Chou, Hung-hsiang, 131
Chuang Tzu. *See* Zhuang Zi
Clarke, Samuel, 51, 222–23
Cognitivism, 31–37
Compassion, 279, 282, 286–87, 294; and morality, 295–96
Confucian concepts
—*jung* (conscientiousness): Dawson and Lao on, 137
—*jun zi* (superior man), 132–33, 158
—*li* (propriety): 133, 134–36, 142, 157; Creel on, 135; Daoists on, 141–42
—*rang* (deference): Dawson and Needham on, 139
—*ren* (humanity): Daoists on, 141–42,

157–60; Dawson, Fu, and Lau on, 136–37
—*shu* (altruism): Dawson, Lau, and Legge on, 137
—*xin* (sincerity): Lau and Legge on, 138
—*yi* (righteousness): Daoists on, 141–42; Dawson and Lau on, 139–40
—*zhi* (wisdom): Lau and Chan on, 138
Confucianism (Confucians), 132–40, 141–42, 144–45, 157–60, 327; *Analects,* 132, 133, 136–39; *The Book of Rites,* 135–36
Confucius, 86, 132–40, 141–42, 148, 150–51, 157–59, 323, 327
Consciousness, 90–92
Conventions, 4–6, 14, 22–23, 27, 33, 41, 48, 55, 63, 65–66, 81, 171, 179–80
Cornford, Francis, 175, 178
Crazy objectivity, 60–61, 68, 242
Creel, Herrlee G., 133, 135, 145–46, 152–53, 158; on Daoist sage, 160, 185
Cudworth, Ralph, 222
Cynicism (Cynics), 298–99
Cyrenaics, 299–300

Daoism (Taoism), 141–47, 292–93, 311–12, 328; contemplative and purposive, 146; and the *Dao De Jing,* 141; as political, 144–47; religious, 154. *See also* Lao Zi; Zhuang Zi
Daoist concepts
—Dao, 142; Lau on, 157; Needham on, 142
—*De* (virtue), 142–43; Lau on, 157
—*wu wei,* 145–47, 311–12, 328; Loy on, 147–48
Dawson, Raymond, 136, 137, 139, 140, 157–59
Deception, verbal and non-verbal, 355–60
Decisions, 260, 309, 311–12, 313–15
Definism, 250–51
Definitions, 250–51; naturalistic, 234–38; Socrates and, 173, 176–77; subjective, 25–26, 50–60, 243–44. *See also* Persuasive definitions
Deikman, Arthur J., 316, 326
Democracy, 163, 167; Aristotle on, 187–88; Plato and Socrates on, 172–74, 181–82
Deontology, 266–68, 369–70; act, 266–67; rule, 259, 266–68. *See also* Prichard; Ross
Desire, 104, 108, 111, 113–14, 298–312. *See also* Buddhism: *taṇhā*
Diogenes, 298–99
Divination, 131, 200–202; augury, 202; extispicy, 202; omens, 201; sortilege, 201–2
Divine command theory. *See* Morality: and religion
Dogmatism, 21, 22
Dostoyevsky, Fyodor, 43–44
Duplicity, 356–60
Durkheim, Émile, 89

Edgerton, Franklin, 293
Egoism: ethical, 261–62; psychological, 71, 222, 313–14; psychological and ethical, 53
Eichhorn, Werner, 132
Emerson, Ralph Waldo, 103
Emotions, 298–312
Empiricism, 223–25, 240
Engel, S. Morris, 207
Engelmann, Paul, 290
Epictetus, 302
Epicurus (Epicureans), 301–2, 305–6, 307
Error theory. *See* Mackie
Evans, Sir Arthur, 161

Farrell, Daniel, 348–49
Fingarette, Herbert, 157
Foot, Philippa, 295; and moral bondage, 37–38; and the object of morality, 54
Frankena, William, 252; and egoism, 53; and the moral point of view, 49–50; and the object of morality, 54
Freud, Sigmund, 45, 77, 219, 296
Function-of-language argument, 32, 36–37, 47
Fung Yu-lan, 134

Gadon, Elinor W., 82–83
Gautama, Siddhārtha. *See* Buddha; Buddhism

Genetic fallacy, 207–9
Gert, Bernard, 354
Gideon, 203–4
Gilgamesh, 194
Gilligan, Carol, 79
God (gods), 44–45, 87–90, 191–207; as creator and owner, 212–14; as enforcer, 192–96; and existence of evil, 203; and love, 215–16; as parent, 214–15; as source of morality and value, 210–19
Goddess, the, 82–83, 95–96, 196–97; and snakes, 201
Godwin, William, 265, 266
Good and evil, 44, 46, 197–99
Goodness, the property, 32–33, 46, 182–84, 224, 235, 238–40
Greek concepts: *agathos* (aristocrat, "good"), 163–65; *demos* (the people), 163; *oikos* (household), 163, 175, 177, 189; *polis* (city-state), 163, 170–71, 175, 189
Grotius, Hugo, 355–56, 358
Guilt and shame, 322–23

Hallucinations, 89–90, 92–94, 95, 205; Murray on, 89; of Saul, Jacob, and Muhammad, 90. *See also* Jaynes
Hammurabi, 84, 85–87
Han Fei Zi, 152–53, 318
Harappa (and Mohenjo-daro), 99
Hard- and soft-liners, 77, 151; about human history, 80–82; about human nature, 77–80, 326
Hāridrumatra and Satyakāma Jabala, 122–24
Harman, Gilbert: criticism of amoralism ("extreme nihilism") by, 46–48, 276, 280; criticism of non-cognitivism by, 34–35; and egoism, 53; as ethical naturalist, 33; on metaethics, 249; as relativist, 26–27
Harmony, 329–40; easy exercises to experience, 336–39
Hedonism, 255, 260, 261, 264–65
Hell (Heaven), 45, 107, 111, 115, 120, 158, 192–96, 198; Sheol, 194
Heraclitus, 115, 169, 170, 182
Herrigel, Eugen, 335
Hesiod, 164–65
Hinduism, 99–106, 308; castes (*varṇa*), 99, 122–25, 128; *Laws of Manu,* 128, 188; *māyā* (illusion), 103; Puruṣa, 99; scriptures, 100–101. See also *Upaniṣads; Vedas*
Hiriyanna, M, 105
Hitler, Adolf, 325
Hobbes, Thomas, 70–73, 75, 221–23; Right of Nature, 269–70; war, 71–73
Homer, 163
Homo sapiens, 70, 75, 80, 90
Human nature, 76–80, 274; and good or evil, 71–76, 148–49, 151–52, 327. *See also* Hard- and soft-liners
Hume, David, 225–32, 375; and *anātman,* 115–16; humanity, 230; impartiality, 61; reason, 226–28; reflexion, 228–30; subjectivism, 59–60, 229; sympathy, 227–30; on virtue, 272–74
Hunt, Morton, 78
Hutcheson, Francis, 224, 230

Ideal observer theories, 61–62
The *Iliad,* 89, 188
Indo-Europeans. *See Āryans*
Inescapability of morality. See Moral bondage
Innate ideas, 76–77
Innocent uses of moral language, 254–55, 257–58
Intersubjectivity, Lovibond and Mackie on objectivity and, 62–63, 242
Intuitionism, 32–33, 35–36, 40, 63–64, 224, 227, 230–32, 234–43; neointuitionism, 241–43. *See also* Moore; Prichard; Ross
Islam, 198–200; Allah, 199; *hadith,* 199; *sharia* (Islamic Law), 199. *See also* The Koran; Muhammad

Jainism (Jains), 106, 107–8, 127, 298; *ahiṁsā,* 108; Mahāvīra, 107–8
James, E. O., 194, 201
James, Susan, 326
Jaynes, Julian, 204–6; on consciousness, 90–92, 95; on hallucinations, 92–94, 95; on language, 342–43; on narratization, 91, 206, 317

Jealousy, 348–49
Jung, C. J., 202
Justice, 56, 73, 85, 96; "Conventional" and "Platonic," 179–81; Cornford on, 175; *dikaiosunē,* 164; divine, 126–27, 165–66, 189–90; as equality, 181, 182; Plato and, 175–82; *yi,* 139. See also *Ma'at*
Ju Xi, 156

Kalupahana, David, 113–14, 127
Kant, Immanuel, 232–34, 256–57; and the Categorical Imperative, 233; on lies, 353–56, 358; and reason, 58, 233–34
Karma (and reincarnation), 101, 105–6, 128, 158, 192, 310; and amoralism, 127; and Buddhism, 111, 117; and Cārvāka, 106–7; and Jainism, 108
Karma yoga, 147, 308–10
Kierkegaard, Søren, 291
Knossos, 161–62
The Koran, 88, 196, 198–200
Kṛṣṇa, 309–10, 333
Kṣatriya, 99, 102, 107, 109

Lakoff, George, and Mark Johnson, on metaphors, 344
Language, 341–52, 360–61; concepts and, 345–48; origin of, 342–43
Lao Zi, 141, 301, 307, 311–12; on Confucian virtues, 142, 159; and symbols, 143–44. *See also* Daoism
Law, 86–87
Leakey, Richard, and Roger Lewin, 81; on language, 342–43
Legalism (Legalists), 86, 151–54, 158, 326–37; Han Fei Zi, 152–53, 326–27; Li Si, 152–53; Qin Shi Huangdi, 327
Leibniz, Gottfried Wilhelm, 76
Lekden, Kensur, 321
Leopold, Aldo, 382
Lewin, Roger, 343
Lies and deception, 324
Locke, John, 76, 115, 212, 223, 374; on rights, 270
Logical Positivism, 30–31, 289–90
Lorenz, Konrad, 77, 78, 81
Lovibond, Sabina, 62–65, 242
Lycan, William, 244–47

Ma'at, 126–27, 194; Wilson, Mertz, and Stone on, 96
Machiavelli, 328–29
MacIntyre, Alasdair, 15, 66, 75–76
Mackie, John, 37–41, 212, 224–25, 231, 238–39, 271–72; and crazy objectivity, 60–61, 68; and the error theory, 57, 278; on evaluations, 50; on inventing right and wrong, 295; and Lovibond, 62–63, 242; as skeptic, 29
Mahābhārata, 101
Mahāvīra, Vardhamāna, 107, 111, 197. *See also* Jainism
Mair, Victor H., 311–12
Mandate of Heaven, 87, 131
Mao Tse-tung (Mao Zedong), 325
Marcus Aurelius, 302–6, 321–22, 334
Marinatos, Spyridon, 161
Masters, Roger D., 76
Matrilineal societies, 82, 143
Me, 126–27; Kramer and Eliade on, 96–97
Meaning, 341–42; descriptive and emotive, 36, 124–25, 251
Meditation, 92, 104, 109–14, 306–8, 330, 331–33
Mencius, 78–79, 147–49, 151, 158–59, 325–26, 327; as moralist, 149
Mesopotamia, 56, 82–87, 194; introduction of male gods in, 82–84; Marduk, 83, 85, 87, 197
Metaethics, 13, 248–52, 362–64
Metaphors, 344, 350
Midgley, Mary, 42
Mill, John Stuart, 256, 271, 376
Mind, like mirror, 147
Minoans, 161
Mio Zi (Moism), 140, 157–58, 322
Mokṣa (release), 102, 107, 109
Monism, 101, 106, 121–22
Monotheism, 100–101, 198
Montagu, Ashley, 78, 81
Moore, G. E., 32, 33, 35–36, 64, 234–39, 244, 250, 253; on goodness, 235, 238–39, 255; on meaning, 235–37, 341–42; the Naturalistic Fallacy, 237;

the open question argument, 235–38, 244; as utilitarian, 237
Moral arguments, 7–12; and interminability, 10–12
Moral autonomy and heteronomy, 57
Moral bondage (inescapability), 37–38, 41, 54–59, 94–97, 225. *See also* Objective prescriptivity
Moral facts, 31–34
Moralism and amoralism (moralists and amoralists), 1–3, 14–19, 42, 43, 46–69, 86, 247, 276–96, 382–83
Morality, 320; and ethics, 16–19, 94, 220, 254; Kant on, 233–34; and law, 86–87; and religion (divine command morality, divine law), 56–57, 87–89, 96–97, 140, 157, 210–19, 222–23, 242
Moral justification, 63–66
Moral knowledge, 35–36
Moral objectivity, 59–63, 127, 178, 189, 230; Anscombe and, 56; Williams and, 17
Moral obligation, 35, 38, 56
Moral point of view, 49, 51, 53, 54; Frankens on, 49–50
Moral realism, 37–41, 59–66, 242
Moral sense, 224–30
Moral truth, 34–35
More, Henry, 222, 239
Moses, 87
Muhammad, 87, 198–200
Mycenaeans, 162, 166, 188–89

Nagel, Thomas, 39–40
Naturalism: ethical, 32–33, 224; Moore on, 235–37; neonaturalism, 244–47
Needham, Joseph, 89, 139, 142–46, 151, 154
Neo-Confucianism, 156
Nielsen, Kai, as act utilitarian, 367; on religion and morality, 216
Nietzsche, Freidrich, 32, 33, 285–88, 297
Non-cognitivism, 30–37, 55, 124, 237, 277–78
Normative ethics, 248–50; 253–74; Theory of Obligation, 258–68; Theory of Rights, 268–72; Theory of Value, 255–58, 265; Virtue Theory, 272–74
Nozick, Robert, 271

Objective prescriptivity, 37–39, 57–60, 277–78, 295, 320
Obligation, theory of, 258–68; act deontology, 266–67; consequentialism, 259–66, 267; rule deontology, 259, 266–68; teleology, 259, 260. *See also* Utilitarianism
Oppenheim, A. L., 87
Ornstein, Robert E., 316

Parmenides, 115, 169, 170
Patañjali, 104
Peloponnesian War, 168
Persia, 167–68
Persuasive definitions, 122–26, 133, 148, 158, 163–64, 177, 181, 293
Pipes, Daniel, 199
Plato, 115, 168, 171–86, 221, 325, 328; and his Academy, 174, 183, 186; and deception, 327–28; on democracy, 172–74, 181–82; Dialectic, 183–84; eristic, 174, 177–78, 183; on goodness, 46; on innate ideas, 76; Ryle on, 174–75; and Socrates, 171–75; Theory of Forms, 182–86
Plato's Dialogues: *Apology,* 171, 174; *Crito,* 171; *Euthyphro,* 210–11; *Gorgias,* 284–85; *Phaedo,* 171; *Protagoras,* 22; *Republic,* 17, 175–86
Plato's *Republic,* 175–86: Adeimantus, 179; Cephalus, 176–77, 190; Glaucon, 178–80; Polymarchus, 177; ring of Gyges, 179; Sachs on, 179–81; Thrasymachus, 177–78
Presocratic Greek philosophers, 168–70
Price, Richard, 230–31
Prichard, H. A., 64, 239–41, 267
Prima facie duty, 240–41, 267–68
Projectivism (projection), 39, 224, 230, 246
Property, 212–13; God's, 213
Protagoras, 22, 170–71, 183

Ramsey, Frank, 290
Rationalism (Rationalists), 221–23;

Clarke, 51, 222–23; Cudworth, 222; More, 222, 239
Rationality, 66–69
Rawls, John, 264
Reasons: and justification, 6; and rationality, 7, 66
Regan, Tom, 6; on animals, 377–80; on inherent value, 378
Reid, Thomas, 230–31
Relativism, 22–28; descriptive, 23–24; of Greek Sophists, 170–71; Harman's, 26–27; naive moral, 24–25; situational moral, 27–28; subjective moral, 25–27
Revelation, 200–205
Ṛg Veda, 99, 100–101
Rightness, the property, 240–41
Rights, 56–57, 253, 268–72; Bentham and Mill on, 270–71; Locke on, 270; moral and legal, 269; negative and positive, 270; in strong and weak sense, 269–70
Ritual, 323–24. *See also* Confucian concepts: *li;* Confucianism
Roe v. Wade, 371–72
Rollin, Bernard: on animals, 379–80; on gestalt shift, 380
Ross, W. D., 239–41, 264, 267–68; on lies, 354
Rousseau, Jean-Jacques, 70–71, 72, 73–75; on pity or commiseration, 74
Ṛta ("cosmic laws"), 127
Ryle, Gilbert, 174–75

Sachs, David, 179–81
Sacrifice, 100–102, 131, 135, 189
Saggs, H.W.E., 82
Sartre, Jean-Paul, 76
School of Names, 149–50; Gong-sun Long and Hui Shi, 50
Schopenhauer, Arthur, 291
Schwartz, Benjamin, 147–48
Searle, John, 343–44
Self: Buddha and Hume on, 115–16; Jaynes on empirical, 91–92; "True," 102, 110–11
Sextus Empiricus, 29–30, 349–51
Shang Yang, 325
Singer, Peter, 6, 282; on animals, 376–80; on applied ethics, 365–66; on intuitions, 239; on rationality and altruism, 67–69
Skepticism, 29–30
Smith, Joseph, 87. *See also* The Book of Mormon
Socialization, methods of, 317–26
Socrates, 89, 168, 170–71, 171–81, 210–11; I. F. Stone on, 172; Kraut on, 173, 181; Popper on, 172; and Protagoras, 22; Ryle on, 174. *See also* Plato
Solomon, Wm. David, 277
Solon, 166–67
Soma, 102
Sophists, 170, 183–84
Sparta, 166–68
Speech-acts, 5
State of nature, 71
Stevenson, C. L., 36–37, 124–25, 126, 252
Stoicism (Stoics), 302–6
Stone, I. F., 172–73
Stone, Merlin, 82, 84, 95, 196–97, 201
Stout, Jeffrey, 2
Sturgeon, Nicholas, 245
Śūdra, 99
Suffering: Nietzsche on, 287. *See also* Buddhism: *duḥkha*
Sumerians, 89
Suzuki, D. T., 329–30
Swinburne, Richard, 200

Taylor, Richard, 243; on metaethics, 249–50
Tennyson, Alfred, 329
Thera, 162
Thomas, Stephen, 208
Thomson, Judith Jarvis, 375
Thucydides, 162
Tolstoy, Leo, 291
Toulmin, Stephen, and Allan Janik, 290
Trojan War, 162, 188–89
Truth, 352–55

Universalism, 21–22, 23, 68–69
Universalizability, 51–53, 68–69
Upaniṣads, 100, 101–6; *Chāndogya,* 105, 106, 122, 127; *Kaṭha,* 103; *Muṇḍaka,* 102–3

Utilitarianism, 261–66, 369–70; act and rule, 265–66; applying, 363; hedonistic, 261, 263; Moore and, 237; objections to, 263–66; Rawls on, 264; Ross on, 264; and the sphere of considerability, 261–62. *See also* Bentham; Mill

Vaiśya, 99
Value: inherent, 378; intrinsic, 255–58, 260, 277; monist, pluralist, and variable accounts of, 255–56, 260; Theory of, 255–58. *See also* Bentham; Mill; Moore
Vedas, 100–102, 106. See also Ṛg Veda
Virtue (and virtues), 232–33, 272–74; and vice, 225–28, 274

Waldron, Jeremy, 270
Warnock, G. J., 54, 242–43, 295
Wasson, R. Gordon, Ruck, and Hofmann, 186
Watt, W. Montgomery, 199
Wernicke, Carl, 315; Wernicke's area, 92, 316
Wheelwright, Philip, 299
Williams, Bernard, 59; on the "amoralist," 276, 278, 279–80, 281; on inescapability, 38; on morality and ethics, 17–19, 254, 276, 278, 279–80, 281
Wittgenstein, Ludwig, 288–91, 331, 342; and amoralism, 290–91; on belief, 206–7; on facts and values, 298; Lovibond on, 62; on philosophy, 289, 341, 350
Wong, David, 277–78
Wood, Ellen Meiksins, and Neil Wood, 171
Wright, Arthur, 153–54
Wu wei (non-action), 145–47, 311–12, 328, 347; Creel on, 145; Guo Xiang on, 145; Loy on, 146–47; Needham on, 146

Xun Zi, 78, 151–52, 157

Yin and *yang,* 143–44, 150–51
Yin-Yang School, 150–51
Yoga, 101–2, 104, 108, 333. *See also* Karma yoga

Zhuang Zi, 11, 28, 141, 143, 145, 147, 159, 294; on Hui Shi, 150. *See also* Daoism
Zimmer, Heinrich, 101–2, 108, 299
Zimmerman, David, 51
Zone of unintelligibility, 216–18
Zoroaster (Zoroastrianism), 87, 197–98; *Avesta,* 197